Ruth C. Carter, PhD, MS, MA
Editor

Managing C and the Org of Information: Philosophies, Practices and Challenges at the Onset of the 21st Century

Managing Cataloging and the Organization of Information: Philosophies, Practices and Challenges at the Onset of the 21st Century has been co-published simultaneously as Volume 30, Numbers 1 and 2/3 2000.

Pre-publication
REVIEWS,
COMMENTARIES,
EVALUATIONS . . .

More pre-publication
REVIEWS, COMMENTARIES, EVALUATIONS . . .

"**A** fascinating series of practical, forthright accounts of national, academic, and special library cataloging operations in action. . . . Yields an abundance of practical solutions for shared problems, now and for the future. Highly Recommended."

Laurel Jizba
Head Cataloger
Portland State University Library
Oregon

The Haworth Information Press
An Imprint of
The Haworth Press, Inc.
New York • Oxford

Managing Cataloging and the Organization of Information: Philosophies, Practices and Challenges at the Onset of the 21st Century

Managing Cataloging and the Organization of Information: Philosophies, Practices and Challenges at the Onset of the 21st Century has been co-published simultaneously as *Cataloging & Classification Quarterly*, Volume 30 Numbers 1 and 2/3 2000.

The *Cataloging & Classification Quarterly* Monographic "Separates"

Below is a list of "separates," which in serials librarianship means a special issue simultaneously published as a special journal issue or double-issue *and* as a "separate" hardbound monograph. (This is a format which we also call a "DocuSerial.")

"Separates" are published because specialized libraries or professionals may wish to purchase a specific thematic issue by itself in a format which can be separately cataloged and shelved, as opposed to purchasing the journal on an on-going basis. Faculty members may also more easily consider a "separate" for classroom adoption.

"Separates" are carefully classified separately with the major book jobbers so that the journal tie-in can be noted on new book order slips to avoid duplicate purchasing.

You may wish to visit Haworth's website at . . .

http://www.HaworthPress.com

. . . to search our online catalog for complete tables of contents of these separates and related publications.

You may also call 1-800-HAWORTH (outside US/Canada: 607-722-5857), or Fax 1-800-895-0582 (outside US/Canada: 607-771-0012), or e-mail at:

getinfo@haworthpressinc.com

Managing Cataloging and the Organization of Information: Philosophies, Practices and Challenges at the Onset of the 21st Century, edited by Ruth C. Carter, PhD, MS, MA (Vol. 30, No. 1/2/3, 2000). " *A fascinating series of practical, forthright accounts of national, academic, and special library cataloging operations in action. . . Yields an abundance of practical solutions for shared problems, now and for the future. Highly recommended."* (Laura Jizba, Head Cataloger, Portland State University Library, Oregon)

The LCSH Century: One Hundred Years with the Library of Congress Subject Headings System, edited by Alva T. Stone, MLS (Vol. 29, No. 1/2, 2000). *Traces the 100-year history of the Library of Congress Subject Headings, from its beginning with the implementation of a dictionary catalog in 1898 to the present day, exploring the most significant changes in LCSH policies and practices, including a summary of other contributions celebrating the centennial of the world's most popular library subject heading language.*

Maps and Related Cartographic Materials: Cataloging, Classification, and Bibliographic Control, edited by Paige G. Andrew, MLS and Mary Lynette Larsgaard, BA, MA (Vol. 27, No. 1/2/3/4, 1999) *Discover how to catalog the major formats of cartographic materials, including sheet maps, early and contemporary atlases, remote-sensed images (i.e., aerial photographs and satellite images), globes, geologic sections, digital material, and items on CD-ROM.*

Portraits in Cataloging and Classification: Theorists, Educators, and Practitioners of the Late Twentieth Century, edited by Carolynne Myall, MS, CAS, and Ruth C. Carter, PhD (Vol. 25, No. 2/3/4, 1998) *"This delightful tome introduces us to a side of our profession that we rarely see: the human beings behind the philosophy, rules, and interpretations that have guided our professional lives over the past half century. No collection on cataloging would be complete without a copy of this work." (Walter M. High, PhD, Automation Librarian, North Carolina Supreme Court Library; Assistant Law Librarian for Technical Services, North Carolina University, Chapel Hill)*

Cataloging and Classification: Trends, Transformations, Teaching, and Training, edited by James R. Shearer, MA, ALA and Alan R. Thomas, MA, FLA (Vol. 24, No. 1/2, 1997) *"Offers a comprehensive retrospective and innovative projection for the future." (The Catholic Library Association)*

Electric Resources: Selection and Bibliographic Control, edited by Ling-yuh W. (Miko) Pattie, MSLS, and Bonnie Jean Cox, MSLS (Vol. 22, No. 3/4, 1996) *"Recommended for any reader who is searching for a thorough, well-rounded, inclusive compendium on the subject." (The Journal of Academic Librarianship)*

Cataloging and Classification Standards and Rules, edited by John J. Reimer, MLS (Vol. 21, No. 3/4,

1996). *"Includes chapters by a number of experts on many of our best loved library standards. . . . Recommended to those who want to understand the history and development of our library standards and to understand the issues at play in the development of new standards." (LASIE)*

Classification: Options and Opportunities, edited by Alan R. Thomas, MA, FLA (Vol. 19, No. 3/4, 1995). *"There is much new and valuable insight to be found in all the chapters. . . . Timely in refreshing our confidence in the value of well-designed and applied classification in providing the best of service to the end-users." (Catalogue and Index)*

Cataloging Government Publications Online, edited by Carolyn C. Sherayko, MLS (Vol. 18, No. 3/4, 1994). *"Presents a wealth of detailed information in a clear and digestible form, and reveals many of the practicalities involved in getting government publications collections onto online cataloging systems." (The Law Librarian)*

Cooperative Cataloging: Past, Present and Future, edited by Barry B. Baker, MLS (Vol. 17, No. 3/4, 1994). *"The value of this collection lies in its historical perspective and analysis of past and present approaches to shared cataloging. . . . Recommended to library schools and large general collections needing materials on the history of library and information science." (Library Journal)*

Languages of the World: Cataloging Issues and Problems, edited by Martin D. Joachim (Vol. 17, No. 1/2, 1994). *"An excellent introduction to the problems libraries must face when cataloging materials not written in English. . . . should be read by every cataloger having to work with international materials, and it is recommended for all library schools. Nicely indexed." (Academic Library Book Review)*

Retrospective Conversion Now in Paperback: History, Approaches, Considerations, edited by Brian Schottlaender, MLS (Vol. 17, No. 1/2, 1992). *"Fascinating insight into the ways and means of converting and updating manual catalogs to machine-readable format." (Library Association Record)*

Enhancing Access to Information: Designing Catalogs for the 21st Century, edited by David A. Tyckoson (Vol. 13, No. 3/4, 1992 *"Its down-to-earth, nontechnical orientation should appeal to practitioners including administrators and public service librarians." (Library Resources & Technical Services)*

Describing Archival Materials: The Use of the MARC AMC Format, edited by Richard P. Smiraglia, MLS (Vol. 11, No. 3/4, 1991). *"A valuable introduction to the use of the MARC AMC format and the principles of archival cataloging itself." (Library Resources & Technical Services)*

Subject Control in Online Catalogs, edited by Robert P. Holley, PhD, MLS (Vol. 10, No. 1/2, 1990). *"The authors demonstrate the reasons underlying some of the problems and how solutions may be sought. . . . Also included are some fine research studies where the researchers have sought to test the interaction of users with the catalogue, as well as looking at use by library practitioners." (Library Association Record)*

Library of Congress Subject Headings: Philosophy, Practice, and Prospects, edited by William E. Studwell, MSLS (Supp. #2, 1990). *"Plays an important role in any debate on subject cataloging and succeeds in focusing the reader on the possibilities and problems of using Library of Congress Subject Headings and of subject cataloging in the future." (Australian Academic & Research Libraries)*

Authority Control in the Online Environment: Considerations and Practices, edited by Barbara B. Tillett, PhD (Vol. 9, No. 3, 1989). *"Marks an excellent addition to the field. . . .[It] is intended, as stated in the introduction, to 'offer background and inspiration for future thinking.' In achieving this goal, it has certainly succeeded." (Information Technology & Libraries)*

National and International Bibliographic Databases: Trends and Prospects, edited by Michael Carpenter, PhD, MBA, MLS (Vol. 8, No. 3/4, 1988). *"A fascinating work, containing much of concern both to the general cataloger and to the language or area specialist as well. It is also highly recommended reading for all those interested in bibliographic databases, their development, or their history." (Library Resources & Technical Services)*

Cataloging Sound Recordings: A Manual with Examples, Deanne Holzberlein, PhD, MLS (Supp. #1, 1988). *"A valuable, easy to read working tool which should be part of the standard equipment of all catalogers who handle sound recordings." (ALR)*

Education and Training for Catalogers and Classifiers, edited by Ruth C. Carter, PhD (Vol. 7, No. 4, 1987). *"Recommended for all students and members of the profession who possess an interest in cataloging." (RQ-Reference and Adult Services Division)*

The United States Newspaper Program: Cataloging Aspects, edited by Ruth C. Carter, PhD (Vol. 6, No. 4, 1986). *"Required reading for all who use newspapers for research (historians and librarians in particular), newspaper cataloguers, administrators of newspaper collections, and–most important–those who control the preservation pursestrings." (Australian Academic & Research Libraries)*

Computer Software Cataloging: Techniques and Examples, edited by Deanne Holzberlein, PhD, MLS (Vol. 6, No. 2, 1986). *"Detailed explanations of each of the essential fields in a cataloging record. Will help any librarian who is grappling with the complicated responsibility of cataloging computer software." (Public Libraries)*

AACR2 and Serials: The American View, edited by Neal L. Edgar (Vol. 3, No. 2/3). *"This book will help any librarian or serials user concerned with the pitfalls and accomplishments of modern serials cataloging." (American Reference Books Annual)*

The Future of the Union Catalogue: Proceedings of the International Symposium on the Future of the Union Catalogue, edited by C. Donald Cook (Vol. 2, No. 1/2, 1982). *Experts explore the current concepts and future prospects of the union catalogue.*

Managing Cataloging and the Organization of Information: Philosophies, Practices and Challenges at the Onset of the 21st Century

Ruth C. Carter, PhD, MS, MA
Editor

Managing Cataloging and the Organization of Information: Philosophies, Practices and Challenges at the Onset of the 21st Century has been co-published simultaneously as *Cataloging & Classification Quarterly*, Volume 30 Numbers 1 and 2/3 2000.

The Haworth Information Press
An Imprint of
The Haworth Press, Inc.
New York • London • Oxford

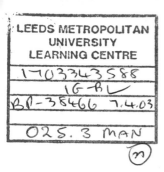
Published by

The Haworth Information Press, 10 Alice Street, Binghamton, NY 13904-1580 USA

The Haworth Information Press is an Imprint of the Haworth Press, Inc., 10 Alice Street, Binghamton, NY 13904-1580 USA.

Managing Cataloging and the Organization of Information: Philosophies, Practices and Challenges at the Onset of the 21st Century has been co-published simultaneously as *Cataloging & Classification Quarterly,* Volume 30, Numbers 1 and 2/3 2000.

The development, preparation, and publication of this work has been undertaken with great care. However, the publisher, employees, editors, and agents of The Haworth Press and all imprints of The Haworth Press, Inc., including The Haworth Medical Press® and Pharmaceutical Products Press®, are not responsible for any errors contained herein or for consequences that may ensue from use of materials or information contained in this work. Opinions expressed by the author(s) are not necessarily those of The Haworth Press, Inc.

Cover design by Thomas J. Mayshock Jr.

Library of Congress Cataloging-in-Publication Data

Managing cataloging and the organization of information : philosophies, practices and challenges at the onset of the 21st century / Ruth C. Carter, editor.
     p. cm.
     Co-published simultaneously as cataloging & classification quarterly, v. 30, nos. 1 and 2/3 2000.
     Includes bibliographical references and index.
     ISBN 0-7890-1312-6 (alk. paper)–ISBN 0-7890-1313-4 (pbk.: alk. paper)
     1. Cataloging. 2. Information organization. I. Carter, Ruth C. II. Cataloging & classification quarterly.

Z693 .M32 2000
025.3–dc21

00-053865

Indexing, Abstracting & Website/Internet Coverage

This section provides you with a list of major indexing & abstracting services. That is to say, each service began covering this periodical during the year noted in the right column. Most Websites which are listed below have indicated that they will either post, disseminate, compile, archive, cite or alert their own Website users with research-based content from this work. (This list is as current as the copyright date of this publication.)

(continued)

(continued)

Special Bibliographic Notes related to special journal issues (separates) and indexing/abstracting:

- indexing/abstracting services in this list will also cover material in any "separate" that is co-published simultaneously with Haworth's special thematic journal issue or DocuSerial. Indexing/abstracting usually covers material at the article/chapter level.
- monographic co-editions are intended for either non-subscribers or libraries which intend to purchase a second copy for their circulating collections.
- monographic co-editions are reported to all jobbers/wholesalers/approval plans. The source journal is listed as the "series" to assist the prevention of duplicate purchasing in the same manner utilized for books-in-series.
- to facilitate user/access services all indexing/abstracting services are encouraged to utilize the co-indexing entry note indicated at the bottom of the first page of each article/chapter/contribution.
- this is intended to assist a library user of any reference tool (whether print, electronic, online, or CD-ROM) to locate the monographic version if the library has purchased this version but not a subscription to the source journal.
- individual articles/chapters in any Haworth publication are also available through the Haworth Document Delivery Service (HDDS).

ABOUT THE EDITOR

Ruth C. Carter, PhD, MS, MA, holds her PhD in History from the University of Pittsburgh and her MS in Library Science from the University of Illinois at Urbana-Champaign. She is the retired Head of the Archives Service Center and Curator of Historical Collections at the University of Pittsburgh, where she also held many positions in automated and technical services including Assistant Director. Dr. Carter is nationally recognized for her expertise and leadership and is a past recipient of the Bowker/Ulrich's Serials Librarianship Award. During 1990-1991 she was President of the Association for Library Collections and Technical Services (ALCTS). Dr. Carter has edited *Cataloging & Classification Quarterly* (The Haworth Press, Inc.) since 1985 and also edits the *Journal of Internet Cataloging* (The Haworth Press, Inc.). She served two terms as a member of the IFLA Standing Committee on Serial Publications and serves on the Pennsylvania State Historical Records Advisory Board.

Managing Cataloging and the Organization of Information: Philosophies, Practices and Challenges at the Onset of the 21st Century

CONTENTS

Foreword:
Managing Cataloging and the Organization of Information

The dogmas of the quiet past are inadequate to the stormy present. The occasion is piled high with difficulty, and we must rise with the occasion. As our case is new, so we must think anew and act anew.

Abraham Lincoln,
in his second annual message to Congress,
December 1, 1862

SUMMARY. This Foreword provides an overview of the two parts of a collection of papers describing philosophies, practices and plans in a cross section of libraries and how their cataloging and technical services managers are dealing with their responsibilities at the beginning of the twenty-first century. Part One includes the National Library of Canada and the Library of Congress. University libraries in Mexico, the United Kingdom, Australia, Canada and Botswana are represented. A survey reports the use of classification systems in Latin American libraries including the factors influencing the selection of a particular scheme. Part Two is devoted to specialized and academic libraries in the United States. One academic medical library, one historical society, and two academic law libraries are represented. Philosophies and practices are described in twelve articles discussing fourteen college and university libraries ranging from the very small to the largest research libraries. *[Article copies available for a fee from The Haworth Document Delivery Service: 1-800-342-9678. E-mail address: <getinfo@haworthpressinc.com> Website: <http://www.HaworthPress.com>]*

[Haworth indexing entry note]: "Foreword: Managing Cataloging and the Organization of Information." Carter, Ruth C. Published in *Managing Cataloging and the Organization of Information: Philosophies, Practices and Challenges at the Onset of the 21st Century* (ed: Ruth C. Carter) The Haworth Information Press, an imprint of The Haworth Press, Inc., 2000, pp. xv-xviii. Single or multiple copies of this article are available for a fee from The Haworth Document Delivery Service [1-800-342-9678, 9:00 a.m. - 5:00 p.m. (EST). E-mail address: getinfo@haworthpressinc.com].

xv

KEYWORDS: Managing cataloging, organization of information, specialized libraries, academic libraries, national libraries

One often hears about cataloging rules, integrated library systems and their database maintenance, subject headings and classification, digitization, markup languages, various practices and techniques. Yet these practical, day to day activities within cataloging, technical services, and digital library units must fit into the library as a whole. They involve resource allocation in terms of staff, equipment, and the acquisition of library resources and cataloging data. Decisions concerning workflow, selection of an automated system or classification scheme, or whether to catalog in-house or to outsource are among the many cataloging related management decisions with considerable implications for the library as a whole. The management of cataloging and other functions concerning the organization of information and the provision of access to the library's local collection along with selected remote resources constitute an essential part of both the cataloging process and the library's administration. While the "stormy present" described by Abraham Lincoln may be more past than present and the sometimes drastic transformations of technical services largely behind us, the present still is a time of adapting to and shaping change.

The Preface in the form of an administrator's point of view and challenges to catalogers by Gloriana St. Clair sets the stage for the following twenty-two articles that make up three issues of *Cataloging & Classification Quarterly* published in two parts. Part One encompasses articles by two national libraries (the Library of Congress and the National Library of Canada) and five articles detailing aspects of the management of cataloging in five academic libraries outside the United States (Australia, Botswana, Canada, Mexico and the United Kingdom are represented). One article provides the result of a survey on the classification systems used by libraries throughout Latin America. Part Two covers four specialized libraries (one medical, one historical society, and two law) and includes ten articles discussing twelve academic libraries in the United States.

Why now? Why at all? Some would say that cataloging and the organization of information is in flux in libraries today. Yes, of course. But life is flux, there is constant evolution. What better time to stop and document the philosophies and practices of a cross section of libraries than at the very onset of the twenty-first century. After a rough period in the 1990s when many libraries made major transformations in cataloging and technical services including the implementation of digital library units and metadata specialists, there is more agreement on the road ahead. Although not a scientific sample or comprehensive in terms of geography or type of library, for example no public or corporate or Asian library is represented, the articles show common themes in terms of practices and their underlying philosophies. Most face similar challenges in the years ahead.

Some of the articles concentrate on a major change such as automation. Others focus on staffing, organization, teamwork, and workflow. Some treat topics connected with digitization of resources or remote resources. Several are comprehensive in the topics treated while others focus more narrowly. All add to our collective knowledge on what is happening in libraries around the world today. Some articles present a guide to "best practice" while others emphasize plans for the future. If there is any single theme it is that catalogers and more broadly, technical services and digital library staff, must be flexible and expect change. Nothing is ever final or forever cast in stone.

In the late 1990s when many libraries faced budget constraints and desired to finance new digital initiatives, they rethought the labor intensive parts of their operations. Often this meant seeking ways to use technology and outside services to reduce staff and streamline operations in technical services. By thinking positively and rising to the occasion cataloging managers can continue to help influence change, not just react to it. The core values remain. The objective is still to connect the patron with the information he or she wants in as timely a manner as possible. The technology that is omnipresent in today's libraries is a tool and also an opportunity. This publication brings home the point that change and technology are accepted and often embraced. In some cases that may even mean returning to some previous practices including inhouse processing as vendors are unable to deliver a timely and cost effective service. Throughout there is a continuing need for imagination, common sense and practicality as one tries to effectively move with the times. The articles in Parts One and Two collectively demonstrate that libraries of diverse types and sizes and regardless of geographic location, face similar challenges and have made amazingly similar decisions, managing cataloging and the organization of information in 2000.

Ruth C. Carter
Editor

Preface:
Chaos, Convenience, and Catalogers

"One thousand additional catalogers would not be enough to deal with the chaos of the Internet," proclaimed Raj Reddy, the co-chair of the President's Advisory Committee on Information Technology, at a meeting last year between representatives from the World Bank and directors of The Universal Library (a futuristic program of Carnegie Mellon's School of Computer Science)–when World Bank leaders, who were trying to address problems around access to and equity of information, wondered if hiring more catalogers would help. The web, with over 800 million pages, grows at a rate of 3 million pages a day. Much of the content there is ephemeral, commercial and individual–only 5-6% has the quality and status that would qualify for library inclusion. Certainly, the web needs the attention of catalogers, but the task is beyond even the mythological challenges offered to Sisyphus or Hercules.

The library of the future, which I often call the digital library, offers many challenges for catalogers. My thesis is that digital library catalogers will have different tasks from those of paper library catalogers. These tasks will require an enhanced skill set and understanding. As an administrator, I will be looking for catalogers whose skills lie in these areas: big picture understanding, technological adaptability and attention to three human passions–convenience, speed and flexibility.

BIG PICTURE UNDERSTANDING

Few librarians predicted the advent of the World Wide Web and the implications it would have for library service. However, those librari-

[Haworth indexing entry note]: "Preface: Chaos, Convenience, and Catalogers." St. Clair, Gloriana. Published in *Managing Cataloging and the Organization of Information: Philosophies, Practices and Challenges at the Onset of the 21st Century* (The Haworth Information Press, an imprint of The Haworth Press, Inc.) Vol. 30, No. 1, 2/3, 2000, pp. xix-xxiv. Single or multiple copies of this article are available for a fee from The Haworth Document Delivery Service [1-800-342-9678, 9:00 a.m. - 5:00 p.m. (EST). E-mail address: getinfo@haworthpressinc.com].

ans who saw that electronic versions of indices and full-text resources would begin to transform service offerings were at least oriented to take advantage of the web. Librarians who believe that the future is digital can best position themselves to prosper in this century.

At NORDINFO in Oslo in 1999, I talked about some advantages of digital libraries:

- Materials are easier to locate with electronic catalogs and indices. For most, 99% of searching is being handled digitally.
- Digital libraries appeal to that human love of convenience.
- Digital resources can be accessed faster.
- Because resources are available more quickly and conveniently, information can be transferred more readily.
- One digital version can serve the entire world.
- Unique collections can be shared with little deterioration.
- If all library costs for acquisitions, processing, storage and access are accounted, the digital library is less expensive.
- Many new functionalities exist.
- Sharing of information from one individual to another is easier.

Catalogers need to begin to think about how their talents can best be used in this new environment. Catalogers' traditional strengths–their organization of information, their understanding about the inherent relationships among disciplines, and their focus on issues of retrieval– are important to having a coherent approach to such a future. Catalogers must be creative, flexible, innovative, and learn first-hand how users seek and use information. Based on traditional strengths and knowledge of information seeking behaviors, catalogers will become risk-takers, develop new cataloging methodologies, and will design and shape access to the digital library.

TECHNOLOGICAL ADAPTABILITY

Technology is the driver for the future. We will have newer, faster, better, more competent machines to do our work. Those machines must be our servants and not our masters. When I was a cataloger and was shortly thereafter engaged in bringing automation into two different libraries, automation often dictated policy. Machine functionalities determined cataloging decisions and circulation policies, rather than having machines serve the library's policy and practice needs. Technology must connect library patrons with the information they need. Librarians must understand technology well enough and be determined enough to make that happen.

Humans are already changing because of their interactions with their machines. Three human emphases are coming to govern the relationships between what library patrons want and what libraries offer. These are convenience, speed, and flexibility. Many librarians (not just catalogers) have certain personal characteristics that stand in the way of their meeting student objectives for library service in the digital library.

CONVENIENCE

As young humans, college students are in the forefront of wanting all their library services to be convenient. Many older humans are also becoming addicted to the convenience of electronic information at the fingertips. Astrophysicists tell us that they are now three percent more productive because both current scholarly work and retrospective scholarly work are available to them electronically. Other disciplines would like to attain that status. In the last few decades, catalogers led by making the library catalog available to students in their dorm rooms, laboratories, and offices. The student response was not gratitude but a demand for full-text to go along with the bibliographic records.

Part of the culture of convenience is the marketing that makes services easy to identify and use. The librarian traits that run counter to the provision of more convenient service might be classed as a kind of fuddy-duddiness. Recently, while visiting the libraries at California Institute of Technology, their web development task force and I had a discussion about why they didn't have moving, flashing stuff on their web pages. They said they had decided against it. Through user testing, Carnegie Mellon students found our local web pages dull and staid. Despite this perspective and information from students, librarians here also decided against a more vibrant and dynamic presence. What turns students on is brand identity and ease of location. Catalogers and other librarians need to be more attentive to the tastes and expectations of the primary target audience because convenience has become a premier constituent requirement. Students don't want to read about it in a packet of orientation information; they want their attention grabbed and riveted, as it can be on the Internet.

SPEED

Another element related to convenience is speed of delivery. The great advantage of digital information is that it can be reached quickly. Faculty rhapsodize about how much time they save in research and teaching when they can find the articles that they need instantly available in JSTOR. Yet, something in the librarian character mandates a more deliberate pace. At a stakeholder meeting for a project called *Library.org*, Jerry Campbell, who identifies himself as one of the great librarian rabble-rousers of all times, remarked that librarians seem to have a gene for slow, deliberate action. He says he has come to accept that, but society around him and the rest of us continues to speed up– as James Gleick illustrates repeatedly in *Faster*.[1]

Certainly, in areas such as organizational change, experts warn that if administrators speed up the process, they will pay in resistance to the ultimate change. Solutions offering quick service need to be grounded in a thorough understanding of user needs and technology, combined with a willingness to adapt new technologies to forge the future digital library and provide access to it. In service areas today, the focus must be on quick service. For example, new books should be sitting in public areas, vying for student attention–not in cataloging.

FLEXIBILITY

As an administrator, flexibility is a quality I value in all library employees at all levels of the organization. Carnegie Mellon's cataloging department recently delighted me by agreeing to create call numbers for valuable off-prints of Einstein articles held in our Rare Books Room, and by offering to undertake the cataloging of a variety of jades, ivories and other objects of art, if good descriptions could be found. The Posner family (donors of the art objects) also pleased me by preferring to have their collection more fully represented in the libraries' main catalog than in an additional, separate database. For the public, the library catalog, accessible worldwide through the web, continues to be the most prestigious address.

The current pace of change is such that flexibility has become one of the greatest virtues. The old virtues of cataloging–authority control, convergence of records under a single entry, and elaborate description–must now give way to new technologies. While web search engines, such as HotBot, Lycos and AltaVista, have many deficiencies by librarian standards, they are what students have come to expect. Cataloging departments now need to put their intellectual efforts into devising more precise search and retrieval systems that have the look and feel of the current student favorites. For almost a decade, Jennifer Younger has been talking with catalogers about conceiving their positions as something much, much more than the cataloging of individual books, serials, and media one by one. In that time, some departments have almost entirely disappeared; others have expanded their range and scope of interest, and so have flourished.

CONCLUSIONS

Chaos reigns in the current digital information environment. The critical path between present practices and digital library management is not a clear one. If catalogers do nothing and know nothing about their future, that future will overtake and obliterate them. Understanding the demands of users of electronic information can make for a more productive and orderly entrée into the digital environment. Research and writing, such as the articles on the future in this special issue, are critical. These authors, many of whom have shaped my thinking as an administrator, lead catalogers forward.

Library patrons, especially traditional age students, need more order so that they can learn to locate information and discern its character and applicability. Catalogers who understand speed, convenience, flexibility, and the implications of technology for their work can create a better information environment. As an administrator, I hope that not just one thousand but many thousands will set their minds towards an orderly and productive information future.

Gloriana St. Clair
University Librarian
Carnegie Mellon University

AUTHOR NOTE

The author wishes to thank Erika Linke, the Carnegie Mellon University Libraries cataloging department and Cindy Carroll for their assistance with this work.

NOTE

1. Gleick, James. *Faster: The Acceleration of Just about Everything.* New York: Pantheon Books, 1999.

NATIONAL LIBRARIES

Managing Cataloging and Cataloging Operations– 2000 and Beyond at the Library of Congress

Beacher Wiggins

SUMMARY. The article focuses on initiatives and innovations undertaken at the Library of Congress (LC) during the past decade and the first decade of the new century that affect LC cataloging–including its implementation of a new integrated library system, its digital resources activities, its adoption of the core level bibliographic record, and its role as secretariat of the Program for Cooperative Cataloging. In reviewing these initiatives, the article underscores the challenges LC faces as the de facto national library in managing cataloging and the organization of information. The author highlights how LC enterprises help point the way for cataloging, both at LC and within the larger library community. *[Article copies available for a fee from The Haworth Document Delivery Service: 1-800-342-9678. E-mail address: <getinfo@haworthpressinc.com> Website: <http://www.HaworthPress.com>]*

KEYWORDS. Cooperative cataloging, core level record, Internet resources, Library of Congress, Pinyin romanization

The Library of Congress (LC), by virtue of its serving as the de facto national library for the United States, holds a unique position in

---

Beacher Wiggins is Director for Cataloging at the Library of Congress.

Address correspondence to: Beacher Wiggins, Director for Cataloging, Library of Congress, 101 Independence Avenue, S.E., Washington, DC 20540.

[Haworth co-indexing entry note]: "Managing Cataloging and Cataloging Operations–2000 and Beyond at the Library of Congress." Wiggins, Beacher. Co-published simultaneously in *Cataloging & Classification Quarterly* (The Haworth Information Press, an imprint of The Haworth Press, Inc.) Vol. 30, No. 1, 2000, pp. 3-17; and: *Managing Cataloging and the Organization of Information: Philosophies, Practices and Challenges at the Onset of the 21st Century* (ed: Ruth C. Carter) The Haworth Information Press, an imprint of The Haworth Press, Inc., 2000, pp. 3-17. Single or multiple copies of this article are available for a fee from The Haworth Document Delivery Service [1-800-342-9678, 9:00 a.m. - 5:00 p.m. (EST). E-mail address: getinfo@haworthpressinc.com].

3

the national and international library communities. It is a position that is acknowledged by its managers and staff as we carry out our work on a daily basis and as we strategize for the future. Probably in no area of the Library's operations is this more true than in cataloging. Since 1902, when LC inaugurated distribution of its cataloging, LC's cataloging has influenced catalogs and cataloging standards across the Nation and throughout the world, forming the basis for cooperative and copy cataloging arrangements. Over the near century of that distribution, the format of those cataloging data has evolved from printed cards to machine readable form on magnetic tape and now via ftp (file transfer protocol). In preparing the LC contribution for this special *Cataloging & Classification Quarterly (CCQ)* issue, the focus will be on initiatives and innovations undertaken at LC during the past decade and the first decade of the new century that affect our cataloging. In so doing, the challenges we face in managing cataloging and the organization of information will be underscored. Further, this review will show how LC enterprises help point the way for us in cataloging, both at LC and within the larger library community, as we move into the 21st century.

One of the exercises that the Cataloging Directorate has been engaged in for a number of years now, not unlike other libraries, is the crafting of Tactical Plans to guide the work of the cataloging divisions and to assist us in better managing our operations. Among the planks in an early 1990s plan was: "Address staff concerns about the future of cataloging and technician jobs." We felt that attention to catalogers' future was warranted because of the vast and swift progression of changes that were and are continuing to occur, not just at LC, but again beyond our institution to the library profession as a whole. Even as we acknowledged the concern of staff by including such an objective in our plan, it is safe to say that most of us Cataloging Directorate managers never felt catalogers' jobs would become obsolete; rather, the thrust of their tasks would likely change. The requisite for the skills of catalogers would only intensify, causing us to reconsider how best to deploy their expertise. I will return to this theme later in this article. But first, to supply some perspective to the topic, it is useful to share some key recent LC initiatives that will affect the future of catalogers, cataloging, and how we manage our cataloging operations and the organization of information.

LC CATALOGING RELATED INITIATIVES

Arrearage Reduction

Since 1989, except for a brief span, the Library's number one priority has been the reduction of its colossal backlog of uncataloged material–our arrearages. LC's arrearages were numbered at nearly 40 million items, in all formats, when the initial arrearage census was tallied. In the ten intervening years, that amount has been reduced by over half, with several arrearage groups eliminated. Our current goal is, by September 2007, to reduce the non-print and rare book categories by eighty percent of their original 1989 tally of thirty-five and one-half million items; for the print materials, we are targeting total elimination of the original four million pieces by September 2004. These are targets we keep prominently before us as we plan for any other new initiatives and as we oversee ongoing activities, including staying current with incoming receipts, which totaled 296,000 monographs alone in fiscal year 1999.

Program for Cooperative Cataloging (PCC)

It is likely that few would refute the contention that a key element in the library profession's resolve to stay abreast of proliferating information will be our ability and willingness to share resources. Toward that end, expanding on its NACO Operations for sharing national authority data, the Library collaborated with other research libraries, along with OCLC and the Research Libraries Group (RLG), in the creation of the Program for Cooperative Cataloging (PCC). In establishing the PCC, LC and the participating institutions reaffirmed what was positive and effective about the well ensconced and widely valued NACO Program and what was then the still evolving National Coordinated Cataloging Program (NCCP).

The PCC emphasizes and provides training with the goal of changing the culture and values of cataloging. The training underscores cataloger judgment and decision making. The training is geared towards engendering a new cataloging mindset. Coupled with this new mindset is the concept of the core level bibliographic record. This record, which exemplifies a level of cataloging with a complement of data elements less than full level but·more than minimal level, was developed by a PCC task group working closely with the library community to ensure that the resulting record would be one that libraries would be willing to accept. The major differences embodied in this record–as distinct from those of a MARC 21 National Level Record–are latitude for fewer notes, fewer descriptive added entries, fewer subject access points, and the granting to individual libraries the discretion to decide whether to give series access in an authorized form. While any institution may adopt the core record, for a record to be coded as PCC core, it is mandatory that every access point in the record be represented by an authority record and that the core record contain a nationally accepted classification number–facilitating the easy integration of these records into any library's catalog. There are several iterations of the core standard now available for use: books, serials (CONSER), computer files, rare books, graphic materials, moving images, music and non-music sound recordings, printed music and music manuscripts, and supplement for multiple character sets.

LC Core Record

After conducting a six-month experiment involving staff from a variety of Cataloging Directorate teams–cataloging materials in a variety of languages, subjects, and formats–LC adopted the core level record standard as the base level of cataloging for its monographs and serials. This decision was based on the distinct gains in productivity that resulted from using the core level record during the experiment. If the Library was going to use the full arsenal of techniques at its disposal to catalog current receipts, as well as continue its successful arrearage reduction effort, embracing the core record as the LC default record was a sound decision. Since the core record is meant to be a dynamic record that can be augmented, as governed by the importance of the particular material, we are assured that our approach will not diminish the quality of the cataloging that we provide our users. In fact, responding to the requests of our public services colleagues, the LC core record routinely includes bibliographical references notes; and, in recognition of our commitment to one of our large user communities, we also determined to include a *Dewey Classification* number, in addition to the *Library of Congress Classification* number that we assign to each record.

Prior to the introduction of the core level standard, LC had begun to look at ways of streamlining its cataloging guidelines and procedures, without introducing deleterious effects. Our efforts to simplify our cataloging and the related guidelines and policies we formulate have been part of our goals for several years now. Accomplishment of this goal will benefit LC, as it meets its mandate to reduce dramatically its enormous arrearages, and will, as well, benefit the library community, which follows much of LC's cataloging policies. To stay on target with our simplification pursuits, as new policies and revision of policies and guidelines are considered, those of us at LC who are responsible for administering and issuing these ask ourselves these questions: Are written guidelines really needed for this situation? If so, what degree of cataloger judgment should come into play? What are the cost implications for implementing these changes?

New Integrated Library System

The Library of Congress ended the century on a momentous note– the year culminated several years of planning for, securing, and finally implementing a new integrated library system (the LC ILS). When the Library began developing its first bibliographic system some thirty years ago, LC was paving the way for the library community to harness the power of the computer to store bibliographic data and then make those data easily retrievable. Henriette Avram was brought on board in the mid-1960s and became responsible for machine readable cataloging as we know it today, underpinned by the MARC format that she created to serve as the container for cataloging data and to function as the vehicle for the transfer and exchange of those data.

It was only in very recent years, however, that it was felt that LC could avail itself of a vendor produced system, rather than build one in house. With confidence that a viable system could be procured that would be capable of handling the massive size of the LC database, the Library started its procurement process in earnest. Managers and staff prepared background information to describe the Library's needs and what would be required in a system commensurate with those needs. We underscored our requirement for a system that would enable us to track our materials; that would provide an inventory of what we had in our collections; that would enable us to convert our manual Shelflist and serials control file to an online database; and that would be sufficiently robust to replace MUMS (Multiple Use MARC System) that had served us well for over a quarter century.

Armed with solid data, LC obtained congressional approval and funding to purchase a system. Early on in this process, we established an LC ILS Program Office to oversee our implementation. Once the system and vendor were identified, the intense and comprehensive planning process went into full swing–preparation to migrate some twelve million bibliographic records and four million authority records; plans to train the three thousand plus staff whose work would shift to the new system; and coordination to install or upgrade PC workstations for all affected staff. Seventy-six LC ILS implementation teams, comprising over five hundred-fifty staff members, were constituted to bring about this mammoth transition, under the direction of six steering groups, nine policy groups, and three technical groups.

With the success of the LC ILS transition behind us, the focus now is how fully to capitalize on our powerful new system. We want to be sure that we do not continue to carry out our cataloging and processing tasks in the same way, if better workflows and more productive ways of performing functions are offered by the LC ILS. To ensure that we take full advantage of the LC ILS, over the next several years, we will concentrate in a formal way on business process improvements (BPIs) for the workflows, procedures, and tasks that we carry out in our new LC ILS environment. Coordination of BPI applications will emanate from our Operations Directorate, after the LC ILS Program Office disbands by the end of 2000. In addition to the areas for BPI consideration that the LC ILS teams identified during the implementation planning phase, we have asked our staff, as they interface with the system, to funnel any other suggestions for procedural and other changes to this office.

Considering its magnitude, we certainly characterize the Library's ILS implementation as a major success; it was, however, not without a few glitches. The cataloging and circulation modules came up first, in August 1999, with the OPAC next. By October 1 of that same year, the acquisitions and serials check-in components were operational. During the first six to eight weeks after the initial phase in, there was a shakedown period during which the system had to be adjusted and fine tuned to accommodate the high level of staff usage against the voluminous database. Staff experienced very slow system response time and system timeouts, causing an intense degree of staff frustration when they were unable to do their work. This period of adaptation was not unexpected or extraordinary for any institution that has installed or replaced a system. Our cataloging teams had contingency plans that they invoked to keep staff occupied. What was reaffirming about this interval was the awareness that staff have a strong desire to work; that they take pride in their work; and that they expect the support from us managers to do their jobs well and productively. We can take comfort from this experience that our staff can and will meet the challenges of the years ahead. As managers planning for the future, we must assure that adequate and appropriate resources are in place to facilitate staff's best and most productive work.

Conversion of LC's Manual Files: Shelflist and Serials

A compelling reason for pushing for the Library's ILS was the need to convert our manual Shelflist to an online mode. An adjunct to this conversion is the conversion of our manual serials check-in file. With a Shelflist consisting of over twelve million cards and sheets, this is an immense undertaking. Much of the conversion is being done under contracts that involve contractor staff's keying data to the LC ILS. Because the data transcribed on the cards and sheets are in a variety of forms, including handwriting that may be difficult or impossible to decipher; and because the cards and sheets contain a mixture of notes, instructions, and other information–some dating to the late 19th century, we must plan for our senior and experienced cataloging technicians to play a substantive and indispensable role in the conversion. Further, since the conversion may take up to ten years to complete, there will be a period during which consultation of the manual files will be required, even while current shelflisting is done online. After shelflist conversion will come shelf compare, where we will need to confirm that all holdings that were listed in the manual files are physically accounted for in the collections.

Pinyin Romanization

After decades of using the Wade-Giles romanization scheme for converting Chinese characters to roman script, the Library has determined that it can now switch to the prevailing standard for Chinese romanization–Pinyin. Considering the estimated one hundred-eighty thousand LC bibliographic records for Chinese titles, the innumerable bibliographic records for non-Chinese works that contain one or more Chinese headings, and the approximated one hundred-fifty thousand authority records for these headings–name, subject, and classification, this is another huge initiative for the Library and our staff. As the Library has done so frequently in the past, we are collaborating extensively with RLG and OCLC to achieve this conversion of Wade-Giles data. RLG has assumed the responsibility for converting the LC bibliographic records by automated means, working with specifications supplied by the Library. Since LC catalogers create Chinese records on RLIN (RLG's database)–RLG's conversion efforts are made easier. OCLC took on the task of converting authority records for Chinese headings–planning to complete the authorities conversion ahead of the conversion of the bibliographic records, helping to address the strong sentiments of the East Asian library community and the community of libraries with large Chinese collections. The Pinyin conversion process holds much work in store for our staff, our partner implementors, and other institutions–reviewing a percentage of the converted records for quality assurance; performing bibliographic maintenance; handling headings that appear on non-Chinese bibliographic records; and dealing with the headings that are not expected to convert properly by machine.

The description of the Pinyin conversion and the two preceding initiatives–the LC ILS and the conversion of the LC manual files–remind us that we must give attention to cataloging quality and to maintenance of our bibliographic and authority data. As a result, we have made plans to establish a bibliographic maintenance unit within our Cataloging Policy and Support Office. This unit will be staffed by senior level catalogers from our cataloging teams, along with specialists from our special format divisions–we will need a broad spectrum of staff to resolve the errors introduced as part of the migration of our cataloging data from our previous system to the LC ILS and to handle the residue of problem records from the Pinyin conversion. We are willing to have this drain from among our most seasoned staff because we recognize the negative impact of not attending to the errors and inconsistencies in the LC ILS that resulted from these several consequential undertakings.

LC Digital Library Futures

The profession is acutely attuned to the importance of digital information–its acquisition and cataloging, its storage and servicing to users, and its use as a medium for preservation. Early on, LC recognized that digital resources are critical to library collections and services, whether the items are born digital or are digitized versions of analog items. Actively involved in this arena on many fronts, LC reached a milestone in 1999 when the Library attained its goal to assemble some five million unique items in its collections in digital form, working in concert with other institutions. Along the way, LC partnered with other libraries and schools to develop a national cooperative digitizing program that helps to ensure easy access to the Library's collections. The Library continued to work with copyright users, copyright owners, and others to resolve the issues surrounding intellectual property rights in an electronic environment.

The Library's digital futures initiative was built on the already digitized American Memory collections of over two hundred thousand items that were being shared in schools and local libraries across the country. Through the coordination of the Library's National Digital Library Program, staff continue to digitize LC's collections of photographs, manuscripts, motion pictures, books and pamphlets, and sound recordings, so that LC can continue to make these collections more widely available over the Internet. Our target now is to secure congressional approval for a budget base that will support the acquisition of hardware and software to build a repository and that will fund hiring staff with the requisite skills to help embrace the digital world.

Electronic CIP (Cataloging in Publication)

In 1993, LC put in place a research and development project to test the feasibility of transmitting electronic manuscripts over the Internet in lieu of mailing the printed galleys. This system supports producing cataloging in publication data completely within an electronic environment–obtaining galleys and manuscripts from publishers for upcoming publications, cataloging them, and transmitting the completed bibliographic records to the publishers via email for inclusion in the printed books. The ECIP Program is now in full production, with the number of participating publishers at one hundred-eighty. Within the decade, it is expected that LC will process the majority of cataloging in publication galleys via the ECIP mode. The ECIP Program offers the prospect of other kinds of relationships with the publishing community for obtaining digital resources; copyrighting them, cataloging them, and servicing them to users. This scenario, of course, presupposes having the requisite repository in place.

LC Bicentennial Conference on Bibliographic Control

Recognizing that there is still much to be determined concerning the most effective means of bringing digital documents, particularly Internet resources, under bibliographic control, LC's Cataloging Directorate is planning an invitational conference in observance of the Library's 200th Anniversary. The Library of Congress Bicentennial Conference on Bibliographic Control for the New Millennium will bring together, in late fall 2000, pivotal thinkers from the library community (technical services and public services librarians), the computing community (computer and information specialists), the library vendor community, and developers of metadata schemes and tools for Internet access. Our aim is to have these experts offer LC insight as we develop guidelines and policies for access to, control of, and retrieval of Internet resources. It is clear that our thinking must transcend traditional methods of controlling these documents and LC wants to fulfill a leadership role in this realm. Invited speakers and attendees will be asked to respond to such concerns as:

- How can libraries discover and provide adequate access to Internet resources?
- How can libraries improve access to Internet resources by combining traditional methods with evolving metadata schemes?
- What is the role of the *Anglo-American Cataloguing Rules* (*AACR*), subject and classification systems, and other standards in organizing and retrieving Internet resources?
- How can libraries best tap into the power of the online library catalog to make it a central stop for access to all materials and information?
- What is LC's role in providing organization to Internet resources and how can it best play out that role?

The conference participants will help LC draft recommendations for strategies and an action plan that will assist LC, *AACR* policy makers, and the library community in better meeting the challenges of providing bibliographic control of Internet resources.

During the conference, we will share what we have in place at LC.

We have a Computer Files and Microforms Team, consisting of only four catalogers and one technician, that is responsible for cataloging tangible and intangible digital materials. The Team consists of staff based on their expertise with a special format, rather than on subject coverage. Clearly, such a small group is insufficient to handle the workload of the tangible computer files alone that arrive on the team daily. The team is plainly too understaffed to deal adequately with Internet resources. Additionally, the team is called on to help determine and influence cataloging policy related to these materials and to participate in special projects, as described below. Our future direction must be to begin expanding responsibility for cataloging Internet resources to all cataloging teams, assigning responsibility to teams for Internet resources based on the teams' subject expertise. This change will offer us more flexibility and give us a better chance to provide appropriate bibliographic coverage for these resources.

One of our success stories that we will report during the conference is our BEAT (Bibliographic Enrichment Advisory Team) activities. Formed in 1992 as a Cataloging Directorate program, BEAT was charged to develop and implement initiatives to improve the tools, content, and access to bibliographic information. As part of its work, it has given special attention to digital and Internet resources. One activity, BEOnline started out with a focus on bibliographic control of business related Internet resources, but has enlarged to include additional disciplines. To aid us in our endeavor to test various options for making Internet resources available through the LC Database, the Library joined OCLC's Cooperative Online Resource Cataloging (CORC) project. Instead of the special software program our staff had written to capture data to form the bibliographic record, we will experiment with using CORC to formulate records for the resources we want accessible through the LC Database. BEOnline has enabled us to gain substantial experience in working with reference colleagues, who identify resources to be cataloged, and with technical staff, who help us develop the means to accomplish this work in a digital environment. I expect BEOnline to serve as the prototype as we disperse responsibility for cataloging Internet resources beyond the Computer Files Team.

Another BEAT activity that we will discuss at the conference is BECites, which is designed to enhance traditional bibliographies by placing them on the Web and including, along with annotated citations, links to the scanned tables of contents, indexes, and back of book bibliographies contained in the sources, as well as reciprocal links between the citations in the bibliography, the scanned elements of the works and their catalog records in the LC Database. We will also, where available, include links to online indexes to journals and other related Web resources.

Cataloger's Desktop

One of the tools that has been made available to catalogers is an online documentation package developed by LC's Cataloging Distribution Service called *Cataloger's Desktop*. LC catalogers have this CD-ROM item loaded on their workstations. Along with the recently added electronic version of *AACR*, the software package allows online display, retrieval, and printing for a broad group of LC-developed cataloging documents: *Library of Congress Rule Interpretations; Subject Cataloging Manuals; MARC 21/USMARC* documentation; manuals and guidelines for cataloging a variety of special format materials; the *CONSER Editing Guide*; and the *NACO Participants' Manual.* Other documents will be added to *Catalogers' Desktop* as they become available, continuing to enhance its utility. As new documents appear in this tool, we will have to consider no longer supporting print cataloging tools–we now have PC workstations that are sufficiently powerful to handle this online package.

Managing Cataloging at LC–2000 and Beyond

With the foregoing review of LC cataloging related initiatives, I will now speak to what we look forward to in managing cataloging and the organization of information at LC in this burgeoning new decade. For me, this has as much to do with how we deploy our staff resources as it does with what techniques we use to bring organization and retrievability to information. We envision adjustments in our cataloging operations at LC such that what our catalogers are engaged in now will likely be different by the end of this decade. For federal libraries, the Office of Personnel Management (OPM) this past decade issued standards revising the job series in the library field. These OPM standards replace outdated ones issued in 1966. Major thrusts of the new standards are automation and how automating functions in libraries have altered library related jobs in the intervening twenty-five plus years. At the time the previous standards were written, automation of library functions was in its nascent stage and bibliographic utilities and other bibliographic electronic networks were nonexistent. Growing sophistication in the application of automation may mean smaller numbers of librarians' performing cataloging as it is done today. But, automation cannot obviate the need for human intellectual intervention.

During the last decade of the past century, we reorganized our cataloging divisions at LC. Eight cataloging divisions form the Cataloging Directorate, which is one of seven directorates in Library Services–a service unit that equates to a department. Library Services was restructured to encompass the traditional library functions carried out by the Library–acquisitions, cataloging, reference, and preservation. Each of these seven directorates functions as a separate operation, with the directors of these areas working closely to coordinate activities and to share in planning the work of the service unit. The realignment of Library Services was a deliberate attempt to bring under one manager, the Associate Librarian for Library Services, full accountability for acquiring, cataloging, serving to users, preserving, and securing the Library's collections. We have found this arrangement to be of tremendous value in managing our traditional operations in a cohesive and more efficient way.

With the reorganization of the Cataloging Directorate, our cataloging operations are now along whole book lines–nothing new for most libraries–so that teams in divisions now perform the full panoply of cataloging and processing tasks (descriptive cataloging, subject analysis, classification, and shelflisting). At the same time, we geared up to take advantage of copy cataloging to a degree that we never had before. We brought up a new integrated library system, with promise of vast improvements in facilitating how we provide access to materials. These changes, along with what has become the explosion of digital resources, have enormous implications for the duties we will ask our catalogers to undertake. Their expertise, professional education, and experience will be needed to attend to professional tasks, e.g., providing authority control and subject analysis; enhancing bibliographic records for greater access; devising methods for more effective and efficient bibliographic control–especially for Internet and other digital materials; ensuring a more responsive interface with public services staff to serve users better; and overseeing teams of technicians who will be performing the more routine tasks associated with cataloging. At the same time, the work of technicians will be altered as well. The training needed by this group of staff will be administered by catalogers. Already acknowledged is the urgency to shore up and buttress the automation and technological skills of our cataloging staff, by moving to our cataloging divisions and teams the expertise and equipment required to operate at optimum levels.

In giving further thought to the changing roles of technicians and catalogers, I have considered looking at some changes in tasks that can effectively be performed by technicians. I would like to see at LC a shift such that certain areas of the bibliographic record would be restricted to technicians. This builds on a proposal that was proffered by the former chief of LC's former Descriptive Cataloging Policy Office, Ben Tucker. At the time he made the proposal, his idea may have been too radical a departure from what has been the norm at LC; now, I think, it may well be time for us to reconsider. What I envision is a different assignment of duties, with a fairly rigid demarcation between what technicians are expected to do versus what catalogers are assigned. One way to accomplish what is proposed is to limit access to certain fields in the bibliographic record. The fields I have in mind for access to be limited to technicians are in the descriptive component of the record.

When close scrutiny is given to the bibliographic record, it is the descriptive area that offers the most meaningful leeway for making a difference in increased production. If technicians are trained to transcribe accurately information from the chief sources of information, there is not much of real substance that catalogers contribute by their additional tweaking to the descriptive fields of the record. Catalogers' value lay in what they add in terms of the access points (descriptive, subject, and classification)–it is on these fields that catalogers' energies should be directed. It is my desire to work with our Cataloging Directorate managers and staff in the next few years to explore our moving in this direction. Beyond the gains in efficiency that should be realized with this approach, there are the opportunities for job enrichment and advancement for technicians. I fully expect such a departure from the status quo to be one that will not be wholeheartedly embraced–myriad problems, along with real and perceived obstacles will be present; nevertheless, I believe this to be a worthy pursuit. Such a change highlights what is professional for catalogers, while expanding the roles of technicians.

What we are likely to be managing by the end of this first decade of the century include:

- fewer book catalogers: efficiencies in cataloging, expanding roles for technicians, and increasing use of contracts for cataloging are likely to offset book catalogers' diminishing ranks
- how to provide increased access to and control of Internet and other digital resources
- how to expand cooperation nationally and internationally to bring about bibliographic control at all levels
- how *the* catalog is defined and used optimally
- how to use standards more effectively to guide our work and ensure that the cataloging records, finding aids, and other navigational tools we create will be interchangeable and useful to all

I view the coming decade with excitement, anticipation, and just a bit of wonder. With a growing universe of information, our primary responsibility of connecting users and information becomes evermore challenging, but nonetheless exciting. We are in a unique place, with incredible promise of opportunities to make a difference through our management of cataloging operations. This is especially so at the Nations's library, the Library of Congress.

The National Library of Canada: Organizing Information for the New Millennium

Liz McKeen
Ingrid Parent

SUMMARY. The authors outline the role played by the National Library of Canada in realizing bibliographic control of Canadian publications, and recount the Library's current and future bibliographic programs at the beginning of the twenty-first century. The historical context is summarized, including the legislative underpinnings of the national bibliography Canadiana, and the development of cataloguing policy and practice traced. The National Library's tradition of bilingual (English/French) cataloguing in accord with Canadian law and culture is explained. The organization of the cataloguing function and programs at the National Library of Canada is elaborated, and the importance of staff and their evolving skills highlighted. The article concludes with an overview of the challenges facing the National Library of Canada at the conclusion of the twentieth century, and its plans to recast the bibliographic dream of former times in the light of technological,

Liz McKeen, MLS, is Director, Bibliographic Access, National Library of Canada, Acquisitions and Bibliographic Services, National Library of Canada, 395 Wellington Street, Ottawa, Ontario, Canada K1A 0N4 (E-mail: (elizabeth.mckeen@nlc-bnc.ca). Ingrid Parent, BLS, is Director-General, Acquisitions and Bibliographic Services, National Library of Canada, Acquisitions and Bibliographic Services, National Library of Canada, 395 Wellington Street, Ottawa, Ontario, Canada, K1A 0N4 (E-mail: ingrid.parent@nlc-bnc.ca).

[Haworth co-indexing entry note]: "The National Library of Canada: Organizing Information for the New Millennium." McKeen, Liz, and Ingrid Parent. Co-published simultaneously in *Cataloging & Classification Quarterly* (The Haworth Information Press, an imprint of The Haworth Press, Inc.) Vol. 30, No. 1, 2000, pp. 19-32; and: *Managing Cataloging and the Organization of Information: Philosophies, Practices and Challenges at the Onset of the 21st Century* (ed: Ruth C. Carter) The Haworth Press, Inc., 2000, pp. 19-32. Single or multiple copies of this article are available for a fee from The Haworth Document Delivery Service [1-800-342-9678, 9:00 a.m. - 5:00 p.m. (EST). E-mail address: getinfo@haworthpress inc.com].

cultural and social forces of today and tomorrow. *[Article copies available for a fee from The Haworth Document Delivery Service: 1-800-342-9678. E-mail address: <getinfo@haworthpressinc.com> Website: <http://www.Haworth Press.com>]*

KEYWORDS. National Library of Canada, Canadiana, national bibliography, bibliographic organization, planning, cataloguing, personnel and/or staff, core competencies, bilingual cataloguing

Celebrating its fiftieth anniversary at the start of the new millennium, the National Library of Canada (NLC) began life in 1950 as an organizer of information, a library without a collection. The dedicated individuals of the Canadian Bibliographic Centre, the forerunner of the National Library of Canada, began to search and film card catalogues in libraries throughout Canada, working in a space fifty feet square on the main floor lobby of the Public Archives of Canada, set off by a few filing cabinets. The task was no less than to compile bibliographic information documenting the literary heritage of the country. From this activity grew *Canadiana: The National Bibliography*, and the Canadian Union Catalogue showing holdings of Canadian libraries, two powerful examples of the value and longevity of organizing information for the use of the country and the world. While these bibliographic tools are still very much in evidence, their look has changed, as have so many other features of the National Library. But no matter how much procedures and mechanisms have changed, organizing information is still a raison d'être for the institution.

The National Library is a research library specializing in Canadiana and Canadian studies, with about 490 staff members. It is also a department in the Canadian federal government. This duality can sometimes be in conflict when serving the interests of the Canadian government and also the Canadian public. The last decade of the century has seen a major downsizing and restructuring of government, including the National Library. The Library consolidated activities, looked for smarter ways to do its work especially by harnessing the potential of the new technologies, and sought partnerships to reach its objectives.

Its work is also done in the context of Canada's two official languages: English and French. Not only does this policy affect its modus operandi, but it also applies to the various National Library of Canada cataloguing policies. Through the use of computer technology and flexible input formats, bilingual access points and catalogue records are created, stored and accessed in ways transparent to the user. The need for seamless access not only to national bibliographic records but also to records from other countries, with their myriad languages and scripts, will grow in the new millennium, as the world's libraries and users are swept by the globalization forces increasingly in evidence in all areas of economic, cultural and social life.

ORGANIZATION OF CATALOGUING AT THE NATIONAL LIBRARY OF CANADA

The cataloguing function in a library must be regarded as one of its fundamental tasks, the lack of which could cause the library's collections to remain inaccessible and its services incomplete. Cataloguing continues to be one of the pillars of the Library's programs, providing users with access to the collections and services, but as well supporting the compilation of Canada's national bibliography, *Canadiana.*

For this reason, cataloguing personnel make up a relatively large proportion of the Library's staff. In 1950, salary expenditures for the newly founded Canadian Bibliographic Centre amounted to $9,240 (CAN) and the total budget for the Centre was only $41,240. In contrast, the salary budget for the National Library of Canada in 1999/2000 amounted to more than $20 million (CAN), with a total expenditure of about $30 million.

The legal deposit provisions of the National Library Act require that Canadian publishers deposit up to two copies of all titles they publish. This legal deposit mechanism has aided immeasurably not only in collecting and preserving Canada's published heritage, but in a very pragmatic way in the compilation of the national bibliography. The National Library is currently seeking clarification of the application of legal deposit to non-tangible Canadian electronic publications.

The Library's cataloguing policies have developed and evolved as its mandate gradually broadened to include supporting the cataloguing operations of other Canadian libraries. For example, while titles listed in the bibliography were originally given a Dewey class number for purposes of listing, a Library of Congress class number was later added, on the premise that *Canadiana* records should serve a variety of types of libraries with different needs and different users. Similarly, so that the *Canadiana* record would serve libraries operating in English and in French, NLC began establishing name and subject headings in both languages. A collaborative partnership with Université Laval began in 1976, to support the work they had begun earlier to compile a French-language list of subject headings, the *Répertoire de vedettes-matière*.

In the early 1970s, the cataloguing function of the National Library was organized on an assembly-line model to take advantage of the efficiencies possible through specialization and division of labour, and to better accommodate the increasing numbers of titles received for cataloguing and the increasing numbers of cataloguers hired for the job. Descriptive cataloguing and LC classification were separated from the assignment of subject headings and Dewey classification, and performed by different staff. Some cataloguing divisions were organized by language (French sections and English sections) while others retained for the most part the format of publication as the organizing principle, resulting in sections for government publications, serials and music. Editing of the bibliographic records for inclusion in the national bibliography *Canadiana* was carried out by another group of staff members.

By the 1990s, with impending budget cuts, the bibliographic access sector of the organization received careful review. In 1993, a consultant was hired to lead the senior and middle managers of the cataloguing area in a re-engineering project, one of several such projects undertaken by the Library. Over the summer of 1993, managers met weekly to rediscover the what, the why and the how of cataloguing at the National Library of Canada. One of the major results of this re-engineering was a reorganization which took place in 1995,[1] which abolished the assembly-line model in favour of integrated teams of cataloguers who complete all aspects of cataloguing (description, subject analysis, editorial preparation of bibliographic records for inclusion in the bibliography) for the titles for which they are responsible. Three divisions were created:

- the Monograph Cataloguing Division for non-government monographs, including music and sound recordings, in all formats and languages. The Monograph Division continues to be organized by language, with English teams and French teams, and a bilingual Music Team.
- the Government Publications and Serials Cataloguing Division to cover these materials, in all formats and languages. It has three

teams: the Federal Monographs Team, the Provincial Mono-graphs team, and the Serials Team.

- the Standards and Support Division to participate in national and international standards development such as the Anglo-American Cataloguing Rules, the MARC formats, library-related activities of ISO (the International Organisation for Standardisation), and the bibliographic activities of IFLA (International Federation of Library Associations and Institutions), as well as to publish Canadian standards such as *Canadian Subject Headings,* a list of English-language headings modeled on the *Library of Congress Subject Headings* but pertaining only to subjects of interest to Canada, *PS8000* Library of Congress style classification schedules for Canadian literature and *Class FC* for Canadian history. The Standards and Support Division also develops National Library of Canada rule interpretations and other policies, provides advice and guidance to NLC cataloguers on the application of bibliographic standards and tools to their cataloguing, provides technical support for the production of *Canadiana* in various formats and maintains databases.

This organization was adopted for a number of reasons. While there had been some savings in the assembly-line model, there had also been many opportunities for bottlenecks to develop along the line. Staff and work processes became specialized to the extent that communication across divisional lines became difficult, and more flexibility was needed. The need for greater timeliness in cataloguing had become more urgent. In the 1990s operations had to be streamlined so that government-wide mandated staff reductions could be accommodated without undue loss of service to Canadian user libraries and researchers.

Organization based on integrated teams of cataloguers and editorial support allows for greater speed in cataloguing priority titles, and fosters communication among staff dealing with the different aspects of cataloguing. Cross-training of staff in several parts of the cataloguing process is actively encouraged, in part to fill the need for greater depth of resources within each team. Organizational flexibility is valued as a means to deal with the many challenges created by emerging publishing technologies, the World Wide Web, and the new economic realities faced by libraries.

At the same time, the Library is attempting to take greater advantage of cataloguing done by others. The National Library is in the fortunate position of hosting the Canadian Union Catalogue on its AMICUS bibliographic management system, so that National Library cataloguers have access not only to source files such as Library of Congress MARC files loaded into AMICUS, but to bibliographic records for the holdings of several hundred Canadian libraries reporting to the Union Catalogue. The Library also uses Z39.50 software to search external databases to increase the number of derived records used.

In 1997, the National Library of Canada published a set of service standards, which for the first time pledged a specific level of timeliness in its *Canadiana* cataloguing.[2] The Library undertakes to list the top priority titles in the national bibliography, i.e., in AMICUS within ten working days of receipt of the item in the Library, and for the remaining current Canadiana, to list at least fifty percent within three months of receipt in the Library. The top priority includes all titles covered under the Library's Cataloguing in Publication program. This commitment to timeliness has helped to focus energies on the need for speed (while maintaining quality and accuracy in the work), and has been for the most part successful in achieving this goal. Cataloguing backlogs, while not yet extinct, are decreasing.

Bibliographic and authority records created by the National Library of Canada are distributed in a number of ways. Canadiana records are available online in AMICUS as part of Access AMICUS, a fee-based service available on the Web, via Z39.50 or via Datapac/Telnet. As well, brief records for the National Library of Canada's holdings are available in ResAnet, a free Web-based subset of the AMICUS database. Canadiana records in MARC 21 format can be obtained by file transfer through the MARC Records Distribution Service. Finally, Canadiana records appear in *Canadiana Microfiche* (monthly) and *Canadiana Authorities* (quarterly with cumulating supplements), and the semi-annual *Canadiana: The National Bibliography on CD ROM*.

The National Library of Canada provides a number of cataloguing programs and services to assist Canadian and other libraries with processing Canadian materials, and to collaborate with Canadian publishers in making their publications known and accessible. One of the most important of these is Cataloguing in Publication (CIP), under which Canadian publishers submit new titles to be catalogued in advance of publication. This preliminary cataloguing data is made available to the publisher for printing in the book itself and appears in the National Library's online database AMICUS, in the next issue of *Canadiana Microfiche*, and in tabloid format called *Forthcoming Books* (in English) and *Livres à paraître* (in French) which are distributed with the monthly Canadian publishing trade journals *Quill & Quire* and *Livre d'ici* respectively.

The CIP program is decentralized, relying on contractual CIP agents to carry out the cataloguing and publisher liaison in different parts of the country, coordinated and closely monitored by the National Library. The National Library's choice of a decentralized model for this key program reflects the geographic, political and business realities of Canada, with its population and publishing industry located in several regions across the country, and the corresponding need for a regional CIP presence. The CIP program has grown steadily from its inception in 1973 and is now averaging some 9,000 titles per year. It covers the output of all of the major Canadian trade publishers and many smaller publishers. It has been consistently noted as one of the most appreciated of the National Library's services throughout the years. Plans for the CIP program at the beginning of the next millennium centre on expansion of the program to cover more online electronic publications, focusing initially on Canadian federal government documents in electronic form. Expansion to other formats such as videorecordings and maps is under consideration.

The National Library also coordinates the Canadian Theses Service to make available the masters and doctoral theses submitted to some fifty Canadian academic institutions, so that Canadian scholarship can be diffused more widely. The National Library contracts with the private sector for the microfilming (and now, digitization) of theses, and the creation of brief bibliographic records for inclusion in the AMICUS database. Some 10,000 bibliographic records for theses are added to AMICUS each year.

The National Library also supports and promotes a number of international programs such as standard numbering systems aimed at controlling and improving access to publications worldwide. The Library serves as the Canadian national centre for the assignment of ISSNs (International Standard Serial Numbers), ISBNs (International Standard Book Numbers) and ISMNs (International Standard Music Numbers). ISSN Canada is located within the Serials Team, so that its work of creating bibliographic records for Canadian serials for the ISSN network can be integrated with the cataloguing workflow in place for the national bibliography *Canadiana*. The current staff of three (some part-time) is thereby able to furnish a fast and efficient service to publishers. The National Library was one of the founding members of CONSER (Cooperative Online SERials) and its serial records appear in the CONSER database which is operated under the auspices of the U.S. Program for Cooperative Cataloging.

The volume of cataloguing done by the National Library for *Canadiana* has grown enormously over the past fifty years. During the first year of publication of *Canadiana* in 1951, about 2,500 bibliographic records appeared. In 1999, close to 60,000 bibliographic and 17,000 name authority records were created. Since the early 1990s, a system of cataloguing levels and cataloguing priorities has allowed the National Library to concentrate its diminishing resources on the highest priority materials. Priority is generally accorded to Canadian titles covered under the Cataloguing in Publication program, federal government publications distributed under the Depository Services Program of the federal government, and Canadiana published within the last two years, especially those in the National Library's areas of special emphasis: Canadian literature, Canadian history and society, and music in Canada. The National Library gives full cataloguing to all CIP materials, titles for the reference collection, and current Canadiana in the areas of special emphasis. A type of core level cataloguing is created for most other Canadiana material. This level more than meets the requirements for the Program for Cooperative Cataloging core level record except for subject headings, which may or may not be included. An abbreviated record sufficient for identification of the title and listing in the national bibliography is created for older materials outside the areas of special emphasis. Most non-Canadiana publications other than reference works also receive abbreviated records.

The National Library of Canada's cataloguing functions have been automated in some fashion since the late sixties, with MARC records available from 1973. The online bibliographic system DOBIS was adopted for use in Canadiana cataloguing beginning in 1980. This shared bilingual bibliographic system was superseded fifteen years later by AMICUS, the Windows-based online system jointly developed by the National Library and CGI Inc. While AMICUS at the National Library of Canada is currently a bibliographic management system, under development are acquisitions, serials check-in, circulation and OPAC modules.

In recent years, NLC has moved into the digital world by developing policies and strategies which allow it to seek out electronic Canadiana for its collections, to archive online networked publications on its own server, and to provide bibliographic access to these materials through both traditional and non-traditional means. For example, the Library has mainstreamed its cataloguing of electronic journals and monographs by creating MARC records for them in AMICUS. It has as well created a Web portal service for Websites around the world dealing with Canadian topics. Canadian Information by Subject (CIBS)[3] is a bilingual service which uses the Dewey decimal classification (although a user need not know or use Dewey) to organize the sites to which it links, and to provide English and French subject indexes to the sites. The National Library has experimented with the creation of Canadian government GILS (Government Information Locator Service) metadata records, and is examining the utility of Dublin Core or other metadata records in this context. The Library has undertaken an active digitization program to digitize parts of its collection of Canadiana so that it can be made more widely available on the Web, and to publish bibliographic tools and other publications on the Web. It has created electronic research tools and finding aids such as listings of notable Canadian children's books from 1975 to the present, guides to various National Library collections such as its literary and music manuscripts, an index to Canadian federal royal commissions, and the *Virtual Gramophone*, a multimedia database of Canadian historical sound recordings. A number of subject-based gateways such as *Celebrating Women's Achievements* and the *Read Up On It* site, an annual guide to Canadian children's literature, provide enhanced digital access to materials in the collection.

THE PEOPLE

The staff of the National Library of Canada comprises members of both official language groups, as well as people with skills in a variety of other languages. It has grown from a handful of individuals to some 490 people housed in four separate locations. Staff engaged in bibliographic access activities have always been a strong component of the Library, and currently number about ninety full-time equivalents. The cataloguing component is comprised of about seventy percent professional librarians, who require a master of library science degree from an accredited university program, and thirty percent library technicians, who generally have a two-year diploma in library technology. It is current practice to assign cataloguing at the abbreviated and core levels to library technicians, and full level cataloguing to professional librarians. This guideline is subject to flexible application, depending on the type of material being catalogued, the abilities of the individual, her/his training, language skills, etc.

Because of changing demographics, in the 1970s the Library, along with other government departments and other libraries in Canada and North America, underwent a period of intense recruitment of new staff, during which many new graduate librarians were taken on. During the eighties this recruitment slowed significantly, and by the mid-1990s almost no external staffing took place. The Canadian government downsizing, with its retirement incentives in effect from 1995 to 1999, created a bulge of early retirements of eligible staff over the age of fifty. As we move into the new millennium, the National Library is faced (as are other institutions in North America) with the prospect of a workforce that will retire en masse over the next several years. One of the major management challenges for the Library in the coming years is to bring on new staff to fill the gap and to ensure that the wealth of knowledge, corporate memory and skills are passed on to the next generation of National Library employees.

In recruiting new employees for the National Library of Canada, it will be important to attract staff with a wide range of language skills to replace the language expertise lost through attrition, and to respond to the growing amount of publishing in Canada of materials in heritage languages other than English or French. In addition to language skills, a number of core competencies have been identified by the Library for its current and future employees, to be acquired through recruitment or training. For example, increasingly sophisticated skills with new and emerging technologies will be needed, sufficient to accommodate new forms of publishing and to move with confidence and leadership into new technological territory for the delivery of library services, including bibliographic services. Other core competencies pertain to the people skills needed for teamwork, leadership, communication and mentoring, and the need for an employee to take responsibility for her/his career, work relationships and goal attainment. Still other important skills involve consultation with user communities, marketing, and the ability to probe user needs and design and deliver services that meet those needs in a timely and satisfactory way. As well, skill in identifying potential partners and partnerships and in developing partner relationships will be highly prized in the coming years. A skills inventory was conducted to identify the skills that staff have now and those that they feel they should have, and plans are underway to address training and recruitment needs.

Because staff is a critical resource in any knowledge organization, success in recruiting and retaining capable staff will be vitally important to the National Library. Among the factors important in staff recruitment and retention is remuneration. The Library Science group in the Public Service of Canada (as in the library profession as a whole) is female dominated in its composition, which has led to a long history of gender-based pay equity disputes based on Canadian federal legislation passed in the 1980s mandating equal pay for work of equal value in enterprises falling under the jurisdiction of the federal government. In 1999, a pay equity dispute originating in 1985 was settled in favour of the complainants, a group of public service employees and former employees in female dominated occupational groups, including the federal librarians and most library technicians. In the year 2000, the Treasury Board (the employer of record for the Canadian federal public service) hopes to introduce a new job classification scheme, the Universal Classification System, to evaluate jobs based on sixteen elements grouped under the broad headings of responsibility, skills, effort and working conditions. It is hoped that this system, designed to be gender-neutral among other things, will go some way towards eliminating wage discrimination.

CHALLENGES FOR THE NEW MILLENNIUM

As we start the new millennium, we recognize that the cultural, economic and social forces around us will have a tremendous impact on the way we do business. Globalization trends have made us adapt our strategies and our thinking, in order to remain relevant and continue to lead in the complex and wide-ranging field of information management. Partnerships are essential; no one library can act alone and hope to manage all its information needs. NLC is pursuing greater international integration and cooperation, for example through efforts to combine the communication format CAN/MARC with USMARC to form MARC 21 in tune with the twenty-first century. We are pursuing harmonization on several cataloguing fronts, notably with the U.S. Program for Cooperative Cataloging, and with the development of the AACR cataloguing rules, all the while retaining the essentials for Canadian national identity and needs, including our bilingual character.

The challenge of the Web at the end of the twentieth century must be very similar to the challenges people in the sixteenth century faced with the printed page which was collocated into something called a book. This process took many years of experimentation and standardization; similarly the Web, its shape and its uses, will evolve into the new millennium. Certainly the Web has become a democratizing force, as was the advent of the book, raising the expectations of our users for more, better and more timely information. Not only must we deliver bibliographic information in more varied and timely ways, as described above, we must also view library processes as building blocks to be arranged in different patterns to meet user needs. Bibliographic records can now be linked to the actual electronic document by the click of a mouse; information from a publisher about a new publication can be downloaded and become the basis for the catalogue record; a directory of publishers on the Web, with location information, can be linked to the publisher's own Website as well as to that publisher's titles described in a library's catalogue. All of this has been or is being put in place. The cards are on the table; we must see how they are shuffled and what hand we wish to play.

The real challenges for information in the new millennium still revolve around the age-old triangle of creators, users and means. As creators of information, we in libraries are but one group of stakeholders in the global village. While various communities create information, it is often the same information in different guises and flavours. We must constantly remain in contact with other creators to benefit from each other's experiences and to avoid reinventing the wheel. Metadata, for example, is created by many information groups for their own purposes, but it is still in large part bibliographic information, and resembles more and more a traditional bibliographic record.

How quickly and inventively we as a library community respond and adapt to the developments in information creation around us will determine our future as a leader in information management. To do this, we must have well trained and capable staff. Transfer of knowledge and expertise among staff and the development and training of staff in new skills will be crucial to meet the challenges of the future.

At the other end of the spectrum from the creators are the users, a heterogeneous group of needs and expectations. The National Library of Canada will spend some time to take the pulse of the Canadian library community and the Canadian people to respond to ever-changing needs, and to make its bibliographic services better known and used. One trend that is clearly in evidence is the need to have a single-window approach to information. The user wishes to have the convenience of finding not only reference to an item or article but almost instant access to the item itself. As more and more documents and publications are available in electronic form, and as finding aids and indexes become more integrated with catalogue records, we can make progress in providing more seamless access to information across disciplines and formats.

Users also expect to receive information in the way that they want it. This means providing a variety of delivery mechanisms, and accommodating many languages and scripts. Even though the National Library focuses on the collection of and provision of access to Canadiana, that material is increasingly appearing in a variety of languages, including the languages of the First Nations. Canada is a multilingual and culturally diverse country, a fact that places great pressures on the ability of libraries to provide the information in the most appropriate way to citizens. The federal government has designated libraries and schools in Canada as nodes serving the Internet-related needs of Canadians across the country. This represents an enormous opportunity for libraries, including the National Library, to be purveyors and intermediaries between the users and the digital information they seek.

This linking of information to the user through the Internet has given new meaning to the term resource-sharing. In the digital environment the National Library seeks to be a leader in the application of digital technologies to library services and the richest resource of Canadian information published in electronic format now and in the future. The Library is examining its access policies and services in the era of Web publishing, to accommodate the fast-paced change in publishing without abandoning the standards so painstakingly established over the years. The goal of resource sharing nationally and internationally is as strong as ever. Technology, the third side of the triangle, will provide the means to improve the creation of information and delivery of services.

Many cataloguing thinkers and practitioners since the pioneering work of Jewett, Cutter and Dewey have shared the dream to provide access to information efficiently and in a form desired by the user. Aided by the technologies available today and the improvements promised for the future, the trained and multidisciplinary staff that will cater to the needs of the user may hope to provide the stellar service that our predecessors envisaged. Let us take up the challenge and make bibliographic information accessible to all.

NOTES

1. Liz McKeen and Ingrid Parent. "Re-engineering as a change agent at the National Library of Canada" in *Alexandria*, 7 (2), 1995, pp. 107-113.

2. "The National Library of Canada's Service Standard Declaration" in National Library of Canada website. [http://www.nlc-bnc.ca/about/eservst.htm] October 10, 1999.

3. "Canadian Information by Subject" in National Library of Canada website. [http://www.nlc-bnc.ca/caninfo] December 13, 1999.

LIBRARIES
AROUND THE WORLD

Defying Conventional Wisdom: Innovation and Culture Change from Down Under

Jilleen Chambers
Jennifer Martin
Beverley Reynolds

SUMMARY. During the last few years, the Technical Services Section of Griffith University Library has undergone widespread and radical change. An ambitious goal of a 50% productivity improvement was a major driving force. The approaches taken to achieve this were three-fold: developing innovative technological solutions to reduce repetitive components of technical services work without sacrificing quality; entering into a mutually beneficial partnership agreement with a preferred vendor; and, instituting a culture change that included high performance, and self managed teams. This paper describes the processes undertaken, and outcomes achieved. *[Article copies available for a fee from The Haworth Document Delivery Service: 1-800-342-9678. E-mail address: <getinfo@haworthpressinc.com> Website: <http://www.HaworthPress.com>]*

Jilleen Chambers is Library Technician in the Serials, Government and Law Team. Jennifer Martin is Librarian in the Monographs Team. Beverley Reynolds is Technical Services Systems Coordinator.

Address correspondence to the authors at: Technical Services, Griffith University Library, Nathan, Queensland 4111, Australia (E-mail to: J.Chambers@mailbox.gu.edu.au; J.Martin@mailbox.gu.edu.au; B.Reynolds@mailbox.gu.edu.au).

The authors would like to acknowledge the support and invaluable assistance of Annette McNicol, the Technical Services Manager, in the preparation of this paper.

[Haworth co-indexing entry note]: "Defying Conventional Wisdom: Innovation and Culture Change from Down Under." Chambers, Jilleen, Jennifer Martin, and Beverley Reynolds. Co-published simultaneously in *Cataloging & Classification Quarterly* (The Haworth Information Press, an imprint of The Haworth Press, Inc.) Vol. 30, No. 1, 2000, pp. 35-50; and: *Managing Cataloging and the Organization of Information: Philosophies, Practices and Challenges at the Onset of the 21st Century* (ed: Ruth C. Carter) The Haworth Information Press, an imprint of The Haworth Press, Inc., 2000, pp. 35-50. Single or multiple copies of this article are available for a fee from The Haworth Document Delivery Service [1-800-342-9678, 9:00 a.m. - 5:00 p.m. (EST). E-mail address: getinfo@haworthpressinc.com].

KEYWORDS. Re-engineering, culture change, technology, innovations, vendors, partnerships, Griffith University

INTRODUCTION

In common with other Australian libraries, Griffith University Library was, and still is, under pressure to increase services to clients and provide access to a wide range of information resources without increases in staff or budgets. In order to meet this challenge, in 1996, the Technical Services Section of the library undertook a bold re-engineering project. What did we do that was different and why has it been so successful?

Griffith University is a multi-campus institution situated in southeast Queensland, Australia and serves over 21,000 students. Four campuses are located in Brisbane, one on the Gold Coast and a new campus at Logan, south of Brisbane. Library services are provided at each campus. The library clientele consists primarily of academic staff, undergraduate and graduate students undertaking studies in a wide range of disciplines ranging from art and music to nursing, engineering and law. Technical service functions, except for serials accessioning and binding, are centralised at the Nathan campus. The combined holdings for the libraries are approximately 850,000 items.

Griffith University prides itself on being innovative and the Division of Information Services, which includes the library, is no exception. As a result of a review of the Technical Services Section conducted in late 1995, a major re-engineering project occurred during 1996. The aim was to create a streamlined, effective organisation with dramatic improvements in the critical areas of cost and timeliness without sacrificing quality.

The Project

Prior to 1994, the Technical Services Section had a fairly traditional structure with separate acquisition and cataloguing sections. Staff job descriptions were narrow and task based. In late 1994, the Section underwent its first restructure and was formed into five teams. Three subject based teams undertook acquisitions, cataloguing (including authority work), and processing of monographs. Serials and legal publications were handled by another team while a fifth team undertook projects and systems work.

The most notable outcome from the restructure was the multi-skilling of staff, particularly library clerical staff and library technicians. However, there was a recognition that simply changing the structure of the Section would not provide the productivity gains that management were expecting. We had assumed that simply changing structures or restructuring roles would bring success; we found, however, (as others had before us[1]), that everything we tried was quickly negated by the very cultural patterns and practices we wanted to change.

In late 1995, the Section was again reviewed, this time by an external consultant who recommended a more radical approach that led to a re-engineering of the section. The goal of the project was very ambitious–50% improvement in productivity. There would be a 50% reduction in staff levels made possible by redesigning processes, and by automation of a number of activities.

Unlike the first review, which was carried out by a committee of elected staff, the re-engineering design was undertaken using a small project team which included the external consultant, the Technical Services Manager and two others. The timeframe for the project was only eight months and input from staff was limited. The consultant was of the opinion that it would be difficult for staff to be involved in a project where they or their colleagues might lose their jobs.

The project team looked at the current processes–at how library materials were selected, acquired, catalogued and processed. Activities were benchmarked in order to provide cost estimates for the current technical services functions. Material and staff costs were collected, and acquisition and cataloguing turn-around times examined.

Input from staff was obtained through focus groups and brainstorming sessions. The team also conducted literature searches, and talked to other libraries, library vendors and system vendors. They challenged all existing models and assumptions on organising and managing a technical services operation with the aim of redesigning, not just building on or remodelling, an existing system. Existing and potential vendor services were explored.

A major goal was to automate as many processes as possible, making technology work for us, by reducing tedious and repetitive work. Where it was more efficient or cost effective to do so, functions would be outsourced. However, the consultant stressed that in order to create the conditions required to achieve and sustain improved productivity, the culture of the section needed to be radically changed.

CHANGING A CULTURE

We cannot deny that 1996 was a very stressful year for staff as management had declared up front that staff numbers would be reduced by 50%. To assist staff in this transition period, change management workshops were conducted and the project team ensured that staff were kept informed of progress. Staff were given an assurance that everyone would be eligible to apply for positions in the restructured section. There would be opportunities for surplus staff to be redeployed to other areas of the library. Interestingly, the majority of staff wished to remain in technical services.

The project team recommended that the section be re-organised into two high performance self-managed teams. This was a radical step and the success or failure of the restructure of the section would depend on the willingness of staff to be involved. Therefore, it was recommended that all positions in the section be made permanent; previously, a high proportion of staff were employed on temporary or fixed term contracts. Permanency was seen as a commitment by management to their staff, and by staff to the new organisation. Team leaders were appointed to each team to facilitate the implementation of the self-managed teams, although the ultimate goal was for the teams to become fully self-managed.

A key feature of the new structure is that teams are encouraged to be pro-active, innovative and committed to excellence within a culture of continuous improvement. Team leaders act as facilitators, coaches and as intermediaries with management. There is a strong emphasis on teamwork and all team members: participate in decision making; set team goals; develop procedures; establish time lines; and chair meetings. Staff take responsibility for the selection and recruitment of new team members.

Within the framework of the team structure, individuals have autonomy in their own jobs. They have responsibility for setting work goals and determining training needs. As part of a learning organisation, everyone is expected to undertake a minimum of ten days work related training per year. This training may be on-the-job training, attending courses, seminars, conferences, or doing private reading or study during work time. Staff are also encouraged to present workshops on topics of relevance to their team including reports on external courses that they have attended.

Sharing of information is emphasised and the Technical Services Manager and team leaders pass on all relevant communications from management or suppliers. Only personal and confidential information is filtered. The philosophy of the section is that staff can only make full and informed decisions about their work when they have full access to all relevant information.

Performance measurement of all aspects of the work of the section is important. The teams monitor their own performance, calculating unit costs, labour productivity, and turn-around times. Staff report on training undertaken, and on continuous improvement initiatives and their outcomes. Individual team members have their performance evaluated annually with six-monthly reviews and one team has instituted 360-degree feedback sessions for all team members including the team leader. A recognition and reward program has been implemented and staff are rewarded for reaching specified agreed targets.

The change in culture has seen the Technical Services Section move from a traditional structure where management is the function of managers to a high performance organisation where everyone is a manager and empowered people work in collaboration. The focus is on people.

PARTNERSHIP AND QUALITY

Along with changing the culture internally, we identified a need to influence the culture external to our organisation–in particular, the nature of the relationship with our vendors. Previously, we had operated in a fairly traditional style, having several preferred library vendors with whom we had excellent relations. Every year we met and negotiated prices, being careful to share the budget allocation equitably. The vendor's role was simply to supply us with the material we requested. However, we wanted to take advantage of the vendors' economies of scale, and develop a full partnership relationship where both parties benefited.

Our goal for monographs was to have the vendor supply us with shelf ready items, with accompanying full Library of Congress (LC) MARC records, wherever possible. We agreed, though, that in-house cataloguing would continue for items that needed special localised adaptations, or where suitable MARC records were not available. Ordering and invoicing were to be totally automated. Orders would be placed directly on the vendor's database and subsequently loaded onto our local system.

For serials, we required a full consolidation service. Our vendor would check-in, claim and end process all issues. A vendor-supplied barcode would assist with check-in on our local system.

Initially, we advertised a Registration of Capability and subsequently a Request for Proposal for the supply of materials and services. Our expectations were to receive 80% of items from our preferred vendors and 20% would be supplied by specialist vendors. The chosen vendors would need to: be willing to enter into a partnership agreement with us; supply shelf ready materials; establish selection profiles and blanket order plans; and be willing to work with us to develop technological solutions that would be beneficial to both organisations. As part of the partnership agreement, it meant that these vendors had to be completely honest with us regarding their profit margins. We, in turn, would ensure prompt payment and minimal return of materials. To protect the vendors, we required all our staff to sign confidentiality agreements. All round, this would require trust and open and honest communication in large helpings.

After exhaustive discussions, we eventually decided to enter into partnership with Blackwells, Oxford and North America for our overseas materials and James Bennett for our Australian materials. To date, we have enjoyed a professional and amicable relationship. The partnership has provided an environment within which alternative approaches to library acquisition practices have been jointly explored, developed and implemented. Our work processes have been revolutionised. Together, we can propose innovative solutions that, in turn, assist the vendor's other clients and ultimately, their business.

As has been noted in the context of Australian business, "innovating enterprises looked two ways–they focussed on satisfying their customers, and they emphasised building a profitable supply system. Another form of assistance was helping to change the culture in the supplier's workplace. Working systematically on the relationship with suppliers did not bring overnight success. Success came through building up the capabilities of the business and in the suppliers, and was based on trust, information and shared interests."[2]

The partnership relies heavily on constant communication. For example, our staff routinely contact our vendor partners by email with agreed response times of 48 hours. At other levels, partnership meetings are held every six months to address any concerns, performance issues, negotiation of terms of trade, and future directions. Teleconferencing has been used to resolve issues of more immediate concern or for development projects.

Blanket Order Plans

The library has been cautious in its approach because it is important that it still has control of the selection of materials and the development of its collection. We are aware of criticism that has been levelled at other libraries in the past for virtually handing over selection to a vendor. Our approach was to have our selection librarians set up profiles for their subject areas in consultation with the vendors.

In the first instance we received New Titles Announcement Service (NTAS) slips or forms instead of materials. We could accept or reject the recommended titles and use this information to subsequently refine the profiles. We have found that in some subject areas, there is such a plethora of materials published that it is very difficult to reach a point where we are prepared to stop receiving forms and start receiving blanket order titles. We have been able to convert to blanket plans in some subject areas.

In the initial redesign, we envisaged 60% of all monographs being supplied as blanket orders. With small budgets and expensive titles, it soon became evident this was untenable. However, with the advent of Collection Manager (Blackwell's web-based database), blanket order plans have become less relevant as selection librarians can select and order, very efficiently, on-line from the profiles they have set up on Collection Manager. This is a cost-effective way of giving selection librarians control of collection management and we no longer need to receive paper forms.

Another area of concern was duplication of materials between blanket and firm orders. We have worked closely with the vendors to eradicate this problem using a combination of profile refinements and system modifications.

Database Quality

Maintaining the quality of our database was a serious concern at the time. Our cataloguers catalogued to international standards and they took pride in maintaining quality records that enhanced access for users. It was agreed that we would only accept Library of Congress records. Blackwells would upgrade certain categories of LC Cataloguing-In-Publication (CIP) records but would not undertake original cataloguing for us. Enhanced Table of Contents (TOC) data were to be supplied by Blackwells and users have found this resource a welcome addition to our catalogue. To date, Bennetts have supplied us with brief records only. The decision was made that all other materials were to be catalogued in-house.

Much work has been done to ensure that records matched correctly, and that confirmation or shipment records, often just brief records, do not overwrite a full catalogue record. We also wanted to maintain a number of local practices. Some materials are ordered under a special code that excludes them from the shelf-ready process. For instance, Australian literature is classified differently from Library of Congress to allow more scope and the Moys system of classification is used for our legal materials.

Authority Control

An integral part of database quality is authority control which is done in-house. We were no longer able to do all the authority work at the time of cataloguing because catalogue records were to be batch loaded into the local library system. Consequently, our cataloguers receive new headings lists daily that they use to review, upgrade and/or amend authority records as required.

A small group from Technical Services has since conducted a project that looked at the value of authority work and how it was undertaken. This group made some interesting findings and the details are available in an article by Jensen, Schulz and Scott.[3] One of the outcomes of this project was the decision to load the Library of Congress subject files. This has proven to be very beneficial in saving work hours. If we had been a United States library, our authority control would not have been quite so problematic and we may even have considered outsourcing this work. However, we wanted to maintain unique Australian headings that enhance our users' access. We had long ago decided to use Pinyin for our Chinese headings while Library of Congress was still using Wade Giles.

Alternate Cataloguing Source

Our philosophy of continuous improvement means that our processes do not remain static. Over the past few years they have been constantly changing, as we look for ways of working smarter. Consequently, we investigated having our vendor supply original catalogue records from a third party. A pilot study was set up and our cataloguers assessed the records supplied. As part of this study, we also benchmarked our own original cataloguing processes and found that our internal processes were more cost effective, and our cataloguing was ot higher quality. However, we would be willing to investigate alternative sources of catalogue records again in the future. The information gained from this trial was shared with our vendor partner giving them useful data to assist in their strategic planning.

TECHNOLOGICAL CHANGES

Technology has played an important role in the changes that have taken place within Technical Services. Given that we wanted to streamline processes as much as possible and reduce the amounts of both manual intervention and repetitive tasks, we investigated technological solutions to assist us. Our aim was to use technology where possible, but we did not want to sacrifice quality for process. A balance was required.

Our approach was to work in stages, particularly with our vendor partner (Blackwells). Monographic ordering was targeted initially and the following gives a step by step approach to present processes.

We examined various existing standards used for the interchange of electronic data (EDI) including BISAC (Book Industry Systems Advisory Committee), the well established fixed length format for books;[4] X12, variable length records and fields for book and serial ordering developed by ANSI ASC (American National Standards Institute Accredited Standards Committee);[5] and EDIFACT (EDI for Administration, Commerce and Transport), developed by the United Nations Economic Commission for Europe. [6]

These developing standards did not meet our needs. We wanted to:

- place orders directly onto the vendor database obviating the need to print orders from the local system or generate a file of orders for transmission to the vendor;

- receive these orders electronically for loading to the local library system;
- accession and invoice electronically when the shipped items arrived;
- receive high quality catalogue records where possible;
- receive shelf ready items (fully end processed with barcode, stamp, tattle tape, spine label) with each full MARC record provided by the vendor;
- identify minimal level or CIP MARC records for upgrading;
- accommodate specific in-house processing requirements, e.g., law titles at Griffith University are classified according to Moys; and
- use error/exception reporting to monitor processing rather than examine every order/item received.

Round table discussions were held with our vendor partners, our library systems supplier (Geac), and staff from the Library System Support and Technical Services Sections. A decision was made to use the existing Blackwells product, MARC with Books, with modification. The bibliographic MARC record would be used as a carrier for related acquisition data, utilising additional 9XX tags.

As a result, some specific programming changes were required to be done by Blackwells so that output from their New Titles Online (NTO) database, and later the web based, Collection Manager database, would provide the desired information. Australian Geac staff proposed programming a new loader which would accommodate both acquisitions and OPAC (main database) updating of the local library system, ADVANCE. Our Library Systems Support staff undertook preparation of specifications for the new loader, with subsequent testing and implementation.

A distinction was made between firm orders and titles supplied under blanket order plans. Staff would place firm orders online on the vendor database, while blanket order titles would be supplied, according to the established profile.

Firm Orders

Processing of firm orders is a two-stage process. We receive a confirmation order record initially, followed by a shipment invoice record.

Confirmation Orders

Firm orders are catalogue checked against the local database. Orders are placed on the vendor database using campus-based logins. Placing an order on the vendor database automatically ensures an electronic order is created. Orders are batch processed daily by the vendor. Orders were initially placed on NTO, but with the integration of the Blackwells US and UK databases, selection librarians and technical services staff now place orders on the web based Collection Manager.

Initial notification of firm orders takes the form of a file of confirmation order records. The bibliographic record on the vendor database is enhanced with the order date, estimated price, number of copies, purchase order number, fund code and any notes (e.g. additional copy, notify requesting staff member on arrival, etc.) (see Figure 1).

Confirmation order files are output to the vendor's FTP (file transfer protocol) site and nominated staff are emailed with file details. Retrieval of files was handled manually during the early stages, but scheduled daily retrieval of files has now been automated with retrieved files being stored locally in a holding directory for 24 hours. Again, nominated staff are emailed with a detailed log of the FTP

FIGURE 1. Confirmation Order Stage

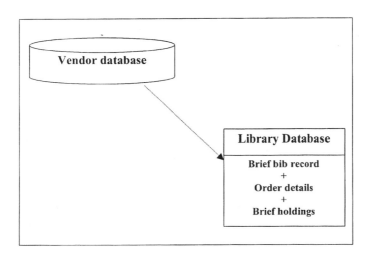

transactions. The delay has been built in, initially to allow time for the vendor to notify us of any potential problems.

A schedule has been established to move files automatically from the holding directory to a designated load directory. Email notification of file transfers to nominated staff also occurs. Using a series of different loader profiles, based on vendor, filename, record type (confirmation or shipment), each profile assigns a number of default values, e.g., currency code, order type, circulation code, etc.

During the load processing, a number of events take place. New orders are created within the acquisitions module of the local integrated library system. Funds are committed with commitment based on the estimated price and the fund used, and the currency conversion is based on the currency of the vendor. Funds have been established to uniquely identify both campus and subject discipline. A system check is also done to ensure that funds are not overcommitted. An acquisitions holdings location, derived from the fund code, is assigned. Concurrently, a bibliographic record is added to the main database following duplicate checking. If the title is already held in the catalogue, the program adds a location statement which includes the campus information, the purchase order number and an 'on order' status. If the title is not already held, a new bibliographic record with location statement is added to the database.

Loads can be run interactively, or, as is the current practice, scheduled to run automatically as a background process. With each batch of records loaded, a nominated staff member receives email notification of the summary results.

Following automatic loading of files, load reports are prepared. They are used to identify any errors, e.g., invalid funds, insufficient funds. These errors are then investigated and corrected by staff. These reports are currently run manually, and placed on an intranet web server where they are accessible to all staff. Automated report generation has been designated as a future enhancement.

Shipment Records

For firm orders, the second stage is the receipt of shipment and invoicing information. When items are ready to be invoiced and shipped by the vendor (weekly), a second file of MARC records containing invoice information is produced. These shipment records contain the purchase order number, fund code, invoice date, invoice number, invoice line number, selling price, number of copies, type of order (firm or approval). These records are identical in bibliographic content to the confirmation records, unless the vendor has upgraded their database record, e.g., replaced a CIP record with a full MARC record, since we received the initial confirmation record.

Files of records, corresponding to invoiced items are placed on the vendor FTP server. Email notification of files ready for pickup is sent to nominated staff. Automated retrieval of shipment files occurs (as for confirmation records) to a holding directory. Loading of shipment files is delayed until the shipment of books actually arrives and is unpacked. This could result in a delay of a few weeks between supply of records and supply of the items, depending on the length of time in transit.

When the shipment arrives together with the paper copy of the invoice, staff responsible for unpacking boxes request that files relating to specified invoices be loaded. The staff member responsible selects the appropriate files from those in the holding directory and the background processor does the rest.

During shipment load processing, the loader uses the purchase order number as the primary match point with bibliographic details (vendor title no., ISBN, LCCN or title) used as secondary checks (see Figure 2). A status of 'received' is assigned to the order. Funds are expended based on the listed selling price in the record and the number of copies supplied. An invoice is built from the invoice number and invoice line number. The main database record is updated with any new bibliographic details. The 'on order' location statement is replaced by a holdings record containing a barcode and, for shelf ready items, the call number derived from the Library of Congress Classification Number (bibliographic tag 050). A default circulation code is also assigned.

Part of the load processing depends on the value of the bibliographic leader character position 17 (Encoding level). The following values are used:

- blank = full MARC record (from LC)
- 8 = CIP MARC record (from LC)
- z = brief packing list record (from vendor)
- any other value = less than full level MARC records

FIGURE 2. Shipment Record Stage

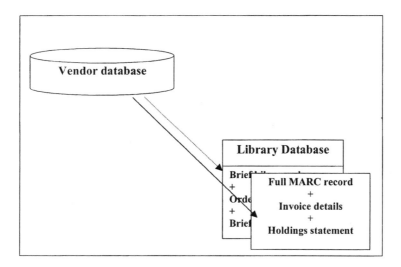

If the record is loaded as a new title, then any encoding level can be accepted, although all which are not full MARC records are reported and are either replaced or upgraded, as appropriate.

If the incoming record to be loaded matches an existing full MARC database record, then the database record is retained (given that we may have made local modifications to the record that we wish to retain). However, certain tags from the incoming record, if present, are added to the existing database record, for example: table of contents (tag 505) and summary notes (tag 520).

Following the load, staff match the 'built' invoice details with the paper invoice supplied, and authorise payment. Shelf ready items are forwarded directly to the appropriate campus. Shipment load reports are used to identify any categories that require in-house intervention in accordance with our total quality management.

There are two categories of items that are not supplied shelf ready–those where Blackwells have been unable to supply a MARC record that meets our specifications, and those requiring local modification. In the first category, where a brief MARC record is supplied, the Australian national bibliographic database, Kinetica, is searched for a full MARC record. If a record is found, it is downline loaded immediately, and used to replace the brief packing list record. As most Australian libraries use the Dewey classification, records retrieved often lack an LC classification number. If this is the case, staff assign an LC number. If a catalogue record is not found on Kinetica, our cataloguers create an original record. In the second category are non shelf ready items, identified at ordering as requiring in-house amendment, e.g., all law items are classified according to Moys. Partial end processing is supplied by the vendor for the foregoing categories.

Blanket Titles

Since provision of titles under Blackwells approval plans is automatic, it was decided that a 'confirmation' order record was not required for these titles. Consequently, only a 'shipment' record is supplied. The process of receipt of the files, loading and invoicing is similar to that for firm orders, except that the loader creates an order and receives the item at the same time. Records for all approval titles are full MARC records and items are shelf ready.

CONCLUSION

The Technical Services Section of Griffith University Library has undergone radical change since 1996. The re-engineering project encompassed three main interacting and interdependent changes. All work processes were critically examined; none were deemed to be sacrosanct. We have used technological solutions, in combination with the development of a partnership relationship with our preferred vendor. Finally, we have undertaken a radical culture change, without which the other facets would have been far less effective.

The process has at times been stressful. Although we defied conventional wisdom, we can now assess these changes, acknowledging that great progress has been made. Together, we have been able to work through, and be released from, an inherent fear of change. Our team members have developed a healthy respect for each other's strengths and learned how to take responsibility for their work. Staff now have a boldness to approach the future with the knowledge that we can grow, develop, and even influence future directions. It is not expected that the future will be 'plain sailing,' but we are prepared to face its challenges.

REFERENCES

1. Terence E. Deal and Pamela C. Hawkins, "Setting the Spirit Free: Tapping Ego Energy," in: *Managing Ego Energy: The Transformation of Personal Meaning into Organisational Success* (San Francisco: Jossey-Bass, 1994) 73-99.

2. Roderick Carnegie and Matthew Butlin, *Managing the Innovating Enterprise* (Melbourne: Business Library in association with the Business Council of Australia, 1993): 66, quoted in Tony Lendrum, *The Strategic Partnering Handbook: A Practical Guide For Managers* (New York: McGraw-Hill, 1995), 197.

3. Paul Jensen, Nathalie Schulz, and Meryn Scott, " The Griffith University Authority Control Project," *Cataloguing Australia* 24, No.1/2 (March/June 1998): 21-35.

4. For a more complete description, see: BISG (Book Industry Study Group) "BISAC" *(http://www.bookwire.com/bisg/bisac.html)*.

5. For a more complete description, see: ANSI ASC (American National Standards Institute Accredited Standards Committee) *(http://www.ansi.org/)*, developer of the X12 standard; and, DISA (Data Interchange Standards Association) ASC X12 *(http://www.x12.org/)*.

6. For a more complete description, see: UN/ECE (United Nations Economic Commission for Europe) "EDIFACT" *(http://www.unece.org/trade/untdid/)*.

Emerging from the Bibliographic Wilderness: Catalogue Automation in the Bodleian Library, University of Oxford

Peter P. Burnett

SUMMARY. This article provides a history of cataloguing and catalogue automation at the Bodleian Library, Oxford University and includes a description of the Catalogue Support Services within the Cataloguing Division of the Bodleian Technical Services Department. The 1995 decision to migrate to Geac and some subsequent development and implementation is described along with staff training for the cataloguing module. The article includes an assessment of the impact of automation and challenges for the future. *[Article copies available for a fee from The Haworth Document Delivery Service: 1-800-342-9678. E-mail address: <getinfo@haworthpressinc.com> Website: <http://www.HaworthPress.com>]*

KEYWORDS. Cataloguing, catalog automation, Bodleian Library, Oxford University, Geac, staff training

INTRODUCTION

The Bodleian Library in the University of Oxford is one of the oldest libraries in Europe, and in England is second in size only to the

---

Peter P. Burnett, BA, MA, is Head of Technical Services, Bodleian Library, Oxford University, Broad Street, Oxford OX1 3BG, England.

[Haworth co-indexing entry note]: "Emerging from the Bibliographic Wilderness: Catalogue Automation in the Bodleian Library, University of Oxford." Burnett, Peter P. Co-published simultaneously in *Cataloging & Classification Quarterly* (The Haworth Information Press, an imprint of The Haworth Press, Inc.) Vol. 30, No. 1, 2000, pp. 51-72; and: *Managing Cataloging and the Organization of Information: Philosophies, Practices and Challenges at the Onset of the 21st Century* (ed: Ruth C. Carter) The Haworth Press, an imprint of The Haworth Press, Inc., 2000, pp. 51-72. Single or multiple copies of this article are available for a fee from The Haworth Document Delivery Service [1-800-342-9678, 9:00 a.m. - 5:00 p.m. (EST). E-mail address: getinfo@haworthpressinc.com].

British Library. It has a continuous history from 1602, the date of its "restoration" by Sir Thomas Bodley, but even then this was a re-foundation on the site of an earlier library. In fact, the first University library of Oxford dates back to circa 1320. In 1610 Bodley entered into an agreement with the Stationers Company, whereby the Stationers undertook to send to the Library every new book that they published. This agreement made the Bodleian Library virtually a deposit library 150 years before the British Museum was founded. The Library has continued to enjoy the privilege of legal deposit since that date, and now contains over 7 million volumes (including 6,500 incunabula), 1.2 million maps, and over 1 million music scores. The collections may be accessed through 29 reading rooms in 12 separate buildings.

The University of Oxford has an even longer history, dating back to the end of the 11th century. The first recorded overseas student was Emo of Friesland in 1190, and in 1214 the title of Chancellor was formally conferred to the *magister scolarum Oxonie*. The earliest colleges date back to the late 13th century and began as medieval halls of residence. The relationship between the colleges and the University has evolved over 800 years and is not a simple one. The University (in the narrower sense of the central institution) provides the curricular framework, sets examinations and awards degrees, while the colleges essentially provide the teaching.

This complex legacy is apparent today within the library environment. In addition to the Bodleian, the University of Oxford has approximately 100 other libraries. These include two further "central" libraries (the Taylor Institution Library and the library of the Ashmolean Museum), 39 college libraries (some of which predate the Bodleian Library itself), and 62 undergraduate lending libraries in the humanities and social sciences (faculty libraries) and in science and technology (departmental libraries). Despite the large number, only five or six of these libraries have more than 5 staff.

Traditionally, these libraries have been either entirely autonomous (as in the case of college libraries) or partially independent (in the case of departmental libraries). Only the central libraries and the faculty libraries have been under the fiscal oversight of a central University Libraries Committee. Since 1997 this situation has been undergoing organisational change following the appointment of the University's first *Director of University Library Services and Bodley's Librarian,* whose remit is to introduce structural integration within the University. Nevertheless it is true to state that developments in library automation have largely taken place in a decentralised environment, characterised by relative library autonomy and a poorly co-ordinated management structure.

Prior to automation, Oxford libraries maintained manual catalogues of variable standards and in different formats. They were often out-of-date and inaccurate, and inevitably dispersed geographically throughout the city of Oxford. The level of cataloguing duplication throughout the system was inevitably wasteful and expensive, and bibliographic access to the wealth of library holdings was laborious and time-consuming.

CATALOGUE AUTOMATION IN OXFORD

The history of catalogue automation in Oxford dates back essentially to the mid-1960s. Indeed the very first Anglo-American conference on library automation took place at Brasenose College, Oxford in 1966. Attended by over 65 British and American University Library Directors, the stated intention of this conference was not only to form the basis of Anglo-American cooperation in the field of library automation, but also to serve a springboard for the development of common practices and policies.[1]

Throughout the latter part of the 1960s and the following decade, the Bodleian Library concentrated on the retrospective conversion of its catalogue of pre-1920 holdings. The history of this project has been described elsewhere, and need not be repeated here.[2] Although essentially a keyboarding project, it was in many ways ahead of its time, having experimented with Optical Character Recognition processes and automatic formatting software, together with techniques of online editing–at a time when batch processing was still the norm. While it would be wrong to give the impression that no developments in automation occurred during the 1970s, it would not be unfair to suggest that little progress on other aspects of automation was made during this period, and AACR and MARC were allowed to pass us by.

During this period the Library did not adopt the MARC format that had been developed at the Library of Congress, and adopted elsewhere. The reason for this is quite illuminating. Between 1969-1971 the Bodleian Library conducted a MARC evaluation project, the purpose of which was to investigate the possibility of automatically producing local catalogue entries from MARC records, (i.e., to extract and manipulate the contents of MARC records to form catalogue entries based on the then-existing and somewhat idiosyncratic Bodleian practices). The final report concluded "it is unlikely that . . . the Anglo-American Cataloguing Rules which underlay MARC would prove tractable to the needs of large machine-readable catalogues," and that "the utility of MARC records in the production and maintenance of working catalogues for large academic libraries was, and is likely to remain, unconfirmed."[3] How wrong that conclusion was! It lost the Library nearly 15 years of automation development.

By 1981 there was a general recognition that Oxford was lagging well behind other libraries in the automation field. Computer science had advanced, costs were coming down, libraries were joining co-operatives and entering programs of shared cataloguing, and national and international standards (including a 2nd edition of AACR) were by this time widely accepted. In 1981 a Working Party was appointed to investigate library computerisation in Oxford, fearing that unless something was done soon the Oxford library service would become increasingly inefficient and old-fashioned. The Report of the Working Party, which appeared in 1983, marks the true beginning of automation in Oxford.[4]

Following the recommendations of the report, three undergraduate faculty libraries, with a total lending stock of c. 150,000 volumes, were subsequently automated between 1985-1987 (using OCLC's LS2000 system), their holdings converted, online cataloguing introduced, and an OPAC mounted. This was considered to be something in the nature of a pilot project, both to ascertain the various implications of automation on services and procedures, and to convince sceptical Oxford minds of the benefits.

As far as the Bodleian Library was concerned, a feasibility study was undertaken between June 1985 and May 1986. It recommended that automation could be phased in, at considerably less expense than had been earlier suggested and that automation would actually be cost-effective, as well as facilitating the provision of an immeasurably improved catalogue.

Stimulated by the success of the Faculty Libraries Pilot Project and the positive and encouraging recommendations of the Bodleian Report, the University decided that we should strive towards the implementation of automated cataloguing in Bodleian in early 1988. By this time, the vision was not simply that of an automated Bodleian Library, but of a University-wide totally automated integrated system, capable of expansion over time to accommodate eventually the cataloguing output from all of the University and college libraries. An Oxford University union catalogue would come, at last, within the bounds of possibility.

In December 1986, a request for proposals (RFP) was sent to tender. After the usual evaluation process, the contract was given in August 1987 to IBM for DOBIS/LIBIS.

Four basic bibliographical principles were to underpin the new union catalogue: (1) any record created by one Oxford library should be usable by another, (2) that records created by libraries outside Oxford should be equally usable, (3) there should be the minimum amount of editing, and (4) there should be a systematic and consistent means of providing subject access to the collection, hitherto generally unavailable in Oxford.

Before online cataloguing could commence in the Bodleian, several preparatory tasks had to be undertaken in advance. At that time, the Cataloguing Division could not boast a single power point, its lighting was wholly inadequate for the introduction of computer terminals and the furniture, while sympathetic with its environment, was totally impractical for the coils of cables about to be introduced. In the space of one year the Bodleian Library (a building complex spanning 4 centuries of architectural styles) was rewired for data transmission, power points were installed, furniture upgraded, and new non-glare uplighting put in place. During the first half of 1988, Bodleian cataloguing staff also had to be trained in AACR2, MARC and LCSH–a significant task when one remembers that Bodleian cataloguers were still applying the rules first drawn up in 1882 (revised 1923) for producing manual catalogue entries, and had very little expertise in any of the standards which had been adopted. Despite the many problems of that period, the result was that on the 13th September 1988 the first Bodleian catalogue entry was created online in the new Oxford Library Information System database (known locally as OLIS).

FROM MANUAL TO AUTOMATED PROCESSING

The implementation of automated cataloguing introduced the completely new concept of "copy cataloguing" in the Bodleian, which inevitably had serious implications for the organisation of cataloguing workflow. Initially, the Bodleian Cataloguing Division was reorganised into the conventional copy cataloguing and original cataloguing units, with clerical staff responsible for the former, and academic-related professional staff undertaking the latter task. We quickly found this to be somewhat inefficient, as this approach necessitated both multiple searching, and double handling of the material. It is commonly accepted that the more times a book is handled for cataloguing purposes, the more inefficient and costly the process. Thus, shortly after the introduction of our Dobis/Libis system in 1988, current cataloguing operations were restructured into English-language and foreign-language units. The English cataloguers undertook both copy and original cataloguing, and were graded at one common (clerical) grade. The distinction between foreign-language copy and original cataloguing was nevertheless maintained, due primarily to the larger differentials in salary then existing between clerical and professional staff.

AACR2, USMARC and LCSH were adopted as the standards for the creation of bibliographic records in Oxford's new Library and Information System. Having decided that the standards should be international ones, the next step was to define and establish a Minimum Cataloguing Level that would be acceptable to the many varied Oxford libraries. A Working Party on Cataloguing Standards was established and an OLIS Minimum Standard was determined, although a Fuller Standard was formulated for the Bodleian and the larger local libraries. Standards and union cataloguing policies are currently maintained through the mechanism of a Cataloguers' Forum, attended by cataloguers from each of the member libraries, and a Steering Committee, chaired by Bodley's Head of Technical Services, which monitors developments locally, nationally and internationally and progresses the decisions of the Forum. The implementation of University-wide AACR2 and MARC standards introduced an extra degree of difficulty for cataloguers, superimposing the complexities of data processing requirements upon the already challenging difficulties of bibliography itself. Training thus became, and continues to be a crucial factor.

Perhaps more significant is the change of mindset that occurred as a result of the introduction of copy cataloguing. An institution that hitherto had maintained total control over its cataloguing rules and standards, now found itself utilising the work of other institutions, and necessarily accepting rule interpretations and conventions no longer under its sole control. Initially it was difficult to convince some cataloguers, and indeed individual librarians, of the need for this change. Exclamations of "Why should we change our practises?" or "We've never done it this way before" were commonplace. Today, we hear few complaints. Staff recognise that common standards do not mean rigidity or inflexibility, or compulsory enforcement of change to achieve bureaucratic uniformity, but rather help us to question the validity of older procedures and help us accept responsibility for and ownership of the system as a whole. Copy cataloguing has now become accepted as the norm, and today cataloguers take for granted access not only a local "bibliographic pool" that holds the weekly files of UKMARC records (converted to USMARC), but also the convenient accessibility of four major external databases (CURL, LOCIS, OCLC and RLIN).

The professional literature has never been slow to characterise the cataloguing fraternity, and labels such as *legalistic, perfectionist, decadent, stern mechanic*, and *pious*, though quite unfair, are familiar stereotypes encountered by most cataloguers.[5] Our guiding principle over this last decade has been **Access** and our philosophy has been to make the computer do as much of the work as possible.

We have adopted a pragmatic approach to copy cataloguing, correcting first and foremost only those parts of the record affecting access rather than tweaking or tinkering for the sake of creating perfect records. Considerations of access have determined our workflows, including the analysis of copyright intake into different priority streams with immediate processing of high-priority materials, and the provision of Minimal Level Records (MLRs) for all non-priority serious, scholarly and academic materials, thereby preserving access to and control of the backlogs ("full access integrity").

In order to enable cataloguers to concentrate on these service aspects, we have adamantly demanded that our online system takes full advantage of the rule-based nature of the MARC format. Not only does our new system (see below) present the USMARC tables with accompanying guidelines for tag and subfield usage, but it also both validates MARC tagging and performs appropriate cross-checking of MARC tags. The system not only indicates MARC tagging errors, but also checks to ensure that non-repeatable tags are not repeated; alerts the cataloguer of the presence of illegal combinations of tags, and reminds the cataloguer if the presence of one tag demands (or forbids) another. This functionality makes the cataloguing process easier and generates greater confidence in the cataloguers.

CATALOGUE SUPPORT SERVICES

From the start of the Union Catalogue project, there were two issues that dominated discussion. The first was training and documentation. It was obvious that the preparation of clear documentation and the provision of timely and appropriate training would be vital to the successful implementation of the system. The situation outside the Bodleian Library was not dissimilar to that inside, where few professional staff were in post, and even fewer were familiar with the modern cataloguing standards. For these reasons training in the cataloguing module of OLIS would have to be rapidly organised and launched on a grand scale (given that it had to reach right across the Oxford library system).

The second aspect that provoked considerable argument within the hitherto autonomous library sector was the issue of whether there should be a central unit responsible for monitoring the bibliographical integrity of the database, and the consistent application of the standards.

After considerable debate, it was decided that these functions should be centralised within the Cataloguing Division of the Bodleian Technical Services Department. This necessitated a further reorganisation of the Cataloguing Division, not only to cope with the new processes of automation but also to accommodate its new University-wide role.

Catalogue Support Services (CSS) was created in 1989 to fulfil 4 main functions or responsibilities: (1) University-wide training and provision of documentation for the cataloguing module of OLIS; (2) University wide database maintenance of OLIS and maintenance of Bodleian's manual catalogues; (3) system-wide authority control; and (4) retrospective conversion within the Bodleian Library, and relevant training and advice to libraries outside the Bodleian in retrospective conversion work.

Since the inception of automated cataloguing, CSS has been central to the success of our cataloguing endeavours in Oxford. In the ten years that have since elapsed the number of cataloguers that have been trained by CSS staff exceeds 500 (if one takes into account staff turnover during this period), and the number of libraries contributing their records to the Oxford Union Catalogue has grown to 88. The OLIS bibliographic database has reached over 3.7 million records (representing over 5.5 million copy or holdings records). The period 1992-1998 has witnessed the retrospective conversion of over 2 million records from the Bodleian Library's post-1920 (non-oriental language) holdings, and significant conversion activity in many of the University's other libraries. CSS staff have played a significant role in these activities also.

One of the great advantages of automated cataloguing is that it enables the process to be broken down into discrete operations: a junior or clerical staff member might add copy or local holdings information; a higher clerical or paraprofessional might perform copy cataloguing; a professional (or in UK terms) an academic-related librarian might be responsible for original cataloguing. Our training was structured at the outset so as to reflect this discrimination of tasks, enabling the cataloguing operation to be performed more cost-effectively.

Given the federal library structure in Oxford and the desire to differentiate training as described above, cataloguing training was highly organised from its inception. Over the period 1989-1994, an average of 10-12 libraries per year joined the system, requiring the appropriate training. In the early days, all trainees were expected to attend general courses offered by our Computing Services Department in DOS, basic hard disc management and general microcomputer usage. In more recent years, this has been replaced by Windows training (though in practice, there are few new staff today lacking this basic prerequisite). This was followed by a detailed classroom-based course on AACR2 and USMARC, consisting of 8 three-hour sessions.

Next came a course on the application of LCSH (2 three hours sessions), covering the use of the Red Books and the structure and application of LC's *Subject Cataloging Manual*. Only after these courses, were the trainees given a hands-on course on the process of cataloguing using Dobis/Libis. This was in fact a further course of eight 3-hour sessions. In other words, before being allowed to catalogue on the LIVE system, a cataloguer would have to undergo a total of approximately 56-57 hours of quite intensive training. This would take place over a 10-week period.

No distinction was made between libraries during the training. This is because even the smallest library, where copy cataloguing might account for almost all the cataloguing output, would occasionally need to create an original record for some of its intake. While some might argue that greater centralisation of processing would reduce the training need, the collegiate structure of the University makes this somewhat difficult, and the political will to restructure the system, to best exploit automated procedures, was not evident.

For those who require some cataloguing knowledge, but not the full level of detail expected of a cataloguer, a separate course entitled *Bibliographic Building Blocks* was created. Again, developed at the operational level and delivered by practitioners, this course provides a basic introduction to MARC, and the OLIS database. It also covers the process of identifying a bibliographic match and adding a holdings record, the creation of Order Level Records (for Acquisitions staff), and the process of accessing external databases and downloading into a separate Potential Requirements File, in readiness for a trained cataloguer to upgrade the item, or use it to replace an existing lower grade record. Modular in nature, staff can pick and mix the modules depending upon the precise nature of their work. And since the modules are run 5 or 6 times per annum, one can attend module 1 of the first course, module 2-3 of the next, and module 4 at a later date. This extension to the basic training programme, with its accompanying documentation, represents a major investment in time and energy. It is, however, as an essential training component within the union environment, which takes the trainee painlessly through the whole process at the appropriate level of expertise.

SYSTEM MIGRATION

In early 1995 the decision was taken to migrate systems. After a selection process lasting approximately 6 months, Oxford selected Geac's standard character-based Advance software for Acquisitions, Circulation, OPAC and Serials registration, but for cataloguing we took the gamble on Geac's Windows-based GeoCAT client software, which, according to the vendor, was scheduled for implementation at MIT in the Summer of 1995. In the event, this did not happen, and we became the development site.

It is not my intention to describe here the fraught and traumatic period of migration that engulfed the Library between April 1995 and

April 1997 (the date when GeoCat/GeoPac was formally released to our cataloguers). However, I do think it informative to discuss in some detail certain aspects of that period, notably the training implications of migrating to new client/server technology.

The first issue to be addressed was Windows 95, since many of GeoCAT's features draw upon standard Windows functions (drop down menus, cut and paste, etc.). At that time, the majority of staff was not familiar with Windows, and had never used a mouse before. Since this period coincided with the then recent much-heralded introduction of Windows 95, we faced an additional problem in that our Computer Services Department (responsible for University-wide computer training) had not yet developed a Windows 95 course and were still Windows 3.1 users. In collaboration with librarians, a course was put together, rather hurriedly, for library staff in March 1996. In retrospect, this half-day course was not adequate, and probably did not prepare library staff well enough for what was to come. The Windows course was delivered in the first quarter of 1996 on the assumption that training in GeoCAT would start shortly thereafter.

In Oxford there were over 250 staff needing training in the use of the cataloguing module, either for full copy and/or original cataloguing, or for adding piece records, or creating bibliographic order records. All would need to be trained in a relatively short, intensive period. The implementation schedule originally assumed that we would take delivery of the new GeoCAT software in January 1996, and after 3 months of testing, enhancing where necessary to accommodate Oxford's federal requirements, and modifying Geac's documentation to fit our requirements, we planned to train staff between April-June 1996, with a view to going Live on July 1st. Of course, we should have known better. Now is not the time or place to detail all the problems we encountered over this period, but I will summarise some of the difficulties: (a) the software was delivered 3 months late, rendering out initial schedule totally redundant and irrelevant; (b) Geac provided virtually no user documentation for their new GeoCAT cataloguing client; and (c) the software was poorly developed, and needed much work to get it to achieve pretty basic functionality. Indeed, this process of software improvement, testing, and revising continued through all of 1996 and well into the first quarter of 1997. We finally went Live on April 2nd 1997. By then, some 85 builds of the GeoCAT software, and 49 builds of the GeoPAC software had been delivered, tested, documented, re-tested and re-documented–by professional Cataloguing staff. This is probably a familiar story to many who have undergone similar migrations during the last few years.

A decision had been taken early on regarding who would do the training. A training team was set up, and a broad division of the work slowly emerged. In practice, the training team, headed by the Head of Catalogue Support, served simultaneously as the group responsible for the Z39.50 cataloguing and authorities module enhancement testing and development. The trainers all came from the Cataloguing Division's operational staff, and were staff who were very much responsible for integrating the technology into ongoing workflow and operations. It was not training organised by committee. This team would train all cataloguers. There was to be no "cascade" training.

During the second quarter of 1996, we made productive use of the delay in receiving the software. We knew that the new system would allow us, for the first time, to make full use of LC authority records (which we planned to load into the system). Since the Authorities Format was virtually unknown to the majority of cataloguers, a training seminar on Authorities (lasting approximately 3 hours) was devised and delivered. MARC refresher courses, reminding staff about recent and ongoing developments in MARC format integration were also written and offered to staff.

It is axiomatic when implementing a new automated system that the selected vendor should be able to deliver good initial training to the customer. We should have satisfied ourselves, and indeed insisted, that the quality of the vendor training met our expectations, and clearly this was a significant omission on our part–since the lack of a structured training package from our vendor was one of the factors contributing to the long period of system implementation.

In fairness, it should be pointed out that the client software was in a state of constant functional development throughout this period, making structured training difficult. It would also be fair to acknowledge that we probably pushed the software harder and further than the average library site.

Nevertheless, we should have ensured that the vendor's trainer was familiar with the problems and scale of operation of a large research library, using US rather than UK MARC, and we should also have insisted that the vendor tailored the training far more to our local federalised environment. All these deficiencies meant that the "training the trainer" model usually adopted when implementing a new system was not as successful as it should have been. Our local training to Oxford cataloguers was, in the event, very successful and well-received, but it was due to the high level of commitment and dedication of our own local training team in assimilating the system subsequent to the initial vendor training.

Planning and scheduling our training was therefore problematic. Having missed our first Live deadline of July 1st, we aimed for a revised deadline of October 1st for starting Live cataloguing–for three reasons: (a) this was the date by which all the bibliographic and other data (e.g., circulation patron records, vendor files, etc.) were scheduled to have been migrated; (b) this was the deadline for the implementation of the Geac Advance character-based modules (Acquisitions, Circulation, and OPAC) to coincide with the beginning of the new academic year; and (c) we had been told by our Systems Department that Dobis would probably not survive beyond the Fall of 1996.

Formal and structured training courses, totalling some 352 contact hours, took place between August and October. Training included not simply the basics of creating original records on GeoCAT, but also accessing the RLIN and OCLC databases–no longer through PRISM or Windows terminal emulation software, but via our Z39.50 cataloguing client, and downloading the records interactively. It meant cataloguers had to learn new procedures for moving in and out of various systems and search windows, familiarising themselves with the differences in each of the external servers and different searches available on each database. Because the trainers had been so closely involved with the evolution of the system functionality over the period they were able to meld their functions into a working environment that fit the larger picture.

October came, and still GeoCAT was nowhere near ready. Our contingency plan was to continue cataloguing on our old Dobis/Libis system, migrate the records overnight to the Geac server, and add the holdings data in Advance the following day. In fact, this procedure was implemented, as GeoCAT only reached full and acceptable functionality some six months later, on April 2nd 1997. It meant, however, that the trainers had to learn and then train cataloguers in holdings-related aspects of the character-based Advance cataloguing module. The use of the classic system for this purpose had certainly never been anticipated.

Following the courses, a training database was made available to staff on which to practise. Cataloguers were encouraged to spend at least one half-hour to one hour per day practising, to ensure they did not lose their newly found skills. Unfortunately, it became evident quite quickly that the software was nowhere near ready to implement on a live production basis, and as new enhancements were introduced, and functionality improved, we realised that formal refresher training was going to be required. This took place in November 1996.

Some statistics might be of interest. Five training manuals totalling 730 pages were written by Catalogue Support Services staff. The first dealt with copy records/pieces; the second on Copy cataloguing/external database searching using Z39.50; the third on original cataloguing; the fourth on ancillary functions, diacritics, spacing and punctuation, and other tools; the fifth on local database maintenance. We have since written documentation for various aspects of authority control and database maintenance.

The first distribution, which took place during the training, totalled 118,730 printed pages. Following numerous rebuilds of the software, and new functional modifications and enhancements introduced between November 1996 and March 1997, new sections were added to the manuals and existing ones expanded. A second distribution of the manuals took place in December, and a third partial distribution again in March-April 1997. These subsequent distributions totalled a further 126,028 pages. This excludes what we termed "CatKits" (folded double-sided handouts on specific topics) and other smaller documentation. In all, a total of approximately 300,000 pages were distributed.

Working in the new Windows 95 environment we recognised early on that one of the great advantages was the ability to run multiple sessions, and to be able to move in and out of diverse applications (multitasking). Although the LC Name and Subject Authority files were available online via GeoCAT, which also effectively contained the complete USMARC formats, with significant amounts of Help, we nevertheless took the opportunity of networking LC's *Cataloger's Desktop*. This allowed us to make available additionally the LC Rule Interpretations, the *Subject Cataloging Manual*, and (again) the MARC formats with the extra benefit of actual examples of MARC usage. However, this too necessitated more training, both to familiarise staff about the product itself, and also to provide suggestions about how best to integrate the usage of the product with the GeoCAT software. Other Windows-based, resource discovery tools were also made available on the cataloguers' workstations (e.g., OED, Bodley's Pre-1920 Catalogue, BL catalogue, BNB).

When the new client-server GeoCat/GeoPac system was finally introduced, it was greeted with almost universal acclaim. Despite the problems described above the functionality of the new software was, and still remains outstanding. The work had proven worthwhile. The period of assimilation was relatively smooth and short, and cataloguing productivity for the calendar year 1998 was, in fact, the highest ever recorded in the Bodleian Library.

IMPACT OF AUTOMATION

The period 1990-1995 witnessed a steady growth in cataloguing productivity. In 1987, the last full year of manual cataloguing, output had peaked at 53,753 items. By 1995, the annual output under DOBIS/LIBIS was averaging 77,000. After a short dip in output during the system migration period, output from the Central Cataloguing Division in 1998 exceeded 87,000 current items. It should be stated that within the Bodleian Library as a whole there are several other cataloguing "nodes." These include the specialist sections (e.g., Music and Map Divisions, Special Collections, Oriental Department) and the separate dependent libraries (e.g., Bodleian Law Library, Rhodes House Library, Indian Institute, and the Radcliffe Science Library). The total Bodleian cataloguing output for 1998 exceeded 110,000 items.

This increase can be explained, at least in part, by the Library's participation in the Copyright Libraries Shared Cataloguing Programme (CLSCP), which started in November 1990. Prior to automation, Bodley's participation in any national co-operative cataloguing programme had not been possible. The advent of automation, coupled with the inexorable growth in copyright intake, made this development both feasible and attractive. The goal of the CLSCP was "to set up and operate a mechanism and agreement for a comprehensive programme of shared cataloguing, for the purpose of maximising the utility to all libraries of the British Library's national bibliographic service and of minimising cataloguing costs in the participating libraries."[6] Under this Programme, the British Library retains responsibility for cataloguing 70% of the national output, while the other 5

Copyright Libraries (Cambridge University Library, Trinity College Dublin, the National libraries of Scotland and Wales, and the Bodleian Library) undertake to catalogue the remaining 30%, or 6% each. Originally the cataloguing responsibility of each participating library was based on the selection of items by publisher. The British Library undertook to upgrade all CIP records, while the non-CIP publishers were divided among all six libraries. From September 1993, the basis on which quotas were allocated changed from publisher's name to title. Bodley's allocation is simply all those titles beginning with the letter M, which amounts to approximately 4,500 titles per annum. The quota includes all printed monographs published in Great Britain, regardless of the language of the text, and all English language items published abroad but received by legal deposit. The scheme currently excludes periodical publications, although discussions are in progress to extend the co-operative process further.

Other factors have contributed to the dramatic increase in productivity over the last decade: in particular, the growth in availability of high-quality external records from both American and British utilities, and the dramatic improvements in mode of access to these records that have occurred in recent years–from a time-consuming and labour-intensive batch process, often involving ancillary software and editing processes to a streamlined, efficient and interactive Z39.50 compliant procedure.

Continuous improvements in cataloguing workflow, the introduction of high specification workstations, the availability of well-designed and functional cataloguing software, and the local loading of the LC authority files are further contributory factors to the dramatic improvements. As a USMARC user, the Oxford libraries follow the US Name Authority file, and have recently started to contribute proposals within the Name Authority Cooperative Program (NACO).

Cataloguers of specialised formats or languages (e.g., Slavic, Sanskrit and music) are, additionally, taking advantage of the easy access via Z39.50 to the catalogues of major institutions, and downloading records from those libraries known to hold major collections in the relevant fields. In this way, the cataloguer can potentially bring together the most productive sources to form his/her own virtual utility. This is an exciting development that should contribute further to increased productivity.

ISSUES AND FUTURE CONCERNS

Although the last decade has been a success story, in cataloguing terms, for the Bodleian Library, there are still many challenges facing us as we enter the new millennium.

As the libraries in Oxford move towards a more integrated management structure, under the new Director of Library Services and Bodley's Librarian, the issue of greater rationalisation of technical service operations will need to be addressed. Rationalisation in the Oxford context need not necessarily mean the creation of one large, monolithic technical services operation, but probably the creation of several larger technical service nodes, or divisional centres, each responsible for logical groups or clusters of departments, so that the operations become more cost-effective and bring together technical and linguistic expertise appropriate to each of the subject clusters.

In times of declining resources and escalating costs, one must not downplay or underestimate the value or importance of efficiency. It is no surprise that decentralisation tends to be in the ascendancy when times are good, but the drive to centralisation is strong when funding is weak. Times are unlikely to improve dramatically in the future, and indeed may worsen as we respond to new demands and expectations within the electronic cataloguing arena. The solution may therefore be to centralise/rationalise certain operations for efficiency and economies of time and money, and to decentralise other operations for service. Larger technical services units will combine staff, use them more efficiently, or reduce staff where necessary. They will allow a reduction in the duplication of reference tools in each unit, the purchase of fewer bibliographic tools such as AACR2, LC Rule Interpretations, (or the elimination of networking overheads and complex IT support costs), far less documentation would need to be distributed, there would be less need for time-consuming training programmes (so enabling other activities to proceed), and less handling of materials overall. With fewer, better trained cataloguers, the internal quality and consistency of the OLIS database would also be improved.

However, in the Oxford environment, such changes are unlikely to be introduced rapidly. Nevertheless, it is heartening to report that within the proposed new Oxford integrated library structure (effective from March 2000) a co-ordinating Director of Technical Services is envisaged.

A further challenge facing the Bodleian Library is that of legal deposit of electronic resources. The next century will see a dramatic increase in the output of exciting and innovative British digital publications in all subject areas. It is vital that legal deposit legislation is extended to include such publications. At the present time we are working with the British Library, the other Copyright Libraries and the British Government to design and build a system that will handle, store, provide access to, and preserve deposited legal publications within a secure networking environment. It is anticipated that not only will such a system protect the publishers' intellectual property rights, but will at the same time result in economies to the legal deposit libraries by avoiding multiple digital deposit arrangements. Planning is still in the early stages, and there still remains the vexed question of long-term preservation of such materials, the precise number of copies to be deposited, and criteria for distribution if more than one copy is to be deposited. Responsibility for the processing and cataloguing of deposited items will depend on the arrangements reached. In any event, methods of loading records into our local system, regardless of their source of origin, will need to be determined.

Other challenges for cataloguers are essentially intertwined with those facing the Library generally. How do we move from an institution that has concentrated, necessarily, on the automation of its internal processes, to one that is more user-oriented and innovative. In recent years Oxford, like other institutions, has witnessed the explosion of electronic information resources. Library users typically have access not only to Web-based OPACs, but networked and standalone access to CD-ROMs, online databases, institutional subject gateways to Internet resources, electronic journals (from a diversity of suppliers), and electronic current content services. The challenge associated with the management of this environment where electronic and paper-based information sources are used alongside each other, is how to integrate access using evolving technologies from the digital library world, in ways which will provide a seamless and transparent service to the user.

In the United Kingdom several projects, under the umbrella of the Electronic Libraries programme (eLib), are investigating different aspects of what has become known as the *hybrid library*: operating practices, possible working models, user issues, impacts on organisational structures, and authentication issues, to name but a few.[7]

Oxford is involved in some of the above projects and has, additionally, developed several local institutional services. Like other libraries, we have developed our Web pages, which serve as a primary gateway to our services, offer links to other library catalogues, local and remote information resources, subject gateways, electronic journals, local digitisation projects, and other sources of information.

Several commentators have identified the traditional skills of the cataloguer as precisely those required for structuring Web sites and managing the metadata required for the organisation of electronic resources. Michael Gorman suggests that "librarians and, especially, catalogers are uniquely qualified to tame the electronic wilderness,"[8] while Vellucci argues "if the goal of libraries is to provide access to information, it is the organisational tools created by catalogers that help the library meet this goal. These tools become even more crucial in the chaotic Internet environment."[9] Brisson wryly observes that the myriad of articles in popular computer magazines that outline the challenges of organising the Web fail to recognise that "what they characterise in these articles is nothing more than what cataloging librarians have methodically practised for decades." He continues: "The authors of these articles don't call it cataloging of course. Increasingly, however, the architects of the Internet–telecommunications specialists, information and computer scientists, and business systems managers–are discovering that cataloging librarians possess a wealth of knowledge and experience in taming the chaotic information domains like those found on the World Wide Web."[10]

This is perhaps the major challenge facing the cataloguing community in Oxford. Although there are numerous digitisation projects underway or completed in Oxford, cataloguers have played a relatively minor part in these activities, not even in the development and maintenance of the metadata standards employed. Vellucci wrote in *American libraries* (1992) that "Future catalogers must extend their view of the organizing process beyond one particular cataloging code or record structure, and beyond the 'item in hand' as the object of bibliographic control."[11] Few catalogue managers would disagree with this sentiment, and would welcome the opportunity to expand their horizon in this way. However, this has been difficult to achieve in Oxford. The reasons for this are several: intake of printed materials has risen inexorably over the last decade, and continues to do so. This has been accompanied by a steady rise in the number of non-print materials, but with no corresponding increase in the numbers of cataloguers. Coupled with the recent migration from DOBIS/LIBIS to Geac, there has been little or no real opportunity for cataloguers to become more involved in the various digital projects taking place within the Library. We have concentrated on what might be termed the less glamorous and more traditional technical services operations, with the result that expertise in imaging, digitization, metadata creation and management have fallen to Systems departments, New Media Librarians, or Web-page experts. Very often exciting projects have been undertaken by staff on short-term contracts. At the conclusion of the project expertise is lost to the Library as the researchers move on elsewhere to their next project-based short-term contract.

Our first and growing priority is the cataloguing of electronic journals. The number available to our users is expanding rapidly as the Library enters into various licensing arrangements with individual aggregators, or subscribes to services brokered by the national negotiating agency, CHEST. Although available titles are listed on a Web page, this is no replacement for access via the OPAC. Our most pressing priority at this time is (a) to develop appropriate guidelines for the cataloguing of electronic resources, and (b) to find adequate staff resources for this to be implemented on a routine and systematic basis.

Associated with this, is the need for us to develop a University-wide policy on cataloguing and making accessible remote Internet resources. The advent of Web-based catalogues not only allows users to retrieve records for Internet resources, but also facilitates retrieval of the actual electronic resource by clicking on a hypertext link. Many libraries have already developed institutional policies for the selection of resources to be catalogued, and the standards to be adopted. Although we have kept abreast vicariously of experiments in this area (e.g., OCLC's Intercat and CORC projects), we have been slow in addressing the problems of electronic resources and the bibliographic implications of recording information about resources that are not held in the collections of the cataloguing library.

CONCLUSION

Ours was a sluggish start at library automation. Some might argue that our entry into the arena was perfectly timed, the delay allowing us to watch from the sidelines as others made all the mistakes. While we might have become involved with MARC, AACR, and integrated library systems somewhat earlier, it is probably true to state that the internal political environment, with its multitude of separate components, would have made it difficult to launch a co-ordinated plan much earlier. However, when things finally did get started, they did so with great speed and efficiency in a way that has been to the credit of the staff involved. They were, and are still, required to learn a lot of new tricks, and do so with great skill and dedication. Much has been achieved in the 12 years since OLIS first became available, and doubtless much more will be accomplished in the new millennium.

NOTES

1. *The Brasenose Conference on the Automation of Libraries: Proceedings of the Anglo-American conference on the mechanization of library services held at Oxford under the chairmanship of Sir Frank Francis and sponsored by the Old Dominion Foundation of New York, 30 June-3 July 1966*/edited by John Harrison & Peter Laslett. London: Mansell, 1967.

2. Michael Heaney, "Publication of the Bodleian Library's Pre-1920 catalogue of printed books on compact disc," *Program*, 28 (2), 1994: 141-153.

3. *The Bodleian experiment in the use of MARC tapes: Report to OSTI on grant no. SI/51/16*. Oxford, Bodleian Library, 1972, p. 20.

4. *Report on the Working Party on Automation in University Libraries.* Oxford, 1983.

5. See for example:

Michael Gorman, "Osborn revisited; or The catalog in crisis; or, Four catalogers, only one of whom shall save us," *American libraries*, 6 (November, 1975), p. 599, 601.

A.D. Osborn, "The crisis in cataloging," *The Library Quarterly*, 11, 1941, 393-411

6. *Shared cataloguing: Report to the principals of the six copyright libraries of the Copyright Libraries Shared Cataloguing Project Steering Group.* (NBS occasional publications,1). Boston Spa, British Library, 1993.

7. See for example:

J.M.N. Hey and A. Wissenberg, "Modelling the hybrid library: Project MALIBU," *New review of information and library research*, 1998, 103-110.

P. Dalton [et al.], "The hybrid library and university strategy: A consultation exercise with senior library managers," *New review of information and library research*, 1998, 43-52.

Chris Rusbridge, "Towards the hybrid library," *D-Lib Magazine,* July/August 1998. Available via <*http://mirrored.ukoln.ac.uk/lisjournals/dlib/dlib/dlib/july98/rusbridge/07rusbridge.html*>.

Also see the eLib projects home page at *http://www.ukoln.ac.uk/services/elib/projects/*

8. Michael Gorman, "The future of cataloguing and cataloguers," *International cataloguing and bibliographic control*, 27 (4), Oct./Dec. 1998, 68-71.

9. Roger Brisson, "The world discovers cataloging: A conceptual introduction to digital libraries, metadata and the implications for library administration." Available via: *http://www.personal.psu.edu/faculty/r/o/rob1/publications/publications.html*

10. ibid.

11. S. Vellucci, "Future catalogers: Essential colleagues or anachronisms?" *American libraries*, 23 (Sept.), 1992, p. 693-694.

Technical Processes
and the Technological Development
of the Library System
in the National Autonomous University
of Mexico

Carlos García López

SUMMARY. This paper will first provide a synopsis of the technological developments to date from the perspective of the technical processes of the Library System of the National Autonomous University of Mexico. Secondly, this paper will explain how the General Directorate for Libraries (DGB) coordinates the development and enrichment of holdings of that Library System. Emphasis will be placed on the Technical Processes Department as being responsible for organizing and processing all the bibliographic material by using a variety of online tools as well as traditional material as the Anglo American Cataloging Rules 2nd ed. and also including standardization developments. Then, the paper will briefly describe the databases that the General Directorate for Libraries has developed: LIBRUNAM, SERIUNAM, MAPA-MEX, TESIUNAM, EUTERPE, CLASE, PERIODICA, and ELECTRONIC JOURNALS. Finally, this paper also describes the computer equipment used to carry out the library activities and services. *[Article copies available for a fee from The Haworth Document Delivery Service: 1-800-342-9678. E-mail address: <getinfo@haworthpressinc.com> Website: <http://www.HaworthPress. com>]*

Carlos García López is Assistant Director Technical Processes, National Autonomous University of Mexico, Mexico, D.F.

[Haworth co-indexing entry note]: "Technical Processes and the Technological Development of the Library System in the National Autonomous University of Mexico." López, Carlos García. Co-published simultaneously in *Cataloging & Classification Quarterly* (The Haworth Information Press, an imprint of The Haworth Press, Inc.) Vol. 30, No. 1, 2000, pp. 73-90; and: *Managing Cataloging and the Organization of Information: Philosophies, Practices and Challenges at the Onset of the 21st Century* (ed: Ruth C. Carter) The Haworth Information Press, an imprint of The Haworth Press, Inc., 2000, pp. 73-90. Single or multiple copies of this article are available for a fee from The Haworth Document Delivery Service [1-800-342-9678, 9:00 a.m. - 5:00 p.m. (EST). E-mail address: getinfo@haworthpressinc.com].

KEYWORDS. Cataloging, technical processes, UNAM, Mexico, electronic journals, library technology

The National Autonomous University of Mexico (UNAM), considered the country's major house of education, has a population of 268,615 students enrolled in all its scholastic levels, from the propaedeutic course of the National School of Music to postgraduate studies. These levels include technical and technical/professional training, undergraduate and graduate education, as well as an extension education called the *Open University System*. There is an academic and research staff of 36,692, and also 26,541 administrative employees.[1]

This not only makes the UNAM the country's largest institution of higher education, but also the most important for its qualified and skillful personnel and for its contribution in the field of research.

Her main objectives are to form outstanding professionals in each field of learning, develop research and promote cultural activities, which makes her a leader among the public universities of Latin America. Furthermore, the National Autonomous University of Mexico is on a level with the most prominent institutions of higher education in Europe and the United States.

To develop education, research and promote cultural activities, the University is resourced with a Library System formed by 141 departmental libraries and one central or main library, which holds one of the largest and most valuable collections in Mexico, made up of 729,514 book titles and 5,443,637 volumes.[2] And the document pieces total are 8,608,408.

The UNAM acquires an average of 120,000 book titles per year; 50,000 of which are new titles in the collection that are classified and cataloged as original cataloging. The remaining 70,000 are other editions or copies that, although new in one particular library, they were previously acquired by another, which helps make them readily available to the user.

The General Directorate for Libraries (DGB) coordinates the development and enrichment of holdings of the Library System. Through its Technical Processes Department, it is also responsible for organizing and processing all the bibliographic material acquired by the 141 departmental libraries, as dictated by The Library System by-laws, in order to maintain an updated information system available for the university community, as well as for the various universities and institutions of higher education and research in the country.

To fulfill this objective, the Technical Processes Department assigns subject headings and performs centralized cataloging and classification. It uses a variety of tools and information sources for these activities, such as:

(a) Validator database, Bibliofile and other catalogs, to assign subject headings
(b) The Anglo-American Cataloging Rules, second edition (AACR2), for the descriptive cataloging standardization. The materials are cataloged with a second description level, and third level when necessary

It also uses the classification system designed by the Library of Congress in Washington, D.C., which fits the organization needs of a university collection.

The MARC format is used to store the bibliographic data in an automated system, for the exchange of information with catalogs of national and international libraries.

Among the contributions made by the Technical Processes Department in helping Mexican University libraries with their task in organizing information, is giving these libraries free access to its automated catalog.

Another important contribution is that, in addition to applying descriptive elements, the bibliographical records recently include the Dewey classification number, which is used by a large number of libraries in Mexico. This helps speed their technical processes.

On the other hand, the General Directorate for Libraries has been working in the development of several automated devices, thought to help in library activities and information services carried out at UNAM and Mexico City, as well as throughout the country.

Thereby, the General Directorate has developed the following databases:

LIBRUNAM The richest book collection in the country is harbored in the National Autonomous University of Mexico; it has approximately 729,514 book titles and 5,443,637 volumes. This vast collection is distributed among the libraries that correspond to the Library System located on the main campus and other branch sites in the Metropolitan area and in several states of the country.

The information compiled in LIBRUNAM consists of bibliographical records that include the Library of Congress classification system, the author, the book title, place of publication, publisher, year of publication and subject matter; furthermore, the user is able to trace the library lodging the needed document.

LIBRUNAM is a database that has been continuously improving. A feature that makes LIBRUNAM unique in the country is that it integrates a subject authority file as well as an author authority file (personal and corporate) in the same system. The professional librarian that is dedicated to cataloging activities benefits with this, as he has the possibility of searching for the topic in English and retrieve the equivalent term in Spanish and vice versa. In the cases of personal or corporate authors, he can also locate the full name, the conventional name, the pseudonym or the initials.

As mentioned earlier, an additional asset for the professionals of a cataloging department, Dewey classification number is added to 11,000 bibliographical records. This helps other university library systems and other such libraries to speed their classifying process.

LIBRUNAM is not only a useful tool for cataloging processes, it also aids reference services, allowing bibliographies to be made on topics of interest to the user, and the library location.

LIBRUNAM is available via Internet to users in general (students, researchers, professors, academic staff and employees). This makes it easily accessible and inexpensive for a wider public, regionally and internationally.

To access LIBRUNAM type: http://www.dgbiblio.unam.mx

SERIUNAM is a union list of serials created by the General Directorate for Libraries (DGB). It contains 48,104 journal titles and 6,553,903 issues from 379 institutions of higher education and research in the country; 143 belong to the UNAM's Library System and 236 to other national entities.

SERIUNAM, multidisciplinary and reference database of serials, is a product of the cooperation of all those libraries interested in sharing their resources. The database is available to the university community and the country's general public. This is a useful tool for educators, researchers and development of culture.

It aims at providing information on the serial resources of each participant library, aiding users interested in locating and retrieving information in the shortest possible time. And at the same time, become acquainted with the bibliographical holdings of the UNAM and member libraries.

The development of bibliographical records is standardized using the Anglo-American Cataloguing Rules. The MARC format is used to create the automated catalog, which makes transferring information to other compatible systems possible.

The cataloging process of serials is centralized at the DGB and carried out by its Union Catalog Department (a branch department of the Technical Services Subdirectorate).

Five professional librarians are currently responsible for the technical processes, observing quality performance.

The SERIUNAM database is enriched by the continual amount of record entries as well as by the elements that compose it, as are: the Dewey classification, the subject headings, journal status, and notes. There may be a first, second, or third cataloging level depending on the descriptive features of each journal; it also features the Library of Congress classification number.

SERIUNAM has been published in two compact disk versions (1985 and 1995). It is also available on-line via Internet on the following web site:

http://www.dgbiblio.unam.mx

MAPAMEX is a union catalog of historic, climatologic, topographic, edaphologic, and geologic maps, charts and plans. It contains 9,834 titles and 46,369 copies. Much of the materials included were works published at the end of the XIX century, produced mostly by the Instituto Nacional de Geografía, Estadística e Informática (INEGI), the Comisión de Recursos Minerales de México, the Instituto Nacional Indigenista (INI), and the Instituto de Geografía of the UNAM, among others. Maps contain data mainly on Mexican territory, although there are references to other countries.

The MAPAMEX database is friendly software. It allows search options by author, title, subject, classification, and scale, by using the Boolean operators.

Among the advantages MAPAMEX offers are: information on library resources; on location of document, direct access to the library for consultation and retrieval; preparing bibliographies, or exporting records to compatible catalogs.

Each library classifies and catalogs the material following international standards, as for example, the Anglo-American Cataloging Rules.

Records are then sent to the Union Catalog of Serials Department of the General Directorate for Libraries, to be reviewed and accessed into the database. It is the General Directorate, which is responsible for coordinating and establishing guidelines for the catalographic records, besides feeding and updating MAPAMEX with information from the libraries.

MAPAMEX can be accessed for consultation on the following Web site:

http://www.dgbiblio.unam.mx

TESIUNAM, also created by the General Directorate for Libraries is a union list of theses. The bibliographical records are a collection of graduate and postgraduate theses from the UNAM, as well as from other institutions of higher education in Mexico that are forwarded to the Central Library to be organized, registered and microfilmed.

TESIUNAM is a database with more than 265,000 records of theses collected from 106 graduate studies given at the UNAM, 147 given at incorporated schools and 58 at non-incorporated schools. It also includes theses from 420 postgraduate studies given at the UNAM, and 27 more given at academic institutions. TESIUNAM contains information that dates back to 1914, as well as a valuable XIX century collection from the School of Medicine; its holdings are not physically housed at the Central Library, but they can be consulted at the Historic Library of the School of Medicine.

The thesis collection is microfilmed to preserve the information and avoid deterioration caused by time exposure, poor quality paper, and bad handling.

A project for the year 2000 considers digitizing the theses compiled in this database. The user could then have direct on-line access.

TESIUNAM is more than an information source; it is a tool that can guide graduate students in research profiles.

The TESIUNAM user can easily retrieve the following information from each bibliographic record:

- Roll microfilm number
- Author
- Title
- School or Faculty

- Profession
- Year of publication
- Number of pages
- Name of thesis advisor

Not all records include the advisor's name, given that the student's thesis director is not necessarily provided.

TESIUNAM has been developed in CD-ROM version, containing information up to 1996. It is also available on-line at the following Web site:

http://www.dgbiblio.unam.mx

EUTERPE is an automated catalog of music scores, developed jointly with the National School of Music of the UNAM with the means of converting it into a union list of printed and recorded music. It currently includes 1,941 records of music scores.

The database can be accessed by:

- Author
- Title
- Series

Advantages:

EUTERPE as a source that will be consulted by more than 200 music schools in the country, and provides documental and bibliographical support.

Cataloging of music materials is carried out following the international standards of the Anglo-American Cataloging Rules. The National School of Music prepares the records that are turned over to the Technical Processes Department to be revised and included in the database.

To safeguard this collection and to ease searching and information retrieval, there is a projection to digitize Mexican printed music with problem-free copyright.

EUTERPE can be consulted at:

http://www.dgbiblio.unam.mx

CLASE is a bibliographic database, product of the National Autonomous University of Mexico, developed in 1975 by the Department of Latin American Bibliography, a subordinate department of the General Directorate for Libraries.

This database contains more than 150,000 bibliographic references obtained from scholarly journals edited in Latin America and the Caribbean. It is specialized in social sciences and humanities and covers the fields of: management and accounting; anthropology; library and information science, communication science; demography; law; economics; education; philosophy; history, linguistics and literature; politics; psychology; foreign affairs; religion; arts; and sociology. It is updated daily with approximately 8,000 new entries per year. Searching may be performed from several access points:

- Author
- Title
- Title of the article
- Institution
- Publication year
- Subject
- Keywords in Spanish

The combination of the above points can be performed using Boolean operators.

CLASE can be consulted on the Internet at:

http://www.dgbiblio.unam.mx

Select "Catálogos en línea" icon

PERIODICA is another bibliographic database created in 1978 by the National Autonomous University of Mexico. The General Directorate for Libraries through its Department of Latin American Bibliography currently manages it. The database contains more than 148,000 bibliographic references of articles published in scientific and technical journals of Latin America and the Caribbean, with several foreign contributions.

The specialized journals in science and technology are compiled in the database that mainly covers the following fields: agricultural sciences; biology; exact sciences; physics; geosciences; engineering; medicine, and chemistry.

PERIODICA includes more than 1,300 scholarly journals, and is daily updated with an average of 8,000 new entries per year.

Information search and location are performed through the following access points:

- Author
- Title

- Journal
- Subject
- Keywords in Spanish
- Keywords in English

And using Boolean operators to combine access points.
PERIODICA can be consulted on the Internet at:
> http://www.dgbiblio.unam.mx
> Select "Catálogos en línea" icon

It should be stressed that all these databases are updated daily on-line by professionals in each discipline and professional library personnel, which guarantees high quality standards.

ELECTRONIC JOURNALS, developed also by the DGB, is an automated catalog of electronic journals which enables access to full text serials on the Internet. This is a new exclusive information service limited to UNAM users, where scientific, technical and humanistic journals can be consulted.

The electronic journal service has been strongly implemented at an international level allowing access to current information. UNAM users are able to consult publications of international prestige, published by editorial houses such as Academic Press, Springer Verlag, Blackwell's, Kluwer Academic, and others.

This on-line catalog, as has been mentioned, contains scientific, technical and humanistic journals of the highest academic quality in a great diversity of disciplines. With this catalog, users will be able to obtain general information on a journal, as well as full text articles; however, this depends on the publisher's access criteria.

The catalog has been developed based on the current subscriptions the UNAM holds on printed publications. Academic specialists of the institution undergo the process of selection. It is important to mention that UNAM users have access to this catalog at no cost, making it a useful tool in teaching and research activities.
Access options to electronic journals are:

- Title of the journal (complete or isolated words)
- Subject
- Editor

Service benefits are:

- Free access to UNAM users
- Current information
- Retrieval of full text, charts, graphics, images and more
- Catalog consultation from anywhere inside or outside the university campus, with only a computer and a modem.

- Minimum time and effort in retrieving documents
- Easy access to collections with the advantage to switch from one catalog to another

The catalog can be consulted at:
http://www.dgbiblio.unam.mx

COMPUTER EQUIPMENT

The General Directorate for Libraries has its own computer equipment, accommodating databases as they grow in size and as informatic resources are implemented.

It is equipped to reduce and optimize response time for library activities, as well as in normal everyday information and consulting services offered by DGB.

The advantage of having databases in different servers is to maintain uninterrupted services in the event that if one malfunctions the rest will continue servicing. To avoid power failures that cause computer system shutdowns and therefore, affect library services, the DGB has its own power plant.

The General Directorate's Computer Center consists of the following computer resources:

A SUN Enterprise 5500, with 1.5 Gbytes of RAM, six 330 MHz processors, 520 Gbytes in hard disk with a 100 MBPS Ethernet interface. The databases stored in this computer equipment are Librunam, Seriunam, Current Contents, and Science Citation Index.

A SUN Enterprise 3500 with 500 Mbytes of Ram, two 330 MHz processors, 520 Gbytes in hard disk with a 100 MBPS Ethernet interface. Stored here are Elsevier's full text journals.

A SUN Spark 1000 server with 256 Mbytes of RAM, four 40 MHz processors, 26 Gbytes in hard disk with a 10 MBPS Ethernet interface.

The databases stored here are MapaMex, Aries Investigadores (researchers), Aries Proyectos (projects), Partituras (music scores), and Catálogo de Libros del Fondo de Cultura Económica (Publisher catalog).

A SUN Spark 20 server with 128 Mbytes of RAM, a 110 MHz processor, 8 Gbytes in hard disk with a 10 MBPS Ethernet interface. The databases that are available here are Tesiunam, Electronic Journals, Clase, and Periodica.

Three SUN Spark Station 10 servers with 64 Mbytes of RAM, a 50 MHz processor, 4 Gbytes in hard disk with a 10 MBPS Ethernet interface. Mapas y Libros de la Biblioteca Central (maps and books of the Central Library), and DGB's Web site are stored here.

Two Local Novell CD ROM networks each with a capacity for 32 compact disks.

Three hundred 486 PCs and a Pentium II with a 10 MBPS Ethernet interface connected to RED UNAM with Internet link.

Two 100 MBPS Cisco switches connected to the backbone of Red UNAM, 20 hubs with 20 and 24 Cabletron and Cisco ports.

ALEPH is the software used to carry out library activities and services. It is an integrated software that automates libraries, with computer applications for acquisitions, cataloging, OPAC, circulation, serial control, authority files, interlibrary loans, and images.

The 330 version of ALEPH is currently used, but migration to version 500 is expected to begin this year or at the beginning of the year 2000, using the ORACLE platform.

·ACTIVITY ORGANIZATION

The General Directorate for Libraries is composed of 5 Subdirectorates: Informatics, Planning and Development, Services, Specialized Services, and Technical. This last subdirectorate is responsible for planning and organizing the technical processes described as follows.

TECHNICAL SUBDIRECTORATE

To conduct each one of its activities, this with high quality and efficiency Subdirectorate is structured in four departments: the Bibliographic Acquisitions Department, Technical Processes Department, Union Serial Catalog Department, and Conservation and Restoration Department.

The Technical Subdirectorate has 51 professional librarians with graduate and postgraduate degrees in library science, who are advocated to bibliographic acquisitions management, subject headings, classification and cataloging. There are also clerical personnel to support in daily routine activities.

TECHNICAL PROCESSES DEPARTMENT

This department is responsible for technical processes under the following procedures:

1. Because technical processes are centralized in this Department, vendors are required to submit photocopies of the bibliographic material purchased by UNAM's Library System.

Photocopies include the title page, the verso title page, table of contents or index, and the Foreword and/or the Introduction, along with the last numbered page, the number of copies acquired, the acquirer's library code, if illustrated or not. These photocopies are delivered directly to the university libraries at no cost.

2. Another procedure is that vendors provide the Marc records instead of photocopies, allowing a faster technical process.

In both cases, after having registered the acquired material, the photocopies or the Marc records are sent from the libraries to the Technical Processes Department.

This Department is subdivided into 6 Department Sections, aiming to optimize resources and to avoid unnecessary procedures. These are described as follows.

LIBRUNAM On-Line Location Section

The activities in this Section consist of locating and verifying on the LIBRUNAM database, that all the acquired titles have been registered. If so, the corresponding record is located, then the bibliographic elements are checked and verified. If identical, each acquired material is assigned an inventory number.

If the work has been registered, but it is a different edition, it is immediately remitted to the corresponding section for its prompt process by qualified professionals. This section has a professional librarian that acts as a supervisor, assisted by six auxiliary librarians.

Section of On-Line Investigation in Auxiliary Sources and Information Transfer

This Department Section looks for information on titles that were not found previously in the on-line location section, using the Bibliofile database of the Library of Congress in the United States, with the purpose of detecting identical titles, original titles (translations of original titles) and other editions.

If identical titles are found, these are recorded in floppy disks (35 records per file in MARC format); they are then processed with a program named TRANSFER, designed and developed by the Informatics Subdirectorate, to translate topics from English to Spanish. After this has been performed, they are ready to be added to the ALEPH system, with the pertinent modifications, as would be the adjustment of Cutter's number, and when the record has been supervised, it is freed to be consulted in LIBRUNAM, which is updated at the same time.

When records of original title (their translations) and other editions are located in BIBLIOFILE, these are printed and sent to the Section of Subject Headings Assignment and Classification.

The main entry (individual or corporate) is also registered complying with the auxiliary sources, and entered in the author authority file. The titles not located in the auxiliary sources are also submitted to the Section of Subject Headings Assignment and Classification.

Four professional librarians form the Department Section.

Section of Subject Headings Assignment and Classification

This Department Section assigns subject headings and classifies bibliographic titles that were not found in the Section of Auxiliary Sources, using the VALIDATOR database and specialized reference works, or by consulting university specialists in each topic.

This Department Section has 4 professional librarians.

Authority File Section

This Section is responsible for validating and updating the subject authority file with each one of the subject headings assigned to the processed materials. It also validates and incorporates new authors to the name authority file using the correct form of personal names and entities in order to control the information in both catalogs, authority names and subjects. The section also creates "See" and "See also" references and scope notes.

Three professional librarians are assigned to the Section.

Cataloging and Classification Section

This is the on-line cataloging section that works with original titles that were not found in any auxiliary source. A cataloger processes an average of 25 titles a day.

Three supervisors and 11 professional librarians who catalog and record entries on the LIBRUNAM database maintain high quality standards.

LIBRUNAM Debugging

One of the high-priorities of the Technical Processes Department is debugging the LIBRUNAM database, to eliminate those inconsistencies that impede the optimal retrieval of information in each and all the different areas of the cataloging record.

This task was developed because of the diverse versions of cataloging rules used, the changes and implementation of internal policies in different administrative periods, and as it happens in any cataloging agency in the world, because of capture errors.

Therefore, this Section corrects all those errors that are reported by the departmental libraries of the system, as well as those reported by the catalogers themselves. This is done with the purpose of maintaining an upgraded quality catalog. Four professional librarians are assigned to these tasks.

Authority Files

Authority files are very important for standardizing bibliographic records. They allow precision in the search and location of information, as well as for the international exchange of that information. The Technical Processes Department has created automated authority files for subjects, names and publishers. At present, they have the following amount of records:

- Subject authority file: 89,388
- Name authority file: 94,167
- Publisher authority file: 21,202

It should be mentioned that the subject authority file has entries in English and in Spanish, which allows for manipulation of the bibliographic records retrieved from different international English speaking resources.

The authority records have the following structure.

Subject Heading in Spanish

It is the subject authority term accepted by the Technical Processes Department, which has been translated from the Subject Heading lists of the Library of Congress of the United States. The translation is carried out with the support of specialized reference books, with the TRANSFER program, and with the aid of Globalink, which is a commercial translator and a part of this program.

Subject Heading in English

It is the subject as it appears in the list of Subject Headings of the Library of Congress of the United States.

SEE REFERENCES (X)

They are synonyms of the authorized heading, which can be employed by the users in different ways. See references are unauthorized terms of the Technical Processes Department, and therefore, are referred to as "See" references.

At the moment, only the Spanish and English topics are being updated in the automated subject authority file; the cancellations and the related terms references are entered directly in the ALEPH system.

Auxiliary Sources Used by the Technical Processes Department

Validator

It is a support tool that is used to elaborate the General Directorate's own authority files, where author entries and subjects are standardized.

This source is an international database elaborated by GRC International and contains 231,000 subjects generated by the Library of Congress in Washington, in other words, Validator stores the Library of Congress' subject headings and 3.9 million records of individual and corporate authors of the Name Authority File.

The tool enables the cataloger to establish correctly access points for subject and author entries according to the Anglo-American Cataloging Rules 2nd edition.

Bibliofile

Another international source used to support the subject assignment, classification and cataloging work.

This database searches titles that the departmental libraries have acquired and locates all those works that corresponds exactly to the same title; titles translated from their original language or other editions. It even detects records of similar titles in order to obtain subjects and classification.

Once the record is located, it is transferred to a floppy disk in MARC format. It is later processed and worked in TRANSFER system for its translation and then entered into the ALEPH system to be modified correctly following the Technical Processes Department policies. Once the record has passed the quality parameters its ready to be accessed in the information service module and for cataloging purposes.

Bibliofile is also used for subject heading assignments, for Library of Congress classification, and for the Dewey Decimal classification. It offers other advantages as using an international automated format as MARC, to allow information exchange among other catalogs in other university libraries, nationally and internationally.

Transfer Program

As previously mentioned the Technical Processes Department uses Validator and Bibliofile as basic tools for assigning subject headings based on the Library of Congress subject headings.

With the need for quality translation of subjects and better control of bibliographic records, the Transfer system was created as an automated program. It was designed jointly by the Technical Processes

Department and the Systems Department of the General Directorate for Libraries at UNAM, as an interface tool with the subject authority file, given its particularity of handling Spanish terms and English equivalents.

The above enables that records from the Bibliofile database including topics in English, when processed by the TRANSFER system, they are translated to Spanish in a consistent and unique form, this way maintaining the standardization in subject headings and the updating of authority files with international quality norms.

Auxiliary Sources Used by the Serials Union List Department

As in the Technical Processes Department, the work of the Serials Union List Department is supported by different international tools, such as on-line databases located in the United States, the National Libraries of Spain and France, compact disks and a variety of printed catalogs, for instance: Bibliofile, ISSN, and Ulrich's.

It's worth mentioning that MAPAMEX, EUTERPE, CLASE, PERIODICA and TESIUNAM are all original cataloging works without the use of any other auxiliary source.

CHALLENGES FOR THE GENERAL DIRECTORATE FOR LIBRARIES OVER THE NEXT FIVE YEARS

Nowadays with technological innovations and the proliferation of data in new electronic formats, we have the opportunity to exploit these advances and enrich our librarian environment and provide access to our databases wherever the user may be located. In addition, the General Directorate for Libraries has the responsibility of integrating and providing information faster and more efficiently to the user. To reach the above mentioned purpose, here are some of the specific or main tasks to perform:

To conclude with the correction process of LIBRUNAM database.

To continue the creation of the authority control catalogs for names and subjects.

Another main objective is to automate the 141 departmental libraries of the Library System.

With the actual computer equipment in combination with the online collective catalog updated and completely cleaned-up, to decentralize technical processes.

Training of the professional staff of the departmental libraries in the use of the Catalog Module of the software ALEPH to introduce them in cataloging procedures.

To add the contents table (help of an index word) to the bibliographic records in order to provide to users the most possibilities of retrieving information.

The departmental libraries have an interesting collection of videos and films that are not cataloged and classified yet. So that will be necessary to create a database that includes these kinds of materials.

Also it will be very important to digitize maps and scores that do not have copyright problems. Thesis will be digitized, too.

NOTES

1. Agenda estadística 1997. México: Universidad Nacional Autónoma de México. Dirección General de Estadística y Sistemas de Información Institucionales, 1997. Pags. 4, 26, 196.

2. Ven y utiliza los servicios y recursos de tu biblioteca. México: Universidad Nacional Autónoma de México. Dirección General de Bibliotecas, 1999. Pag. 32.

Role Changes:
Cataloguing, Technical Services
and Subject Librarianship
at the University of Botswana Library

Rose Tiny Kgosiemang

SUMMARY. The University of Botswana library (UBL) was formed in 1971. It started automating its processes in 1990, which has led to changes in workflow, roles and staff allocations. In the processes of automation, acquisition and cataloguing have been merged. The paper examines changes that have occurred since the merger of acquisitions and cataloguing. It compares practices of the manual era and the automated period. Lastly, it outlines lessons learned; problems encountered and makes some recommendations. *[Article copies available for a fee from The Haworth Document Delivery Service: 1-800-342-9678. E-mail address: <getinfo@haworthpressinc.com> Website: <http://www.HaworthPress.com>]*

KEYWORDS. University of Botswana, organization for cataloguing, cataloguing workflow, technical services

INTRODUCTION

A Brief Description of UBL Structure

The University of Botswana Library is organised according to subject librarianship. In August 1983 the Library changed its organisa-

---

Rose Tiny Kgosiemang is Assistant Librarian, Technical Services, University of Botswana, Gaborone, Botswana, South Africa.

[Haworth co-indexing entry note]: "Role Changes: Cataloguing, Technical Services and Subject Librarianship at the University of Botswana Library." Kgosiemang, Rose Tiny. Co-published simultaneously in *Cataloging & Classification Quarterly* (The Haworth Information Press, an imprint of The Haworth Press, Inc.) Vol. 30, No. 1, 2000, pp. 91-109; and: *Managing Cataloging and the Organization of Information: Philosophies, Practices and Challenges at the Onset of the 21st Century* (ed: Ruth C. Carter) The Haworth Information Press, an imprint of The Haworth Press, Inc., 2000, pp. 91-109. Single or multiple copies of this article are available for a fee from The Haworth Document Delivery Service [1-800-342-9678, 9:00 a.m. - 5:00 p.m. (EST). E-mail address: getinfo@haworthpressinc.com].

tional pattern from functional to subject organisation.[1] This decision was taken in the light of the decisions which had been taken in the 1979/80 academic year, when the library staff had participated in the evaluation of the library and its functions.[2] Under the functional organisation, only a few staff were involved with technical processes, while under subject librarianship all subject librarians catalogued and classified all materials within their subjects. Subject librarians, each having a degree in a subject area, service a faculty. They are assigned subject responsibilities, which include collection development, subject content analysis, user education, faculty liaison and others. Externally, Subject librarians liase with the faculty, while internally they liase with the Technical Services division of the library, which is also organised according to faculty teams.

An Overview of the Previous Acquisitions, Cataloguing and Subject Librarians' Practices follow.

ACQUISITIONS

This is the unit of the library responsible for making all materials acquired for various collections of the library available. As such, the unit performs a wide variety of tasks associated with library acquisitions including pre-order searching, ordering, receiving, invoicing, record maintenance, opening of boxes, triggering, stamping, accessioning/barcoding, pocketing, sorting/distribution of books.

From 1983-1997 Acquisitions was a separate unit from cataloguing with its own Co-ordinator. The unit co-ordinated the acquisitions activities, including the following:

- Processing of orders generated by Subject librarians.
- Maintaining an order file for all the materials ordered and received.
- Receiving, collating and accessioning of new books.
- Preparing invoices for payment.
- Maintaining an order file containing order slips for all the materials placed on order.
- Communicating with Book Dealers on matters relating to payment of invoices.
- Maintaining an accession card for all materials received, accessioned and classified.

On receipt of materials from book dealers 2 slips (1 accession + 1 flimsy) were pulled from the order file and stamped with date of receipt and price. The flimsy one was put back in the order file so that before the book is processed and put on the shelf its status would be known. The accession card was placed in the book and taken to the Subjects' offices.

- sorting out new books according to faculties and distributing them to Subject librarians
- generating the accession cards and maintaining the accession card file

CATALOGUING

This is the section of the library responsible for making new materials physically ready for customer use. It is responsible for the bibliographic integrity of all purchases, gifts and non-book materials added to the collection. This includes editing records of new books and other materials that already had records in the library database, creating original bibliographic records for those items without records in the library database, assigning call numbers for items that required original cataloguing, maintaining all authority records, and correcting any errors found in the database.

From 1983-1997 the Cataloguing unit of the University of Botswana Library co-ordinated all the cataloguing activities of the library including :

- editing scripts for books catalogued by Subject librarians
- co-ordinating the typing of stencils for the production of cards
- establishing and maintaining quotas for filing and dropping of cards. The library maintained author, title, subject, class number and shelf-list cards. The author and title cards were inter-filed in one alphabetical sequence. An extra card was made and sent in batches to the South African national library for inclusion in the Union catalogue
- training of staff on the filing of cards according to ALA Filing Rules, 1980
- production of cataloguing manuals
- ensuring that books were properly catalogued and classified, also

- The Cataloguing Co-ordinator and designated staff were responsible for the production of the Accessions list, which was distributed to other libraries locally. The accessions list was one of the methods the library used to inform the university community and other institutions of additions to the collection.

In 1984 the library introduced the catalogue card service. The service was introduced as a means to speed up technical processing and avail to Subject librarians more time for collection development and improvement of the index to subject catalogue.[3] Card sets also eliminated various cataloguing styles which made co-ordination and close monitoring especially vital if standards were to be maintained.[4] All books coming from Blackwells, the library's major book, came with card sets. The production of cards locally for books coming from other dealers and for Botswana Collection materials continued.

This production of cards locally for books coming from other book dealers came to an end in 1992 when the library was about to be fully automated. The card sets continued coming with books even when the library was automated. The cards stopped coming in 1995 and were replaced by a single flimsy card with bibliographic details, which still come with the book.

Subject Librarians

Subject librarians were assigned subject assistants who were responsible for checking orders in the card catalogue, order files, books in, books in print and for descriptive cataloguing. They were each assigned a cluster of subjects based on their subject knowledge. Subject librarians were responsible for the following:

- collection development activities
- production of subject bibliographies as a means of informing the university community and other agencies of materials in the collection in a specific subject
- cataloguing, classification and subject indexing
- faculty liaison
- maintenance of name and subject authority files. They were used for authority control of headings and their standardisation. The online authority files replaced the manual authority files when the library was automated
- supervision of Subject assistants

Acquisition Activities

For every item that was ordered Subject Librarians kept a record on a card referred to as a notification card. If the title was recommended by an academic member of staff details of the title ordered were noted including the name of the staff who recommended the title, and the date on which the title was sent to the Acquisitions unit. The notification card was then filed in trays in the Subject Librarian's office. When material had been catalogued and shelved, this notification card was sent to the relevant academic department.

Cataloguing Activities

The card sets service introduced, brought about changes in roles performed by Subject librarians.

- from 1989/1990 cataloguing and classification were major aspects of Subject librarians' duties
- 1989/1990 establishment of centralised cataloguing

This was done to facilitate cataloguing and classification activities. It was also felt that, that would leave Subject librarians enough time to pursue content analysis for subject index catalogues; reference and bibliographic instruction and establishment of regular and strong liaison links with academic departments.[5]

- in 1990/1991 descriptive cataloguing became a major aspect of Subject assistants with the direct supervision by the Cataloguing Co-ordinator
- in 1990-1991 classification and indexing continue to be one of the major activities central to subject librarianship[6]
- in 1993/1996 cataloguing process was done online. All the Assistants doing cataloguing were based in cataloguing section

Only books without CIP were sent to Subject librarians' offices for subject indexing which included classification, allocation of thesaurus terms and subject group codes.

- in 1997 Subject assistants were transferred permanently to the Cataloguing section

The following cataloguing procedure dates back to 1989, the time when Subject librarians still did cataloguing till 1997 when Subject assistants were transferred to Cataloguing section and were supervised by the Cataloguing Co-ordinator.

When books were received from Acquisitions they were first checked against the notification card file then from the card catalogue.

1. New books from Acquisitions would arrive in the subject offices. In the Subject Librarian's offices they were checked against the card catalogue/library database. Duplicates/new editions were noted in pencil in the book by the Subject Assistant.
2. Books with card sets/slips were passed straight to the Subject Librarians. Subject Librarians' role was (i) allocate Subject Group codes, (ii) classify/check classification, and (iii) allocate thesaurus/check thesaurus terms.
3. Prior to automation, books without card sets were catalogued in scripts and were checked by Subject librarians who did subject cataloguing. After the library automation sources from which bibliographic details were searched included international databases. If records were found for them they were printed out. If the record found was for an earlier edition, details of the current edition would replace those of an earlier edition such as the ISBN, imprint, etc. For those without printouts input worksheets were completed.
4. Books at (3 above) were then passed to the Subject Librarians to (i) allocate Subject Group codes (ii) classify and (iii) allocate thesaurus terms. Details were written on the printouts/input worksheets.
5. Once the Subject Librarians had finished with books, they sent them back to the Cataloguing section

Subject librarians understood that their role did not just end when orders were submitted at Acquisitions. They had to keep on checking the status of their orders. They also understood the importance of the currency of materials ordered that as soon as books came they had to be processed immediately and made accessible to the public. Occasionally there were titles without card sets, whose subject content was difficult to determine in which case they would be left on the shelves for sometime before their subjects could be determined.

When all material had been catalogued and cards for the material had been filed in the card catalogue, the order file was cleared.

Supervision

The supervision of Subject assistants by Subject Librarians dates back to 1983, the year in which subject librarianship came into practice at U. B. Library. This supervision included training them on descriptive cataloguing and in using bibliographic tools to identify bibliographic details of books. Assistants were taught how to search orders in the card catalogue for records before preparing titles for ordering and to search the card catalogue again when new books arrived in the workrooms before they were catalogued. This was done in order to avoid assigning different class numbers to copies of the same title. It was the responsibility of Subject Librarians to ensure that the information provided for ordering was correct. Subject assistants were also trained on how to produce faculty newsletters, which informed the faculty members about new items added to the collection.

ROLE OF AUTOMATION

The library automated its functions in 1993. In January 1993 Acquisition module started operating[7]. The cataloguing module became fully automated later the same year. The Online Public Access Catalogue was made available to the public in 1994.[8] Library automation brought about many changes in the library as a whole. Among the many changes that took place the following were noted:

1. Although card sets coming with new books were no longer filed, the UBL received new books supplied with cards until 1994. When the filing of cards came to an end in 1993, the library had started automating and for every new material that was received and added to the database a catalogue update in the form of a book was produced to assist library customers. The printed catalogue was also used as a back up in case the system went down. In 1994 the card sets were replaced by one flimsy slip bearing

details of the book. Information on the cards was used to guide Subject librarians in their subject cataloguing.

2. Subject Assistants were transferred to the Cataloguing unit in 1997.

3. All the technical processing that previously took place in the workrooms supervised by Subject Librarians became the responsibility of the Cataloguing unit except in cases where original cataloguing of materials was required.

4. Checking cataloguing, class numbers and subject analysis quality and approving new subject terms and classification numbers were also affected by automation.

5. The order file in Acquisitions was dismantled and replaced by online acquisitions.

6. The notification card was discontinued. The notification card played a very important role in informing the Subject Librarians about the materials ordered. Its discontinuation denied them the opportunity to even know the titles they had on order. If a lecturer would come looking for any materials he had requested through them, it would not be easy for them to know the status unless assisted by Technical services staff or unless such materials had been treated as rush orders. In which case the material would have been hand delivered to them.

The notification card also assisted both the Subject Librarians and their Assistants in determining whether the titles selected were duplicates or not. Its discontinuation robbed Subject Librarians of the only method they could use to determine whether their selections were duplicates or not. As a result, the number of duplicate orders returned to Subject Librarians every month is high and it affects their monthly outputs. Where urgent processing of orders was requested by academic staff the orders were separated from others and were presented to Technical Services for urgent ordering.

The following activities were eliminated:

- filing book recommendation forms
- checking catalogue and order files for selected items
- filing out and filing in notification cards
- adding accession numbers, class numbers and entries to card sets from Blackwells
- typing stencils for books without card sets

- typing cards for subject index
- filing in all types of catalogues
- separating books received with card sets from those without
- checking new books against the card catalogue

Merging of Acquisitions and Cataloguing into Technical Services

The advent of modern technology in libraries creates possibilities to streamline and re-design work processes in order to service the customer effectively. Not only did the manual practices end but the Library Management together with the Automation Committee decided that both acquisitions and cataloguing units should be merged into one division, Technical Services. It was felt that merging the two divisions and centralising their operations in an automated environment would eliminate duplication of efforts, especially that an integrated database would bind all functions together. It was also felt that merging would enable customers to be able to trace the materials they are looking for easily.

In 1998 the library merged its acquisitions and cataloguing units into Technical Services. It recognised the fact that for an organisation to succeed it required highly motivated, personally responsible, clearly focussed experienced people in every position, at every job, working together for maximum results.[9] Five main factors, which necessitated the merger, an issue that has been under discussion since 1995, include the following:

- the need to streamline technical services functions
- to avoid duplication of efforts, a factor that has already been mentioned in the text
- cost-effectiveness in terms of human resource allocation
- the ability to track materials from acquisitions to cataloguing
- the advantages of an integrated database which binds all functions together and makes it possible for one record to be used for order, receipt, cataloguing and OPAC

The Technical Services division provides technical processing (acquisitions and cataloguing) for all the materials acquired for the University of Botswana Library collections.

Working Arrangements

Making a division like Technical Services successful takes more than just individual effort–it takes teamwork.[10] Technical Services is using teams to accomplish many tasks. Staff has been re-organised into faculty teams: Education, Faculty of Engineering Technology, Humanities and Social Sciences. Teams are made up of support staff organised according to the available tasks headed by professional members of staff. Each team is responsible for the processing of materials in their respective faculties starting from the pre-order stage until they are ready for access by customers.

Team Roles

Each team is made up of groups of people performing three different roles. The first group does pre-order searching, opening of boxes, triggering, stamping, pocketing and barcoding. The second one handles online ordering activities until the orders are sent out to the suppliers. The last group does editing and cataloguing.

ACQUISITION

Pre-Ordering

This is one of the Acquisitions stages whereby orders recommended by Subject Librarians and/or teaching staff are submitted to TSS for processing prior to ordering. Orders may be presented in the form of pre-selection slips, selections from publisher's catalogues, recommendation forms or printouts from other sources, such as the Internet or book reviews. They are dropped in subject boxes kept in the TSS Co-ordinator's office to be attended to. They are then collected from the boxes by Assistants responsible for pre-order searching according to the Faculty from which orders originate.

The orders are checked in Motswedi-wa-Thuto, the University Library database to see if they are not already in the system. If available, a mark is made on the form either in the form of a tick, a class number or a statement saying "on order." If titles are not found in Motswedi, they are searched in Book-In-Print to verify their bibliographic details after which they are sent to the Deputy Librarian for approval. Every title that is placed on order must be in support of either the undergraduate, postgraduate courses, research or be a standard reference source, a new area of potential interest to undergraduate, postgraduate or lectures or have a favourable review on Botswana, be on the reading list, etc. That ensures that funds are spent on the right materials.

After all these have been done, orders are placed on order on-line. A monthly acquisition form is completed to indicate the number of orders and the amount committed. Each Subject Librarian is expected to order at least 110 orders per month. This cut across the subjects that one orders for. The 110 are based on the 2,000 yearly acquisitions target.

Ordering

The TSS Co-ordinator considers orders after the Deputy Librarian has approved them. As indicated above this ensures that money is spent correctly. It is also at this stage that an indication of the supplier is made.

All titles that are ordered on-line carry a message that says "on order." Orders with this message appear in the OPAC. The reason for presence of these messages in the OPAC is for the customers to know the status of records.

Receiving On-Line

Receiving on-line involves the scanning of the barcode of the newly received title onto the system. After scanning the barcode the message that says, "received and awaiting cataloguing" is automatically printed in the OPAC. What does this mean to the library customer or even to a member of the staff? To the library customer it means the book has been received, but it has not been catalogued. As indicated in the text above when new books are received they are first sorted according to faculties.

CATALOGUING

This unit is responsible for making new materials physically ready for customer use. It is also engaged in the production and maintenance of a database of bibliographic records.

When new books come from Acquisitions they are loaded into a trolley and searched in the library database by the Cataloguer. Books with all bibliographic details in the database are edited, have shelf-references, barcode numbers and subject group codes added to them. If they do not have all the bibliographic details they are searched in other international databases such as Library of Congress catalogue, Ohio Link and others. If no information is found for them in all the databases they are sent to Subject Librarians for subject cataloguing which includes assigning the classification number, thesaurus term and subject group code. Therefore, it is possible that a book that has been received and is waiting cataloguing could be in the Subject Librarians' office. When Subject Librarians are through books are sent to Technical Services for original cataloguing by Assistants.

After all the cataloguing has been done by the Assistants, the Heads of teams who are the senior members of staff in Technical Services do the final stage of editing. This process enables them to establish the accuracy and quality of records bought and downloaded into the University of Botswana Library database as well as records that are given original cataloguing. This is the only chance the supervisors have to access the work of their Assistants and determine how much assistance they need to improve on their cataloguing skills.

When all the editing is complete, books are passed on to General Assistants for spine labelling. Finally, they are cross-checked by a selected group of staff to ensure that they have been correctly spine-labelled and then are sent to the shelves to be accessed by customers. Besides monitoring and supervision of staff in their respective faculties, Heads of teams or Team leaders are also responsible for quality control of the database. Occasionally they go over the authority files trying to detect database errors and making corrections as they go along.

Teamwork: Its Benefits

Although team members have clearly defined roles, working in teams would enable them to utilise the strengths of each member to achieve best results. Not only would working in teams help them achieve their goals but it would also enable them discover the strengths of their colleagues as well as ways of improving working relationships in order to accomplish team goals. However . . . "for teamwork to be successful, teams and individual team members need to have shared goals; a sense of commitment; the ability to work together; mutual accountability; access to needed resources such as computers and necessary skills."[11] Everyone must be focussed toward the same defined goals.

Delegation and Empowerment

Before this arrangement was put in place senior staff in Technical Services and Diploma holders each took turns supervising other members of the division. It was a very difficult task to supervise the work of more than twenty people and monitor their movement. That was so because once the number of subordinates increases the quality of supervision becomes increasingly ineffective.

For the daily routine tasks that senior staff had to do together such as the general orderliness of the workroom there was too much duplication of efforts, confusion and sometimes misunderstandings. Also noticeable in the section was lack of commitment among staff. Although people had responsibilities, they had limited authority to manage their work. It was as though their contribution was not recognised or acknowledged. That way no one could be held responsible for anything.

This new arrangement enhances team development, personal development and leadership performance. It also promotes positive feelings of self-respect and self-fulfilment. It provides possibilities for staff empowerment that would not be available to individual employees. This can only be achieved through delegation. According to Berryman-Fink and Charles B. Fink delegation involves the assignment of a job, as well as the accompanying authority and responsibility for doing that job, for an employee who is held accountable for the performance of the job. It is getting things done through others.[12]

Among the middle management supervisors and heads of teams there are some staff to whom the TSS Co-ordinator delegated some responsibilities. Whereas some of those people enjoyed and managed to apportion their time among the tasks assigned, there are some who were very negative and could not balance the tasks at all. Their failure to balance the tasks was reflected in their low output and the backlogs that accumulated in their work areas. What is not clear however, is whether the assignments included communicating the specific results expected, then empowering and motivating the subordinate to achieve the results, monitoring the person's progress, and evaluating performance upon the completion of the task.

Lessons Learned

This working arrangement was a fairly new experience to most people in this Library, more especially Acquisitions and Cataloguing units. Teamwork meant different things to different people. After having this set-up for a year it is obvious that the only thing that was clearly understood by everyone in the section was the objective of the library, that our mission is to support teaching and research by making resources available to users as quickly as possible. The logistics of carrying that out does not seem to have been clearly understood. What happened for example was that, if the Science group doing pre-ordering ran out of orders and book boxes to open they had to look around and see which group doing the same thing needed help. The same thing applied to other groups.

The following are some of the areas that did not seem to have been clearly understood:

Responsibility for Accomplishing Tasks

- It did not seem to be clear to staff that as individuals they were each assigned tasks which they were expected to accomplish. Some people wasted a lot of time playing on the mercy of others to assist them or hoping that the Co-ordinator would instruct others to assist them.
- It was not appreciated that only in cases where individuals had bigger work loads than others that one would expect people with such workloads to be assisted, e. g., faculties with more staff doing selection such as the Social Science faculty would generate more orders than faculties of Education, Engineering and Humanities where there are only a few Subject Librarians. However, one still has to work and be assisted only when necessary. Someone's ability to perform well under pressure is the one that earns hiS/her credit during evaluations.

Supervision and Accountability

- Staff assigned supervisory roles did not seem to understand what the roles entailed. For example, the Head of a team was expected to ensure that the person doing pre-ordering and opening of boxes of new books always had orders and new books to process at all times. He had to liase with the responsible Subject Librarians to ensure that orders are always available. But if the Subject Librarians were not generating orders as expected then the Co-ordinator had to be informed. But in some cases the person doing pre-ordering would just concentrate on processing new books. When they are finished and there are still no orders he would assist members of other teams.

Although this is good team spirit it does not do justice to the budget allocated to that faculty. At the end of the year failure to finish the money allocated to a faculty is blamed on the Co-ordinator of Technical Services whose job is to constantly appraise Subject Librarians on their commitments and remaining balances on budgets allocated their faculties. The Co-ordinator in turn would blame the Head of the team who would also try to blame others below him for his lack of supervision. The same thing applies to the cataloguers. Before they could go on assisting others they should have made sure that everything was in order, and if not, informing Heads of their teams. At the end of the day every member is accountable for making sure that the objectives of the section and those of the institution are realised. Lastly,

Involving Supervisors in the Evaluations of Their Subordinates

- At the end of the first round of this arrangement Heads of teams were not involved in the appraisals of their subordinates. On trying to find an explanation to their exclusion from evaluating their subordinates it became clear that even the Co-ordinator did not realise that a mistake had been made and that each Head of a team had to assess the people he supervised. It was embarrassing to be left out at the time of evaluation.

With time and practice this current arrangement will not only benefit the Technical Services division, but it will bring with it opportunities for more delegation and empowerment. Berryman-Fink and Charles B. Fink note that delegation and empowerment are essential parts of any manager's job and that understanding the advantages, process, problems and ground rules of delegation and empowerment can make this role more comfortable and more effective.[13]

It is indeed a better way of developing staff through delegation and empowerment. It will empower the team leaders to be more positive, more confident, and more effective team members, communicators and problem solvers. It is believed that teams are better problem solvers, they have a higher level of commitment, and include more people who can help implement ideas.[14] Working together in teams is a more effective way to accomplish important tasks.

Before the merger, the library had a tradition of rotating junior staff after every two years. They were deployed to Public Services while those at Public Services were deployed to other areas such as Acquisitions and Cataloguing, later Technical Services. That arrangement affected productivity in the library, and in particular, Technical services. More time was spent training staff and supervising them closely so that they became experts in their work. But before the section could benefit from the skills imparted onto the new staff member that staff member was deployed to other sections. Rotation is fine if we want people to do many things; if we want the job to be done, however, a large part of the workforce must spend more time doing what they do well. The practice is no longer maintained in the library.

Problems

The Technical Services division has been faced with different types of problems:

Lack of Space

- Due to lack of space in Technical Services it has not been possible in the section to redesign the floor space in order to enable team members to sit together and to facilitate logical workflow.
- Space constraints also hamper housekeeping efforts. Sometimes these cause conflicts which need to be resolved before people can concentrate on their work and it ultimately affects productivity in the division.

Lack of Equipment

It is impossible to provide everybody in Technical Services with a desk on which to operate due to lack of space. There have been people without computers to function and as a result such people had to go round the sections every day trying to see if there is a spare computer so that they may have something to work with. The time they spent looking for spare computers and desks could have been used effectively in the division.

Unsatisfactory Performance by the Computers

The problem of the slow response time by the network affects the whole library. Sometimes Technical Services staff have to process their work manually since computers slow down progress at times. On the other hand if records processed manually are orders it becomes difficult to trace them afterwards and creates duplicate records.

At the time of writing this paper, the University of Botswana Library had bought new software, the INNOPAC software. Technical Services staff had already been trained on MARC structure and cataloguing in INNOPAC.

CONCLUSION

It is not yet clear whether this merger will be a success or not due to the fact that it is a new experience. Its success would depend on several factors: proper prior planning, this includes among other things, clear written goals, detailed plans and organised schedules of activities the teams follow every working day; the teams' commitment to quality work; communication–the teams members' ability to interact effectively with one another; proper guidance and direction by the team leaders. Also, the leaders' ability to delegate some of the tasks to their subordinates in the division is crucial. This is so because it is through delegation that they would be able to grow and develop in some areas that they are not presently familiar with. Whereas some members would find that challenging, exciting and an opportunity to do something different, others would find that threatening and frustrating.

Recommendations

1. The practice in the Library has been to offer in-service training to staff according to tasks they perform. In Technical Services

for example, people doing cataloguing cannot do acquisitions because they have not been offered acquisitions training. Likewise, those doing acquisitions cannot catalogue because they have not been trained in cataloguing. We all know how specialisation can be boring. It limits one's knowledge to the same task. Also, it affects productivity in the sense that if one who has been trained in one aspect cannot perform, the others who have been trained to do other tasks cannot replace him or her easily without having to go through the same training.

Therefore, it is recommended that in future, all Technical Services staff should receive training on all aspects of Technical Services. This would reduce boredom and the pressure of work that is always felt when more staff from one section are sent out for training.

2. In the new building, the Technical Services space should be designed to allow teams to sit together. That will make supervision and communication easy for team leaders.
3. It is also recommended that teams should have regular meetings to report on progress, their performance, problems experienced and how they may be resolved. That will reduce tensions and conflicts that seem to be reigning in the section.
4. Lastly, Supervisors are urged to supervise subordinates and act responsibly at all times to avoid being copied wrongly.

NOTES

1. University of Botswana annual report, 1983. p.146.
2. Ibid.
3. University of Botswana Annual Report 1985. p.108.
4. Ibid. 1981/82. p.108.
5. Ibid. 1989/90. p.60.
6. Ibid. 1990/91. p.71.
7. Ibid. 1992/93. p.45.
8. Ibid. 1994/95. p.41.
9. Neil Matthies. Peak performance systems. Phoenic seminar. Manitoba: Life-long Learning Centre, [1993]. p.1.
10. Kent, Petersen. Critical issues: building a committed team. University of Wisconsin-Madison. 1993.
11. G. L. Maeroff. Team building for school change: equipping teachers for new role. p.514.

12. Cynthia, Berryman-Fink and Charles, Fink. The manager's desk reference. New York: American Management Association, 1996. p.68.

13. Ibid.

14. Neil Matthies. Peak performance systems. Phoenix seminar. Manitoba: Lifelong Learning Centre,[1993]. p.1.

BIBLIOGRAPHY

Berryman-Fink, and Fink, Charles B. *The manager's desk reference*. 2nd ed. New York: American Management Association, 1996.

Katzenbach, J.R. and Smith, D. K. *The wisdom of teams: Creating the high performance organization*. Boston, MA: Harvard Business School Press, 1993.

Maeroff, G.L. *Team building for school change: Equipping teachers for new roles*. New York, NY : Teachers College Press, 1993.

Matthies, Neil. *Peak performance systems*. Manitoba: Lifelong Learning Center, [1993].

Peterson, Kent. *Critical issues: Building a committed team. Excerpted from a presentation given at NCREL's Urban School Leadership Mini-Conference in July 1993.*

Phoenix Seminar papers presented at the North Central Regional Educational Laboratory's Urban School Leadership Mini-Conference [University of Wisconsin-Madison], in July 1993.

The Organization
of the Cataloguing Function
at McMaster University

Cheryl Martin

ABSTRACT. Many technology-related changes in technical services have affected not only what we catalogue, but how access is provided. At the McMaster University Library, there have been many changes in the organizational structure and composition of the Bibliographic Services division in the past few years. This paper will document the management of the cataloguing and maintenance functions and the organization of information at a Canadian academic library. Future trends and how the library is planning for them are also discussed. *[Article copies available for a fee from The Haworth Document Delivery Service: 1-800-342-9678. E-mail address: <getinfo@haworthpressinc.com> Website: <http://www.HaworthPress.com>]*

KEYWORDS. Technical services, catalogue maintenance, organization of information, cataloguing, McMaster University

INTRODUCTION

Most of us who entered the library field ten or more years ago could not have imagined that we would be doing some of the things that we

---

Cheryl Martin is Director of Bibliographic Services, McMaster University Library, Hamilton ON L8S 4L8 (E-mail: martinc@mcmaster.ca).

The author would like to acknowledge the assistance of Donna Thomson in the preparation of this paper.

[Haworth co-indexing entry note]: "The Organization of the Cataloguing Function at McMaster University." Martin, Cheryl. Co-published simultaneously in *Cataloging & Classification Quarterly* (The Haworth Information Press, an imprint of The Haworth Press, Inc.) Vol. 30, No. 1, 2000, pp. 111-121; and: *Managing Cataloging and the Organization of Information: Philosophies, Practices and Challenges at the Onset of the 21st Century* (ed: Ruth C. Carter) The Haworth Information Press, an imprint of The Haworth Press, Inc., 2000, pp. 111-121. Single or multiple copies of this article are available for a fee from The Haworth Document Delivery Service [1-800-342-9678, 9:00 a.m. - 5:00 p.m. (EST). E-mail address: getinfo@haworth pressinc.com].

111

now accept as routine. It doesn't seem that long ago that we wrote our cataloguing out or typed it in card catalogue format, taking note of indentations in the proper places, and of the numbering systems for subject and added entries.

Of course, many libraries are still producing and using card catalogues; they are widely used in both small and large libraries. However, the role that technology has in our daily lives could not have been imagined by any but the most forward-thinking. Information technology has largely been developed and managed by programmers and systems analysts, but librarians are doing more of this work, as well as providing the structure and gateway to access the growing body of knowledge that is available electronically. The speed of change in the past few years has been exhilarating, if overwhelming to some. Many recent articles have discussed this trend. Karyle Butcher has described it as a completely different world than that of the pre-1990s: "there is no such thing as an 8 to 5 workday. They [librarians] not only work longer hours, but the work they do covers such a range of responsibilities that their daily jobs are segmented into a myriad of duties . . . One of the most common pleas heard in the profession is the desire to have time to reflect and think."

In technical services, these changes have had profound effects on the way that we do our work, and even how we approach it. For many cataloguers, being able to look at shelves of print tools and know exactly where to find a particular rule, interpretation or class number was part of the body of knowledge that we acquired as we gained experience. Now we consult electronic sources with indexes, keyword searching, and links between databases. In some cases the print tools have disappeared entirely; those with access to tools such as Cataloger's Desktop and Classification Plus have almost everything they need to catalogue on a daily basis in electronic form, right on their own desktops.

We have had to rethink almost everything that is done in technical services, as we moved from card catalogues to databases. There has also been a great change in information storage methods; we have recently had to deal with CD-ROMs, electronic serials, and web sites. The acquisition of these new formats has begun to affect the structure of the rules themselves, and provided new challenges to staff members who must learn how to deal with these new formats.

At the McMaster University Library, there have been many changes in the organizational structure and composition of the Bibliographic Services division in the past few years. This paper will document the management of the cataloguing and maintenance functions and the organization of information at a Canadian academic library.

ORGANIZATION OF THE DEPARTMENT AND ITS FUNCTIONS

This paper deals primarily with the organization of the Bibliographic Services department of the McMaster University Library. The Library consists of three units: Mills (arts and humanities), Thode (science and engineering), and Innis (business). The Health Sciences Library is part of the Faculty of Health Sciences, and is separately administered and funded. While there is a great deal of cooperation and consultation between the two libraries, they are physically and administratively separate. The Horizon database is shared, but each library catalogues its resources separately, except for a small number of electronic resources that are paid out of a common account.

Virtually all materials for the Library are ordered, catalogued, and processed by the Bibliographic Services Department. The only exception is the archival collections which are catalogued in the Research Collections Department. Collection-level archival records have recently been added to the catalogue. These were converted by Bibliographic Services staff from records that had existed only in a text file.

The Director of Bibliographic Services reports to the University Librarian, and is a member of the senior management team along with the Assistant and Associate University Librarians. The Bibliographic Services division is organized into three sections: Database Development (ordering and copy cataloguing), Original Cataloguing, and Catalogue Services (maintenance and authorities). There are a total of 21 staff members. All are library assistants except the Director and the supervisor of the Database Development section, who are librarians. Job descriptions do not require that assistants be library technicians, but many of them have a two-year college diploma in library techniques. Several also have undergraduate and in some cases graduate university degrees.

Staff members in the division have developed flexibility and adaptability to changes in workflow levels. In some months, ordering levels are quite low, and this affects the work in Database Development.

Both of the other sections have backlogs of work; in some cases these are quite large. Staff from Database Development has frequently been seconded to Catalogue Services to assist with various projects, and to Original Cataloguing to cover short-term leaves. Recently it was decided to move a permanent position from Database Development to Catalogue Services, to help with serials maintenance. As workflows change throughout the academic year, staff members need to be flexible in their work assignments, and more willing to move between sections and to perform a variety of tasks.

Most libraries have had to struggle with declining budgets and an increased need for resources for the last several years. The situation at McMaster is similar to that at other academic libraries: increased enrollment, a need to purchase resources in ever-expanding types of formats, rising serials prices, and a much-reduced staff complement. Ontario has always had a five-year high school program, but the Ontario government is phasing out the fifth year of high school. Beginning in 2003, students from both the old five-year and the new four-year programs will be entering a university. In addition to the regularly occurring economic and financial crises, Ontario universities are trying to find ways to deal with the implications of this "double cohort."

In 1994, there were 143 FTE staff members in the University Library; at the end of 1999, the total number is 118, a reduction of 17.5 percent. There were no layoffs: the reduction was accomplished through attrition and retirements. As a staff member left, the position was examined to see if it could be eliminated or consolidated with others. The position of Director of Bibliographic Services was created in March 1999 by the amalgamation of two positions: those of Director of Processing Services and the Principal Cataloguer. It was determined that these two functions could be effectively performed by one person when the incumbents in these two positions retired. Several other positions were eliminated or filled with contract staff when the incumbent retired or left.

The Original Cataloguing Section, and the creation of original bibliographic records, was historically the exclusive preserve of librarians. Early in the 1990s, library assistants began to move into these positions. As librarians retired, their positions were eliminated; other librarians were moved to public service positions when librarians there retired or left. One public service librarian who was formerly a member of the section spends one day a week in the department, cataloguing German and science materials. Because these two areas of expertise are lacking in the section, it was possible to arrange a split appointment so that she could continue to catalogue these materials.

SKILLS NEEDED FOR CATALOGUING

The skills needed to work effectively in cataloguing have changed drastically over the last few years. When automated systems and MARC coding appeared, cataloguers needed to learn how to type, created their own records in the database, and had to worry about the indexing and retrieval implications of database records. Maintenance was done online, and shelf lists were no longer needed. Many cataloguers retired or fled to public service at this point. Now much more cataloguing is done by non-librarians, partly due to economic considerations and partly because the quality and amount of copy is much greater. McMaster's shelf list only recently left the department. Conversion projects had destroyed copy and volume information that had to be re-entered from the shelf list; this project has just been completed. Even so, it was difficult for the staff to begin to depend entirely on the online shelf list. Many notes and annotations had been made on the cards, and some staff members believed that effective shelflisting could only take place with the help of those notes. We have made provision for a file of classification and cutter exceptions, which can be consulted, manually or in the future on our web page.

All libraries are in the process of dealing with electronic resources. These may be monograph or serial, new or continuing a print product, and in a variety of formats which are accessed on the web or from a library server. As well, the concept of describing things that are not physically in the library has meant a change in the philosophy of what the catalogue is. It has become a record of what the library has access to, not necessarily what is physically held in the building. At McMaster, we have formed a task force to look at technical and public service issues related to electronic resources. This group is developing cataloguing procedures and guidelines, and will make recommendations about what should be available in the catalogue, on the library's web page, or in both places, and also look at public service issues of access and display. At the time of writing, the task force has just issued an interim report which will recommend workflows and procedures based on the format of the item, and whether it is available from an individual library workstation, from a server, or from the Internet.

One by-product of the growth in electronic resources is the increase in serials maintenance. This has been compounded at McMaster by the implementation of online serials check-in in 1999. Many problems that were hidden in the Kardex are now being discovered and must be resolved. We have had only one person involved full-time in serials maintenance. Her duties include recataloguing titles that have split or combined, plus all of the other maintenance tasks such as frequency changes, holdings changes, closing holdings for titles that have ceased, and documenting missing issues. In addition, she was to absorb the maintenance work on electronic serials; this included adding information for the electronic version to the print copy, and creating a new record for the electronic version when the title or content varied from the print.

The growth in maintenance for government documents serials has been the largest of any category. Many government documents that were available in print are now only available on a web site, and users often have trouble determining where to go to find the next issue, especially if we have not entered the URL in the bibliographic record. The total workload in serials maintenance has increased to the point that one person cannot manage to complete it in a timely manner, and it is not likely to decrease in the near future. As mentioned above, we have created a new position with responsibility for serials maintenance, so that there will be two people assigned to this function full-time.

Our Horizon system affects cataloguing workflow and organization. All cataloguing processes use 486s with Windows 95. We have found that the system response time is quite slow and staff cannot work as quickly as they would like. There are also numerous PC crashes and slowdowns, mostly because of the large amount of memory needed to open the separate program modules needed for cataloguing, searching, acquisitions, and serials. Pentiums have been ordered and are to be installed in the near future, which should ameliorate this problem.

One serious problem with Horizon is the inability to print laser spine labels on regular label stock. Staff must use a word processing program to produce the labels and print them out on a laser printer. The call number is handwritten in the back of each book by the cataloguer, so that staff producing the labels can see the call number in order to type it using the word processing program. While this system works, it is not very efficient or cost-effective.

DEPARTMENT ORGANIZATION ISSUES

At McMaster, both the original cataloguing and database maintenance functions are performed by teams of non-librarians. Each team shares the function of team leader in a two- or four-month rotation. All members of both teams report directly to the Director. The derived cataloguers have a librarian supervisor.

The team function and the lack of close supervision have meant that the staff members themselves must take greater responsibility for keeping up to date with rule interpretations, cataloguing issues and trends, and workflow management. As the functions of director and principal cataloguer have been amalgamated into one, other staff members have had to take a greater role in problem solving and in identifying potential problems or conflicts. This has been a difficult transition; the assistants have many years of practical experience, but do not have the theoretical knowledge that is expected of the principal cataloguer. The emphasis has changed from reacting to changes decided by the principal cataloguer, to identifying potential changes or problems and bringing them to the attention of the Director for discussion and resolution as a team. As in many other organizations, staff members here are being asked to do more, do it faster and more efficiently, and be-able to change at a moment's notice. This will be one of the challenges of managing the cataloguing function in the coming years: to motivate people who are asked to do more and more with less and less, and to continually react to change in a positive way.

The organization of cataloguing staff into teams has been a positive development, overall. Many of the activities of planning projects and workflow, dealing with changes in cataloguing and classification practice, and working to resolve problems can be done more easily in a collaborative environment. The original cataloguers have been a team for several years. The Catalogue Services staff members have been a team for just over a year, so their experience of teamwork is much shorter. It has been a valuable experience for the teams to participate in the planning of their own projects and to evaluate their progress. It does take a great deal of time, especially at the beginning of the team process, to work out both personal and professional conflicts so that the team can function properly and achieve its goals.

PARTICIPATION IN SHARED PROGRAMS

McMaster Library does not participate in any shared cataloguing programs. Our original bibliographic records and holdings for other materials are sent to OCLC and to the National Library of Canada, mostly for interlibrary loan purposes. OCLC is our primary source for bibliographic records, except for Canadian government documents, which are searched on AG Canada (formerly UTLAS and then ISM). Until recently, non-US libraries could not participate in NACO and PCC. Now that it is possible, Canadian libraries will likely look at the advantages of participation.

We will seriously consider implementing core bibliographic record standards within the next year. Many of our decisions about bibliographic standards are based on the idea of a core record, but are not officially at "core" standard. A decision to implement the core standard would involve staff whose work might be affected, from all departments. A reduction in access points would definitely have implications for access and retrieval that would affect public service staff, and this step would have to be carefully considered.

THE FUTURE

It's difficult to even imagine where we might be in ten years; thinking back ten years, it would have been impossible to imagine where we are today. Electronic products are only one of the areas that have experienced great change, and although it has taken some time, we now have rules and procedures to deal with this material. Hopefully in the next few years, it will become easier to deal with these and other formats that emerge. Cataloguers have become more adaptable to changing formats. When this first began to happen, particularly when sound recordings became compact discs and filmstrips became videos, many did not know how to cope. Now we seem to be more capable of dealing with changing formats, and the rules are adapting to these changes.

Much thought has gone into looking at cataloguing and MARC coding systems to ensure that they meet the needs of future library users. The International Conference on the Principles and Future Development of AACR provided a starting point for us to reflect on the philosophy behind what we do, and to think about alternative ways in which the rules could be structured. The recently published report "Revising AACR2 to Accommodate Seriality" has forced us to rethink our basic beliefs about the rules that we use every day. The documents coming from these initiatives are far more radical than anything that was proposed in the 1970s when AACR1 was being revised, although cataloguers may not have thought so at the time! Most of us are now agreed that we need to develop a code which is flexible enough to cover any formats and materials that are in existence now, and any that might be developed in the future. The amount of time that it took for us to receive any definitive guidance on how to deal with electronic materials has been instructive for all of us. At McMaster, much time and effort has gone into acquiring electronic materials, but access to these materials has mostly been available only through an alphabetic list on the library's web site. We must find ways of adapting our policies and procedures to new materials in a more timely manner, so that we can provide access to them through the catalogue.

Economic pressures are not likely to decrease. At McMaster as well as at other institutions, there is a perception on the part of those outside the library that electronic resources will replace print, so libraries won't need more space or staff, and will probably need less money in the future. Even now, senior administrators are finding it difficult to justify additional space for collections. The National Library of Canada has just conducted a collections space study because they were having space problems. As Irene Szkundlarek stated recently in *National Library News*, "the Library currently holds 17 million items and the number continues to grow by more than half a million items per year." The move of libraries full throttle into the digital age has led some to predict that digitizing collections would be a panacea for library storage problems, "[however] the precentage of titles published in print format has remained high at 95 percent."[3] We will need to continue to work to ensure that we have enough space, staff, and money to provide the resources that our users need. Some materials will never be available in digital format, and some are more useful in paper or other formats. The cost of electronic resources will likely decrease, but some resources may remain prohibitively expensive, especially if they do not receive sufficient use to be cost-effective.

The pressure to do more, better, and faster is not likely to decrease either. Our users want material to be available as quickly as possible, no matter what the format. They also do not want to have to try to determine where to look for materials; they want it all in one place. Many of our users are not even in the building when they are searching our catalogue or accessing electronic materials through our web site. The task of providing easy access to all of the library's materials, whether they are physically held by the library or not, will continue to challenge us.

Integrated library systems will also have to keep up with advances in MARC and in information technology. At McMaster, we are still using a system that will not be able to cope with subfield versus in subject headings until late 2000. This lack of forward thinking is unacceptable now and will be even more detrimental to our ability to function and to serve our users if it continues.

We are in the process now of deciding what electronic resources will be accessible from our web page and our catalogue, and which ones should only be in one place or the other. We have recently begun to acquire aggregator databases of full-text journals; we do not have the staff or resources to create an original bibliographic record for each title, but know that these resources cannot be used effectively unless there is a record for each journal title in the catalogue, with a hyperlink to the journal site. We hope to explore other possibilities for providing access to aggregator titles, such as vendor-supplied MARC records. In the interim, if we do not hold the journal in print, we download a record from OCLC for the electronic version. If we have a print version, we add the information about the electronic version to the record for the print copy.

McMaster's technical services departments are not unique in that they are staffed by people with many years of experience, who have performed their duties quickly and efficiently for many years. Many of these people are within ten years of retirement. As they leave, they may or may not be replaced, depending on the economic pressures of the time. If they are replaced, it will be by younger staff members who may be more energetic and eager to learn new things, but who will not have the same level of experience or the ability to perform some functions as quickly. It will be a management challenge to utilize staff capabilities and to develop the capabilities of newer staff members.

As we look to the future, we are excited and eager for the changes which must continue to take place. It has become increasingly difficult to justify activities that do not provide immediate value to the user, and in some ways this is a good thing. It is a positive step to examine processes that have existed for years, to see if they can be done differently, or not done at all. It can, however, be difficult to find a balance between ensuring that users' needs are met, and continuing to do things that need to be done, even if the immediate value c█ seen. We still need to document our procedures and ensure tha█ basing our decisions on national and international standards, e█ seems time-consuming and wasteful to others. We must still maintain an accurate authority file, although some question the time and cost involved. Some people see change as a threat to their jobs or to the way things have always been done. If it is seen as an opportunity to learn something new, to eliminate processes that don't really add much value, and to simplify the increasingly difficult journey that users must take to figure out what we have and where it is, then change should be seriously considered. Technology can be used to eliminate time-consuming processes such as typing and filing catalogue cards, and to make global changes to enormous numbers of bibliographic records in an instant. Most of us would rather not have to do either one of these things manually, ever again. The challenge will be to keep up with developments and to respond to them.

REFERENCES

Butcher, Karyle. "Reflections on acaemic librarianship," *The Journal of Academic Librarianship* 25: 350-353.

Hill, Graham R. *McMaster University Library Report 1999*. Hamilton, ON : McMaster University Libraries, Nov. 1999, p.7. (Also available at: http://www.mcmaster. ca/library/general/lib-plan/lib-plan.htm)

Hirons, Jean, with the assistance of Regina Reynolds, Judy Kuhagen and the CONSER AACR Review Task Force. *Revising AACR2 to Accommodate Seriality: Report to the Joint Steering Committee for Revision of AACR*, Apr. 1999. (Available at: http://www.nlc-bnc.ca/jsc/ser-rep0.html)

The Principles and future of AACR: Proceedings of the International Conference on the Principles and Future Development of AACR. Jean Weihs, editor. Ottawa: Canadian Library Association, 1998.

Szkundlarek, Irene. "National Library of Canada conducts collections space study," *National Library News* 31/11 (Nov. 1999), p. 6-7.

Classification Systems
Used in Latin American Libraries

Filiberto Felipe Martinez Arellano
Orlanda Angelica Yañez Garrido

SUMMARY. It is taken for granted that the Dewey Decimal Classification and Library of Congress Classification are the most used classification systems worldwide. However, LIS literature does not include studies or research reports about classification systems currently used in Latin American libraries, and the reasons behind their adoption. This paper shows the results of an e-mail survey carried out among Latin American libraries to learn what were the classifications systems used in them, as well as some of the reasons that motivated them to select those classification system. *[Article copies available for a fee from The Haworth Document Delivery Service: 1-800-342-9678. E-mail address: <getinfo@haworthpressinc.com> Website: <http://www.HaworthPress.com>]*

KEYWORDS. Latin America, classification, Dewey Decimal, LC classification

INTRODUCTION

Bibliographic classification systems are an option that libraries have been using for ages to organize their collections. This option

---

Filiberto Felipe Martinez Arellano, PhD, is Head of the Library Science College, National Autonomous University of Mexico, Mexico D.F. (E-mail: felipe@servidor.unam.mx).

Orlanda Angelica Yañez Garrido is in the Library and Information Studies Graduate Program, National Autonomous University of Mexico, Mexico D.F. (E-mail: orlanda@selene.cichcu.unam.mx).

[Haworth co-indexing entry note]: "Classification Systems Used in Latin American Libraries." Arellano, Filiberto Felipe Martinez and Orlanda Angelica Yañez Garrido. Co-published simultaneously in *Cataloging & Classification Quarterly* (The Haworth Information Press, an imprint of The Haworth Press, Inc.) Vol. 30, No. 1, 2000, pp. 123-136; and: *Managing Cataloging and the Organization of Information: Philosophies, Practices and Challenges at the Onset of the 21st Century* (ed: Ruth C. Carter) The Haworth Information Press, an imprint of The Haworth Press, Inc., 2000, pp. 123-136. Single or multiple copies of this article are available for a fee from The Haworth Document Delivery Service [1-800-342-9678, 9:00 a.m. - 5:00 p.m. (EST). E-mail address: getinfo@haworthpressinc.com].

123

allows library patrons to find a particular item they are looking for in the stacks, but also, more importantly, it allows library patrons to find together, in an unique place, a set of books about a particular subject to browse them.[1] Additionally, Ghikas has mentioned that classification is a tool that "became a very efficient route to move about the collection."[2] Classification should seriously be considered more than a simple tool to organize materials on the shelves. In this way, library patrons will have a variety of items to satisfy their information needs.

Bibliographic classification systems used by most of the libraries worldwide are the Dewey Decimal Classification and the Library of Congress Classification, commonly called LC Classification. This fact has been frequently mentioned in the LIS literature and at professional meetings approaching technical services issues; however, there are no reports or studies that had considered what classifications systems are being used by Latin American libraries. Likewise, there is no understanding about factors influencing library decisions for selecting a determinate classification system.

Taking into account the above mentioned, it was considered interesting and worthwhile to carry out a study for gaining understanding about library classification systems used by Latin American libraries. Moreover, because the decision to use a particular classification system has substantial implications for managing cataloging production and access, the study also explored some of the reasons for the libraries selection of the classification system they currently are using. This paper shows the main results of that study.

FACTORS INFLUENCING THE ADOPTION OF A LIBRARY CLASSIFICATION

As mentioned earlier, the library classification systems most commonly used by a large number of libraries worldwide are the Dewey Decimal Classification and the LC Classification.

The Dewey Decimal Classification was created by Melville Dewey in 1873 and published for first time in 1876. Currently, the 21st edition of this classification system is available for those libraries that have adopted it. About this system, it has been written that "[t]he Dewey Decimal Classification is the most widely used library classification system in the world. It is used in more than 135 countries and has been translated into over 30 languages. Recent translations in progress or completed include Arabic, Chinese, French, Greek, Hebrew, Italian, Persian, Russian, Spanish, and Turkish. In the United States, 95% of all public and school libraries, 25% of all college and university libraries, and 20% of special libraries use the DDC. In addition, Dewey is used for other purposes, e.g., as a browsing mechanism for resources on the World Wide Web."[3]

The Dewey Decimal Classification has been published in four volumes, the first one includes its introduction and tables, the second and the third contain the classification schedules, and the last one its index. At the present time, there also exists an electronic version of the Dewey Decimal Classification. Moreover, there is an abridged version of this classification. Its notation is based in ten main classes, which are divided, on a decimal form, going from general to particular topics. These characteristics makes Dewey Decimal Classification a logic and easy system to use for anyone.

As indicated by its name, the Library of Congress developed the LC Classification System. Its schedules were published along several years, from 1899 to 1940. LC classification includes 21 main classes, which have been published in 45 volumes and in CD version. Kao points out that the "Library of Congress Classification System is the second most widely used system in the United States," and is used by most academic libraries and special libraries.[4] Many of these libraries used the Dewey System originally, but changed to the Library of Congress System in the late 1960s and early 1970s. It is important to point out that this system was created for the utilitarian purpose of arranging a particular collection, that of the Library of Congress. For these reasons, this classification mainly satisfies LC's needs, and does not always shows a uniform and nemotecmics subdivision for all the subjects included in it.

In a survey carried out by Nichols among California libraries, she found that public libraries tend to use the Dewey Decimal classification, while large academic libraries prefer the Library of Congress Classification, with both systems being the most common among the libraries that participated in the survey.[5]

There are also other bibliographic classification systems, like the one being used by the National Library of Medicine, the Universal Decimal Classification and the Colon or Faceted Classification; however, the use of these classification systems has not been widespread among libraries.

Regarding the factors that have influenced the selection and adoption of one or another system, they can be divided into two main categories: easy use, and administrative and economic aspects. Some of the disadvantages that have been attributed to the LC Classification are its great extension and the lack of manuals to guide the user through its application. Also, the lack of an index was a shortcoming until the emergence of the "Combined Index to the Library of Congress Classification Schedules" took place. Another disadvantage attributed to this system, particularly for Latin-American libraries, is the existence of schedules only in English. This can be a limitation for managing and applying this classification system and therefore, it also would be considered a factor that affects its adoption.

Certainly, the set of shortcomings and disadvantages attributed to the LC Classification system, mentioned above, are some of the factors that have limited its selection and influenced the adoption of the Dewey Decimal Classification instead. Nevertheless, as it has been pointed out by Godden,[6] "In the mid-1960s and early 1970s there was a move to reclassify library collections from Dewey to LC. This was especially popular among college and university libraries. Reasons given for adopting the LC system included the availability of complete LC cataloging and the expansiveness of LC in accommodating new subjects." Likewise, in an article of that time, Welsh (1967, p. 351) cites the following opinion: "any title which has an LC card and LC classification number [i.e. "Call number?"] could be handled by a clerk."[7]

These arguments are not at all true although having the classification number in the LC records makes it easier to classify the material, but they also imply further work. Consequently, these factors also have influenced the adoption of the LC Classification in some libraries, particularly in those having a scarce number of personnel for technical services.

Furthermore, the existence of diverse bibliographic tools generated by the Library of Congress to support the cataloging by copy by the distribution of catalog cards and the National Union Catalog publication in the first half of this century; the generation and distribution of automated registers, microfiches and CDs including LC cataloging during the second half of the century; and at the present time the availability of catalog records through the Internet, are among factors influencing the adoption of the LC Classification System.

Another factor that has influenced LC adoption is the one pointed out by Welsh "There is evidence, however, as reflected in inquires to the Library [of Congress], that one of the considerations in some cases is the assumption that adoption of the Library of Congress classification schedules will be a necessary condition for using its bibliographic services at such time as they are automated."[8]

Finally, Hill makes reference to various elements that should be taken into account when adopting a library classification system, such as: library management, the collection, the users, classification system features, and the technological one.[9]

According to all the above mentioned, it can be shown that the classification system selection is highly influenced by administrative aspects. Moreover, the existence of tools that support classification activities is an important factor. They affect the time and the personnel to perform library classification and also the economical resources needed for that. Likewise, the kind of library, the collection size, and its future development represent additional factors having some influence on the classification system adoption. Nevertheless, a classification system selection can also be influenced by fashionable trends or simply imitation. In other words, if a library uses a particular classification system, the rest of the libraries will also use it.

Methodology and Libraries Background

As earlier mentioned, the purpose of this study was twofold. First, to know what library classification systems were being used by Latin American libraries, and second, to gain understanding about the reasons for their choices. These choices are management decisions that can greatly affect the cataloging process and also a library's original cataloging contributions to shared databases or made available through their own online catalogs.

To achieve the study purpose, an e-mail survey was carried out among Latin American libraries. This approach was chosen because e-mail is a quick way of communication that allows an immediate and easy response for respondents. Surveyed libraries were selected using directories such as World of Learning (44th ed., 1994), World Guide to Libraries (12th, 1995), and World Guide to Library, Archive and Information Science Associations (1990). All kinds and sizes of libraries were considered; however, those with large collections were preferred. It should be noticed that the sources for obtaining library data were not the most updated, which would be considered a shortcoming of this study.

One hundred ten questionnaires (Annex) were sent to libraries from 17 Latin American countries. The questionnaire included seven questions inquiring by library type, library size, stack access, classification system used, edition of classification schedules, reasons for selecting the current classification system, and if the library had plans for changing its current classification. The survey was carried out between September and December 1998. Of the 110 questionnaires that were e-mailed, 35 (32%) of them were sent back due to nonexistent addresses. There were 63 libraries (58%) from 14 countries that responded to the e-mail questionnaire. Nevertheless, there were no answers from Honduras, Panama and Paraguay.

Table 1 shows the number of questionnaires received from each one of the different countries included in the survey. As it can be observed in Table 1, the greatest number of responses received was from Brazil, 28 questionnaires (44%), and from Colombia, 12 questionnaires (19%). Regarding Brazilian libraries replys, it should be pointed out the questionnaire was sent to the coordination of a library network, called Antares, which relayed the survey throughout the network, increasing the answer rate.

Survey Results

The first survey question inquired about the library type. Study findings (Table 2) show that of 62 libraries replying to the questionnaire, 33 were university (52%), 17 specialized (27%), 6 respondents marked university and specialized (9%), none school, 2 public (3%), and 5 other type (10%). Four of these last ones were national libraries and the other one stated to be a community library.

The next question was about library size. Size was measured by the number of volumes held by the library. Results dealing with this question are included in Table 3.

As it can be observed in Table 3, most of the library owned holdings from 10,000 to 50,000 volumes (36%). Another significant number of libraries held less than 10,000 volumes (17%). Findings in regard to library size showed that more than a half of the libraries held small collections.

The next question inquired about type of stack access. Results from this question are shown in Table 4. It is important to indicate that some

TABLE 1. Number of Questionnaires Received Per Country

COUNTRIES	NUMBER OF QUESTIONNAIRES RECEIVED	
Argentina	2	(3.2%)
Bolivia	1	(1.6%)
Brazil	28	(44.3%)
Chile	2	(3.2%)
Colombia	12	(19.0%)
Costa Rica	1	(1.6%)
Cuba	1	(1.6%)
Ecuador	3	(4.8%)
El Salvador	1	(1.6%)
Guatemala	1	(1.6%)
Nicaragua	1	(1.6%)
Peru	3	(4.8%)
Uruguay	5	(7.9%)

TABLE 2. Library Type

LIBRARY TYPES	NUMBER OF QUESTIONNAIRES RECEIVED	
University	33	(52.4%)
Specialized	17	(27.0%)
University-Specialized	6	(9.5%)
School	0	
Public	2	(3.2%)
Other	5	(7.9%)
TOTAL	63	

TABLE 3. Library Size

NUMBER OF VOLUMES	LIBRARIES	
Less than 10,000	11	(17.5%)
10,000 to 50,000	23	(36.5%)
50,001 to 100,000	7	(11.0%)
100,001 to 200,000	7	(11.0%)
200,001 to 400,000	4	(6.4%)
400,001 to 600,000	3	(4.8%)
600,001 to 900,000	3	(4.8%)
more than 900,000	4	(6.4%)
No answer	1	(1.6%)
TOTAL	63	

TABLE 4. Stack Access Type

Stack Access	Libraries	
Open	40	(63.5%)
Closed	12	(19.0%)
Mixed	10	(15.9%)
No answer	1	(1.6%)

respondents marked two options, that means they use a combination of open and closed stack access. Open access to stacks was a general policy among libraries. Of 63 library respondents, 40 had open stack access (63%), and only 12 libraries (19%) a closed stack policy. Additionally, ten libraries (16%) mentioned they had a mix of open and closed stack access.

Table 5 shows figures dealing with the classification system used by libraries that replied to the e-mail questionnaire. As it can be observed, libraries overwhelmingly indicated they were using Dewey Decimal Classification. There were 32 libraries indicating they were using DDC (50%). Furthermore, 7 libraries mentioned they were using DDC together with another classification (11%). Only 8 (12%) of the libraries that said they were using Library of Congress Classification. Additionally, there were 9 libraries that answered they were using other classification systems (14%). Among them, 2 mentioned they were using Faceted Classification and the other ones particular classifications.

Also, it was considered important to know what edition of the classification system the libraries were using. Table 6 includes figures dealing with this question. There was a general agreement concerning which edition of the classification schemes they used. The most relevant finding was that of 32 libraries mentioning that they use the Dewey Decimal Classification, 24 follow the 20th edition (75%).

Regarding library plans for changing the classification currently in use, there was a strong trend to maintain the same classification system. Only one library mentioned its plans for changing the current classification system. It was thinking over changing from the Dewey Decimal Classification to the Library of Congress Classification.

Finally, libraries wrote their reasons for having adopted the current classification. There were a variety of answers which can be explained by the fact this inquiry was an open question. Most of the libraries participating in the survey included one or more reasons for using

TABLE 5. Classification System Used

CLASSIFICATION SYSTEMS	LIBRARIES	
Library of Congress Classification	8	(12.7%)
Dewey Decimal Classification	32	(50.8%)
Universal Decimal Classification	7	(11.1%)
Other	9	(14.3%)
Combination:		
Dewey and Universal Decimal	2	(3.2%)
Dewey and Other Classification	5	(7.9%)
TOTAL	63	

TABLE 6. Edition of the Classification Systems Used

CLASSIFICATION SYSTEMS	EDITION	ANSWERS
Library of Congress	1998 CD-Rom	4
	4a ed.	2
	1996 ed.	2
	TOTAL	8
Dewey Decimal	21a ed.	4
	20a ed.	24
	18a ed.-20a ed.	1
	1995 ed.	1
	No answer	2
	TOTAL	32
Universal Decimal	1998 ed.	1
	1997 ed.	1
	2a ed. Portuguese	3
	2a ed.	2
	TOTAL	7
Other	1998 ed.	1
	1997 ed.	1
	1994 ed.	1
	1978 ed.	1
	No answer	5
	TOTAL	9

their current classification system (92%). Just five questionnaires were sent back without being answered (8%).

Library responses included diverse reasons for adopting the current classification. Most of the reasons were related to Dewey Decimal Classification since it was the most used in Latin American libraries. However, there were some reasons for rejecting DDC and adopting another classification system. Library reasons were divided into the following categories: classification system characteristics, user needs, library collection, and administrative policies.

In regard to the classification system characteristics, the following reasons were stated:

1. It is flexible, easy to use and practical (6 answers)
2. It is a detailed classification (5 answers)
3. The general coverage of Dewey (3 answers)
4. It allows the generation of national bibliographies by subjects (2 answers)
5. It is simple, short numeric notation (2 answers)
6. The latest editions include Spanish versions (2 answers)
7. It does not include a large specificity for subjects (2 answers)
8. It is not updated in several areas; the system is incomplete (2 answers)
9. Flexible enough to combine the different editions (2 answers)
10. Dewey was saturated in certain areas (2 answers)
11. The terms have been translated into Portuguese (1 answer)
12. Its multidisciplinary nature is right for an on-line catalog (1 answer)
13. LC is more open to a larger number of categories and it tends to be less saturated (1 answer)
14. Each new edition of Dewey changes considerably in regard to the previous one (1 answer)

The second set of reasons were focused on user needs and they included:

1. Easy to understand by the users (4 answers)
2. It is better to use a system that patron has been managing (1 answer)
3. The most adequate one for the library service (1 answer)
4. Due to university exchange programs, it is important for students to use and understand the system they will be using in the United States.

The third category of responses included those related to the library collection. The following reasons were expressed:
1. It is the one that better represents the content of our collection (3 answers)

2. It is useful for the great amount and diversity of subjects included in a library (2 answers)
3. For its adaptability to the system of open stacks (1 answer)
4. Dewey is not adequate for specialized and/or university libraries (1 answer)
5. It is practical for a library system that is being developed to manage the reading room and the reference service (1 answer)
6. Because of the international characteristics of the institution (1 answer)

In regard to administrative policies, the next reasons dealt with were mentioned:

1. The system was adopted since the beginning (5 answers)
2. It is currently the most widely used system (4 answers)
3. It is the most widespread system in Latin America (4 answers)
4. It is the same system used by other institutions (4 answers)
5. It is the most adequate system for the library services (3 answers)
6. There is a professional agreement on its adoption (1 answer)

Finally, all the libraries indicated they do not have plans for changing the classification system they arc using. Just one mentioned that it had previously used the Universal Decimal Classification and the collection had been reclassified some years ago with Dewey.

CONCLUSIONS

The goal of this study was to learn what library classifications systems were being used in Latin American libraries and what were some of the reasons for their adoption.

The study found that Dewey Decimal Classification is the most common classification system used in Latin America. More than half of the libraries surveyed stated that they use it. The Library of Congress Classification and the Universal Decimal Classification were also used but they are not widespread.

More than a half the library holdings are small, less than 50,000 volumes, which would be a possible explanation for the adoption of the Dewey Decimal Classification. It seems this assumption is supported by the statements included in the collection reasons for adopting a classification system.

Regarding the library type, the study found that more than half of the surveyed libraries were university, and over a quarter were specialized. Literature on library classification reveals these library types are usually associated with use of the Library of Congress Classification system. Nevertheless, in Latin American libraries most university and specialized libraries are using the Dewey Decimal Classification.

Although in some other parts of the world university and specialized libraries usually use Library of Congress Classification instead of Dewey Decimal Classification, in the case of Latin American libraries their collection size could justify the effective use of DDC. Likewise, statements given in the user reasons for adopting a classification system seem to support the successful use of Dewey Decimal Classification. Library opinions state that the current classification systems are functional and easy for patrons to understand.

A large number of mentioned reasons for adopting a determinate classification system were focused on the classification systems characteristics. This fact leads us to think about the user role in the adoption of a classification system. It seems the user factor has not been considered totally in comparison to classification characteristics and collection size.

The results of this study represent a first approach to the use of library classifications in Latin American libraries. Therefore, results show a general portrait of these issues. The next reasonable step is to carry out studies that included a greater sample of Latin American libraries to validate the findings of this study. Likewise, it is reasonable to consider and to test some association or correlation among the variables included in future studies. Certainly, this study would have some shortcomings; however, it contributes to the understanding of Latin American libraries. Moreover, it establishes the foundations to carry out further research on this subject.

NOTES

1. Irene P. Godden, *Library technical services: Operations and management.* (San Diego, CA: Academic Press, 1992). Cites Paul Dunkin.

2. Mary W. Ghikas, "Setting classification policy," in *Classification of Library Materials: Current and Future Potential for Providing Access.* (New York: Neal-Schuman, 1990)p. 126-135.

3. A brief introduction to the Dewey Decimal Classification. (1999). *http://www. oclc.org/oclc/fp/about/brief.htm* Accessed, November 10, 1999.

4. Mary Lou Kao, *Cataloging and Classification for Library Technicians*. (New York: The Haworth Press, Inc. 1995).

5. Elizabeth Dickinson Nichols, "Classification decision making in California Libraries," in *Classification of Library Materials: Current and Future Potential for Providing Access*. (New York: Neal-Schuman, 1990), p. 146-173.

6. Godden, Library Technical Services, 1992, p. 173.

7. William J. Welsh, Considerations on the adoption of the Library of Congress Classification, *Library Resources and Technical Services* 11(3):345-353.

8. Ibid., p. 351.

9. Janet Swan Hill, "Classification, an administrator's perspective, *Cataloging & Classification Quarterly* 21(2):69-73 (1995).

REFERENCES

A brief introduction to the Dewey Decimal Classification. (1999). *http://www.oclc.org/oclc/fp/about/brief.htm* Accessed, November 10, 1999.

Ghikas, Mary W. (1990) "Setting classification policy." In Classification of Library Materials: Current and Future Potential for Providing Access (pp. 126-135). New York: Neal-Schuman.

Godden, Irene P. (1992). Library technical services: Operations and management. San Diego, CA.: Academic Press.

Hill, Janet Swan. (1995). "Classification, an administrator's perspective." Cataloging and Classification Quarterly, 21(2), 69-73.

Kao, Mary Lou (1995). *Cataloging and classification for library technicians*. New York: The Haworth Press, Inc.

Nichols, Elizabeth Dickinson (1990). "Classification decision making in California Libraries." In *Classification of Library Materials: Current and Future Potential for Providing Access* (pp. 146-173). New York: Neal-Schuman.

Welsh, William J. (1967). Considerations on the adoption of the Library of Congress Classification. *Library Resources and Technical Services*, 11(3), 345-353.

ANNEX. Classification Systems Used in Latin American Libraries Survey

We are carrying out a survey about classification systems used in Latin American libraries. The survey results will be used only for research purposes and your answer will be anonymous. Please reply to this message and thank you for your participation.

RESPONDENT NAME ————————————————————————————
POSITION ——————————————————————————————————
PLACE ———————————————————————————————————————

1. Library Type
____University
____Specialized
____School
____Public
____Other. Please define

2. Library Size
____Under 10,000 volumes
____10,000   to   50,000   volumes
____50,000   to   100,000   volumes
____100,000   to   200,000   volumes
____200,000   to   400,000   volumes
____400,000   to   600,000   volumes
____600,000   to   900,000   volumes
____Over 900,000 volumes

3. Stack Access
____Open
____Closed

4. Classification system used
____Library of Congress Classification
____Dewey Decimal Classification
____Universal Decimal Classification
____Colon Classification
____Other. Please define

5. What edition of your classification system are you using?

6. What are the reasons your library adopted the current classification system?

7. Is the library planning to use a different classification system?
____NO
____YES
        What Classification system?
        Why?

SPECIALIZED LIBRARIES

Bibliographic Access Management at Lane Medical Library: Fin de Millennium Experimentation and Bruised-Edge Innovation

Dick R. Miller

Chance favors only the mind which is prepared.

–L. Pasteur, 1854

SUMMARY. This paper surveys four aspects of Bibliographic Management at Lane Medical Library, Stanford University Medical Center. First, a capsulized overview of the current scope and organization provides context. Second, counts of selected form/genre headings statistically present the extent and nature of databases maintained and illustrate our emphasis on form/genre. Third, descriptive summaries of selected policies and practices currently in effect illustrate how staff are

---

Dick R. Miller, MLS, is Head of Technical Services, Lane Medical Library, Stanford University Medical Center, Stanford, CA 94305 (E-mail: dick@stanford.edu).

The author is indebted to Nancy Austin, Mary Buttner, Maria Feng, Mary Love, Pamela Murnane, Jo Wang, Randy Woelfel, and others for their support and willingness to experiment in what continues to be a collective effort. In recognition of this joint effort 'we' is used throughout this paper.

[Haworth co-indexing entry note]: "Bibliographic Access Management at Lane Medical Library: Fin de Millennium Experimentation and Bruised-Edge Innovation." Miller, Dick R. Co-published simultaneously in *Cataloging & Classification Quarterly* (The Haworth Information Press, an imprint of The Haworth Press, Inc.) Vol. 30, No. 2/3, 2000, pp. 139-166; and: *Managing Cataloging and the Organization of Information: Philosophies, Practices and Challenges at the Onset of the 21st Century* (ed: Ruth C. Carter) The Haworth Information Press, an imprint of The Haworth Press, Inc., 2000, pp. 139-166. Single or multiple copies of this article are available for a fee from The Haworth Document Delivery Service [1-800-342-9678, 9:00 a.m. - 5:00 p.m. (EST). E-mail address: getinfo@haworthpressinc.com].

139

attempting to improve bibliographic access and prepare for future retrieval systems. Because many of the positions taken may be controversial, discussion includes how the impact of differences is minimized in external systems. Last, selected new and/or experimental initiatives explore near future projects to further extend and enhance bibliographic control. The potential of these options derives from a more flexible integration and deployment of traditional and digital library resources focused on domain-specific user needs. A conjectural conclusion identifies the need for radical changes in the scope and structure of bibliographic control necessary to utilize rapidly evolving technologies effectively. Lane's ongoing XML MARC experiment suggests the feasibility and necessity of replacing MARC with a less arcane scheme and posits the concept of organic bibliography as the basis for a more robust bibliographic infrastructure. *[Article copies available for a fee from The Haworth Document Delivery Service: 1-800-342-9678. E-mail address: <getinfo@haworthpressinc.com> Website: <http://www.HaworthPress.com>]*

KEYWORDS. Digital materials, XML MARC, form/genre, component parts, organic bibliography

CURRENT SCOPE AND ORGANIZATION

Lane Medical Library[1] is one of the leading medical school libraries as indicated in the annual statistics compiled by the Association of Academic Health Sciences Libraries Directors.[2] A tradition of innovation,[3] has accelerated with the appointment of an information scientist, Tom Rindfleisch, as director in January 1997. The resultant blending of professional cultures has produced beneficial synergies in developing strategies to help the library combine technology and service gracefully. A newly approved facility should further accelerate this trend. Lane has a budget of $5.3 million and now has five divisions:

1. Administration
2. Computing and Networking Systems (split from Technical Services in 1997)
3. Instructional Facilities Operations (established in 1999, partially by external transfer)
4. Public Services
5. Technical Services

Technical Services is changing rapidly and consists of five closely inter-related functional areas:

1. Acquisitions and Serials (merged in 1991 due to budget cuts; subsequently Collection Development and Digital Licensing were added)
2. Bibliographic Management
3. Digital Materials (established 1997)
4. Information Systems Development (approved fall 1999)
5. Library Automation (established 1983 as Systems Dept., cf. 2 above)[4]

Bibliographic Management attempts to provide exceptional access to resources in the health sciences. Each successive challenge brings an opportunity to analyze and further enhance an evolving, flexible bibliographic framework, thus providing relative stability. Three regular FTE and other staff balance quality and quantity in building databases to support this effort:

1. Head of Technical Services (approx. 20%)
2. Bibliographic Access Manager (100%)
3. Bibliographic Access Librarian (50%; temporary until retirement of incumbent)
4. Specialist IV (50%; serials)
5. Specialist II (100%; monographs, component parts)
6. Specialist II (50%; digital materials, processing)
7. Specialist II (10%; archives, history of medicine; reports in Public Services, although bibliographic work reviewed in Bibliographic Management)
8. A half time Library Automation position and two positions in Digital Materials include a "contribution to bibliographic management" in their job descriptions. A part time Specialist IV in Serials does special projects related to cataloging as time permits.
9. Liaisons in Public Services help integrate handling of Reserves, Reference, and Archives/History of Medicine. Most Technical Services staff have a reference or information desk assignment.
10. Various students, interns, volunteers–sometimes funded by salary savings during vacancies.

To refocus Technical Services' direction, a new Digital Materials position was substituted for the Bibliographic Access Manager position when the incumbent resigned in 1997. The Bibliographic Access

Librarian became the Manager. When the lost position was reinstated in 1999, a new Manager was hired. The interim Manager refilled the Librarian position half time as a step toward gradual retirement. Recruitment and retention are receiving increased attention recently. Due to several promotions, all Technical Services staff are at the Specialist level II or higher reflecting the increasing complexity of digital materials, where "use judgement" has taken on new meaning. There is less review of "regular" cataloging to permit greater focus on emerging formats.

Staffing has been indirectly augmented and the magnitude of the databases significantly expanded by various batch loads: (1) converting minimal level serials records from the National Library of Medicine's (NLM) Serhold database to MARC in 1986 to jumpstart database creation, (2) loading University of Minnesota Biomedical Library records into a local resource file in 1988, (3) loading records from the University of California, Los Angeles' IMMI[5] in 1995, (4) a retrospective conversion project with Retrolink Associates in 1998, (5) loading digital image records from the University of Utah[6] in 1999, (6) and most recently bibliographic data mining of digital materials' component parts, which will be described in a future paper.

Lane currently uses the Carl System, with considerable local enhancements, and has partnered since 1992 with the Jackson Library of Stanford's Graduate School of Business in sharing library automation. Since Lane only has one physical branch, we use Carl's branch feature to establish virtual collections: ACCESS (for material not owned), ELANE (for digital materials), RSERV (grouping of locations for Reserves), FLRC (Fleischmann Learning Center and Informatics Lab collection), PER (periodicals locations), etc. We export to RLIN (used since 1977), Socrates (the Stanford union catalog), the California Digital Library (serials only), and NLM (Serhold). A request for proposal is in preparation for a new integrated library system anticipated for 2000.

DATABASES MAINTAINED

Table 1 uses Nov. 1999, counts of selected form/genre headings to illustrate the range and distribution of records in our three databases and thus the breadth and depth of the collections. Undercounting varies depending on the degree of success in retrospective application.

The headings illustrate Lane's emphasis on form/genre explained under content enrichment sections below. Form/genre headings have essentially replaced form subheadings and reliance on fixed fields for nature of content and bibliographic level and type.

Table 2 illustrates the distribution of Authorities records by type. Lane has a policy of relying on bibliographic headings when authority records would not provide additional information, thus counts vary considerably.

SELECTED POLICIES/PRACTICES OF INTEREST

To focus on the state of Bibliographic Management at Lane, descriptions of various policies and practices with their rationale illustrate areas which differ from general practice. Lane attempts to describe and provide thorough access to its physical holdings, licensed digital materials, and selected high quality, free Internet resources. Lane also strives for complementarity with the NLM's databases, particularly in regard to selection of component parts, i.e., they generally should not be included in Medline.[7] The intent is to eliminate duplication of effort and duplication in results in future combined searches of both resources.

Record Import/Export

In considering the relationship of Lane's records to our bibliographic utility, RLIN,[8] several factors suggested that local qualitative enhancements could be undertaken without negative impact on the union catalog.

1. Lane is "downstream" from utilities; only 3% of traditional records are original; thus most often there are other records available for download which follow Library of Congress (LC) practice. Internally, certain locally "enhanced" records are given a code which translates to a lower encoding level when exported to RLIN.

2. Locally programmed import/export filters permit efficient flipping of headings from local to national forms and vice versa. This same mechanism flips obsolete MeSH to the current form and adds a subfield indicating 'local' to all exported form/genre

headings. Thus, Lane's exported records follow LC practice more closely than our internal version.

3. Many values are mapped from fixed fields and textual occurrences to indexed entries and keywords as described below. This semi-automated approach with human verification makes possible some practices which would otherwise be too labor intensive to be feasible. It also makes encoded data visible and searchable by users.

4. RLIN retrieval is enhanced when additional headings, fields, etc., are added due to cluster indexing. Thus, many of Lane's records provide original access in RLIN. No complaints relating to Lane policies have been received, suggesting that content enhancements are valued more than digressions from LC policy, perhaps noticeable only to catalogers?

As with most libraries' online catalogs, current policy implementation reflects desired features, and vestiges of past practice can rarely be eradicated completely. Despite a relatively small database and much retroactive batch processing, only some of the policies discussed below can be considered fully implemented retrospectively. Loading retrospective conversion records was a set-back in authority control, although ongoing heading consolidation often yields unique information for the authority file.

Language

The current language of science and medicine is English. Lane has elected to consider English as the language of our databases. To enhance retrieval we translate many foreign language titles, providing additional keywords in English. We enter foreign corporate names under English usage or translation with cross-references from the original language.[9] A local field for language as subject supplants language subheadings. Indexing of the language of text, obscured in the fixed fields and field 041, will be addressed in migration to a new system. For staff convenience authority records include language codes. Textword authorities carry language codes for variants likely to occur in English text.

In earlier periods Latin, French, and German were the chief languages of science. To reflect this importance in our historically rich collection, the vernacular heading becomes a cross-reference and ref-

TABLE 1. Database Composition by Selected Form/Genre

Form/Genre Heading	LML[1]	ETC[2]	AUT[3]
[# records]	140,000	53,586	43,000
Archive Material	2,008	-	-
Collection	289	-	-
Subunit	55	-	-
Internet Resource[4]	3,082	6,551	3,572
Component[5]	47	53,586	-
Article	-	35,704	-
Chapter	-	23,640	-
Book	124,475	-	-
Atlas,Cartographic	5	-	-
Atlas, Epidemiologic	13	-	-
Atlas, Pictorial	2,667	-	-
Serial[6]	12,718	-	-
Periodical[7]	10,851	-	-
Photograph	2,080	300	-
Videocassette	440	56	-
Congess	14,328	39	-
Govt Pub, Local	241	1	-
Govt Pub, State	1,266	-	-
Govt Pub, Federal	4,674	152	-
Govt Pub, International	1,599	-	-
Legislation[8]	190	18	42
Case, Legal	16	5	-
Manuscript, Handwritten	815	-	-
Manuscript, Print	1,345	1	-
Print Reproduction	2,396	575	-
Rare Material, Pre-1401[9]	3	1,130	-
Rare Material, 15th Cent.	17	371	-
Rare Material, 16th Cent.	419	6	-
Rare Material, 17th Cent.	638	-	-
Rare Material, 18th Cent.	1,696	7	-
Rare Material, 19th Cent.[10]	4,152	179	-
Rare Material, 20th Cent.	276	8	-
Chronology	79	63	-
Letter	180	469	-
Practice Guideline	56	1	-
Autobiography	335	30	-
Biography[11]	1,024	407	-
Biography, Collective	285	139	-
Biographical Information	951	5,219	2
Personal Narrative	314	287	-
Portrait	859	2,793	4
Cartoon	11	15	-
Classical Work[12]	153	2,058	7
Fiction	51	3	-
Historical Work	5,193	10,042	-
Nurses' Instruction	742	-	-
Popular Work	628	121	-
Thesis	3,658	33	-
Translation	2,687	392	-
Case Report	434	276	-
Comparative Study	23	27	-

TABLE 1 (continued)

Notes:

[1] LML represents Lane's main database of books, serials, audiovisuals, etc. Four classification schemes exist (Old, LC, Archives and Learning Resources); we are reclassing old history and reference to LC. Also, 305,000 items link to these records. An estimated backlog of 25,000 monographs remains.

[2] ETC is a database of monographic component parts mostly from books and serials. A backlog of approx. 13,000 articles by Stanford authors and 7,000 portraits exists.

[3] AUT is our Authorities database. Cf. Table 2 for details.

[4] Over 13,500 Internet Resources currently comprise about 13% of the records in the databases; most of this growth occurred in 1999. In Authorities, Internet Resource is the primary form/genre term used.

[5] The value 47 represents component part serials included in the main database to keep all serials together.

[6] Includes approx. 2,700 current titles and 47 component part serials. A backlog of about 2,700 titles with an estimated 27,000 items remains for barcoding.

[7] Includes approx. 2,197 current subscriptions. All print periodicals are shelved alphabetically by title keyword; local fields carry normalized bibliographic and physical sort titles.

[8] Legislation is used on uniform titles for laws, but coded in a separate 'type' field.

[9] The ETC value mostly represents IMMI records; host titles not held.

[10] Consists mostly of pre-1850 titles.

[11] Biographical headings, including Portrait, are now assigned to authority records which contain a qualifying URL.

[12] Classical Work represents material cited by an author or reference as being classic, seminal, a milestone, landmark, etc. Many of these qualify due to inclusion in the standard Garrison & Morton (with a 510 field). A project to add remaining numbers is underway.

erences in this language and those in all languages of science are retained or made. However, to eliminate clutter, for example, cross-references for an Italian corporate body in Dutch are moved to a non-indexed field in authorities.

Authorities–Proactivity

Lane has taken the proactive stance of establishing authorities in advance of occurrence in bibliographic records in selected areas. We establish medically related Stanford corporate and personal names when announced. Similarly, we anticipate other in scope names by monitoring selected web sites, checking reference resources, or scanning articles with histories of corporate names or key scientists in a discipline. It is easier to construct a group of related names all at once than to craft that family piecemeal based on random individual instances. Thus, it is easy to validate headings in existing authorities when works containing them are received. Scanning indexes for prob-

TABLE 2. Authorities by Subcategory

Code	Type	Count
MeSH[1]	Medical subject headings	18,963
MSUB	MeSH subheadings	797
LaSH	Lane subject headings	84
LSUB[2]	Lane subheadings	1
LaFG[3]	Lane form/genre/format headings	230
Series	Series entries	1,959
Person	Personal names	10,412
Corp[4]	Corporate names	8,714
Utitle	Uniform titles	97
Conf	Conference names	155
TWA[5]	Text word authorities	742
NWA	Name word authorities	17
GWA[6]	Geographic word authorities	0
NUM	Numeric word authorities	21

[1]Includes topical and geographic headings, as well as language subheadings which are treated as headings.
[2]The only local subheading is 'no subheading' which is used in our XML MARC experiment to positively identify the absence of topical subheadings to improve display.
[3]Lane form/genre/format headings are exported as local, although many match those of the Library of Congress and/or NLM publication types.
[4]Includes nearly 1,000 medical schools of which 378 are extant.
[5]More information on the various word authorities is included in the section on New Directions.
[6]Defined but none established.

lematic areas is often more fruitful than one heading at a time efforts. We also include many 5xx links which are lacking from LC records.

Authorities–Selectivity

In order to focus on substantive enhancement, authority records are established only for selected bibliographic entries.[10] Authorities are generally limited to the biomedical area, but selectively include other areas as needed to support local entries; such records tend to be less extensive than in scope ones. Authority work in the ETC database is limited to famous people and names which have authorities established for the LML database. Generally, we establish headings in these cases:

1. Conflict resolution
   A bibliographic entry is considered the *de facto authority* until a conflict occurs.
2. Known (not necessarily occurring) variants which are *not likely to co-file*

Many of LC's variants are of limited value in retrieval and actually clutter indexes with multiple similar headings making selection among them more difficult. Lane transfers such cases to an 'unindexed variant' field.

3. All Stanford related names

Eventually, we hope to include all past faculty and graduates of the School of Medicine regardless of whether they have published. Names do not need to occur bibliographically to merit an authority record.

4. Famous people

Inclusion of notable persons permits identification of key contributors to the history of medicine by searching the authority file.

5. Most corporate names

The frequency of name changes and the desirability of the file serving as a directory of health-related organizations is the basis for this decision. We do not do authorities for all low level subordinate bodies.

6. Limited conference names

Due to their ephemeral nature, only major ones and those with significant changes or variants are established. Further, we avoid corporate name/title entries, with a preference for separate name and title entries which can stand alone in separate indexes. To avoid confusion of whether a conference name might be interpreted as a title, all are indexed as both names and titles. Linkage between conference name changes would better be handled by links between bibliographic records as proceedings occur most often as single works.

7. Series

Serial records are considered *de facto* series authorities with *no duplication* permitted. We established all series for a time, but recently revised our policy to establish an authority when a conflict occurs, a title changes, or variants are involved.

8. Uniform titles

We establish uniform titles sparingly when many manifestations of a work occur, such as for classics, religious works, and > 4 editions. Recently, we have focused on computer operating systems, databases, languages, systems software and networks. For conflict resolution of serial titles, we create most uniform titles in the bibliographic file alone as *uniform entries* which flip to field 130 upon export. Creating a separate authority record in each of these cases of conflict resolution would be prohibitive and of dubious value. We treat serial "authorship" by moving field 245 ^c information to notes.

9. Medical Subject Headings (MeSH)
   Annual MeSH-MARC updates from NLM, which exclude supplementary chemical terms, are batch-loaded using ftp (file transfer protocol). We have established a limited number of Lane Subject Headings (LaSH), mostly local geographics.

10. All form/genre/format
    Cf. Table 1 for a sampling of Lane's practice in this area. We use the singular predominantly to distinguish form from topical subjects (e.g., Portrait (155) vs. Portraits (150)). When we establish a separate form index, we plan to add plural cross-references.

Authorities–Content Enrichment

Lane views authority records as serving the dual roles of *authority control* and *informational resource*, with the retrieval value of informationally rich records rivaling or exceeding the value of significant cross-references. We introduced this rather ambitious policy gradually via batch loads and manual projects relating to specific categories of information. Some examples of policies for inclusion and projects reflect this:

People

1. Brief biographical sketches of famous people.
   These are added on an ad hoc basis, often paraphrased from a work in hand, reference source, or the Internet. We avoid evaluative statements and include source increasingly.

2. Stanford faculty profiles.
   Data from all Stanford Biomedical Faculty Research Interests[11] were extracted with database control numbers (which do not appear online) to permit a perl[12] script to retrieve specific database records. An agreement with the database producer provides for automated updates of changes in the source database via email. Thus, retrieval based on authority records leads to exten-

sive profiles of the current faculty database, which also includes an option for a Medline search of the author's works.
3. Educational credentials–including institution, degree, and date when readily available.
4. Birth and death dates.
   As files grow, temporal context will prove increasingly valuable in studying historical and contemporaneous influences. Dates also provide clues to users of works' currency. Dates of intellectual contributions might serve these purposes better.
5. Affiliations (coded as latest or former)– including institution, appointment, and dates when readily available.
6. Selective references for materials not held or not included in the database (e.g., an obituary).
7. Uniform Resource Locators (URLs), selectively.
   E.g., Biographies from the Nobel Institute and Profiles in science from NLM.

Organizations

1. Historical sketches of organizations
   We emphasize name changes, dates of existence, and scope of activities with an eye toward their value as keywords. We recast many cryptic, non-public LC notes into public fields, as well as adding unique information.
2. Topical and geographic subjects and form/genre-like headings for type of organization, e.g., California Orthopedic Association has headings for Orthopedics, California, and Societies, Medical.
3. URLs for organizations whenever they can be identified.
4. Dates of existence under various names.
   We routinely add dates to clarify when organizations existed under various names, using angle brackets when the range is incomplete, e.g., <1846>-<1853>.
5. Selective references for materials not held or not included in the database (e.g., an article describing the history of an organization, although these are preferably done as component parts).
6. Hierarchies for names entered under subordinate subdivisions.
   In anticipation of future, enhanced browsing of collapsed hierarchies of corporate names, special attention focuses on providing omitted intervening levels and including references for changes in higher level names. We are considering inversion of subordi-

nate entry names to emphasize the key element, rather than the organization type, e.g., 'Technical Services Dept.' instead of 'Dept. of Technical Services.' While description is valuable, slavish adherence can be counterproductive. Scattered LC cross-references of the type 'Technical Services, Dept. of' occur.

Topics

Lane has modified 1,513 MeSH records (identified by keyword 'meshx') by adding local shadow fields which are carried forward when new versions of MeSH are overlaid. NLM's non-print references were fielded separately to prevent indexing of these machine-generated variants which clutter indexes, e.g., Child Rearings see Child Rearing. Other useful variants are duplicated as local to improve subject searching. Keyword access to notes is very useful to staff in assigning MeSH and will be useful to users once we have tighter control of indexing. Local additions include:

1. See references, often common names of diseases.
2. See also references to a limited extent (the relationship of broader and narrower terms to MeSH's hierarchical tree structures needs further review).
3. Notes providing historical context, e.g., when discovered or first described.
4. URLs for LC country studies.
5. MARC country codes for staff use.
6. Codes for NLM's checktags indicating general terms, age groups, experimental animals, publication types (treated as form/genre), and historical period.

To support future topical and geographic indexes of organizations, we assign MeSH to corporate authorities.

Types

Lane has established 230 form/genre headings, initially by reviewing and harmonizing candidates from several sources:

1. NLM's publication types
2. MeSH form subheadings

3. Published lists[13]
4. General material designators[14]
5. MARC fixed fields for bibliographic level and type, nature of contents, Festschrift, fiction, government publication, etc.

We emphasize *type* as an equally legitimate aspect of user-oriented bibliographic control, particularly in opposition to the obscure, mostly unutilized fixed field encoding found in MARC. Although extensive broader and narrower cross-references were made to collocate related headings, a hierarchical list using the following categories is useful:

1. Bibliographic format of material, e.g., Monographic Series
2. Issuing body/issuer aspects, e.g., Consensus Development Conference
3. Production aspects, e.g., Facsimile
4. Organization and arrangement of content, e.g., Price List
5. Biographical aspects, e.g., Funeral Sermon
6. Genre/theme/style, e.g., Fiction
7. Bibliographical relationship, e.g., Translation
8. Methodology employed, e.g., Case Report

Lane applies form/genre when a work *is or includes a* particular heading. The singular is used primarily to distinguish from the plural of the "same" heading which is often a topical heading. Table 1 represents a sampling of the variety of headings with their relative frequency.

Extending Lane's emphasis on form/genre, many categories of authority records receive similar 'type' headings in a local field, e.g., Schools, Medical for a specific school, and similarly, Government Agencies; Hospitals, Teaching; etc. We plan to augment current keyword access with a future 'type' index. Most 'types' are MeSH headings, although we need to indicate this is the authority record, possibly as a form/genre of topic, i.e., topics which can serve as types of organizations. The subtle distinction between 'type' for other form/genre headings added for corporate names needs review at Lane.

Bibliographic Records–Proactivity

Lane conducts an annual review of bibliographic records for all current serials, checking for acronyms, new issuing bodies or publishers, frequency changes, variant titles and missed title changes. We add or revise many elements which have changed since the previous year or are not present or clear from the first issue of changed titles.

Bibliographic Records–Simplification

Lane recognizes a subset of MARC tags[15] which we attempt to supply and maintain, preferring to focus on content and quality. We review newly announced tags for feasibility of application and gradually apply them retrospectively. Coordinate indexing permits minimal use of precoordinated headings (e.g., author/title entries), and elimination of series entered under personal or corporate names (fields 400, 410, 411, 800, 810, and 811 are not recognized). Field 440 will be eliminated when switching systems in favor of 490/830. Some fields have restrictions on permitted values (e.g., 035 restricted to OCoLC, DNLM, and a few others). We use the generic complex linking entry note (580) more often than difficult to code reproduction (533) or original version (534) fields.

We use *title main entry* for all serials and series. This and *successive entry* (since periodicals are cited as published) were retrospectively implemented in about three years in the late 1980s, and the entire periodicals collection re-alphabetized. In 1999, we softened entry policy to recognize *latest entry* for classed reference serials, where minor and arbitrary changes hover about a single, revised work with the latest version most often cited. This eliminates confusion resulting from too many similar records.

Bibliographic Records–Integration

We implemented a web catalog in Sept. 1997, and took advantage of extensive, explicit, inter-record linkages added over many years. Most 76x-78x linking entry fields contain Lane's control no., and these fields are included for editions of monographs, omitting the title when it has not changed (e.g., 780 12 ^w90B2486). Local definition of a ^w for 440/830 supports hotlinks from analytics to the host serial. Rigorous use of 773 ^w will allow display of book chapters and periodical articles from host records, although currently this link retrieves sibling records only as the host record resides in a separate database. Separate component part records are preferred to lengthy contents notes (505), which we try not to duplicate.

Lane adopted the format of Medline's source field for consistency in field 773 (host record). However, in attempting further integration it is problematic to include only abbreviated title entries when the host can be searched in the same index under both abbreviated and unabbreviated titles. Ideally, title phrase indexing for both ways would retrieve components and analytics along with the host title.

Lane considers field 856 a relational field and has over 13,000 hotlinks to web sites and fulltext which are highlighted by clickable thumbnail images in the web catalog. Archival collection records contain links to their finding aids, and we have begun adding links from personal authorities to portraits. Quarterly runs of LinkChecker identify links needing attention.

Bibliographic Records–Content Enrichment

Errors of omission may be the most insidious system short-coming. Lane espouses that bibliographic records should carry as much information as feasible. In addition to the following types of enhancements, component parts records provide otherwise lacking access.

People

We include the first five authors (not editors) as well as all Stanford authors. Component parts records, although similar to Medline records, carry authors' full names as they appear; however, we do not do authority work on an individual name basis. For more consistent name searching, databases, e.g., Medline, should record names as they appear with automatic generation of normalized forms. This is easier when deriving description from fulltext than when keying.

Organizations

Due to the increasing importance of the source of serials, we include the publisher for all current serial titles and aggregator for all digital titles in an RLIN-defined field, e.g., 797 2 ^aHighWire Press. or, 797 2 ^aMD Consult (Firm). We are also considering automated conference name geographic qualifier flips to improve consistency.

Topics

Lane has gradually converted to following Medline instead of cataloging policies in regard to McSH.[16] This culminated with a project to strip form, language, and geographic subheadings from topical MeSH completed in Feb. 1997, two years prior to a similar restructuring at NLM, which brought cataloging and indexing practices closer. Our computer program changed 55% of LML records and 27% of ETC records, and the same processing applies to newly loaded records to prevent adulteration. The program also reads titles and LC subjects to enhance existing MeSH, e.g., the strings elderly and geriatr# trigger appending 'Aged.' Similar procedures cover other age groups, male, female, human, experimental animals, etc. Since MeSH are required in LML, the loader supplies a searchable placeholder 'nomesh' when they are lacking entirely. Staff encountering this code may supply the needed heading(s) or change the code to 'nomeshx' indicating the need for further assessment. These semi-automated procedures make the extra access feasible, although staff review programmed changes.

At the same time, we implemented primary, secondary, and tertiary codes (1st indicator of 650), defaulting existing headings to primary. Tertiary is locally defined to cover MeSH check tags and exported as secondary. We add many additional secondary headings manually, although not as many as Medline includes. Special efforts to add geographic headings reflect the importance of epidemiology, social and travel medicine.

In the ETC database, only Garrison & Morton titles routinely receive MeSH. This mixture of records with and without subject headings needs further study, although the minimal records provide improved keyword access.

Annually, some attempt is made to apply new MeSH retroactively, either by keyword searching or by reviewing entries under a term which has been split.

Types

Lane treats form separately from topic. Bibliographic display and retrieval benefit from equal treatment for form/genre/format. Lane addresses title display with uniform entry parenthetic qualifiers, notably (Online) and (Print/Online), and general material designators (GMDs). Improved retrieval is based on repeatable form/genre headings. See Table 1 for examples.

MARC fixed fields have become increasingly complex with the addition of fields 006 and 007. Lane uses neither, relying on the *repeatability* of form/genre headings. We assign a heading representing each format involved, e.g., Computer File and Serial for a digital serial. To partially accommodate MARC, we defined a local value for 008:23 of 'e' for all *digital materials* (computer files or textual) exported as an 006 (additional material characteristics) and 000:06 local value 'x' for online textual materials exported as 'a'. We assign as many other form/genre headings as needed, following NLM publication type practice rather than MeSH practice of assigning only the most specific ones. Ideally, the most specific term could be retrieved from any level of a hierarchy.

Whenever a *novel heading* would be useful, it is coded with second indicator 9 to indicate lack of an authority. We review these later for consideration as permanent headings or cross-references.

Title Abbreviations

All periodicals and all current serials contain indexed standard title abbreviations.

Collection Development Statistics for Serials

To keep statistics parallel with title changes, serial records carry collection development data. This includes price data since 1986, circulation statistics since 1993, reshelving statistics since 1996,[17] Institute for Scientific Information (ISI) impact factors,[18] indicators of duplicate subscriptions on campus, prior selection evaluation codes, and electronic usage (defined and currently available for Ovid titles, but not yet loaded). We display some publicly:

- Circulated (this yr)
- Circulated (total)
- Reshelved (this yr)
- Reshelved (total)

Locations

A virtual location anchors summary holdings for digital serials. However, since the same location is not repeatable in RLIN, we must establish several codes intended to display identically to cover cases where multiple versions are available, e.g., Ovid and Highwire.

Bibliographic Records–Scope Expansion for Digital Materials

Three departments cooperate to control digital materials: Acquisitions/Serials (e.g., licensing, maintaining accurate subscription numbers, and dealing with vendor changes), Digital Materials (e.g., operational deployment, formatting changes, and software issues), and Bibliographic Management (e.g., coordination with print resources, cataloging, and linkage management). In three cases a *CGI directory* (common gateway interface) simplifies management by isolating technical data from the bibliographic record, which contains a simple link to the directory: (1) long URLs that may break, which have also been problematic when exported to other systems, (2) perl scripts required to bypass login and various authorization sequences, and (3) perl scripts to perform canned searches for web pages without a static address (i.e., created on the fly from a database).

Lane established the *eLane data repository* to provide a stable home for digital materials owned or locally controlled. Examples of such resources include: a book written in residence by our honorary curator of archives,[19] a collection of newsletters and email covering our hospitals' merger, and two editions of Stanford's medical school catalog. The latter presents the challenge of indexing the current edition for web access and the superseded edition for archival web searching. We are adding some metadata to improve the site index, although we consider linked cataloging records the richest and most flexible metadata. A database will soon replace the school catalog, creating a more significant archival problem. We are investigating how to handle this, potentially by adding an annual snapshot of the database to the repository.

Bibliographic Records–Scope Expansion for Component Parts

Cataloging and indexing have been segregated for too long. To complement Medline coverage[20] and to utilize in experimenting with tighter bibliographic integration, we created a MARC-based component parts database, ETC. Each record contains a form/genre heading 'Chapter' for components of a book, 'Article' for a component of a serial, both for components of analyzed serials, etc. ETC contains records for difficult to verify articles, material on topics in which Lane has traditional collection strengths, Stanford publications predating Medline coverage, key Garrison & Morton articles,[21] and records for digital materials created via bibliographic data mining. This automated method of building MARC records will be described in a future paper.

NEW DIRECTIONS

New and/or experimental initiatives with potential for supporting integration of both traditional and digital resources into user-focused, domain-specific environments are in various stages of study or experimental implementation. The following describes selected areas of concentration, some of which may prove supportable and some not. All could contribute to a sturdier and more logical foundation upon which to build flexible future systems.

Intranet Documentation

A fledgling Intranet established in 1997 in Technical Services needs more development to support system transition and the coherent coordination of bibliographic policies with database decisions regarding indexing and display. This will provide opportunities for staff to develop HTML skills, force updating of documentation, and permit direct linking to examples in the databases.

Authorities Enhancements

Computers facilitate change, but general practice limits changes in authority headings. Additional authorities enhancements at Lane are partially underway or being considered to provide more options in support of future database functionality and to influence attitudes by example.

Word Authorities

Keyword searching is popular and deserves increased attention. Preventing errors of omission could be easily accomplished by the use of word authorities. Lane's collection of word/phrase authorities will support adding a cross-referencing structure into an experimental keyword index with links to entries in medical dictionaries. We review terms encountered in day-to-day work that may cause retrieval problems and add authorities, e.g, spelling variants (pediatric/paediatric; intern/interne), word elisions (health care/healthcare; long term/long-term), archaic or obsolete variants (homeopathy/homoeopathy; physician/physitian), irregular plurals (ameba/amebae; also amoeba/amoebae), slang (cocaine/crack), misspellings or common typos (helath/health), acronyms (coronary artery bypass graft/CABG/pronounced cabbage), grammatical forms (fever/febrile), thesaural relationships (mountebank/quackery), etc. Semantic support could be interactive to index more accurately when multiple meanings are reflected, cf. invalid (not valid) and invalid (sick person). This example illustrates the potential of word authorities to improve keyword searching: bloodletting (blood-letting)/phlebotomy/bleeding/venesection.

This supplements the Specialist Lexicon, part of the Unified Medical Language System (UMLS),[22] from NLM, which contains thousands of additional terms with relationships. One problem area has been duplication with variants which occur in MeSH, which we have generally avoided, but which would potentially exclude many useful keyword references. These efforts would improve both recall and precision, although more could be done to provide computer support for semantic precision in a technical area such as medicine.[23]

Volatile Data

We download current data from university files for circulation purposes. We plan to append selected elements (e.g., phone no., dept., etc.) from these records for a subset of faculty/staff to authority records, or create a minimal level record when no match is found. While this would further improve the authority file's directory role, the project is stalled pending resolution of encryption problems relating to the university ID. It is needed for matching, but should not be displayable. Once all faculty/staff are included, we would link records to the local Internet who is directory service.

Series Simplification?

Since unnumbered series can be considered collective uniform titles, and numbered series are nearly indistinguishable from serials, Lane is considering experimental mapping of authority records for numbered series into the serial format. Similarly, unnumbered series can be treated as representing bibliographic collections, potentially replacing series authorities with bibliographic records. This would keep all information about works together.

Uniform Title Clarifications

Uniform titles function in the role of a collective title. The choice of adding linking entry fields between editions, adding a variant title (246), or creating a uniform title needs clarification; this is complicated by links between changed uniform titles. We are investigating uniform titles for academic courses and monitoring cases of "named" surveys, censuses, examinations, programs, projects, etc., due to the variance that exists in practice. These are addressed partially by MARC's *ambiguous headings*.[24] More consideration of indexing aspects and review from the user perspective are needed.

Lane does not use "Laws, etc." Instead, a combination of geographic (1/710/651) and form/genre "Legislation" (655) decouples jurisdictional aspects from form/genre. The relation between geopolitical corporate names, geographic topics, and uniform titles remains problematic judging by the multitude of extant codings found in catalogs.

Cross-Index Relationships

The value of bibliographic relationships became clearer with the introduction of hypertext. To further meld our bibliographic and authority data, we believe relationships need more attention, particularly in the area of cross-index relationships. MARC allows coding these relationships and has a list of relator codes,[25] but such linking is the exception, cf.:

    Person to Topic
        150   ^aAlzheimer Disease
        500 1   ^aAlzheimer, Alois,^d1864-1915.
           A form/genre term for the eponymous aspect is in order.

    Person to Person
        100 1   ^aMayo, Charles Horace,^d1865-1939.
        500 1   ^aMayo, William James,^d1861-1939,^ebrother.

Person to Organization
    110 2 ^aMayo Clinic.
    500 1 ^aMayo, Charles Horace,^d1865-1939,^efounder.
    500 1 ^aMayo, William James,^d1861-1939,^efounder.

Topic to Form
    150   ^aClinical Trials
    555   ^aClinical Trial

This concept extends to identification of relationships of variants to the entry version (e.g., language of variant) and other inter-index relationships, e.g., a uniform title for an academic course with a personal reference (500 ^efaculty). Dates of relationships should be an integral part of the relationship. The relationship between buildings, corporate names, and geographics presents similar problems. Conference name/title entries might better be de-coupled, e.g., a "Symposium of the Medical Library Association" could have an authority or be entered uniformly without an authority:
    111 ^aSymposium (Medical Library Association) . . .
    510 ^aMedical Library Association,^esponsor.
Relationship authorities could be devised for formalizing these types of relationships, as well as those identified by tag or indicator in MARC linking entry fields (76x-78x).

Indexing Enhancements

Lane anticipates eventually having indexes structured by type of data. For example, a title index would consolidate titles, series, and title linkages. A title would occur once with an indication that a subordinate list of analytics, component parts, and/or links exist. Similarly, MeSH headings would appear with an indication that subheadings and see also references are displayable with more granular hit counts. See references would display the same results in the main sequence, although indicating the preferred heading. Although more authority work would be needed, a corporate name index could be devised with multiple access points to the same hierarchy, e.g., National Library of Medicine (U.S.) could be found with indication of subordinate headings either under its name or its parent, National Institutes of Health (U.S.) and so forth. A more comprehensive view of information management is needed to build a sound infrastructure for future systems.

Bibliographic Enhancements

A project dubbed Extra-Med will investigate methods to establish virtual appends to external bibliographic records, principally to Medline records, which may lack data elements of local interest. A search matching added subjects, keywords, names, notes, etc., would invoke a script to link to the appropriate record and co-display it with local added elements in the result set.

Digital Materials Management

Digital licensing variations suggest the need for authorization by individual resource or category of resource. Our current reliance on Internet protocol-based authentication and planned replacement of this with encrypted kerberos authentication accommodates user or user category. Potentially, a scheme of resource restriction categories could be incorporated into an authorization script in conjunction with authentication. Such access coding could reside in the bibliographic record and/or in metadata appended to individual resources.

In 1999, Lane converted its classroom videotaping to a digital video process. We anticipate that as this service matures, bibliographic issues will arise. Content indexing utilizing voice recognition to allow a textual search to position a user in a relevant segment of a video make this very appealing. The need for uniform titles for courses mentioned above is also relevant in this endeavor.

We expect the eLane repository to grow rapidly. Since many fulltext resources will be deployed in different ways, much work needs to be done to consider whether a single repository can provide a substrate for multiple services/interfaces.

Electronic Data Interchange (EDI)

We anticipate EDI issues relating to maintaining bibliographic parity with external systems. We have provided our control numbers to our serial vendors, but it is likely we will need their numbers in our records. The recent trend of publishers' bundling groups of titles for marketing purposes portends more difficulties. We may need to create a collection record, although we do not want to lose attribution of price and usage to individual titles, particularly for digital materials.

Domain-Specific Interfaces

In 1999 Lane began operating SHINE,[26] a web-based integrated information environment that delivers knowledge resources for clinical decision support and continuing education. This system responds to queries with separate matches from various databases and fulltext resources. Hits for fulltext display with the tables of contents for context. An experiment may involve merging results based on relevance ranking or other sort criteria with a clear indication of which resource contains each citation, although maintenance of context might be problematical. Meanwhile, we are updating content and adding more resources. A project to generalize SHINE will permit building similar interfaces for other domains (e.g., ophthalmology, oncology) more readily. Integrating databases and fulltext presents indexing options which need further study. Bibliographic control, particularly of versions, is fundamental to maintaining currency and accuracy. Another experiment will involve adding Lane's databases as a resource, which requires the flexibility of XML for incorporation into this integrated environment.

XML MARC

Initial experiences in our ongoing XML (Extensible Markup Language) MARC project called Medlane has lead us to believe that it is feasible to convert bibliographic and authority formats to XML.[27] While results of our experiment are pending selection of a search engine vs. database indexing of over 200,000 XML records, the need for libraries to put their offerings directly on the Internet is clear. MARC, in essence a proprietary format, is at odds with open systems and impedes, rather than promotes, librarians' ability to redeploy information flexibly. Needs change rapidly, and XML records can be reformatted and manipulated far more easily than MARC since presentation is separate from content. Currently, 'library information' is under-utilized due to its segregation from mainstream web resources, and in danger of becoming marginalized. We need to move into this arena aggressively and begin dealing with more advanced aspects of bibliographic management, e.g., intuitive representation of multiple linkages and navigational options to authority records, bibliographic records and digital content. An even less prestigious role awaits us, if we fail to recognize this millennial opportunity.

ORGANIC BIBLIOGRAPHY?

Libraries were aggregrators long before the word became popular in digital parlance, and are excellently placed with a tradition of non-bias to play a premier role in the future. The more the web grows, the more evident shortcomings of its organization become. Our experience in delineating XML elements from their attributes in the Medlane project suggests that the potential exists to define a simple, yet comprehensive, bibliographic structure. The inherent simplicity results from describing *works* (anchored by titles), *aspects* (associated names, topics, geographics, languages, form/genre, time factors, words/ phrases, and a few others), and *relationships* amongst these. XML provides built-in portability since hardware and software systems are not involved, thus eliminating the need for a "communications" format. Groups of special libraries with a bias for action could cooperate to demonstrate the feasibility of such an XML-based substitute for MARC.

Further simplification of bibliographic complexity results from overlaying a set of *hierarchical relationships* (e.g., work/analytic/ component; collection/subunit; subject/subheading; organization/ subdivision; genealogical relations) with a set of *temporal relationships* (e.g., title changes; name changes; reviews; citations of earlier work). Controlling these via *relationship authorities* facilitates defining inter-related relationships. Such a web-oriented network of relationships would capitalize on their apparently pervasive 'natural' patterns, *organic* at least in the sense that humans repeat the same patterns over and over. Further, the same patterns apply for bibliographic (work to work) and control (authority to authority) relationships, as well as interrelationships between the two (work to authority and vice versa).

Although much effort remains, much has already been accomplished, including a German conference in 1982 on hierarchical relationships,[28] Tillett's thesis on bibliographic relationships,[29] Garfield's historiographs based on citation practice,[30] as well as NLM's elegant topical semantic network.[31] More recently, Leazer and Smiraglia's emphasis on relationships[32,33] and the University of Michigan Digital Library's elaborate work on ontogenic relationships[34] illustrate how critical such an infrastructure is. Librarians need to better understand and exploit these fundamentals to provide the flexibility, extensibility and robustness necessary for library-based systems to be viable in the heterogenous information environment of the 21st century.

REFERENCES

1. Lane Medical Library: *http://www-med.stanford.edu/lane/*

2. *Annual statistics of medical school libraries in the United States and Canada.* 1997/1998.

3. This example of free Medline access before it became routine is indicative: Peter Stangl, Gloria Linder, and Valerie Su, "The Impact of unlimited online access to medical literature on the Stanford medical community" In: *Health information for all.* 1988: 103-10.

4. Dick R. Miller, "Change and the maintenance of systems relationships at Lane Medical Library, Stanford University Medical Center," *Igaku Toshokan* 1995; 42(4):405-14.

5. Index of medieval medical images in North America: *http://www.medsch. ucla.edu/som/neurobio/immi/immihtm1.htm*

6. Spencer S. Eccles Health Sciences Library, Knowledge Weavers: *http://www medlib.med.utah.edu/kw/*

7. Cf. Medline description: *http://www.nlm.nih.gov/databases/medline.html*

8. Research Libraries Information Network: *http://www.rlg.org/rlin.html*

9. This implies that foreign language headings and references should be all foreign, instead of part English, e.g., Deutschland. Kaiserliches Gesundheitsamt, not Germany. Kaiserliches Gesundheitsamt. Catalogs in different countries may prefer a language other than English. A parallel authority system by language would permit automatic expansion of searches by inclusion of references in other languages; efforts in maintaining such a system could distribute the work by language expertise.

10. Elizabeth E. Fuller, "Variation in personal names in works represented in the catalog," *Cataloging & Classification Quarterly* 1989; 9(3):75-95. This study found that over 80% of personal names occurred in only one form in a random sampling from a large library catalog.

11. Faculty research directory in biomedical & biological sciences: *http://www. med.stanford.edu/school/bluebook/*

12. Perl stands for Practical Extraction and Reporting Language, a simple yet powerful computer language especially useful for parsing text.

13. E.g. *Thesaurus for graphic materials. II, Genre and physical characteristic terms,* 1995.

14. Cf. *Anglo-American cataloging rules.* 2nd ed., 1988 rev.

15. Our approach is supported indirectly by a recent study reported on the MARC List Serve which found that only 33 tags were used in more than 1% of 4 million LC records.

16. Application of MeSH for medical catalogers: *http://www.nlm.nih.gov/tsd/ cataloging/ catmesh.html*

17. Usage statistics not stored in the bibliographic record include the year of the volume and the date of use.

18. For an essay on impact factors, consult: *http://www.isinet.com/hot/essays/7.html*

19. John L. Wilson. *Stanford University School of Medicine and the predecessor schools: An historical perspective*, 1999. *http://eLane.stanford.edu/wilson/*

20. For a fuller description of the ETC database see: *http://www-med.stanford.edu/lane/database/cat_lois_etc.html*

21. Jeremy M. Norman, ed. *Morton's Medical bibliography: An annotated checklist of texts illustrating the history of medicine (Garrison and Morton)*, 5th ed. Scolar Press, 1991.

22. Cf. UMLS description: *http://www.nlm.nih.gov/research/umls/umlsmain.html*

23. William O. Robertson, "Quantifying the meaning of words." *JAMA* 1983 May 20; 249(19):1631-2.

24. *MARC 21 format for bibliographic data. Appendix E, Alphabetical list of ambiguous headings. Feb. 1999.*

25. *USMARC code list for relators, sources, description conventions, 1997.*

26. For background consult: *http://shine.stanford.edu/* Access to content is restricted.

27. MEDLANE Experiment - MARC to XML: *http://lanelib.stanford.edu:8080/~dmiller/*

28. *Hierarchical relationships in bibliographic descriptions.* Gesamthochschulbibliothek Essen, 1982.

29. Barbara Ann Barnett Tillet, *Bibliographic relationships: toward a conceptual structure of bibliographic information used in cataloging.* Dissertation, UCLA, 1987.

30. Eugene Garfield. *Citation indexing: Its theory and application in science, technology, and humanities*, Wiley, 1979. Page 94 contains an historiograph illustrating citation relationships.

31. Cf. UMLS semantic network factsheet: *http://www.nlm.nih.gov/pubs/factsheets/umlssemn.html*

32. Gregory H. Leazer. "Recent research on the sequential bibliographic relationship and its implications for standards and the library catalog: an examination of serials." *Cataloging & Classification Quarterly* 1996; 21(3/4):205-20.

33. Gregory H. Leazer and Richard P. Smiraglia. "Toward the bibliographic control of works: derivative bibliographic relationships in an online union catalog," In: *Proceedings of the 1st ACM International Conference on Digital Libraries*, 1996, p. 36-43. *http://www.acm.org/pubs/citations/proceedings/dl/226931/p36-leazer/*

34. UMDL Ontology Concept Descriptions: *http://wwwpersonal.umich.edu/~peterw/Ontology/ontology.html*

Technical Services in Twenty-First Century Special Collections

Ellen Crosby

SUMMARY. Special collections libraries are evolving to include electronic resources in addition to the papers, books, photographs and artifacts that have been collected in the past, and technical services must evolve and change as well. This overview examines new and traditional duties and staffing. New responsibilities will include managing electronic rights and resources, preparing scanning and digitizing projects, overseeing online catalogs, and developing metadata standards. Staff will need thorough grounding in fundamentals of technical services work, as well as the ability to cooperate across departmental boundaries. The special collections library will become an important information portal in the twenty-first century. *[Article copies available for a fee from The Haworth Document Delivery Service: 1-800-342-9678. E-mail address: <getinfo@haworthpressinc.com> Website: <http://www.HaworthPress.com>]*

KEYWORDS. Special collections, archives, digitizing, MARC, EAD, metadata

As we approached the end of the twentieth century, we saw the functions of technical services in libraries evolving and changing. In

Ellen Crosby, BA, MLibr, PhD, is Head of Cataloging at Indiana Historical Society and Adjunct Assistant Professor in the School of Library & Information Science, Indiana University.

Address correspondence to: Ellen Crosby, PhD, 450 West Ohio Street, Indianapolis IN 46202 or (E-mail: ecrosby@indianahistory.org).

[Haworth co-indexing entry note]: "Technical Services in Twenty-First Century Special Collections." Crosby, Ellen. Co-published simultaneously in *Cataloging & Classification Quarterly* (The Haworth Information Press, an imprint of The Haworth Press, Inc.) Vol. 30, No. 2/3, 2000, pp. 167-176; and: *Managing Cataloging and the Organization of Information: Philosophies, Practices and Challenges at the Onset of the 21st Century* (ed: Ruth C. Carter) The Haworth Information Press, an imprint of The Haworth Press, Inc., 2000, pp. 167-176. Single or multiple copies of this article are available for a fee from The Haworth Document Delivery Service [1-800-342-9678, 9:00 a.m. - 5:00 p.m. (EST). E-mail address: getinfo@haworthpressinc.com].

addition to the physical resources contained within our walls, we provide access to resources in electronic formats that may or may not be stored at our institutions. Many technical services departments are even responsible for creating new resources in electronic form. The true excitement of the twenty-first century comes out of newly developing technologies. Resources once available only to those who could visit them in person are now accessible to anyone who has a computer and the means to download images. We make manifest the connection between the past and the future through scanning and digitizing archival resources.

Broadly speaking, technical services work is everything done "behind the scenes" to prepare library materials for use by the public. In her introduction to the second edition of *Library Technical Services: Operations and Management*, Irene P. Godden cites two definitions of technical services. The traditional tasks of technical services in all libraries, according to Mortimer Tauber, involve "the operations and techniques for acquiring, recording and preserving materials." More broadly, Karen Horny notes that technical services "provide access," both physical and bibliographic, and that "all other aspects of library service depend upon the efficiency and accuracy with which this work is accomplished."[1]

In this article I will discuss current practices of technical services departments and suggest future directions. I will focus on such institutions as university and state archives, historical societies, public and privately funded archival and manuscript repositories, and rare-book or photograph collections. I exclude museums, in which the emphasis is on creating planned displays and programs to present information. In libraries and archives, *our* emphasis is on creating catalogs and finding aids that allow researchers to identify materials, draw conclusions, and make their own connections.

As an example, I offer my own institution. The Indiana Historical Society is a private, nonprofit educational organization whose mission is to collect, preserve, interpret, and disseminate the history of Indiana and the Old Northwest. The William Henry Smith Memorial Library is one division, others being Publications, Education, Marketing and Community Relations, and Administration. There are three major collecting categories, encompassing approximately sixty-five thousand printed items, seven thousand manuscript and archival collections, and one and one half million photographs. There are also several thousand maps, broadsides, videorecordings, microfilms, and artifacts.

The library is currently staffed by eighteen professional librarians, archivists, and conservators, as well as seven clerical and support staff. The Cataloging Department (i.e., "technical services") includes a full-time cataloger for printed materials, a half-time cataloger for manuscripts, and a three-quarter-time clerical assistant. The department head doubles as library systems administrator and also catalogs approximately one-quarter time, handling maps, photographs, and videorecordings–everything not a book or a manuscript,

I will use the term *special collections libraries* to refer to the broad range of similar institutions, and I will amplify Tauber's and Horny's definitions to include additional specific tasks. As new materials are received, they must be registered or accessioned, processed, and cataloged. Other activities such as preparing finding aids, digitizing and microfilming, running the online catalog, creating the library webpage, and linking to other sites may also be considered technical services tasks. I exclude direct public service from consideration, although serving the public is certainly the goal of all technical services activities.

In special collections libraries, identifying and acquiring materials and accepting donations may be curatorial responsibilities that lie outside the technical services department. This is the case in my institution. Curators must identify desirable acquisitions and ▮▮▮▮▮▮d to work with sometimes reluctant donors or sellers. On the ▮▮▮▮▮▮d, as people move from family homes, become more mobile, ▮▮▮▮▮py smaller living spaces, they willingly decide to give up family documents to libraries and archives. The curators then graciously accept these unexpected offerings.

Once materials have been accepted, technical services operations begin. Registration of acquisitions is difficult and time-consuming because a detailed accession record is an essential part of documenting the provenance of an acquisition. The registrar must identify the source, value, and previous owners of materials and prepare deeds of gift and letters of acknowledgment. The accession record may exist both as paper files and as a database. Disposition of various parts of an acquisition to various collections may be necessary.

Physical materials must be prepared for use. A manuscript collection or corporate archive seldom arrives in a condition to be consulted by researchers. Basic processing includes ascertaining the scope of the collection and discerning the arrangement intended by its creator(s). Duplicate and extraneous material is noted and discarded; staples and other metallic fasteners are removed; folded pages are flattened; newspaper clippings may be photocopied onto acid-free paper. A finding aid is prepared to describe the creator of the collection and place the person or organization in historical context. The contents of the collection are described, with some indication in the finding aid of which storage unit contains the various topics or dates.

In addition to such basic practices as staple-pulling and refoldering, more sophisticated conservation is possible. My institution enjoys the luxury of full-time, professionally trained conservators who clean and stabilize fragile materials, repair torn pages, and perform complex treatments such as removing stains and residues left by tape. In other institutions, however, sophisticated conservation may not be possible. Reboxing without refoldering may be all that can be done with existing resources. Even in an age where all information is expected to be digital, the simple preservation of the physical item as artifact will be important to future scholars.

Newspapers are a good example of an information resource that cannot be preserved without reformatting. Microfilming preserves the information content and the appearance of the item, but the process often destroys the physical object. Microfilm has some advantages over digital formats–it has proven to be physically stable, and the technology needed to view the image is relatively simple. Special collections libraries have long been engaged in comprehensive microfilming projects; this work must continue in tandem with scanning and digitization efforts.

Two sometimes conflicting goals motivate scanning projects. Scanning to preserve an information resource that would otherwise be lost requires time, high resolution, and a great deal of storage space, even with image compression. Scanned images have some advantages over the originals. A high-resolution scan can aid scholarly investigation by displaying erasures and enhancing faded traces of ink that cannot be seen in the original. A high-quality image made freely available, however, may be vulnerable to unlicensed uses. A low-resolution scan, as chosen by my institution for public access, provides enough information for the average student or scholar. We make another scan or a photographic reproduction for publishers and others who need high-quality images.

To serve the needs of contemporary scholars, special collections libraries must identify electronic resources in addition to the traditional formats discussed above. Reference librarians have used the *National Union Catalog of Manuscript Collections*, OCLC, and RLIN to discover the existence of collections related to their own. Now, however, we can–and have the responsibility to–provide more direct access to remote collections. The special collections library's website should include links to other repositories where complementary or otherwise valuable resources have been identified.

The American Memory Project at the Library of Congress is a good example of the kind of resource that can be developed. In addition to "Today in History," the site includes a Learning Page that provides guidance for students and teachers. The Collection Finder allows searching for collections by broad topic areas. A search button allows the user to search for all instances of a topic found in items within the collections. A successful search will lead to a finding aid or to a digitized image.

A typical example of the home page of a state historical society was developed by the Ohio Historical Society. Its page features an article about a historical topic, information about the Society and its programs, and links to resources for teachers, to online exhibits, and to the online catalog of the OHS collections.

In the state of California, four complementary projects make up the Online Archive of California, a searchable online union database that includes finding aids to archival collections in institutions throughout the state. The project was designed to create a prototype for collections of encoded finding aids using Encoded Archival Description (discussed below). This site features an SGML toolkit and other information for library professionals, as well as an introduction for the public to research using primary sources.

The Research Room site developed by the National Archives and Records Administration provides links for quick access to frequently requested materials as well as information about NARA and its holdings. Through this site, library users can access NUCMC via the Library of Congress Z39.50 gateway to the RLIN database.

If budgets allow, commercial indexes can be a valuable component of good service. Available to subscribers online, *America: History and*

Life is a bibliographic reference to the history of the United States and Canada from prehistory to the present. Published since 1964, the database consists of almost 400,000 bibliographic entries with abstracts selected from more than 2,000 journals.

Another commercial index available online is *ArchivesUSA*. This database includes and updates several print publications: the *Directory of Archives and Manuscript Repositories in the United States*, the *National Union Catalog of Manuscript Collections*, and the *National Inventory of Documentary Sources–US*.

To take advantage of these and other commercially available resources, special collections librarians must learn to negotiate rights and contracts for services, and they must become sophisticated about user authentication issues.

In addition to creating and identifying online resources, archivists have begun to create virtual repositories of electronic records. Congressional hearings have called for an electronic depository system that would be a digital analog to the Library of Congress. The challenges are many but not insurmountable. Information producers hope to retain rights and control over their intellectual property, while others fear that changing technology will make archived information impossible to retrieve. Technical services librarians will need to participate in these debates.

The heart of technical services has always been cataloging and the catalog, a fact that will remain true in the future–well beyond the twenty-first century. Shared cataloging, first proposed by Charles Coffin Jewett 150 years ago, has become the foundation of the modern library world. Special collections libraries can make significant contributions to the goal of universal bibliographic control by creating records for their unique holdings. Contributing new records to bibliographic utilities can, to some degree, offset the costs of membership. The Program for Cooperative Cataloging established by the Library of Congress is an international effort to increase the quantity and the quality of bibliographic records by providing useful, timely, and cost-effective cataloging that meets mutually accepted standards. The NACO and SACO projects, in particular, provide an opportunity to special collections libraries to create name and subject headings based on their holdings. Even though the volume of cataloging we do is relatively small, my library staff has joined the NACO project because we have the resources to establish many Indiana names. When we need new subject headings for materials in our collection, we send proposals through a SACO liaison or directly to the Library of Congress.

Format integration has both enhanced and hampered access to manuscript and archival collections. The loss of the specialized AMC format stung the archival community, and redefining what were "archival" as "mixed" collections led to some confusion at first. But adding the archival control byte (leader 08) and making all fields and subfields available in all formats has led to richer catalog records for all types of materials treated as collections. For example, the ability to use the date and note fields specified in archival cataloging standards has enriched my own records for photographic collections. Furthermore, development of new fields in the MARC record has improved access to archival collections by making it possible to link finding aids and scanned images directly to the bibliographic records.

Recent discussion of creating what proponents call "Earth's Largest Library" has touched upon enhancing the information contained in MARC records by adding promotional material prepared by publishers and booksellers. While some features of the Earth's Largest Library proposal will be difficult to accomplish, enhancing bibliographic records should not be. Vendors are already distributing cataloging copy enhanced with table-of-contents information; dust jacket art and blurbs can be displayed as easily as other scanned images if we choose to do so.

Archival institutions that used to consider themselves and their collections unique have begun cooperating to create standards for finding aids that will allow their collections to be shared and searched consistently. While the MARC community was working on format integration, archivists were developing the Encoded Archival Description (EAD), a structured encoding standard for machine-readable finding aids such as inventories, registers and indexes.

Developers of the EAD wanted to present the complex and interrelated descriptive information found in archival finding aids in such a way that users could perceive the hierarchical relationships in the data and would be able to navigate from one level to another. Another goal was to index the various elements of an archival description consistently. When EAD is widely adopted, users of archival finding aids will enjoy the same predictability of information and structure that has always been present in bibliographic description. Additionally, encoded finding aids allow keyword access to locate folders or items previously hidden in container lists. This standard structure has also enabled searching among pools of networked finding aids.

Very recently, archivists have incorporated XML coding in EAD finding aids in order to facilitate Internet access. XML allows later versions of Web browsers to display EAD-encoded finding aids in their native SGML without requiring helper applications. A good example can be found at the Cornell University Division of Rare and Manuscript Collections. The application uses XML if the information seeker's browser is compatible; otherwise HTML coding is created dynamically. The Online Archive of California (discussed above) also uses EAD coding. These two applications demonstrate both the consistency and the local customization that cooperative standards make possible.

For other internet resources, various metadata schemes have been developed to facilitate discovery and retrieval. The Dublin Core (DC), named for the site of the first planning meeting at OCLC headquarters in Dublin, Ohio, is a prime example. DC was originally intended to be applied by creators of Web resources, but instead has been more widely adopted for formal resource description in libraries, government agencies and commercial organizations. DC elements provide the same kind of authorship and "publication" information traditionally found in bibliographic description.

Dissatisfaction with current commercially produced web indexes has led to a project to catalog Internet resources using OCLC's cooperative cataloging model. In the Cooperative Online Resource Catalog (CORC) project, librarians identify resources that are appropriate additions to their collections, then use intelligent software to derive bibliographic information from the website's content. CORC offers MARC record output, which can then be shared by other libraries, and automated creation of custom pathfinder pages.

Cooperation in standards development will become increasingly important in the twenty-first century. We have lost the nineteenth century convenience of the card catalog–a standard user interface found in all libraries. Returning to some consistency, where users can predict their results when they confront the library catalog, is essential. The job of configuring the OPAC has moved out of the library systems office and into the realm of the technical services librarian. Catalogers understand the implications of choices about indexing and display; as catalogers themselves, Martha Yee and Sara Shatford Layne are "painfully aware of information riches locked away in our records and not yet extricated by catalog systems."[2] The International Federation of Library Associations (IFLA) is working to develop sorely needed standards for OPAC displays.

Whatever the interface, the OPAC is here to stay. Even the smallest special collections library will be expected to provide computerized access to its own collections as well as to the rest of the world. Integrated library system vendors are beginning to recognize and court the special collections community, tailoring products to provide more of the specialized features and functions that special collections researchers need. For example, many integrated library systems now incorporate a component for indexing and displaying scanned images.

What kind of people will be needed in the twenty-first century technical services department of a special collections library? All staff members will need to have computer skills and history skills, but in addition they will also need professional education with a solid grounding in principles. Internships and on-the-job fine-tuning can give practical experience. Special collections libraries–by their very nature unique–will require trained catalogers to prepare local records. Cross-departmental and cross-disciplinary cooperation will become more important. Catalogers should learn HTML and SGML/XML as well as MARC; archivists should learn MARC as well as EAD.

Staffing in my own institution splits functions among several departments–curatorial, conservation, preservation imaging, and cataloging. Our curators seek and acquire materials to support the library collections, and staff members of the printed, visual, and manuscripts departments process and prepare finding aids. The cataloging department creates bibliographic records in both OCLC and our local online catalog. Materials in need of conservation are treated by the conservation department.

In my institution we are currently scanning photographs and connecting the scanned images to collection-level bibliographic records in the online catalog. The scanning work is done in the Preservation Imaging Department, which has extended its activities from microfilming newspapers to scanning and digital photography.

The goal of technical services work at the cusp of the millennia is to create an environment that will put libraries at the center of the information landscape. With online catalogs and digitized images of our own resources, links to catalogs of other institutions, and carefully developed home pages and pathfinders, special collections libraries can become a "portal of choice" for information seekers.

NOTES

1. Irene P. Godden, ed., *Library Technical Services: Operations and Management*, 2nd ed., (San Diego: Academic Press, 1991), 1, quoting Mortimer F. Tauber, ed., *Technical Services in Libraries*, (New York: Columbia University Press, 1954): 4, and Karen L. Horny, "Technical Services Librarians: A Vanishing Species?" *Illinois Libraries*, 62 (1980): 588.

2. Martha M. Yee and Sara Shatford Layne, *Improving Online Public Access Catalogs* (Chicago: American Library Association, 1998): 4.

Cataloging @ 2000:
Over 100 Years of Change
at The University of Colorado
Law Library

Georgia Briscoe
Karen Selden

SUMMARY. The University of Colorado Law Library has provided access to its collections for over 100 years. This article recaps the evolution of those efforts with emphasis on current issues such as defining a cataloging philosophy, cataloging Internet resources in a Web catalog, using genre terms, and using the Internet to increase productivity. Major historical trends in cataloging law collections in general are also discussed. *[Article copies available for a fee from The Haworth Document Delivery Service: 1-800-342-9678. E-mail address: <getinfo@haworthpressinc. com> Website: <http://www.HaworthPress.com>]*

KEYWORDS. Law libraries, cataloging legal materials, cataloging philosophy, Web catalogs, MARC field 856, genre terms, MARC field

Georgia Briscoe, AMLS, University of Michigan; MA, University of San Diego, is Associate Director and Head of Technical Services, University of Colorado Law Library, Fleming Law Building, Room 190, CB 402, 2405 Kittredge Loop Drive, Boulder, CO 80309.

Karen Selden, MLS, Simmons College, is Catalog Librarian, University of Colorado Law Library, Fleming Law Building, Room 190, CB 402, 2405 Kittredge Loop Drive, Boulder, CO 80309.

The authors acknowledge the assistance of their colleagues at the University of Colorado Law Library, especially Barbara Bintliff and Rob Richards.

[Haworth co-indexing entry note]: "Cataloging @ 2000: Over 100 Years of Change at The University of Colorado Law Library." Briscoe, Georgia, and Karen Selden. Co-published simultaneously in *Cataloging & Classification Quarterly* (The Haworth Information Press, an imprint of The Haworth Press, Inc.) Vol. 30, No. 2/3, 2000, pp. 177-195; and: *Managing Cataloging and the Organization of Information: Philosophies, Practices and Challenges at the Onset of the 21st Century* (ed: Ruth C. Carter) The Haworth Information Press, an imprint of The Haworth Press, Inc., 2000, pp. 177-195. Single or multiple copies of this article are available for a fee from The Haworth Document Delivery Service [1-800-342-9678, 9:00 a.m. - 5:00 p.m. (EST). E-mail address: getinfo@haworthpressinc.com].

655, cataloging Internet resources, use of Internet in cataloging, University of Colorado Law Library

INTRODUCTION AND HISTORY

The University of Colorado Law Library's efforts to provide access to its collection since the late nineteenth century illustrate the challenges that have faced all libraries during this time period. These universal challenges involve moving from manual, simplistic physical control of relatively small local collections to the automated and sophisticated intellectual control of both local and remote resources that patrons expect and demand from today's libraries. In addition, the Law Library coped with challenges specific to cataloging legal materials, such as cataloging looseleaf materials, microforms, and computer files, and the development and refinement of the Library of Congress classification schedules for legal materials. The details of the Law Library's journey through the twentieth century, including the impact of trends in cataloging legal materials and the implementation of new initiatives, are presented below.

The University of Colorado Law Library is fairly representative of most midsize academic law libraries[1] with a long history. The Law Library has been an integral part of the law school since the school's founding in 1892. This relationship is necessary in the profession of law, because a law library is comparable to a laboratory, where research must be conducted before any practical application is possible. For the law student, learning to effectively use a law library is essential. Access to the library collection is therefore vital.

As in most law libraries over 50 years of age, the University of Colorado Law Library's original collection had neither descriptive cataloging nor classification. "The opinion was widely held that because of the nature of law books, both the staff and the patrons of a law library could keep the entire collection in their heads, making the catalog a needless bother."[2] Collections were comparatively small, consisting of traditional Anglo-American legal works, often in large sets with very good indexing. They were also easy to organize and shelve by form and/or jurisdiction. The major groupings included: statutes, cases, treatises arranged alphabetically by subject or author, and journals. An acquisitions record was kept in accession number order, and one of the law professors was generally responsible for the collection, with a secretary assigned to daily maintenance.

As is typical with most academic law libraries, the University of Colorado Law Library was originally a branch of the University's main library, with ordering and processing handled at the main library. Descriptive cataloging was regularly performed at the Law Library from the early 1960s, when the first professional cataloger was hired. Card sets were manually typed, with added entries typed in red.

With the services of a professional cataloger available and the collection growing rapidly, it was decided that class numbers should be added to the volumes for more efficient access. Classification was not attempted prior to 1965 because law collections were considered to be self-classifying and the Library of Congress had not published a standard classification schedule for legal materials. In the absence of an LC schedule, some of the larger Anglo-American law libraries developed their own systems.[3] The University of Colorado Law Library chose to use the Harvard Law Classification System for most of their titles. The first fully developed Library of Congress classification scheme for American law, *Subclass KF (Law of the United States)* was published in 1969. However, it was deemed most expedient for the University of Colorado Law Library to continue to use the Harvard system since the catalog cards had recently been upgraded with Library of Congress subject headings and Harvard Law School published annual volumes of their acquisitions,[4] which could serve as a source for copy cataloging. In addition, at this same time the small staff of four in the Law Library was busy planning for a new law library building, leaving little time for a reclassification project.

In order to comply with standards set by the American Bar Association's Section on Legal Education, the Law Library became autonomous from the University's main library in 1983. As a result, the Law Library's collection grew greatly as titles in subjects closely related to law (for example: political sciences, social sciences, philosophy, criminology) were added to ensure a well-balanced collection in the now independent library. A greater need for bibliographic control was evident. The Law Library's cataloging department also became fully autonomous. It was time to join a bibliographic utility. OCLC was selected because the University's main library used it and because RLIN, the only viable alternative, was considered most useful only for the largest law libraries. The OCLC contract was signed in 1988.

New, energetic leadership in the library forged ahead. With a major step taken by joining OCLC, it was also a good time to consider reclassifying the collection and automating it. CARL, the Colorado Association of Research Libraries' home grown automated library system, provided a strong impetus. CARL was viewed as an afford- able automation system, which would provide the basic modules of an integrated system and become the standard for patrons of all libraries in Colorado. If reclassification could be combined with converting the shelflist to machine-readable records, the stage would be set for join- ing CARL and leaping into the modern law library scene. However, the reality of the situation understandably involved a long, expensive, and tedious process of many baby steps rather than progress by leaps and bounds. Instead of converting and classifying the collection in- house with a very small staff, the Law Library solicited competitive bids to complete the project. OCLC was awarded the contract, and the shelflist was prepared, drawer by drawer, for mailing to its Dublin, Ohio headquarters. OCLC returned each shelflist card with an LC call number penciled on it and spine and pocket labels paper clipped to it. While outsourcing the project was a cost-effective and efficient meth- od of retrospectively converting and classifying the collection, it was not without problems. OCLC staff could not read many of the cards because they were illegibly handwritten. Different editions of works received greatly different class numbers, and many shelflist records were converted without being classified. These problems occurred primarily because many records in OCLC were without LC numbers, a consequence of the long time taken to complete the LC law sched- ules. To make a long story short, the Law Library's cataloger was left with years of problem-resolution, which continues to this day.

Retrospective conversion allowed the Law Library to contribute its records to CARL in 1989. All CARL libraries, including the largest academic libraries in Colorado, loaded their MARC records into a giant database called the "superbib." This database was stored on one large Tandem computer located in Denver, 30 miles south of the Law Library's location in Boulder. CARL seemed like a miracle in those early days of automation because patrons no longer had to rely on the old divided card catalog. As the years passed, however, the superbib became a beast unto itself, with bugs and glitches predominating. CARL became unreliable in its ability to withdraw the MARC records exclusive to the Law Library or any other participating library. Even- tually, shelflisting became impossible, circulation lost thousands of dollars in fines, and authority control was never developed. The Law

Library's Head of Technical Services finally declared she was unable to provide bibliographic control with CARL.

The entire Law Library faculty agreed it was time for a change. A similar decision was brewing at the University of Colorado's main library. This allowed the two libraries to jointly write the 102 page *Request for Proposal for a Library Automation System and Related Services,*[5] in 1992-93. After a lengthy, state-regulated process, it was determined that the Law Library and the University's main library could not share an automation system and still remain autonomous. Innovative Interfaces Inc. (III) was eventually independently selected as the new integrated library system by each library.[6] The Law Library selected III because it most closely met the library's requirements and had a proven record of performance in law libraries.[7] In 1994, the Law Library's MARC records were extracted from CARL and sent to Blackwell North America, Inc. for authority control and deduping. A DEC 2000 computer was purchased from III, and Innovative staff loaded the MARC records and the turnkey software on the machine before delivery. While migration from CARL to III gave the Law Library reliability, stability, flexibility, and robustness in its automated catalog, the new database was only as good as the data it contained. The many problems needing "clean-up" after the migration[8] were mainly the result of "dirty" data, which was extracted from CARL's superbib. III's administrative module made this "cleaning" easier by allowing lists of bibliographic records to be created, sorted, and rapidly updated by almost any MARC field or subfield tag. The Law Library's Innovative system was named LAWPAC.

With the migration to III complete, technical services processes were reorganized and streamlined, and workflow made more efficient. The OCLC database is searched for titles to be ordered, and matching records are immediately downloaded into LAWPAC, with an order record automatically attached. When the volume arrives, the order record is edited and the book sent directly to cataloging. Most importantly, patrons can access full bibliographic information of what is "on order" and "in process."

Since the early 1990's, a paraprofessional staff member has performed copy cataloging under the guidance of a professional cataloger, who handles original cataloging and difficult copy cataloging. Standards in the most recent editions of the *Anglo American Cataloging Rules (AACR)* for description, the *Library of Congress Subject*

Headings (LCSH) for subjects, the *Library of Congress Classification* schedules for classification, and the *U.S. Machine Readable Cataloging (USMARC)* for data format are all adhered to very closely. Authority control has been performed weekly since 1994.

UNIQUE ISSUES OF LAW CATALOGING

Legal materials have always presented unique challenges to catalogers. The first book published to assist the "person who undertakes to catalog a law library," was Elsie Basset's *A Cataloging Manual for Law Libraries,* published in 1942. In 1984, Peter Enyingi and Melody Busse Lembke, of the Los Angeles County Law Library, produced a major work, *Cataloging Legal Literature*[9] to assist law catalogers. That title covers LC descriptive and subject cataloging, but does not handle classification.

One of the major challenges in cataloging legal literature over the years has involved selection of the main entry. Because so many primary and secondary legal materials are the product of a corporate body, it was often the main entry, until the publication of AACR2.[10] "Although the concept of corporate authorship was abandoned, AACR2 continued to prescribe corporate main entry for several categories of work said to "emanate" from corporate bodies. Included are laws, decrees of the chief executive that have the force of law, administrative regulations, constitutions, court rules, treaties, court decisions, legislative hearings, and religious laws."[11] These legal materials may still be entered under corporate bodies but the addition of form subheadings such as "Laws, statutes, etc.," "Constitution," and "Treaties, etc.," has been replaced by uniform titles. Because these conventions continue under the guidance of the newest edition of the *Anglo-American Cataloguing Rules*[12] (AACR21998), law library catalogers have of necessity become proficient assigners of uniform titles.

AACR2 also allowed primary legal publications to receive main entries under: (1) jurisdiction governed; (2) emanating corporate body; (3) a heading that would match most closely with citation practice; and (4) title. This practice also continues in the newest edition, AACR21998. The formerly revered title page is therefore not the preferred source of main entry and a law cataloger must often struggle to determine a corporate emanating body or jurisdiction, the nature of a legal publication, or the legal process that produced it. Debates among law catalogers over the entry choices have been frequent and have required many LC rule interpretations for clarification. In the last decade, online catalogs have diminished much of this concern over main entry as they allow for more access points and take away the importance of the "main" entry. However, "law librarians must make certain that the unique access points needed for law materials are included in the database, and they must insist that system designers utilize this information in the most advantageous way."[13]

With the constant need in law to be current, it is not surprising that many titles are published as a looseleaf service. Law libraries have traditionally treated looseleafs as serials for acquisition, check-in, and accounting purposes, but for cataloging purposes, they are usually monographs. Adele Hallam's book on this subject has been very useful to law librarians.[14]

Law Libraries traditionally have large percentages of their collections in microform. The University of Colorado Law Library is representative with approximately one third of its titles in microfiche, saving both space and money for mainly outdated and less-used materials that are still very necessary for legal research. For the last fifteen years, titles received by the Law Library in various microformats are given full bibliographic control including LC classification. For large sets, such as those published by Congressional Information Services or Law Library Microform Consortium, MARC records are purchased whenever they are available.[15]

Since the mid 1980s, government documents have also been integrated into the library collection at the University of Colorado Law Library with full LC classification. Many law libraries are not this fortunate, using only sudoc numbers with partial or no descriptive cataloging. The Law Library is a partial government depository,[16] receiving only twelve per cent of available titles because the University's main library, located on the same campus, is a full depository. The inconsistency in format distribution (subsequent issues of the same title may be received in paper format, microfiche, CD-ROM, and by means of the Internet) of government document serial titles is a special challenge for both cataloging and check-in. At the Law Library, when this occurs, the format of the first received issue is cataloged with notes added for additional formats and the holdings statement and check-in record displaying the format of each issue.

Computer files, especially the full-text databases of WESTLAW and LEXIS, have been a very important part of the law library scene since the 1980s. A surge of activity to provide cataloging for individual files of these mega databases occurred in the late 1980s when the University of Minnesota Law Library cataloged the files of WESTLAW and the State University of New York at Buffalo Law Library did the same for LEXIS. The University of Colorado Law Library did not participate in this experiment, which was suspended in 1991 because of the transitory nature of the online texts. Today these efforts are being revived by non-law libraries, which endeavor to catalog LEXIS-NEXIS databases with hotlinks into their new Lexis-Nexis Universe services. The Law Library may participate in this project in the future if stability can be shown and advantages will outweigh disadvantages.

After the Library of Congress published classification schedules for foreign law jurisdictions,[17] most libraries faced a gigantic series of reclassification projects. Completion of these projects was simplified at the University of Colorado Law Library because the retrospective conversion and automation project of the early 1980s caught England, Canada, and the general law titles. Each of the other jurisdictions have been tackled as mini-projects, using whatever staff can be freed from their already full job assignments. The University of Colorado Law Library's reclassification efforts, like those of other smaller law libraries, have benefited greatly from Web access to other law libraries' catalogs. The Internet allows law libraries with strong foreign law collections and the resources to undertake massive reclassification projects-such as Yale and Georgetown-to share their work with the whole law cataloging community. At the University of Colorado Law Library, it is expected that reclassification will be ongoing for several years to come, competing for staff time with cataloging Internet resources.

THE LAW LIBRARY'S CATALOGING PHILOSOPHY

In 1997, the Law Library created and adopted a formal Cataloging Philosophy,[18] reproduced below:

Titles are catalogued into the collection of the University of Colorado Law Library to meet the Law Library Mission:

The primary mission of the University of Colorado Law Library is to provide materials and services that support the instructional and research programs of the faculty and students of the School of Law. Further, as the largest collection of legal information resources in the state of Colorado, the Law Library offers its resources and services to assist the University and legal communities and the public in meeting their needs of legal information.

*The Law Library is committed to pursuing opportunities afforded by the cooperative organization of resources in order to establish and maintain appropriate resources for **optimal access** and use of legal resources. The Law Library is also committed to exploring **creative alternatives to conventional procedures** as it plans, develops, and provides information, materials, and services to its targeted communities.*

[bolding added for emphasis in this version of document only]

Toward this end, the library adheres to the Anglo-American Cataloguing Rules (AACR2R1998), the Library of Congress Subject Headings, the Library of Congress Classification System, and the practices of the Online Computer Library Center (OCLC). However, "(s)ince the primary reason for adopting any subject classification scheme is to arrange your books on the shelf in such a way that like material will be found altogether,"1 class numbers and subject headings will often be altered to provide *optimal access*. Optimal access for Law Library patrons means classing titles on similar subjects in the same location as much as possible. It also means adding as many access points as is reasonable. Modifications to cataloguing of the Library of Congress and members of OCLC are therefore common. The Head of Faculty Services is the most knowledgeable faculty member to be consulted for classification and subject questions in the Law Library collection.

1 Benemann, William, AALL Spectrum, October 1997, p.14.

The Law Library's detailed, written cataloging procedures[19] reflect this philosophy. Recent projects that combine the use of new technology and procedures to enhance patrons' access to legal materials include: developing and enhancing a web-based catalog; cataloging Internet-based resources; developing and using new genre terms to enhance access to electronic resources; and using the Internet to increase productivity. A brief description of each of these projects follows.

THE WEB-BASED CATALOG

In early 1998, the Law Library formed a committee to create policies and procedures for the design and display of the new web-based III catalog, LAWPAC on the Web.[20] The composition of the LAWPAC on the Web Committee reflects the Law Library's service-oriented philosophy, in which the Public Services department and the Technical Services department consistently collaborate and cooperate in order to meet the needs of the Law Library's patrons. In this case, the Head of Public Services, the Technical Services Librarian (who maintains the Law Library's Technical Services website and web-based LAWPAC's customizable pages), the Catalog Librarian, and the Government Documents Technician were chosen to create a useful and user-friendly catalog display tailored to the needs of the Law Library's patrons. The formation of this committee is also an example of the Law Library's long-term commitment to the use of new technology and innovative approaches to deliver legal information to its patrons. The committee meets monthly to tackle design, display, and access issues that arise through continued use of and enhancements to the web-based version of the catalog.

CATALOGING INTERNET-BASED RESOURCES

Creation of the Law Library's policies and procedures for cataloging Internet-based resources was a natural task for the LAWPAC on the Web Committee. With the existence of a web-based catalog came the ability to provide hotlinks to information of interest to the Law Library's patrons. Indeed, the existence of web-based OPACs allows catalogers to focus their efforts on access to materials and not just on the traditional description of materials. In a posting to the INTERCAT (OCLC Internet Cataloging project) electronic mailing list,[21] Allison Zhang, the Webmaster/Electronic Resources Librarian at the University of Rochester's Rush Rhees Library, insightfully summarized the emerging issues this new technology presents to catalogers:

With new development[s] in library system technology, we are able to catalog and provide direct access to Internet resources through the OPAC. The nature of the OPAC has changed. It is no longer an inventory list but rather what we have access to. It has moved from a list or a finding aid to delivery mechanism to contents. Catalogers' role[s] [have] changed too. We are not just describing the resource, we are providing access to it.[22]

Matthew Beacom, the Catalog Librarian for Networked Information Resources at Yale University, phrased the same sentiment more succinctly in a posting to the AUTOCAT (Library cataloging and authorities discussion group) electronic mailing list:[23] ". . . whether we like it or not the catalog has become a document delivery tool in addition to its traditional functions."[24]

The LAWPAC on the Web Committee enthusiastically took on the challenge of creating an OPAC that would both describe and access materials for the Law Library's patrons. The issues involved in creating such a catalog include:

1. How will the Law Library provide access to Internet-based resources?
2. What Internet-based resources will the Law Library provide access to?
3. How does the Law Library want to display hotlinks to and information about specific Internet-based resources?

Because the answers to these questions are highly influenced by each library's needs and resources, there are no right or wrong answers. In addition, the answers depend upon such factors as new methods to improve patron access and information display, changing cataloging rules, and new software enhancements. Indeed, the answers to these questions have changed for the Law Library even since early 1998, and will undoubtedly continue to change in the future in response to such influences. Thus, the Law Library's Policy Statement and Procedures for Cataloging Internet Resources,[25] which documents these decisions, is an evolving "work in progress." What follows is a sketch of the major policies that the committee adopted to address the issues mentioned above.

1. How will the Law Library provide access to Internet-based resources?

Libraries can provide access through subject-oriented web pages,
which are linked to the automated catalog and maintained and updated
by library staff. Indeed, the Law Library began creating such pages in
1994 to provide access to many legal and non-legal Internet-based
resources.[26] While such web pages are useful for patrons, the maintenance often becomes laborious and time-consuming for the staff members involved. However, the committee also recognized the value of
providing direct access to Internet-based resources at the "point of
need"–from the bibliographic record retrieved during an OPAC
search. Thus the committee decided to provide hotlink access to websites via individual bibliographic records using the MARC field 856.

MARC field 856 is used to provide the electronic location and
access information for electronic resources. More simply, this is the
field that provides the hotlink to a website from an individual bibliographic record. However, using this field to create hotlinks requires a
commitment to local editing for three reasons. First, MARC field 856
has experienced relatively recent and significant changes. In 1997,
important indicator values were added,[27] while the status of subfield u
(the subfield that stores the URL or PURL, and is required to create a
hotlink in the bibliographic record) was changed in January 1999.[28]
Originally repeatable, subfield u became non-repeatable, requiring
that a separate 856 field be created for each hotlink that was desired in
a bibliographic record. In order to meet current MARC standards and
create useable hotlinks, copy-cataloging records created prior to January 1999 will usually require at least some local editing.[29] In addition,
OPACs differ widely on what 856 subfields they can display, and in
what order. Thus, it is imperative to know the display conventions
affecting one's catalog in order to format useable hotlinks and user-
friendly displays of hotlinks and associated information. The Law
Library's cataloger and copy catalogers faithfully edit indicators and
multiple occurrences of subfield u, while also editing records to enhance the hotlink and associated public information displays. Finally
URLs, and even PURLs, can easily change, making a commitment to
periodic link checking a must. The Law Library uses Microsoft Front
Page to check the approximately 400 URLs and PURLs stored in
LAWPAC's bibliographic records. The software is used monthly to

generate a report of links that **might** be broken. On average, the Law Library's monthly report contains 12 to 15 links. Manual inspection of these possible broken links yields an average of 3 to 5 links that are actually broken. The false reports of broken links usually result from a server being down or busy, and sometimes from a PURL server taking a long time to redirect the user's query to the underlying URL. Whenever a broken link is discovered, a new URL or PURL must be found and placed in subfield u in order to re-establish a valid, useable hotlink in the bibliographic record.

    2. What Internet-based resources will the Law Library provide access to?

Generally, the only Internet sites that the Law Library's catalog provides links to are those offering full-text materials. This policy stems from the belief that patrons usually want and value access to the material itself, rather than related items or finding aids. The Law Library is a selective GPO depository, and increasingly these paper-based federal government resources are also available in web-based versions. Often the copy cataloging record for a hard copy GPO item contains a URL or PURL for the web-based version of the title. Indeed, GPO websites account for the bulk of the Law Library's cataloged Internet-based resources. The cataloger and copy catalogers do not make a conscious effort to find Internet-based resources, but do add hotlinks if a web-based version of a title is discovered.

    3. How does the Law Library want to display hotlinks to and information about specific Internet-based resources?

III software enhancements have greatly improved the MARC field 856 display options in LAWPAC on the Web. Indeed, the introductory text that appeared above the hotlink became completely customizable, and each library could choose which 856 subfields to display, and in which order. In response, the LAWPAC on the Web Committee decided the hot linked URL or PURL from an 856 field's subfield u will always be the first piece of information to display. The URL or PURL will be followed by the text in two other subfields, as applicable: subfield 3 (Materials specified) [for example, Vol. 60 (1995)-] and subfield z (Public note) [for example, Adobe Acrobat Reader required]. The phrase used to introduce the URL or PURL was customized to fit this new display format, while experimentation led to the discovery that the text in subfields 3 and z can be displayed, in most cases, in separate, non-hot linked boxes below the hot linked URL or PURL.[30]

USE OF GENRE TERMS TO ENHANCE ACCESS TO ELECTRONIC RESOURCES

Another question that the LAWPAC on the Web Committee addressed is:

How can the Law Library enhance access to electronic resources?

The committee favored the use of form/genre headings in the MARC field 655 (Index Term-Genre/Form field) that would clearly describe the format of Internet-based resources for patrons. Unfortunately, none of the genre/form heading thesauri listed in the *USMARC Code List for Subject/Index Term Sources*[31] included terms to describe electronic resources. However, the committee discovered a thesaurus of genre terms for legal materials being developed by the AALL (American Association of Law Libraries) Ad Hoc Committee on Genre Terms for Legal Materials, under the auspices of the Cataloging and Classification Standing Committee of the AALL Technical Services Special Interest Section.[32] AALL is sponsoring the thesaurus' publication by William S. Hein & Co. in early 2000. The eventual goal is to have the thesaurus listed as an official source for genre terms in the *USMARC Code List for Subject/Index Term Sources*. The LAWPAC on the Web Committee submitted three terms with brief definitions to this project, and the Law Library's cataloger and copy catalogers currently use these terms in the MARC field 655, supplying **local** in subfield 2 as the source of the term.[33] The three terms are: **Electronic journals; Internet resources; and World Wide Web resources**.

Using the first term in a subject search creates a list of all electronic journals in the Law Library's catalog, while using the other two terms creates a list of all Internet-based resources in the catalog. Developing and using these terms increases patrons' access to the Law Library's electronic resources, while contributing these terms to the thesaurus of genre terms for legal materials project is a worthwhile way to share these ideas with other librarians.

USING THE INTERNET TO INCREASE PRODUCTIVITY

Yet another example of the Law Library's Technical Services Department employing creative alternatives to conventional procedures is the department's enthusiastic use of the Internet to increase productivity. Examples of the Internet's use in cataloging include using Z39.50 connections to search databases such as WorldCat or the web-based catalogs of other libraries for helpful classification or subject analysis guidance; providing TCP/IP connections to bibliographic utilities such as OCLC and RLIN; performing FTP data transfers to OCLC and the vendor that compiles our monthly acquisitions list; verifying the validity of URLs and PURLs in MARC 856 fields; and the creation of an Internet-based Technical Services Home Page.[34] The Technical Services Home Page includes a detailed, current version of the Law Library's Technical Services Procedure Manual,[35] as well as links to dozens of useful reference tools arranged by subject area (Acquisitions, Cataloging, Government Documents, Needs and Offers, Preservation, Serials, etc.). Integrating these online tools and processes into the cataloging workflow has increased productivity by minimizing interruptions and speeding the work pace, thus getting materials to patrons in a more timely manner.

CONCLUSION

Like all law libraries, and especially law libraries, the University of Colorado's Law Library has experienced a tremendous amount of change during the twentieth century. Patrons who first experienced the Law Library as a collection with no descriptive cataloging, classification, or physical catalog could never have dreamed of the changes brought on by different and evolving classification schedules and automated library systems, as well as access to the Internet. Margaret Maes Axtmann, Assistant Director for Collections and Technical Services at the University of Minnesota Law Library and President of the American Association of Law Libraries for 1999-2000, characterized the impact all of these factors continue to have on technical services departments in all types of libraries:

Coinciding with the increasing complexity of the [Technical Services Librarians'] work is the increasing demand for enhanced services. This "more, better, faster," or MBF mentality is a natural response to the rapid developments in automation. Librarians and patrons are demanding better bibliographic access, which can be provided with enhanced MARC records. We also have the ability to provide online access for our staffs and patrons to the catalogs of other libraries and to publisher databases. We can mount indexing and abstracting services as part of our OPACs, and we can provide gateways or direct access to Internet resources, Gophers, web sites, and full text databases. Who will organize these resources on the Internet and in our institutions? Document delivery, both physical and electronic, is another aspect of the MBF pressure. If the library doesn't own an item, how quickly can we get it and deliver it to the user? Whose responsibility is it to perform this function, and how can we find the time to create the tools and databases to produce these services? What is the impact on the staff of the increasing speed and volume of the work?[36]

Obviously, these questions Axtmann raised in 1997 will follow catalogers into the twenty-first century, demanding answers that will continue to change catalogers' roles and libraries' services. Indeed, this situation gives credence yet again to the saying "the only constant in life is change." Although no one can even begin to guess what specific changes the next century will bring to libraries in general, law librarians anticipate the further refinement of the Library of Congress classification scheme for law in the near future with the addition of theocratic law schedules.[37] On a local level, the University of Colorado Law Library plans to begin the new century by completing some major reclassification projects (especially JX to JZ and KZ), classifying the last bastions of items in the collection that are still organized and shelved by form and jurisdiction (state statutes and reporters), and adjusting cataloging practices for participation in an electronic regional union catalog. With the University of Colorado Law Library's commitment to exploring creative alternatives to conventional procedures, the Law Library is poised to tackle all new challenges, currently anticipated or not, by taking advantage of whatever new technologies and procedures evolve during the twenty first century.

NOTES

1. Midsize law libraries are considered to have 300,000 to 400,000 volumes. See the American Association of Law Libraries website (AALLNET), *About AALL Academic Libraries,* at the following URL: <http://www.aallnet.org/about/opportunities.asp>.

2. Miles O. Price, "Selection and Training of Law Catalogers," *Law Library Journal* 45 (1952): 297.

3. Examples include: *Los Angeles County Law Library Classification Schedule, Class K, Law,* which was developed by Miss Elizabeth Benyon, Senior Assistant in Charge of Preparations, originally published in 1951. *Yale Law Library Classification,* by Frederick C. Hicks, 1939. *A Classification Scheme for Law Books,* by Elizabeth M. Moys, 1968. *Manual for Canadian Libraries,* by Shih-Sheng Hu, 1966. *Stanford Law Library Classification,* by John Henry Merryman and Rosalee M. Long, 1968.

4. Harvard Law School Library, *Annual Legal Bibliography,* 1961-81.

5. The RFP is available from the authors.

6. From 1994 to the end of the century, every major academic library in Colorado migrated to Innovative Interfaces, Inc.

7. The serials module of III was developed using legal serials, which are some of the most complex of any subject area. More academic law libraries use III for their ILS than any other, according to *Law Library Systems Directory* (Littleton, Colo.: Fred B. Rothman & Co., 1996) pp. Index 11-14.

8. Briscoe, Georgia, "Migration: a Natural Growth Process for Libraries," Colorado Libraries, 20(1994): 27-31.

9. Melody Busse Lembke and Rhonda K. Lawrence, *Cataloging Legal Literature* (Littleton, Colo.: Fred B. Rothman and Co., 1997).

10. *Anglo-American Cataloguing Rules.* 2nd ed., 1988, rev. Ed. Michael Gorman and Paul Winkler. (Chicago: American Library Association, 1988).

11. Cecilia Kwan and Phyllis Marion, "Cataloging and the Online Catalog," *Law Librarianship: A Handbook for the Electronic Age* (Littleton, Colo.: Fred B. Rothman & Co., 1995) p.352.

12. Joint Steering Committee for Revision of AACR, *Anglo-American Cataloguing Rules.* 2nd ed., 1998 Revision (Chicago: American Library Association, 1998).

13. Cecilia Kwan and Phyllis Marion, "Cataloging and the Online Catalog," *Law Librarianship: a Handbook for the Electronic Age* (Littleton, Colo.: Fred B. Rothman & Co., 1995) p. 359.

14. Adele Hallam, *Cataloging rules for the description of looseleaf publications : with special emphasis on legal materials.* 2d ed. (Washington, DC: Library of Congress, 1989).

15. OCLC's Major Microform Project is a good source and CIS has produced MARC records of most of their titles starting from 1970 to date.

16. Law passed in 1978 enabled accredited law school libraries to become depositories.

17. United Kingdom and Ireland (KD in 1973), Canada (KE in 1976), Germany (KK-KKC in 1982), the Americas (KDZ, KG-KH in 1984), France (KJV-KJW in 1985), Europe (KJ-KKZ in 1989), Asia and Eurasia, Africa and Pacific Area, and

Antarctic Regions (KL-KWX in 1993); as well as schedules for general law (K in 1977), and law of nations (KZ in 1998).

18. University of Colorado Law Library, "Cataloguing Philosophy," *Technical Services Manual*, 1 November 1999, <http://www.colorado.edu/Law/lawlib/ts/man/catphil.htm> (21 January 2000).

19. University of Colorado Law Library, *Technical Services Manual*, 19 November 1999, <http://www.colorado.edu/Law/lawlib/ts/man/contents.html> (21 January 2000).

20. University of Colorado Law Library, *LAWPAC on the Web*, <http://lawpac.colorado.edu/> (21 January 2000).

21. Subscribe to INTERCAT at the following URL: <http://www.oclc.org/oclc/forms/listserv.htm>.

22. Allison Zhang, <azhang@rcl.lib.rochester.edu> "Re: Call for Input," 6 July 1999, <http://www.oclc.org/oclc/forms/listserv.htm> (6 July 1999).

23. Get more information about AUTOCAT at the following URL: <http://ublib.buffalo.edu/libraries/units/cts/autocat/>.

24. Matthew Beacom, <matthew.beacom@yale.edu> "Re: CC.DA/TF/OPAC Displays." 8 July 1999, <http://ublib.buffalo.edu/libraries/units/cts/autocat/> Available via E-mail: LISTSERV@LISTSERV.ACSU.BUFFALO.EDU/Getpost autocat 61453 [1999, July 8].

25. University of Colorado Law Library, "Policy Statement and Procedures for Cataloging Internet Resources," *Technical Services Manual*, 18 January 2000, <http://www.Colorado.EDU/Law/lawlib/ts/man/intcat.htm> (21 January 2000).

26. These subject-oriented web pages are accessed from the *University of Colorado Law Library Home Page* at the following URL: <http://www.colorado.edu/Law/lawlib/>.

27. Cataloging Distribution Service, *USMARC Format for Bibliographic Data* (Washington, D.C.: Library of Congress, 1994) Update No. 3 (July 1997).

28. MARBI, "Proposal No. 99-06: Repeatability of Subfield u (URL) in field 856," 11 December 1998, <http://lcweb.loc.gov/marc/marbi/1999/99-06.html> (21 January, 2000).

29. For a concise listing of commonly used MARC field 856 indicators and subfields, as well as examples and explanations of most frequently encountered editing changes, consult "Most commonly used 856 indicators and subfields," by Karen Selden and Mary Strouse, at the following URL: <http://www.Colorado.EDU/Law/lawlib/ts/linking/856no1.htm>.

30. For more discussion of these III capabilities and the detailed procedures the Law Library uses to create these displays, please refer to the most recent version of the University of Colorado Law Library's "Policy Statement and Procedures for Cataloging Internet Resources," available at the following URL: <http://www.Colorado.EDU/Law/lawlib/ts/man/intcat.htm>.

31. Network Development and MARC Standards Office, "The USMARC Code List for Subject/Index Term Sources," (27 December 1999) <http://lcweb.loc.gov/marc/relators/re9806su.html#top> (21 January 2000).

32. The draft version of the "Thesaurus of Genre Terms for Legal Materials" is available at the following URL: <http://www.aallnet.org/sis/tssis/stndcomm/catclass/gnredrft.htm>.

33. For detailed definitions of these local genre terms and specific procedures for their use, please refer to the most recent version of the University of Colorado Law Library's "Policy Statement and Procedures for Cataloging Internet Resources," available at the following URL: <http://www.Colorado.EDU/Law/lawlib/ts/man/intcat.htm>.

34. University of Colorado Law Library, *Technical Services Home Page*, 17 November 1999, <http://www.colorado.edu/Law/lawlib/ts/index.html> (21 January 2000).

35. University of Colorado Law Library, *Technical Services Manual*, <http://www.colorado.edu/Law/lawlib/ts/man/contents.html>.

36. Margaret Maes Axtmann, "I'm Dancing as Fast as I Can: Life in the Fast Lane of Technical Services," in *Toward a Renaissance in Law Librarianship* (Chicago: American Association of Law Libraries, 1997), 118.

37. "New Standardized Form Division Tables for K Classification Schedules," *Cataloging Service Bulletin* no. 85 (summer 1999): 8.

Information Resource Management: Transitions and Trends in an Academic Law Library

Eloise M. Vondruska

SUMMARY. Over the last three years, there have been changes in management, organization, staffing, and services at the Pritzker Legal Research Center (PLRC) of Northwestern University School of Law. The methods for acquiring and cataloging information resources have been redesigned. These changes coincided with new management, a change in the name of the technical services department, a migration to a new library management system, and a new name for the law library. The bibliographic services organization and workflow before and after the migration are described. The cataloging and bibliographic services activities will continue to be reevaluated. The goal of the bibliographic services department is to align with the 21st century mission of the PLRC to be an integral component in supporting the scholarly, teaching and learning needs of faculty and students as the law school becomes *the* law school for a changing world. *[Article copies available for a fee from The Haworth Document Delivery Service: 1-800-342-9678. E-mail address: <getinfo@haworthpressinc.com> Website: <http://www.HaworthPress.com>]*

KEYWORDS. Academic law libraries, technical services, cataloging, resource management

---

Eloise M. Vondruska, MS, is Associate Director for Bibliographic Services, Northwestern University School of Law, Pritzker Legal Research Center, 357 East Chicago Avenue, Chicago, IL 60611 (E-mail: e-vondruska@nwu.edu).

[Haworth co-indexing entry note]: "Information Resource Management: Transitions and Trends in an Academic Law Library." Vondruska, Eloise M. Co-published simultaneously in *Cataloging & Classification Quarterly* (The Haworth Information Press, an imprint of The Haworth Press, Inc.) Vol. 30, No. 2/3, 2000, pp. 197-213; and: *Managing Cataloging and the Organization of Information: Philosophies, Practices and Challenges at the Onset of the 21st Century* (ed: Ruth C. Carter) The Haworth Information Press, an imprint of The Haworth Press, Inc., 2000, pp. 197-213. Single or multiple copies of this article are available for a fee from The Haworth Document Delivery Service [1-800-342-9678, 9:00 a.m. - 5:00 p.m. (EST). E-mail address: getinfo@haworthpressinc.com].

197

BACKGROUND AND HISTORY

From its earliest mention in 1891,[1] and for the next one hundred years, the library at Northwestern University School of Law focused on building collections rated for excellence in their range of materials. In the several years following the hundred-year mark, however, the library has undergone changes in organization, management, and services with the purpose of creating a legal research center focused on excellence in its range of information resource services for the law school. While the first one hundred years was about buildings and collections, the 21st century mission of the legal research center at Northwestern University School of Law is about services and access to information.

The Pritzker Legal Research Center (PLRC) serves a Northwestern University Law School community of over 600 JD enrolled students. The collection numbers over 600,000 volumes of materials on Anglo-American law, international and foreign law materials, rare book items, and a large collection of U.S. government documents. These legal materials are stored in three buildings from different periods of Law School construction (1926, 1959, and 1984). The buildings are connected physically and share a single entrance/exit for library use. The collections in the three buildings are part of one organizational unit, the PLRC.

The history of resource management and cataloging practices at the Law School library falls roughly into three periods: from its beginnings until about 1980, the pre-NOTIS era; from 1980 until 1998, the NOTIS era; and from 1998 until present, the post-NOTIS era. The focus of this paper is on recent transitions and trends, especially from 1996 through the migration process from NOTIS to Voyager, and until the present. However, a description of the law library's pre-NOTIS and NOTIS eras is appropriate, since so much of the recent activities and trends have been shaped by the foundation of those years.

Card catalog records of the law library's holdings have existed for the collection since its beginning in the late 19th century. The shelf list includes handwritten, typed, printed, and computer-produced catalog cards. The shelf list was closed to new entries with the migration to a new library management system in 1998, although the physical shelf list still resides in the cataloging staff area. The law library only began using an online system for technical services activities (NOTIS) in

1980. All titles acquired from 1980 onward were represented online, but retrospective holdings were accessible only via the card catalog or by shelf browsing. Local subject headings had been created for use in the card catalog.

Because the Library of Congress (LC) schedules for law were in development but not done, much of the collection acquired before 1980 was classified using two different schemes, but not the LC schedules. Represented in the collection still today are foreign legal works classified according to the *Yale Law Library Classification*[2] developed by Frederick C. Hicks (also known as "Hicks numbers"), and international legal works classified according to the *Classification for International Law and Relations*[3] by Kurt Schwerin (also known as "Schwerin numbers"). Currently acquired materials are classified according to the Library of Congress classification scheme, or, the Superintendent of Documents scheme for United States government documents. All materials classified according to LC also have a locally created location code. This location code is placed on the spine label above the call number, is present in online records and identifies where the material is shelved in the three buildings that make up the PLRC. An example of this is the location code for Anglo-American monographic treatise material: MON (for monograph). A monograph on U.S. trials would have the location, MON, the LC class number KF 224, etc.

ONLINE ERA

In 1980, the School of Law received a major foundation grant[4] to recatalog, reclassify, and automate the bibliographic records of the law library collection. The goal was to recatalog the entire collection according to the *Anglo-American Cataloguing Rules*, second edition (AACR2),[5] to reclassify materials into the Library of Congress classification scheme when possible, to apply Library of Congress subject headings and name authorities, and to create online bibliographic records in NOTIS. To accomplish these goals, the grant money was used to add staff, equipment, and access to RLIN, the Research Libraries Information Network.

The grant money did not cover the entire conversion project. At the conclusion of the grant funding, the Law School continued funding for a special projects librarian to work on recataloging and reclassifying the remaining offline materials. By 1996, there remained over 30,000 monographic titles and several thousand serial titles that were not represented in the online catalog. With the increased emphasis on access to materials in the late 1990s, the Law School generously funded two projects in 1997 and 1998 that allowed for additional retrospective conversion. This funding was used to purchase outsourced retrospective conversion of foreign and international law monographs from TALX Corporation, as well as bibliographic records for selected United States government documents from MARCIVE, Inc. The approach to retrospective conversion flip-flopped from in-house in 1980 to outsourced in 1997, but the result was an almost 100% online database. By virtue of planning and luck, the database records from these two outsourced retrospective conversion projects were loaded into the NOTIS database in time for the NOTIS to Voyager migration in 1998. The remaining offline serial titles are being added to the Voyager database and all holdings should be in the online catalog by May 2000.

In-between these two retrospective conversion projects were other innovations and challenges in technical services for the library. The law library has participated in the use of national bibliographic utilities since 1980. The RLIN bibliographic database was the primary source for cataloging copy from 1980 to 1989, but OCLC has been the primary source since 1989 when a single dedicated OCLC terminal was acquired. Several years later a second OCLC terminal was added. By 1997 both of the dedicated OCLC terminals were replaced by the use of OCLC Passport for Windows on staff PCs. A cataloging activity unique to the PLRC is the cataloging of the archival collection of the American Bar Association (ABA). In 1985, the headquarters of the American Bar Association became the upstairs neighbor of the Law School. The Law School arranged to provide for the cataloging and storage of the ABA archives in the library. Cataloging staff devised an expanded table of numbers for ABA section and committee names based on the limited Library of Congress classification schedule for the ABA. Cataloging of the ABA archives continues to be a part of the work at the PLRC.

RECENT INFLUENCES

In 1996 and 1997, with vacancies in the positions of director and the associate directors for public services and technical services, three new managers were appointed at the law library. This included the associate dean for library and information services, and two associate directors of the law library, one responsible for public services activities, the other for technical services activities. Despite the authority work caused by corporate body name and serial title changes, at the time of appointment of the new manager of technical services, that department was rechristened bibliographic services.

In the background of these changes, two other scenarios external to the law library had direct influence on the reshaping of services and staffing in the law library. The first was the appointment of a new dean for the law school in the 1995-1996 academic year. Stronger emphasis on the access to and delivery of electronic information resources was requested. The second was the fact that in early 1996 Northwestern University began a review process to replace the locally created, much loved, and long-used library management system, NOTIS. Migration to a new library management system meant all acquisitions, cataloging, and circulation processes would likely change, along with the look and feel of the online public access catalog (OPAC). The selected library management system also would require technology upgrades and staff training in preparation for implementation of the new system.

Another name change came in that of the law library itself. The generosity of a gift to the Law School from the Pritzker Family and the Pritzker Foundation was acknowledged when the law library was named the Pritzker Legal Research Center in April 1999. Looking back at this constellation of changes, one can see that a new foundation had been laid down in the mid-1990s to support the organizational, staffing, and services changes that developed rapidly and continue to occur.

Before these transitions began in 1996, the law library used NOTIS for acquisitions, cataloging, and circulation. The bibliographic services staff, like NOTIS technical services staff in other libraries, loved working with NOTIS. Cataloging activities had become increasingly sophisticated yet simplified through the use of CLARR, the cataloger's toolkit.[6] Bibliographic records were imported and exported to OCLC with the push of a button by catalogers who had use of a PC, but many staff still used IBM 3180 "dumb" terminals. Staff used a shared-access departmental personal computer for e-mail, word processing, and Internet use beginning only in 1993. For most of the staff, Windows were still something to look out of, instead of being something one looked at on the desktop. In the acquisitions area, staff members were proficient in the use of NOTIS order data screens and with the serial check-in abilities and limitations of NOTIS. Online fund accounting on NOTIS had been in use since 1991.

In recent years, staffing in the bibliographic services department was notable for its longevity of service, including one staff member who worked until her nineties, retiring in 1996. Several other staff members began their employment in the department in the 1970s. Many other staff had received their five- or ten-year service awards. The department staff represented loyalty to the Law School, expertise with NOTIS, and cooperative attitudes.

Cross training of bibliographic services staff for activities within acquisitions and cataloging areas had been in place for several years before the migration to a new library management system. This cross training was needed to provide for the daily provision of essential services where staffing levels represented a one person to one activity expertise. Each bibliographic services staff member wrote a procedure manual to document workflow in NOTIS prior to migration to Voyager. As a matter of fact, the writing of the manuals started before the system migration was announced. However, the process of reviewing and scripting activities before the migration reaped benefits in the migration year and in the system implementation year.

Technical services activities encompassed three units: acquisitions, cataloging, and special projects; the principal activity of the special projects unit had been retrospective conversion of the remaining off-line shelf list records into online records. Twelve staff members report to the head of bibliographic services. All the bibliographic services librarians had traditional training and education in library science degree programs. Several of the librarians had additional graduate degrees in subject areas.

ENDEAVORING TO DO OUR UTMOST

The Endeavor Voyager library management system was selected in September 1997 by Northwestern University administration for use by all Northwestern University libraries. The University Library on the Evanston campus includes main subject collections and branch libraries. The Law School's Pritzker Legal Research Center and the Medical School's Galter Health Science Library are on the Chicago campus. Even though they are separate administrative units, these

Libraries have a long history of cooperation, including the use of a shared database in NOTIS. Day One of system implementation for all Northwestern University libraries, using all modules, was targeted for August 10, 1998. The transitional year of 1997-1998 was notable for planning, testing, and training. Representatives from all the Northwestern University libraries served on implementation planning committees focused on the overall systems migration process, technical issues, and on each of the Voyager modules: acquisitions/serials, cataloging, circulation, and OPAC. Each Northwestern library, in turn, had to plan and train for implementation within each of those libraries. During 1997-1998, changes in procedures and staffing were much talked of, anticipated, and worried over. Meanwhile, day-to-day work continued to be performed on NOTIS. The migration year was valuable in that it provided time to get comfortable with the idea of change.

MIGRATION TO A NEW LIBRARY MANAGEMENT SYSTEM

Managers held several preview orientation sessions of all Voyager modules with law library staff members throughout the year before implementation. This timing gave the staff the opportunity to preview their daily online tasks and how they would work, or not work, in the new system. The migration to a new integrated library management system all at once was a radical departure from the gradual integration of NOTIS. At the law library, NOTIS use had been incorporated in stages (online technical services in 1980; online circulation in 1991) with minor upgrades as they occurred.

The planning, testing, and training of the migration year consumed a lot of time and energy. Workflow redesign was thought about, but not tested out, prior to implementation, because time was at a premium that year. It was also known that the software version that was available during the migration year would be different from the version to be installed at implementation. This was another reason to avoid detailed workflow redesign before implementation. In addition, law library desktop equipment had to be upgraded from dumb NOTIS terminals to smart PCs for all staff, because Voyager would require each staff member to have a PC. Training was imperative to insure success with the new computer equipment before Voyager was implemented.

Extensive staff training was scheduled prior to Voyager use. In the law library the summer of 1997 was designated as the Summer of

Skills Building.[7] The training team consisted of class instructors and peer group tutors. Librarians and paraprofessional staff members from public services, bibliographic services, and the law school's information technology staff served as the instructors and tutors. Topics that had to be taught and mastered included PC Fundamentals, Windows 3.1, Netscape, Word, Excel, and HTML. While not all of these topics were required for use with the new system, the availability of PCs opened up the training platform for staff to learn some of these other PC applications. After that training, and with the replacement of NOTIS terminals by PCs with NOTIS access, the staff were better prepared for the implementation coming the next summer. In early 1998, supplemental staff training was provided on Windows 95, the scheduled operating system for the Voyager environment at the law library. The Voyager orientation sessions also gave the staff the impetus to refine their newly acquired Windows skills, while continuing to work with NOTIS, although now on PCs.

During the summer of 1998, NOTIS bibliographic, patron, and circulation transaction files were migrated into Voyager. Several weeks of system configuration by systems managers at each of the Northwestern University libraries followed the data migration. With the completed system configuration, Voyager implementation occurred as scheduled on August 10, 1998. All Northwestern University libraries began to use all Voyager modules that day.

IMPLEMENTATION OF A NEW LIBRARY MANAGEMENT SYSTEM

The next challenge became recreating or modifying established NOTIS technical services procedures to take advantage of Voyager's new capabilities. The NOTIS database remained accessible, but only as a resource. Staff had to jump right in and create data in Voyager. The timing of implementation was critical especially at the PLRC, since the Law School's academic year started the same week as system implementation. Academic calendars for other schools in the University started later in August or in September. A major concern was the checking-in and routing of serials for faculty use and the general collection because the data migration and implementation process had created one-time workflow bottlenecks and backlogs. Acquisitions order data did not migrate to the new system, and would need to be entered manually. Check-in records (and their supporting publication pattern records and purchase orders) needed to be created for the law library's collection, which is more than three-fourths serials in nature. This required acquisitions-cataloging staff crossover beyond the established cross training backup system already in place.

A strategy to create check-in records was planned. The check-in project became the highest priority in bibliographic services post-implementation. Cataloging and special project staff were trained and supervised by acquisitions staff to create records for the least complicated serials, i.e., daily newspapers, law reviews, and other serial titles with simple, regular, publication patterns. Acquisitions staff handled the irregular serial publication types prolific in legal publishing. Serial check-in records were created based on two criteria: (1) titles routed to faculty were handled first; (2) titles received most frequently were handled next, i.e., dailies, weeklies, monthlies, etc. Within several months the majority of the needed check-in records had been created. Cataloging and special project staff energies were redirected to cataloging; acquisitions staff focused on all the other procedures of acquisitions.

In the cataloging unit, tasks that had been mechanized by the cataloger's toolkit had to be analyzed and modified for Voyager. With the assistance of staff at the University Library, new macros were created to import OCLC records into Voyager. Because the law library became a Name Authority Cooperative (NACO) participant in 1997, it was important to continue that participation in Voyager. Macros to export Name Authority records for NACO from Voyager to OCLC were established. Another OCLC-related process that needed rethinking was attaching the library's holdings symbol to OCLC records. During the NOTIS years, University Library systems staff sent computer tapes of law library catalog records to OCLC for loading and attachment of the law library's holdings symbol to OCLC records. The law library became responsible for updating OCLC records locally. The method of online updating in OCLC by the catalogers was selected, as it accommodated the low volume of new titles added.

Work-saving opportunities in the Voyager cataloging module appeared in the use of templates and macros. The Voyager system offers the ability to create and store templates for the four types of record components: bibliographic, authority, holdings, and item records. Installed as files on the local PC, each Voyager operator can save and use templates as needed. Catalogers created and used the templates initially. The catalog librarian subsequently worked with each acquisitions staff member to install templates suitable to each individual's work. The catalog librarian also developed the use of macros. Using a commercial software product, and inspired by the work of Auburn University's macros for Voyager, macros were created for local needs. One example of this is the macro to retrieve a bibliographic record by bibliographic record ID number. The macro reduces five steps and mouse clicks to a single sequence using one keyboard command. Again, the catalog librarian worked with each acquisitions staff member to develop macros for use in the acquisitions/serials module. While only sometimes a time-saver, the macros are always an ergonomic benefit, since they save on wrist motion and the use of a computer mouse.

The high-level of customer satisfaction that the PLRC cataloging staff experienced in using the Voyager catalog module was particular to our situation. The tools and templates available to the PLRC in NOTIS were limited. Voyager gave the PLRC staff new efficiencies in cataloging. However, the University Library catalog department had been making different use of tools and templates in NOTIS. Cataloging in Voyager became less efficient and more time-consuming at the University Library.

One other add-on software program installed on all staff PCs was one to print Voyager screens, since Voyager does not have a print option on each and every screen. These screen prints were invaluable for training purposes and problem resolution. In the first months of implementation, the bibliographic services staff succeeded in wrestling Voyager into a tool for daily performance of essential activities that had been done in NOTIS.

STAFFING NEEDS

By the spring of 1999, the economies and costs in terms of staffing and workflow in the Voyager library management system were apparent. The work of shifting staff and realigning procedures in bibliographic services to match those economies and costs came next. Other factors that had been ongoing with the new law school and library management were the emphasis on services combined with an acquisitions budget that was not able to keep pace with the increase in cost of serials. The migration year was also the serials review year. The library's collection development committee evaluated each serial title that came up for renewal. With an increased portion of the acquisitions budget being spent to acquire serials and electronic resources, the monograph acquisition rate declined.

It became apparent that new skills were needed in the bibliographic services department after several months of Voyager use. There were some NOTIS-based products that were not available with Voyager as canned ready-to-use products. One example of this was the new acquisitions list. In the NOTIS environment, computer tapes of newly cataloged titles were printed by a commercial service in the form of a printed new acquisitions list, distributed monthly to the law faculty. There was no canned report for this in Voyager; one would need to be created. Because Voyager uses a relational database it has a wealth of information that can be used for collection management. However, many of the queries and reports for this kind of information would have to be custom-produced. Even with the prospect of additional canned reports coming from the system vendor in the future, there would be interest and need for local information requiring local programming. The law library had no history of library systems analysts or computer programmers on staff. All NOTIS development work for Northwestern University had been performed at the University Library.

After six months of use of the new system, it became obvious that getting comfortable with the idea of change was not the same as being comfortable with the fact of change. That required flexibility, and a lot of encouragement. Some staff members were more at ease with the new system than others. Not all were early adopters. It became time to work with staff on expanded training to achieve new levels of job mastery in Voyager. The staff was experiencing the same kind of "changes in relationships that come with the introduction of a new 'family member'."[8] This time Voyager was the new member of the family, and it had moved in and taken over.

STAFFING CHANGES

It was time for realignment of responsibilities in order to use each individual's skills to optimum benefit in tandem with the features of the new library management system. It was decided that job audits should be performed for each position in bibliographic services, examining what work each person was responsible for, and how the library management system and workflow helped or hindered staff to succeed in their work. This job audit process was discussed with the bibliographic services staff at the start of the process.

At the start of this process, the special projects unit consisted of a catalog librarian, assisted by one of the library clerks from the cataloging area who handled the remarking of reclassified and recataloged materials. In the cataloging area, there was a catalog librarian, two cataloging assistants, and two cataloging clerks. The librarian handled original cataloging, electronic resources, and complicated copy cataloging. One of the cataloging assistants did MARC copy cataloging, including upgrading CIP records to full level. The other cataloging assistant focused on database maintenance activities, processing withdrawals, transfers, corrections, and maintaining the department's cataloging resource materials, i.e., the MARC and other documentation received in print version. While the one cataloging clerk already mentioned processed all reclassified materials, the other cataloging clerk did the physical processing of all new materials.

In acquisitions, the day-to-day activities were supervised by the acquisitions librarian, and supported by five library assistants. An acquisitions assistant handled the finances and accounts for the purchase of collection materials. Of the two serials assistants, one acted as serials manager to place orders and claim materials; the other serials assistant checked-in new materials and routed material to law faculty. Another acquisitions assistant handled monograph orders and receipts. There was also an acquisitions assistant who supervised the bindery activities, which are substantial in a collection that is mostly serials.

After the job audit, it was decided to continue the special projects staffing at the same level. However, there needed to be adjustments between acquisitions and cataloging. As it developed, no additional staff positions were needed, but specific staff shifts were needed. Because of the declining level of receipts of new monograph materials, there were fewer new MARC copy titles. With the efficiencies in cataloging in Voyager, and with the level of monograph ordering declining, it appeared that one person could handle both MARC copy cataloging for monographs and acquisitions ordering and receipts for monographs. This revamped position became the monographs assistant position and followed an unanticipated resignation by the monographs acquisitions staff member who returned to school to complete a degree program. The cataloging assistant who handled MARC cataloging became the monographs assistant, known colloquially and affectionately by co-workers as the "acqualoger."

Serials check-in was the area that proved to be the "black hole" in the new system because of the great amount of time and large number of steps involved in setting up and creating check-in records. Also, future releases of the software were scheduled to incorporate more and more steps into the check-in process, including the creation of the item record. The routing of serial materials to the law faculty is an important service in the PLRC, which requires daily processing. With the law collection being predominantly serials, the serials check-in assistant became overburdened and a second serials check-in position was defined. This change still added no new positions to the department because the monographs assistant position shifted to become the second serials check-in assistant.

Another unanticipated vacancy occurred with the retirement of the other cataloging assistant, following twenty-seven years of service. The processing of database maintenance information performed by this cataloging assistant was divided among several members of the bibliographic services department, depending on the nature of the activity. Our new need was for staff who could work with the library management system and its relational database, and staffing was reconfigured accordingly. An individual with a master's degree in computer science has been added to the bibliographic service department staff, in the position of the library management systems specialist. This position marks a new category of staff with a different kind of education than has been hired traditionally at the PLRC. The focus of the new position will be to develop customized reports for management use, as well as to devise new information products and services in an environment that is increasingly web-oriented.

During this time of staffing realignment, other activities came into the department. Traditionally, the heavy volume of loose-leafs were filed by a commercial service, and supervised by a public services staff member. The transfer of the loose-leaf filing supervision from public services to bibliographic services had been explored before the new system was in place in order to accommodate reorganization in public services. The structure of the Voyager acquisitions module data screens makes the check-in data for loose-leafs complex to interpret, and required the expertise of serials staff who work with this kind of data routinely. It seemed like a natural transition to move this activity to bibliographic services. The outsourced, commercial service was continued, but the supervision of the activity moved to the bindery assistant.

While acquisitions staff assumed this responsibility for loose-leafs, adding an activity to the bibliographic services department, another realignment occurred that resulted in transferring the cataloging of some U.S. government documents to government documents staff, part of the public services department. MARCIVE records are imported into the database on a regular basis. Bibliographic records are created upon import for certain U.S. government documents acquired by the PLRC as a partial depository library. The government documents library assistant, after training and review by catalog staff, now performs MARCIVE copy cataloging for selected items. The government documents library assistant accepts the MARCIVE copy, completes the holding record information, and creates an item record with barcode information. These materials never come into the cataloging area now. Statistics are kept for this cataloging activity, and reported with other cataloging statistics. Cataloging staff now refer to the government documents area as a cataloging "satellite."

Just as library management systems lend themselves to a single technical services interface that combines acquisitions/serials and cataloging functions for highest performance and efficiency, it seems as though technical services departments, too, are moving in the same direction. The lines between what is an acquisitions activity and what is a cataloging activity, while sometimes clear, at other times overlap. It is useful to have someone with a cataloger's training initiating the bibliographic record required to support purchase order activity. It is useful to have catalogers share an understanding of subscription data from the acquisitions records.

NEW DIRECTIONS

Other adaptations in cataloging and dissemination of information continue. In 1996 the School of Law received a gift of some of the United States Supreme Court papers of Associate Justice Arthur J. Goldberg, a 1930 alumnus. It was decided to share these Supreme Court papers, a unique resource, through digitization of the papers.[9] However, special processing and funding were needed to process these materials, since the PLRC staff had no experience with archival collections. Traditionally, all archival collections had been sent to the archives of Northwestern University for processing and retention.

A grant from the Illinois State Library funded this digitization project. The funding allowed the PLRC to retain outside experts to help with a "best practices" approach to the digitization project. For this project, several agencies collaborated. Personnel from the University Library provided significant assistance. University Archives prepared the first container list of the collection. Contract archivists enhanced the container list with item level descriptions of those materials that were digitized. The project director at PLRC prepared an Excel spreadsheet for purposes of numbering items to be digitized (to ensure that each item had a unique item number) and connecting item number with item description. An outside vendor digitized selected items creating an archival TIFF file for each image. From the archival TIFF images, additional derivative images were prepared in a variety of formats (GIF, JPEG, PDF) for use on the PLRC's web page.

Other transitions in cataloging include the adoption of the OCLC PromptCat service. This outsourced activity to deliver catalog records of new monographic acquisitions, along with setting the library's holding symbol on OCLC records, will streamline internal processing. The PromptCat records will be enriched by Table of Contents (TOC) data supplied by Blackwell's Book Services, the primary book vendor for the PLRC. The Voyager OPAC presents TOC data as a special tab in the OPAC, and permits searching of the TOC field. This provides additional information resources finding tools for the online catalog users. Blackwell's will transmit the TOC data to OCLC electronically. OCLC will add the TOC data to the PromptCat records sent to the PLRC electronically on a weekly basis.

The Voyager system also has the capability of linking bibliographic records to Internet sites, via the 856 field in the MARC record. Several electronic resources are linked in the NUcat Voyager online catalog[10] and on the PLRC web page.[11] This includes both Internet access subscription resources, such as the LegalTrac database, and some full-text journal resources such as are available from Oxford Online. The catalog librarian has received on-the-job training to design and work with web resources, and has played a pivotal role in the cataloging of electronic resources and creating the links to these kinds of resources. This level of this kind of cataloging activity will only increase in the coming years.

Another feature of the new library management system soon to be incorporated into the library's acquisitions workflow is Electronic Data Interchange (EDI). The PLRC plans to use EDI whenever possible for the communication of purchase orders, claims, and invoices between the acquisitions staff and vendors and publishers.

CONCLUSION

The inevitability of change and technological developments will mean that there will be other transitions for the PLRC in the 21st century. It is likely that the current library management system will not be in place for the tenure that NOTIS had at Northwestern. The NOTIS run of eighteen years is almost infinity, technologically speaking. The shelf life of today's library management systems will likely be much less than that of the pioneering library management systems, such as NOTIS. In a services-oriented organization, it is important to "not let technology become a limitation to our perspectives."[12] Services should be designed based on needs and imagination, on service to the library user, and not just on what is technologically feasible.

NOTES

1. James A. Rahl and Kurt Schwerin, *Northwestern University School of Law–A Short History* (Chicago: Northwestern University School of Law, 1960), 69.

2. Frederick C. Hicks, *Yale Law Library Classification* (Yale University Press: 1939).

3. Kurt Schwerin, *Classification for International Law and Relations* (Dobbs Ferry, NY: Oceana Pub., 1969).

4. Ann Wiley Van Hassel, "Current Comments: Northwestern University School of Law Receives Grant for Library." *Law Library Journal* 74(1): 225, 1981.

5. *Anglo-American Cataloguing Rules*, 2d ed., edited by Michael Gorman and Paul W. Winkler (Chicago: ALA, 1978).

6. Gary L. Strawn, *User's guide to accompany CLARR, the cataloger's toolkit* (Evanston: Northwestern University, 1995).

7. Northwestern University Law Library Training Team, *Summer of Skills Building* (Chicago: Northwestern University Law Library, 1997).

8. Kathryn Luther Henderson, "The New Technology and Competencies for 'The Most Typical' of the Activities of Libraries: Technical Services," *Professional*

Competencies–Technology and the Librarian, edited by Linda C. Smith, p. 31. (Graduate School of Library and Information Science, University of Illinois at Urbana–Champaign: 1983), 31.

9. Christopher Simoni, email message to the author, 03 October 1999.

10. Welcome to NUcatWeb: Catalog of the Northwestern University Libraries. <URL: *http://www.nucat.library.nwu.edu* > (1999)

11. Northwestern Law Pritzker Legal Research Center. <URL: *http://www.law.nwu.edu/lawlibrary/*> (1999)

12. Karen L. Horny, "New Turns for a New Century: Library Services in the Information Era," *Library Resources & Technical Services* 31(1):11 (Jan./Mar. 1987).

ACADEMIC LIBRARIES

Exploding Out of the MARC Box: Building New Roles for Cataloging Departments

Judith Ahronheim
Lynn Marko

SUMMARY. A new, less catalog-centric model for library services has begun to develop. There are places within this new model for catalogers and cataloging departments to contribute in new and more challenging ways than has been the current practice. Catalogers will need to apply old skills in new ways and departments will have to restructure in order to facilitate their service. Management of these new departments requires emphasis on different skills from those used in traditional departments. *[Article copies available for a fee from The Haworth Document Delivery Service: 1-800-342-9678. E-mail address: <getinfo@haworthpressinc.com> Website: <http://www.HaworthPress.com>]*

KEYWORDS. Cataloging, metadata, library management

Judith Ahronheim has recently become the University of Michigan Library's Descriptive Metadata Specialist, after having been Head of their Original Cataloging Unit for seven years. She has made a number of metadata presentations to both library and non-library audiences in recent years.

Lynn Marko is Head of Monograph Cataloging Division at the University of Michigan Library, a position that she has held for many years. She has been an active participant in all seven Dublin Core Metadata Workshops and has published several articles and given many talks on the wider view of cataloging.

[Haworth co-indexing entry note]: "Exploding Out of the MARC Box: Building New Roles for Cataloging Departments." Ahronheim, Judith, and Lynn Marko. Co-published simultaneously in *Cataloging & Classification Quarterly* (The Haworth Information Press, an imprint of The Haworth Press, Inc.) Vol. 30, No. 2/3, 2000, pp. 217-225; and: *Managing Cataloging and the Organization of Information: Philosophies, Practices and Challenges at the Onset of the 21st Century* (ed: Ruth C. Carter) The Haworth Information Press, an imprint of The Haworth Press, Inc., 2000, pp. 217-225. Single or multiple copies of this article are available for a fee from The Haworth Document Delivery Service [1-800-342-9678, 9:00 a.m. - 5:00 p.m. (EST). E-mail address: getinfo@haworthpressinc.com].

EXPLODING OUT OF THE MARC BOX

The University of Michigan Library has a long and rich tradition of a well supported research library collection which also has been well supported in terms of bibliographic control. At this point, bibliographic control services are somewhat distributed with cataloging occurring centrally through the monograph and serials divisions as well as area program services. In addition, cataloging services are provided beyond traditional technical services in maps, archives, and special collections. Monograph Cataloging Division has responded over the years to very real administrative and service pressures to provide cataloging services that are responsive to user needs. Such services required of the department include not backlogging newly acquired material, but cataloging it promptly through continuously improving copy cataloging techniques and modified minimal level original cataloging, called Brief Record Cataloging. Over the years, original cataloging has become the province of highly trained support staff which has allowed the development of change and growth oriented roles for the professional cataloging librarian. In this article, we will describe some of the change and growth opportunities that we have seen and outline a vision for the cataloger and cataloging department for the next decade.

Much of the recent literature relating to cataloging focuses on process improvement. We learn how libraries organize their work processes, either within the library itself or in association with outside vendors through the purchase of goods and services. We also learn how libraries continuously seek to enhance their services and provide high quality, low cost service to the Community which they serve.

The cataloging function in our department, as is the case in most large, research libraries, has undergone its share of cost studies, service review, evaluation, and cost containment efforts over the years. This presents a dual challenge to today's manager, to contain costs while pursuing innovation. In this challenge, there is opportunity. Even though cost, efficiency, accuracy and adherence to standards are important parts of what we do, we feel that catalogers and cataloging have very important additional contributions to make to the new information environment.

As libraries add networked digital resources to their collections, a new library infrastructure has begun to develop. While the catalog continues to play a role in the identification of useful information, it must share that function with a wide array of additional tools, some vendor provided, that operate using different principles and vocabularies of description. Looking at this wider information universe, we need to make certain that while we are providing programmatic support for cataloging services, we carve out resources for new initiatives. How one manages the traditional pressures of production along with participation in the information universe, is always going to be a challenge. And how a library determines it will meet those challenges, also determines the shape of the organization structure that is going to be used.

The cataloging department of even the near future is going to need to develop some new skills as new models of organization emerge within the rest of the library and the university. Flexibility of staff and their view of their core assignment is going to be a key component of success. Collaborative models within and in association with other departments are going to need to be encouraged and fostered. Project orientation and management skills will be another important component. This will necessitate a flatter supervisory structure that is characterized by collegial relationships which have trust as both a hallmark and primary component.

In addition, the ability to change in response to these developments will determine how effective, integrated, and forward looking the department is as it provides services to support legacy print, electronic, and web-based resources. In this article, we hope to focus on the elements of that cataloging department of the future This will be a department that provides tools to manage those resources and which contains staff members who combine traditional cataloging skills with new tasks, expertise and relationships.

METADATA SPECIALIZATION

If the library's service posture is not to become fragmented and chaotic, methods must be devised that relate description, discovery, and delivery tools to one another in some fashion that makes sense to users. In addition, the ease of moving from one resource to another within a network raises user expectations of interoperability, of being able to take information from one resource and apply it in another. Central to these sense-making and cross resource functions is the type of information we call metadata. Libraries will need to develop expertise in understanding how a multitude of profit and nonprofit communities have chosen to structure their resources and resource descriptions with a view to making them work together. One title for someone with this expertise is "metadata specialist." Such an individual will work collaboratively, as a member of a project team, either integrating existing resources into the library system or helping in the resource's creation. As part of this function, the specialist facilitates the bringing of independently developed resources under the Library's umbrella by encouraging the development and use of standardized management tools.

For a cataloger or other technical services staff member to become such a specialist, he or she will need to develop or strengthen him- or her-self in several ways. First and foremost he/she must develop a broader vision of the information universe and an acceptance that MARC/AARC2 will not be the best answer for every problem. Second is to cultivate an understanding of the development of non-library-based descriptive traditions and an awareness of new developments in taxonomies and hierarchies specific to specific knowledge domains. Further, catalogers need to develop greater comfort and understanding of formats like image and sound based resources, not just filtered through AACR2 colored glasses, but in all their capabilities and granular richness. For example, the CIMI extensions to Dublin Core include emphasis on aspects of the objects they describe that are not emphasized in AACR2 desciptions. Or, in fields in biological specimen databases where taxonomic description is a major access point, but whose richness and relationships are not reflected in standard library description.

Catalogers are already experts in the interactions of one search and delivery system: the MARC/OPAC one. We know the effect changes made in a MARC record will have on public displays and on system response to searches in the OPAC. Now, as metadata specialists, we need to learn about other systems that exist and are being developed, so that we can make similar predictions about how our records will display and index in those systems and how other systems' metadata will display and index when shared with ours. As standard search tools integrate, through standards like Z39.50, we will also need to be aware of the impact of our decisions on those more generalized displays.

In addition, catalogers moving into these broader metadata realms, need to be far more proactive than we have been in the past. We need to be able to place ourselves on development and deployment teams and make the case for our value to them. We need to seek out projects as they develop and insert ourselves into the planning process. This requires the development of new kinds of cross community people skills.

As part of projects that create or mount resources, we need to learn effective ways to manage projects: making reliable estimates to time and funding needs, identifying goals, scheduling, breaking projects down into smaller tasks, sharing workloads, working with partners from different intellectual traditions respecting what each partner brings to the table, knowing what to do when project directions change midstream, defining change control issues to managers, identifying missing tasks, contingency planning, developing milestones, getting commitment from people you don't manage, moving from project into general production, reporting project status to others, and serving several masters at the same time. Our collaborative skills need to be raised to a higher level. Equally important, we need to be prepared to accept responsibility for the projects of others with a collaborative mindset. We need to learn a new culture that encourages sharing rather than control.

ADMINISTRATIVE SUPPORT

Getting from here to there, is a long, and thoughtful process. The first thing that is needed is a library vision and a vision of, in particular, the services that the library is going to offer. Furthermore, administrative support and understanding of the demands of the information environment is needed and that means attendance at conferences that are not necessarily always library conferences and as a result have a higher level of expense that we are used to for registration fees. Attendance at these conferences is not always comfortable because we are not among known colleagues but among professionals who have their own language, their own jargon, and their own ways in which they relate to one another. We need to extend beyond our library domains and in so doing cultivate a common point of view over a period of time with non-library information professionals in non-library communities.

The second step in all this is, frankly, to bring it home. Going to conferences is often a challenging and career enhancing experience that creates excitement, but if there is no opportunity at home to use the new information, the new skill set, the new tools, there isn't an opportunity to solidify the new skills through practical application. The institution needs to provide the support, not just for travel to non-library conferences, but also to be willing to provide practice experiences for the attendee who returns from such trips needing a way to begin applying the new knowledge learned. Small pilots provide hands-on experience that speaks louder than any number of training sessions and workshops.

STANDARDS

The network accessibility of databases has presented new challenges to communities outside as well as inside the library profession. Practitioners operating in a wide variety of fields now attempt to locate and share information that resides in other practitioners' databases. Equally importantly, the idea of the "reusability" of research data is being encouraged by that major grant funder the Federal Government.[1] Such impelling forces have begun to encourage a variety of commumities to come together in an attempt to standardize the description of resources in their particular fields. Thus we see standards developing in the art museum community, the natural history community, and more broadly, in the Internet community as a whole. But we cannot contribute if we do not participate, and we cannot participate if we are not willing to make use of the standards being developed. Any improvement in the consistency of description of resources benefits us because we can develop more consistent processes for handling the descriptions and using them in conjunction with others to provide users with comprehensible description and access to resources.

This does not mean we should translate all data into MARC/ AACR2. It is important for us, as we move into new information arenas, to understand when MARC/AACR2 is not appropriate and to develop comfort levels with other schema that will allow us to choose tools that are appropriate to the description and access problems that face us. Staff need to have comfort with a variety of schema. Such comfort allows staff to make effective decisions on appropriate schema use for differing purposes.

As librarians begin to participate in the development of new descriptive standards with other communities, we bring to the table a wealth of experience and tradition from our own profession. Perhaps the most valuable contribution we can make to standards discussions is a respect for the long-term value of both the resources and their descriptions. Our experience in maintaining descriptions over long periods of time and incorporating new functionality into systems while retaining older forms has useful lessons for other practitioners. As a profession, we have thought about these complexities and, even when our solutions are not perfect fits for others, we can offer them the benefit of our experience in having extensively thought about them. Librarians have made significant contributions, for example, to the development of GILS, FGDC, and Dublin Core descriptive standards.

POSITIONING

How do we position catalogers to provide this new kind of service? We need to identify for ourselves what are the long term values of cataloging that have meaning beyond the library field and which values we are ready to compromise on or discard. Outsourcing need not be the enemy. Deciding when local customization is truly necessary and when acceptance of other's work is acceptable should be a basic component of planning and strategy development. But that transfer of work should not mean that catalogers are let go. Freeing up catalogers to do more complicated work means that you can customize where the added value means something to users. For example, if we believe that authority control is a vital part of the value we add, we need to be prepared to make that case in the criteria we require in outside resources and we need to be willing to work with others investing time in designing tools that will apply authority control outside a pre-existing resource that we cannot control.

We need to participate in non-library conferences where standards are being developed and make connections with actors from other traditions. And to do it at lower functional levels, rather than just at the upper management level. If we are asking catalogers to represent a library point of view, they need to begin talking to people other than librarians. That means attending and listening carefully to presentations by practitioners of the fields we are attempting to serve. This activity enhances the metadata specialist's ability to speak the language of fellow team members and gives him/her greater legitimacy in the eyes of co-workers.

We need to find out what the rest of our local community is doing. The ready availability of inexpensive software for creation of databases means that valuable collection-worthy resources are being developed under someone's desk. If you don't know that someone, you don't know it's there. Getting that data out where others can find and use it provides a value-added service that is not collection-based, but yet still partakes of the Library's mission. But finding such resources requires much greater involvement in our user communities and the building of a higher level of trust with resource creators that we will respect their efforts and perpetuate their purposes as well as our own. Long-term, the building of such relationships and services means there will be a greater chance of preserving these resources when their creators move on to other things. However, upon accepting these resources, we make a commitment to maintenance, whose burdens can be *intense*. It therefore behooves us to take care in our decisions and to encourage standards-based development at every opportunity.

MANAGEMENT

Getting metadata specialists into such productive relationships means they have to be respected by team members. While some of that respect will develop from the specialist's contribution to the group, the specialist starting out needs something even more important: the demonstrated respect of her institution. If what she knows and does is not valued there, it will show to others and what she does will not be valued elsewhere.

Managing a department that contains these types of specialists becomes more and more complex. Before, skill sets were uniform and a manager could easily judge competence and effective work. New, varied skill sets involve more trust. A manager must understand at some level the work and it must make sense, but the manager must also trust the specialist to do the job and sometimes even to judge the necessity of the job. Such a manager must have comfort with staff expertise that surpasses her own, yet manage her own expertise in such a way as to remain aware of the technical, budget and system pressures facing the staff

The constantly changing information universe that doesn't allow itself to be statically organized can revitalize a department. The dynamism is very real and it can become a part of the Cataloging Department life and work. Our production environments with all their cost pressures, service pressures and requirements for redundancy in response to reliability expectations can be reinvented on a far more dynamic model. We ask ourselves and our staffs to apply the fundamentals of our knowledge based experience in this new and exciting world. It's hard. It's risky. It's a challenge. And we love it.

NOTE

1. See proposed amendments to OMB Circular A-110, "Uniform Administrative Requirements for Grants and Agreements with Institutions of Higher Education, Hospitals, and Other Non-Profit Organizations." (http://www.gcdis.usgcrp.oov/policies/a-110rev.html).

Cataloging
at the University of Massachusetts
Amherst Library

Patricia Banach
Melvin Carlson, Jr.

SUMMARY. The paper deals with the cataloging operations at the University of Massachusetts Library that take place in three departments in the Collection Management Cluster. Recent changes in cataloging routines came as a result of new technology, as well as the manner in which cataloging staff are utilized. Also noted are the cooperative efforts in which the library is involved and the possible future in cataloging electronic materials. *[Article copies available for a fee from The Haworth Document Delivery Service: 1-800-342-9678. E-mail address: <getinfo@haworth pressinc.com> Website: <http://www.HaworthPress.com>]*

KEYWORDS. Cataloging, catalog, University of Massachusetts Amherst, workflow, electronic resources

Patricia Banach is Associate Director for Collection Management, W.E.B. Du Bois Library, University of Massachusetts Amherst, Amherst, MA 01003. She holds an MLS (1972) from Simmons College and an MA (1979) from the University of Massachusetts Amherst (E-mail: banach@library.umass.edu).

Melvin Carlson, Jr. is Head, Cataloging Department. He holds an MS (1966) from the University of Illinois, Urbana-Champaign, an MA (1979) from the University of Massachusetts Amherst and a DLS (1989) from Columbia University (E-mail: melvinc@ library.umass.edu).

[Haworth co-indexing entry note]: "Cataloging at the University of Massachusetts Amherst Library." Banach, Patricia, and Melvin Carlson, Jr. Co-published simultaneously in *Cataloging & Classification Quarterly* (The Haworth Information Press, an imprint of The Haworth Press, Inc.) Vol. 30, No. 2/3, 2000, pp. 227-239; and: *Managing Cataloging and the Organization of Information: Philosophies, Practices and Challenges at the Onset of the 21st Century* (ed: Ruth C. Carter) The Haworth Information Press, an imprint of The Haworth Press, Inc., 2000, pp. 227-239. Single or multiple copies of this article are available for a fee from The Haworth Document Delivery Service [1-800-342-9678, 9:00 a.m. - 5:00 p.m. (EST). E-mail address: getinfo@haworthpressinc.com].

If one were to review an organization chart of cataloging operations at the University Library, University of Massachusetts Amherst campus from twenty-five years ago and a chart from today, one would note that the organizational structure of those operations has remained stable. Cataloging was and still is done centrally in three departments within the Collection Management Cluster (formerly called the Technical Services Division). The organizational structure is perhaps the only constant in a sea of change.

ORGANIZATION

The Cataloging Department is responsible for cataloging the following types of materials: serials and monographs needing original bibliographic records; materials with incomplete OCLC copy; monographic continuations; microforms; CD-ROMs; electronic resources; scores and sound records; East Asian languages. The department is currently staffed by seven MLS catalogers, three cataloging assistants and a department secretary. The cataloging assistants are "grade 16" level staff, the highest non-professional personnel category in the library. Each cataloger has subject and/or language specialties and the paraprofessionals work in a team arrangement with a cataloger, particularly on special projects. The Information Processing Department is responsible for Library of Congress cataloging copy and English language OCLC copy with subject headings and classification. The department also handles database maintenance, both retrospective and current barcoding and linking, and end processing. Information Processing is staffed by two librarians, seven grade 16 cataloging assistants and seven FTE grade 12 library assistants. Some serials cataloging (LC copy, title changes, full OCLC copy) is also done in the Serials Section of the Acquisitions Department by a grade 16 cataloging assistant.

CATALOGING POLICIES AND PROCEDURES

The Library's cataloging policies and procedures adhere to national standards (AACR2 rev. and LCRI) and the Cataloging Department has recently contacted the Library of Congress to arrange for NACO training. The only exceptions to national standards are the treatment of University of Massachusetts Amherst theses and dissertations, and a small storage collection of Latin American materials. Theses and dissertations are cataloged according to an in-house standard that includes a special classification and subject scheme. The classification keeps all theses and dissertations classed together by degree level and provides a subject approach based on the subject of the department in which the degree is taken. We also provide Library of Congress subject headings for all of these works. The other example of non-standard treatment relates to a closed collection of Latin American materials that are represented in the OPAC with a minimal cataloging record and shelved by a numeric sequence. The library's holding symbol for these titles is set on OCLC if there is an available record. This approach was taken because we perceived that the materials might be little used and we did not have staff available to fully catalog them in the foreseeable future. If a patron requests a title from this collection, the item is fully cataloged for the general collections.

Aside from the non-standard treatment of the two categories noted above, the Library avoids variations from national norms due to unsuccessful past experiences. Certain variations to standard cataloging were attempted to provide quicker access to library materials or to provide better service to the Library's patrons. The cataloging of general pamphlets for many years was done with a minimal record and an abbreviated classification scheme. Another attempt involved classifying national bibliographies in a special number based on the Library of Congress classification. Both of these experiments proved to be confusing to patrons and librarians alike. The special handling required more cataloging and processing time than was necessary for the usual routine procedures. These variations were abandoned; items cataloged in these ways were then recataloged following usual cataloging routines.

SHARED CATALOGS

Following national standards has become increasingly important, not only because it leads to cost efficiencies, but also because libraries, including the UMass Library system, are participating in linked and virtual catalogs. The UMass Library catalog is part of the Five College shared catalog in a two database configuration. The Five College consortium consists of Amherst, Hampshire, Mount Holyoke and Smith Colleges and the University of Massachusetts Amherst. The Five Colleges have a long history of resource sharing and reciprocal borrowing which is now supported by two Innovative Interfaces, Inc. Innopac catalogs in which the catalog user chooses to search either the UMass Amherst Library catalog or the combined catalog of the other Four Colleges. With a single keystroke, the search can be repeated in the other catalog. In order to ensure that reciprocal searching is effective, both catalogs are indexed identically and a Five College Cataloging Committee meets regularly to agree on uniform cataloging practices.

While the Five Colleges have had shared catalogs since 1984 (they first shared an LS/2000 system), the trend today seems to be a link across disparate systems in what has come to be know as a virtual catalog. The UMass Amherst Library is a member of the Boston Library Consortium[1] (BLC) which has recently been negotiating to link the catalogs of their 16 members. If the BLC successfully accomplishes their goal, the combined resources of all of their members will be searched simultaneously and a deduplicated result set will be displayed for the library user. This is an ambitious project which underscores the necessity of adhering to national standards to maximize consistent data retrieval.

OUTSOURCING

Like other libraries, the University of Massachusetts Amherst Library has employed outsourcing as a tool to accomplish cataloging and cataloging related work which we felt could be more effectively and efficiently accomplished by outside agencies. The primary example of outsourcing at the UMass Amherst Libraries is authority control. The Library used Blackwell North America's authority control service until 1998 when it was sold to OCLC. Since then we have been doing very limited in-house authority control, and searching, with increasing urgency, for an acceptable alternative vendor. The considerable flux that has occurred during the past two years in the authority control service area has led us to delay making a decision on which service to use. What has become clear is that a service, once outsourced, is virtually impossible to perform in-house without significant staffing support. We are hopeful that we will have identified and contracted with an acceptable authority control vendor early in 2000.

Another more limited foray into outsourcing relates to our East Asian collection. When the Library's East Asian language cataloger retired in the late 1980s, the Library attempted to survive without one. One of the Library's catalogers worked with students of native language ability to catalog some monographs and serials and had the cataloging cards produced by a local vendor. The process had its limitations and it was also time consuming. To expedite the number of titles cataloged, the Library contracted with OCLC to produce catalog cards based on OCLC printouts supplied by the Library. Cards were a necessity because the East Asian collection, about 15,000 titles, was and is the only cataloged collection not fully represented in the online catalog. By this method several hundred titles were processed and made available for circulation.

Although this solution accomplished the goal of eliminating a cataloging backlog, it was not really very satisfactory. It still took a lot of time to administer this project and the cataloger involved, who had extremely limited knowledge of East Asian languages, spent the majority of her time on this project. A much more satisfactory, and creative solution was achieved when the Library hired an East Asian cataloger in 1996. The cataloger's appointment is at the University of Massachusetts Amherst, but her salary and expertise is shared among the libraries of the Five Colleges. This cataloger not only provides cataloging for each of the libraries of the Five Colleges, but also participates in collection development and provides reference services for each of the Five College libraries. This appointment requires that this individual know the interests of the faculty in each institution, as well as each library collection.

CHANGES IN PROCEDURES AND STAFFING

Although at the outset of this paper, we stated that the organization of cataloging has remained constant in our library, even through a major reassessment of the Library's organization as a whole which occurred throughout 1998, what has changed substantially in recent years is the *way* cataloging is done in the University of Massachusetts Library system.

The beginning of this change dates to 1995 when a cataloging task force was appointed to evaluate the level of scrutiny being focused on Library of Congress cataloging copy. The impetus for the task force's review was a cataloging backlog which resulted in some materials being cataloged as long as a year after receipt. Also, not even considered as a part of the backlog, was a substantial number of gifts kept in storage, and fed very slowly into the regular cataloging mix. As the backlog showed no sign of diminishing, and as the prospects for adding more cataloging staff were nil, the task force was charged with looking at how cataloging efficiency could be improved within the existing staffing complement.

At the time the task force began its review, Library of Congress cataloging copy was rigorously scrutinized by high level paraprofessional cataloging assistants. They were guided by detailed procedures which specified which fields in the MARC record were to be edited (virtually all of them) and what changes were required. Although the Library was a participating member of OCLC, and had recently migrated to an Innovative Interfaces Inc. online catalog (Innopac), we had a unique workflow which was based on in-house use of the Library of Congress MARC tapes to control the amount of material sent for cataloging. New receipts were entered into the workflow management system by keying in LC card numbers or ISBNs. These data elements were searched against an index to the MARC tapes and a controlled number of LC MARC edit sheets were produced and matched against books in the backlog. All editing was done manually on these paper edit sheets and then the changes were keyed into OCLC by input staff. The bibliographic records were subsequently extracted from OCLC and tape loaded to Innopac.

Because all LC copy was edited on paper worksheets, it was possible to accumulate the worksheets and evaluate the changes. A week's worth of worksheets was accumulated and the nature of the corrections was analyzed. After much discussion and considerable debate, it was decided that many of the changes being made had little or no impact on the retrieval of the record in an online catalog search (i.e., few indexed fields had serious errors). Consequently, the LC copy editing guidelines were radically changed and a new type of standard was applied to LC copy: "streamlined cataloging." Those whose work was most affected found these changes difficult to accept at first. They had developed considerable expertise and had long been encouraged to be very meticulous in their work. Some of them saw the changes as a devaluing of the quality control they had so long striven to maintain. This concern was shared by some members of both the professional and classified cataloging staff. However, all understood that the greater good to be achieved in reducing the backlog was the overriding goal. Also emphasized was the new benefit of allowing the cataloging assistants to work on more challenging OCLC member contributed copy. Although the "streamlined cataloging" procedures were introduced in May 1996, it was not until October 1996 that the cataloging assistants actually started turning their attention to OCLC member contributed copy, such was the backlog of LC copy to over-come.

The effect of channeling OCLC contributed copy to the cataloging assistants was a concomitant rise in the complexity and difficulty of the cataloging sent to the professional catalogers in the Cataloging Department. Where previously the catalogers reviewed and edited all OCLC contributed copy, under the new guidelines only foreign language OCLC copy and OCLC copy lacking subject headings and/or classification went to the catalogers in the Cataloging Department. This made all of their work much more difficult but also far worthier of their talents. The result of these changes was a gradual decrease in the backlog. Materials in the backlog were also prioritized so that the former policy of cataloging materials in order of receipt, however long that took, was modified such that science materials were given highest priority. It was painfully apparent that keeping recent science mono-graphs in a cataloging backlog for 6 months to almost a year was a serious disservice. Consequently science materials were culled ahead of other materials as a separate category. This led to achieving the goal of cataloging science materials on receipt months before that goal was achieved in other categories.

Other workflow changes were implemented subsequent to the deci-sion to perform streamlined cataloging on OCLC copy. In April 1997 catalogers and cataloging assistants discontinued manually editing paper worksheets and keying changes on OCLC for subsequent tape-loading of records to Innopac. Instead, all editing of bibliographic records was done directly on the Innopac system. This change not only saved at least three weeks time lag while tape loading occurred and materials were held, but also resulted in fewer OCLC searches per title cataloged. In the old workflow, OCLC was searched once at the point of record download into Innopac as part of the ordering process, again on receipt of the materials, to print an OCLC edit sheet, and again to call up the record to perform the input. In the new workflow, the record is downloaded from OCLC into Innopac and not searched again at all if it is an LC record. If it is an OCLC member contributed record, it is searched once more immediately prior to cataloging and the existing Innopac record is overlaid with the latest version in OCLC at that time.

Another key element in the progressive change in the way cataloging is performed and staffed occurred in March 1998 when a reclassification review of all support staff in the then Technical Services Division was completed by the University's Human Resources personnel. This review resulted in the reclassification of six library assistants to a higher classification. The result was that these staff members were authorized to perform streamlined LC copy cataloging, whereas in the past they were engaged primarily in data input and processing, and linking item records to bibliographic records. This reclassification substantially increased the pool of staff authorized to perform cataloging functions. In April 1999 a final change in workflow occurred in which, for most categories of materials, the cataloging review and the barcoding and linking were combined instead of being performed as separate operations by different people.

IMPACT OF TECHNOLOGY

Although changes in cataloging standards, and changes in the level of personnel assigned to various categories of cataloging were key factors in improved throughput time, another crucial element was the introduction of better technology. In 1995 all of the catalogers and cataloging assistants were provided with new PCs for the first time. The ability to open multiple sessions in a Windows environment enabled the cataloging staff to cut and paste a name heading from an authority record into an access point in a cataloging record both quickly and with no chance of typographical error. It also enabled them to cut and paste the call number from the bibliographic record into the item record where it is indexed, again with speed and guaranteed accuracy. This particular capability was crucial to the integrity of the new workflow previously described. Beyond the editing advantages of a Windows environment, the functionality of the PCs opened up a whole new range of possibilities. The library purchased multiple licenses to *Catalogers Desktop/Classification Plus* and networked the product. Training sessions were conducted and the catalogers in particular began to make increasing use of these online tools. As more LC schedules have been added to *Catalogers Desktop*, fewer and fewer paper copies of the LC schedules have been requested by the catalogers. Whereas in 1995 virtually every cataloger had a full set of LC schedules, now there is but one full set in the Department. Individual catalogers may still prefer a paper copy for their primary cataloging specialty, but far fewer paper copies are purchased. Multiple subscriptions to the Library of Congress *Cataloging Service Bulletin* were reduced, and fewer copies of AACR2 revised have been purchased.

Besides the externally produced and purchased cataloging tools available from the desktop, the catalogers have also benefited from the development of a Cataloging Department homepage. The Cataloging Department homepage has proven to be a resource that brings together information from a myriad of resources, including foreign language dictionaries, specialized format cataloging guidelines, Library of Congress files, other libraries' catalogs, to name but a few of the categories available for quick access.

The final step toward taking full advantage of an online networked environment for cataloging dates to January 1999 when the last group of cataloging staff, the recently upgraded library assistant category, received PCs to replace the Wyse 160 terminals they had been using. With all staff performing any level of cataloging having access to the Library network, it was decided that the two inch thick in-house cataloging manual should be converted from paper format to html for web-based access. A task force was charged to review the existing paper documentation, and convert all up-to-date procedures from Word versions to html versions using conversion software. Any documents considered to need correction are referred to the Cataloging Coordination Advisory Group, a group of six including the Heads of both the Information Processing Department and Cataloging Department, for discussion and revision. By November 1999, the manual was well along in its html coding and links were being created among documents. The net result will be a manual in which it is much easier to refer from one document to another related one, and 21 copies of every revision will not have to be distributed in paper format. Further, since not everyone who received a revised page of the manual always found the time to file it appropriately, the users of the new web-based manual will always be assured that they are referring to the current version of a policy and not a superseded one.

BACKLOGS ELIMINATED

The advent of technology based efficiencies, coupled with rethinking and revising cataloging standards has resulted in eliminating the previously existing backlogs. Also part of the equation is a flat acquisitions budget over several years which resulted in an erosion of monographic buying power as serials consumed an ever larger share of the acquisitions funds. The net effect of this combination of circumstances has been a change in attitude about cataloging priorities. Whereas in the past the cataloging operation seemed to be in a continual stage of siege in which any request for cataloging assistance was met with understandable resistance, today cataloging is in the enviable position of being able to catalog collections never before represented in the catalog. A primary example of this new responsiveness was the willingness of the Cataloging Department to begin cataloging unique or rare materials in the Library's Special Collections Department. Just one example of the materials cataloged from that department included a series of anti-slavery pamphlets that had not been reflected in OCLC or in the Library's own catalog. Another project undertaken by cataloging assistants in the Information Processing Department is the cataloging of United Nations documents also never before listed in the Library's online catalog. There are still other collections which need to be considered for cataloging (maps, microform analytics, NASA reports, pre-1976 U.S. government documents) as time and resources permit.

ELECTRONIC RESOURCES

It seems that the cataloging backlogs were eliminated just in time, as the library now confronts an entirely new type of cataloging not even considered in this library in 1995. Electronic journals and selected scholarly web sites have now expanded the scope of the library catalog beyond what is physically owned to what is electronically available. The Library has been cautious in opening what could be a floodgate when it comes to "cataloging the Internet." Our cataloging policies in this regard have evolved incrementally. The first category of material we tackled was electronic journals to which the library has paid subscriptions. It took an extended period of time to begin cataloging ejournals because of a lengthy debate over the one record vs. two record approach. The pros and cons of both approaches were discussed with public services librarians and the virtue of a single entry vs. the vice of overly complex records was debated. Ultimately, it was decided that separate records were best in an environment where the content of the online and paper versions of a resource seem to increasingly diverge. After the first round of cataloging our paid electronic journals was complete, we extended the cataloging policy to include those ejournals free by virtue of print subscriptions. Most recently, in September 1999, we have further extended the cataloging policy at the request of the science reference librarians, to include selected scholarly web sites.

Because the Library now has a web-based OPAC, Innovative Interfaces Webpac, the effect of cataloging electronic resources is that library patrons can directly access many full text resources by clicking on the URL in the cataloging record. Of course, with the cataloging of web-based resources came the continual need to maintain the URL's. Although the library's cataloging policy for electronic resources is quite modest and contained, the library also subscribes to the Marcive service for tape load of government documents records from the Government Printing Office (becoming a misnomer?). The GPO has abandoned print in favor of electronic versions of many of their publications and this policy has introduced hundreds of URLs into the catalog. In order to cope with the maintenance, a series of programs and procedures were developed that allow a paraprofessional to extract all records having URLs from Innopac, convert the file to html, employ web checking software to check the links, and then a report of broken links is output. These links are searched on the web, corrections made, and then referred to a cataloger for review. In this way broken links are kept to a minimum.

The next challenge for serials catalogers are those elusive titles included in aggregator databases such as InfoTrac and Lexis/Nexis. Some of the reference librarians in our Library have lobbied for inclusion of these electronic journal titles in our online catalog. While sympathetic to their request, the immense challenge of cataloging potentially thousands of electronic serial titles which are added and dropped with abandon, which are contained in whole or in part, and which do not have consistent periods of coverage, has proven to be a formidable obstacle to catalogers. However, the recent offer of the Tri-Colleges Consortium[2] to sell cataloging records for the titles contained in Lexis/Nexis and to maintain those titles to the extent possible, has been very enticing. We are currently discussing with our reference librarians the implication of purchasing these records and loading them to our online catalog. Since the only viable way for us to maintain the accuracy of these records is to delete them en masse and reload them when Tri-Colleges provides the next update, we feel that we made a wise choice when we decided to use the separate record approach to cataloging electronic journals.

The predominance of the World Wide Web as an information resource has posed a dilemma for libraries in trying to decide which resources to represent in the library catalog, and which to represent on the library homepage. The question is posed concerning whether students and other library users will continue to use the library catalog or whether they will gravitate toward the library homepage to the exclusion of the catalog. While not every resource or link on the library's homepage necessarily needs to be represented in the library's catalog, we suggest that ejournals and scholarly websites should be cataloged. Moreover, as the list of electronic resources continues to grow, well beyond the capability of simple alphabetic listings on web pages to provide meaningful access, the catalog becomes increasingly important. Electronic journals and scholarly web sites are much like any other growing and unwieldy collection. When it was a small, manageable number of titles and sites, a simple arrangement on the homepage was adequate. However, trying to represent the same set of titles in both the catalog and on the homepage becomes a large double maintenance effort unless the data is maintained only once. In the UMass Library several initiatives have been undertaken to leverage the cataloging records and extract them from the OPAC for use on the library's homepage. Several projects of this sort have been successful. In one case, new books in various subject categories are extracted on a regular basis from the library's OPAC and automatically converted to html for display as a new books list on the science branch libraries' homepages. The same routines are used to create new books lists for subject specific homepages maintained by some of the Library's bibliographers. In another case, serial titles targeted for cancellation were extracted from the OPAC with price data from the order record, automatically converted to html using software written for that purpose, and displayed on the library's homepage for faculty response. Projects of this sort, which leverage the cataloging record, make it relatively simple and very cost effective to maintain the data in the catalog and also display it on the library homepage.

CONCLUSION

Perhaps the most striking aspect of this overview of current cataloging practice and recent cataloging history at the University of Massachusetts Amherst is the capacity of the cataloging staff to adapt to an exceptional amount of change while continuing to provide organized access to an ever widening array of resources. The stereotype of catalogers set in their ways and bogged down in detail is not born out by the reality of cataloging at the onset of the new millennium at the University of Massachusetts Amherst, nor is it likely to be valid elsewhere. In the information age, with the overwhelming amount of electronic data proliferating, cataloging staff and their critical skills, are needed now as much as ever.

NOTES

1. Members of the Boston Library Consortium are: Boston College, Boston Public Library, Boston University, Brandeis, Brown, MBL/WHOI, MIT, Northeastern University, State Library of Mass., Tufts University, UMass Amherst, UMass Boston, UMass Dartmouth, UMass Lowell, UMass Medical Center, Wellesley College.

2. The Tri-College Consortium is comprised of Bryn Mawr, Haverford, and Swarthmore Colleges.

Pursuing the Three Ts:
How Total Quality Management, Technology, and Teams Transformed the Cataloging Department at Penn State

Marie Bednar
Roger Brisson
Judy Hewes

In truth, an inefficient or unproductive cataloging department is a failure of management. Libraries that do not devise means to use the accumulated expertise of their catalogers in innovative ways are wasting an invaluable human resource.

–Michael Gorman, 1995

SUMMARY. Beginning in 1992 the University Libraries at the Pennsylvania State University embarked on a program to formally transform

Marie Bednar, MLS, MA is Cataloging Coordinator in the University Libraries at the Pennsylvania State University, University Park, PA.

Roger Brisson, MLS, MA, is Digital Access Librarian and Selector for German Language & Literature in the University Libraries at the Pennsylvania State University, University Park, PA. He is in the PhD program in History at Penn State, and is currently writing his dissertation.

Judy Hewes, BA is Cataloging Coordinator in the University Libraries at the Pennsylvania State University, University Park, PA.

[Haworth co-indexing entry note]: "Pursuing the Three Ts: How Total Quality Management, Technology, and Teams Transformed the Cataloging Department at Penn State." Bednar, Marie, Roger Brisson, and Judy Hewes. Co-published simultaneously in *Cataloging & Classification Quarterly* (The Haworth Information Press, an imprint of The Haworth Press, Inc.) Vol. 30, No. 2/3, 2000, pp. 241-279; and: *Managing Cataloging and the Organization of Information: Philosophies, Practices and Challenges at the Onset of the 21st Century* (ed: Ruth C. Carter) The Haworth Information Press, an imprint of The Haworth Press, Inc., 2000, pp. 241-279. Single or multiple copies of this article are available for a fee from The Haworth Document Delivery Service [1-800-342-9678, 9:00 a.m. - 5:00 p.m. (EST). E-mail address: getinfo@haworthpress inc.com].

241

its organization following the principles of Continuous Quality Improvement, or, as it is more commonly known, Total Quality Management. The process by which the Cataloging Department underwent reorganization into teams is described, as well as its strategic use of computing technology in rationalizing and streamlining its workflows. In creating an organizational restructuring that permitted a more rapid and flexible response to new assignments and changing conditions, the Cataloging Department positioned itself to effectively assume new responsibilities as emerging formats and other library materials were acquired or made accessible to library patrons. The essay concludes with a frank assessment of the lessons learned in undergoing reorganization, as well as weighing the successes and failures experienced by the Cataloging Department. *[Article copies available for a fee from The Haworth Document Delivery Service: 1-800-342-9678. E-mail address: <getinfo@haworthpress inc.com> Website: <http://www.HaworthPress.com>]*

KEYWORDS. Total Quality Management (TQM), Continuous Quality Improvement (CQI), library management, library technology, cataloging management, teams

INTRODUCTION

Typical for a large university library in the early 1990s, the Cataloging Department at Penn State University processed several thousand items monthly. Depending on the month, between eight and fifteen thousand books, microforms, videos, audio CDs and cassettes, computer software, to name only the most prominent formats, passed through its workflows for cataloging before going on to the stacks of the many departments, branch and campus libraries that make up the university library system. Appearing in one or more of several dozen languages, these materials spanned the universe of human knowledge, ranging in topics from the most popular to the most esoteric. Not only were they accurately described and given a placeholder for future use in terms of inventory control, they also received intellectual analysis of their content and were provided with specialized headings from a complex controlled vocabulary. The department included a highly skilled staff with the ability to work quickly while simultaneously possessing a sharp eye for detail and accuracy; they needed to be comfortable working in numerous languages; and a broad enough understanding of the universe of knowledge was needed to adequately contextualize the materials processed in terms of their respective subject matter.

In the early 1990s a large number of cataloging departments in academic libraries found themselves confronted with numerous challenges, symptomatically expressed in an increasingly negative reputation for being able to adequately manage the flow of library materials acquired for their respective institutions. Although the work of the some 50 staff employed in the Cataloging Department at Penn State, as at other university libraries across the country, represented a significant accomplishment by any measure, what had originally been the quiet murmerings of administrators in the 1980s steadily rose to a vocal call for sweeping reform of cataloging practices. With the publication of Carol Mandel's and Dorothy Gregor's article "Cataloging Must Change," published in the April 1, 1991, issue of *Library Journal*, an open and often divisive national debate ensued. Setting aside the question whether the critics of existing practices were correct in their characterizations, by the early 90s it had become clear that cataloging departments were experiencing serious challenges in managing the flow of materials through their departments, and in their ability to respond to additional needs of patrons and the staff of other library departments. These challenges could be characterized in part by the seeming inability to address the growing backlogs resulting from long-entrenched cataloging practices and workflows.

Because of the similarities in confronting intractable obstacles by private industry and the technical service units in academic libraries, the management techniques emanating from Total Quality Management (TQM) principles appeared to offer a viable approach to tackling the chronic problems facing cataloging departments. As with many areas in industry, cataloging involves the flow of materials through discrete processing steps, and it employs definable tasks carried out by staff of varying qualification levels and experience. Throughout the 1990s a rich literature developed on the application of TQM principles for library administrations, indicating a clear interest in applying these principles in library environments. As at other academic libraries across the country at that time, the Universities Libraries at Penn State followed the lead of university administration in implementing Total Quality Management. This article will investigate how Penn State addressed the challenges of its own cataloging department by implementing TQM, the reorganization into teams, and strategic use of innovative computing technology. It should be noted at the outset, however, that this article should be regarded as a specific application of TQM within a particular context. As such a general knowledge of TQM and strategic planning will be assumed, though important principles will be explicated within the Penn State context as the narrative proceeds. There are now a number of introductory articles on TQM, as well as its use in libraries, and readers interested in obtaining general background before reading this article should consult these articles first.[1]

THE CRISIS IN CATALOGING

In their article, Gregor and Mandel succinctly outline the issues that cataloging departments had increasingly encountered in the latter half of the 1980s.[2] Though using a provocative title for their article, the two authors in reality cogently outline the factors leading to the problems that cataloging departments were facing at the time. Throughout the eighties most academic libraries had gradually migrated to online catalogs, adding new functionality and features as they became available. At the same time, with the growth and increasing effectiveness of library consortia and the national cataloging utilities, cataloging departments adapted and harmonized their work processes to the needs of these larger cataloging organizations.

To promote the sharing of records, inter-institutional cataloging standards became increasingly important, and these were added to the local policies and procedures used by cataloging departments. Gregor and Mandel astutely advocate what many others with less tact were also proposing: that catalogers spend less time following complex rules, a number of which were considered unnecessary, and spend more time developing the skills to better address the issues surrounding an increasingly complex online environment. The claim was that many of these rules may have been important for the older card-cataloging environment (or for the earliest generation of online catalogs, which had much in common with card catalogs), but for the newer catalogs with sophisticated keyword searching, authority control, and multiple headings, many of the rules still being adhered to were no longer believed to be relevant. The need for close conformity to Library of Congress practice, as well as striving for absolute consistency, seemed to have taken on self-supporting values in their own right, becoming a drain on professional and departmental resources, and requiring significant training programs.

At the same time, while shared cataloging continued to grow in both importance and quality, cataloging management in many libraries seemed incapable of adapting workflows to take productive advantage of the records made available by the cataloging utilities. Cataloging departments appeared to be self-absorbed, spending an inordinate amount of time attempting to maintain local practices and 'traditions.' Gregor and Mandel believed that a professional's time could be used more productively than in assuring that a little used rule interpretation or local policy, with virtually no impact on searchability, was applied. In the online environment, with its powerful and transformational searching capabilities, many of these rules originating from the era of card catalogs simply lost their value. In any case, there appeared to be much truth to the claim that a small but noteworthy percentage of these rules provided little benefit in better finding needed materials.[3]

Other factors, however, also played a role, factors that were not mentioned in the critical literature of the time. With hindsight one can recognize without much difficulty that the perceived soaring costs of cataloging had much to do with the high overhead resulting from still primitive computing technology (where little of the cataloging process was actually automated[4]), from the procedural and computing requirements of the cataloging utilities, and from the need to create records of a high national standard following complex rules. The perception that cataloging had become too costly because of inefficient methods and wasteful workflows was thus only partially true. A well-known tenet of TQM theorists was once again being demonstrated: that ineffective processes, as well as poor management, were more the culprits in creating cataloging backlogs, and not those who were the brunt of the critical literature at the time, the catalogers themselves.[5]

The MARC record that included full AACR2 cataloging is in reality a result of addressing a number of needs from several constituencies. By satisfying these constituencies, and by closely following LC practice, catalogers were in effect laying the foundation and developing the monumental international bibliographic databases, the large regional union catalogs, and the interconnected local catalogs (through the Z39.50 protocol) that have so transformed the current library landscape. Key aspects to insuring the success of large-scale cooperative cataloging were still undergoing development in the utilities, and hence their impact were only beginning to be noticed (prominent examples being the CIP program, the development of cooperative cataloging programs NACO and BIBCO, and, perhaps most importantly, the uploading of large datasets of retrospective cataloging from ARL libraries).

Library administrations thus often unfairly laid blame on cataloging departments for problems that had little to do with cataloging management or staff themselves. For example, the relatively primitive computing environments based on the legacy mainframes and 'dumb' terminals added significant procedural and workflow overhead to the cataloging process. Indeed much of the 80s and early 90s could be characterized as a time where a relatively tense relationship existed between technical services and computing systems staff. It often took years before even minor changes or system enhancements could be implemented by systems staff programmers (or by the library software vendor), since programming for the legacy mainframes was a monumental task. A typical problem dealing with system architecture was the inability for the various modules of an 'integrated' library system to share data. This inevitably meant the rekeying of data, which considered in terms of the several thousand records created monthly had a substantial impact on cataloging productivity.[6] Indeed, the shortcomings of the cataloging modules of the legacy mainframe software resulted in significant additional work on the part of cataloging staff.

While the above factors all contributed to the growing cataloging backlogs in the 1980s and early 1990s, the addition of new formats and more comprehensive levels of cataloging also played a noteworthy role. As powerful new searching capabilities of online catalogs were being added to successive upgrades of local library systems, the value of providing enhanced access to whole bodies of library material took on a new significance for library administrations. While serious discussion occurred at national meetings on the benefits of adding tables of contents to records, for example, the lack of institutional support allowed this to be implemented with only a minor impact on overall database quality. Formats that were formerly not cataloged at all or had possessed only a minimal presence in the main dictionary catalog, materials like microforms, maps, audio-visual materials, and large collections, suddenly rose significantly in value in light of the potential of the online environment. Here too a novel feature of online catalogs was little recognized by library administrations: the value of cataloging records rose noticeably as a library commodity once the catalog was transformed from a card to an electronic format. Not only could they be manipulated and searched in a far more powerful manner in the online environment, but with the click of a button they could also be multiplied and shared among a larger library community. The recognition of the enhanced value of these records by library administrations was an important factor in prioritizing the cataloging of neglected bibliographic formats, but few administrations were willing to increase the budget for this additional cataloging work. In any case, the apparent inability of cataloging management to effectively adapt to a rapidly changing environment made it difficult to justify expending additional resources to catalog these materials. A typical result was to simply add a large body of uncataloged material to a cataloging department's backlog as the recognition of providing access to them grew in value, without providing the additional resources to process the material.

Gregor and Mandel, as well as the more trenchant critics of the time, did play a positive role with their calls for change in compelling cataloging departments to take pause and reflect in a more fundamental manner about their raison d' être vis à vis a library's overarching mission in serving its patrons. It was becoming increasingly clear that cataloging departments could take greater strategic advantage of emerging computing and telecommunications technologies, as well as to streamline workflows by making use of the rapidly developing shared cataloging culture. Until the mid-1990s, little thought had been made in systematically employing technology to rationalize cataloging processes. In order to effect these changes, however, it was necessary to develop organizational and management structures where change would become a central part of this restructuring. Since private industry had embraced continuous quality improvement techniques to address the challenges of continuous environmental change, it seemed natural that libraries would look to these management strategies in addressing similar challenges.[7] But in order to come to terms with the competing tensions of taking advantage of new opportunities to enhance quality and the pressure coming from administrations to cut costs, cataloging management needed to carry out a sweeping assessment of its mission, values, and priorities vis à vis the 'customers' it served. These customers needed to be better defined and characterized in terms of primary and secondary customers, and internal and external customers. Equally subject to the challenges outlined by writers such as Gregor and Mandel, Penn State also realized by the early 90s that a radical rethinking of its cataloging operations was in order. Following the lead of the university's recent commitment to Total Quality Management, the University Libraries recognized the opportunities that arose with integrating these management techniques into its own operations.

PENN STATE'S RESPONSE TO THE CRISIS

The Cataloging Department in 1990

The situation at Penn State at the beginning of the 1990s was much like that characterized above. Though there was not a serious backlog of current incoming materials without cataloging copy, there were growing numbers of materials with minimal or incomplete records in the OPAC. In addition, several categories of materials, such as the nearly 20,000 rare books, were in a perpetual state of cataloging limbo, with no realistic plans in sight to provide full access to them. The Cataloging Department was guilty of taking the easy way out in addressing its responsibilities to its constituencies by handling large amounts of current materials with copy and doing full original cataloging on some priority titles but by postponing full cataloging of and gradually accumulating backlogs of hard-to-catalog titles.

In the early 90s the Cataloging Department possessed a layered, five-level hierarchical structure, with two sections responsible for cataloging–the Original Cataloging Section and the Bibliographic Processing Section (copy cataloging). Responsibilities, as well as the decision-making sphere of each of the hierarchical levels were very carefully circumscribed. The paraprofessional supervisors, under the direction of the librarian section head, generally made operational and procedural decisions. The large nucleus of the staff was made up of long-term library employees; a significant number had been working in the department for well over ten years, and some for over twenty years. Almost the entire staff was composed of permanent full-time employees, with the department making little use of student labor. Turnover among cataloging faculty was noticeably higher. In addition to their responsibilities with original cataloging, faculty supervised higher-level paraprofessionals and made cataloging policy decisions. The large copy cataloging staff (each person was responsible for copy cataloging of monographs, as well as another more complex format) was organized into three administrative groups supervised by paraprofessional staff. In addition to this organizational structure, another, task- and format-related structure emerged. There were eleven workgroups that cut across primary administrative lines and included faculty and staff from the entire department. These cataloging workgroups included Audio-Visual, Conference Proceedings, Microforms, Sets, Documents, Serials, Rare Books, Computer Files, Maps, Music, CJK and Juvenile materials. Until the department reorganized, these workgroups functioned only in an advisory and monitoring capacity; actual cataloging work was not structured around them. It was these workgroups, however, that later laid the groundwork for the eventual evolution into format teams and the dissolution of the hierarchical organization.

The cataloging process itself was based on an elaborate division of labor between five paraprofessional grades of staff and faculty catalogers. Each grade level performed defined tasks and was compensated according to those tasks. As a result, work that could not be completed at a particular level was referred to a higher grade-level for completion, all the way to the faculty catalogers. The non-supervisory staff had very little input into decisions on how the work was done. They were told exactly what to do and how to do it. In principal, this elaborate system of referrals was well developed and functioned like clockwork. At the time, the department was certainly proud of this complex workflow, and in many ways rightly so. The primary purpose of this organization was that the various levels of staff did routine cataloging based on qualifications and experience, including basic descriptive cataloging, and that faculty catalogers did only the most complicated work, such as subject analysis, assigning call numbers, and more complicated types of descriptive cataloging. However, handoffs and rework led to significant bodies of material being referred up the hierarchy for completion, sometimes going through several pairs of hands before finally being cataloged. Delays at each level, based on the concentrations of incoming material, were an integral part of the workflow and considered unavoidable. Increasing numbers of materials requiring referral all the way to the professional staff led to not insignificant backlogs accruing in the Original Cataloging Section. A large number of these referrals were a result of very minor aspects of a record requiring attention. As the TQM analysis groups began to look at processes throughout the library, it was becoming increasingly clear that the Cataloging Department was ripe for reorganization and the adoption of TQM principles: prioritizing goals and objectives, flattening the organization, empowerment of staff, reducing rework, streamlining processes, and focusing on the customer's needs.

CQI AND REORGANIZATION INTO TEAMS

TQM/CQI at Penn State

At the beginning of the 1990s, the entire university embraced Total Quality Management as a means of improving services provided to the university community, and at the same time it embarked on a sweeping program to increase the efficiency of its operations. As at other academic institutions, Penn State used the term Continuous Quality Improvement (CQI), rather than Total Quality Management, to better connote the ongoing process of change in committing to systematic, long-term improvement of its services. The management concepts that were introduced to faculty and staff proved to be a model that addressed the areas and issues the university as a whole had recognized to be problematic. Library administrators, in particular the Associate Dean for Information Access Services (technical services), gave full support to the concepts of TQM/CQI from the start. In the early 1990s, the Libraries, as in all other units of the University, were asked to come up with a permanent 10% operating budget reduction over several years. Cutting positions was part of the University Libraries' strategy to generate the needed savings. TQM, with its strong emphasis on streamlining processes, reducing workflows as well as handoffs, and a general promise of doing more with fewer people, seemed a promising method for striving to become a leaner and more productive organization, particularly for the very process-intensive technical services operations.

In July 1992, a two-day library retreat led by specialists from Oregon State University introduced the concepts of CQI to the university faculty and staff. Within that same year the University Libraries moved to introduce CQI concepts. The first quality team in the library was formed in the Cataloging Department to address issues involving pre-order searching. All staff were given a large notebook filled with orientation materials and essays on the various aspects of CQI. The Cataloging Department, as well as in other units in the library, began to develop a reference shelf devoted to TQM/CQI, which provided reading material for staff interested in learning more about such pertinent topics as working in teams, developing mission statements, TQM management principles, benchmarking, quality control, and the like. The university's Human Resources Development Center began offering workshops and classes on a number of CQI-related topics, and library administration encouraged staff to participate in these activities. By providing learning materials, and by emphasizing the need to make continuous staff learning a central part of CQI, the library had taken the first steps in formalizing the transformation to a *learning organization*.

CQI in Cataloging

The Cataloging Department as a whole began the CQI process by preparing its own mission and vision statements. Identifying shared values for the department was also part of this process. All staff and faculty were present at the mission/vision development meetings and contributed to identifying core values and the future direction of the department. The importance of shared values and a strong sense of working towards a common goal are often emphasized in the literature on teams.[8] It is critical that these initial activities involve *everyone* equally in the department, and that such steps as devising a mission statement or developing shared values are not delegated to work groups. In preparing for the anticipated reorganization, over a period of several months cataloging management embarked on an active, ongoing discussion of key aspects of CQI. For staff it represented quite a novel undertaking discussing, in open meetings, notions like who were the department's 'customers,' or what were the key values informing the staff's work. The shift from a hierarchical organization based on authority to a learning organization based on collaboration and empowerment was a radical shift in orientation for staff, and it required several months of adjusting for them to begin feeling comfortable working without the security of the structure inherent in a hierarchically organized department.

It should be noted that by no means did the CQI process proceed as smoothly as outlined in the management literature (or in the very brief analysis found in this essay, for that matter), and the difficulties encountered should not be underestimated. Except for the meetings of the copy cataloging section, the policy meetings of the faculty librarians, and the management meetings, the department as a whole was unaccustomed to regular meetings. As the CQI process gradually gained momentum, meetings became more frequent and they grew significantly in number. Staff who had developed a daily routine of cataloging-related activities now found themselves with an irregular schedule composed of ongoing meetings, close collaboration with colleagues, workshops, briefings, and the like. Many staff, to put it bluntly, reacted hostilely to these meetings, as well as to the very idea of teams. Having worked more or less independently within a large department for the past several years, the idea of working in a small, close-knit group was an uncomfortable thought for many. In addition, the language now employed in describing work processes seemed strange and gimmicky for many staff. At the time many participants attending these meetings found the exercises pointless and, as one reads frequently in the literature, criticized the CQI initiative as a passing fad. With hindsight one can only reflect back with humor on the almost burlesque manner in which many of these meetings proceeded. Whole meetings could be devoted to such trivial-seeming discussions as to whether the department had 'customers,' what a customer was, and in identifying the department's primary and secondary customers. Indeed, one could regard this as a reflection of how far the department needed to develop in its transformation into a true service orientation, for it took staff a good deal of effort to first admit that it even served 'customers,' and then to begin to understand the consequences of what followed from such a customer orientation. It should be mentioned here, however, that as an academic institution staff did not typically think in terms of having 'customers' at that time. Nevertheless, this process should be regarded as serving an important function, and that it took staff so much effort to conceptualize what it meant to have 'customers' was symptomatic of how removed the department was from being a truly responsive service organization.

In retrospect, one could perhaps fault those leading the CQI process at the time for not placing enough value on the need to *learn* communication skills for staff not accustomed to working closely in groups and making important decisions as part of a collaborative process.

This is a common problem in making the transition to an organization based on continuous quality principles. Communication and social skills are often neglected during the process, all too often they are simply assumed, and for these reasons one needs to be especially sensitive to the crucial role that learning and developing such skills play for successful staff interaction. Several workshops were held on the topic of working in teams, but in most cases communication was dealt with only cursorily during these sessions. The importance of communication skills could in any event be readily measured during CQI implementation at Penn State, since in general staff became markedly more proficient in productively communicating ideas in groups over time.

Though the difficulties of these early stages in the process require frank discussion, it should be emphasized that most staff acknowledged constructive progress throughout the CQI implementation, and today the large majority would affirm that, viewed as a whole, the transition to continuous quality principles was an important one for the future of the department. The process of finalizing the departmental mission and vision statements spanned over several months, but embodied in this work were numerous productive discussions that led to a more focused understanding of the Cataloging Department's purpose. Most importantly, this discussion was carried out, in varying degrees, among all staff. The version of the two statements developed at these challenging meetings have stood the test of time and have served the department well over the years, helping to chart the course of the department's activities since then. The following is the final version of the mission statement as it was approved by the department in 1993:

The Mission Statement of the Cataloging Department

July 29, 1993

To assist in meeting the mission of the Pennsylvania State University Libraries, the mission of Cataloging Services is to provide timely and accurate access to materials of the University Park, CES campus, Behrend, and Great Valley library locations. On a broader scale, we provide leadership in descriptive and subject cataloging, and consider it vital to maintain holdings and bibliographic information in The CAT and shared databases to support international resource sharing. We

provide friendly and quality service to the faculty, staff, and students of the University; the citizens of the Commonwealth; and other libraries, nationally and internationally.
We accomplish our mission by:

- *Creating and maintaining quality bibliographic records and authority control according to local and national standards for The CAT and other shared bibliographic databases;*
- *Contributing to the ongoing development of The CAT;*
- *Maintaining and providing physical access to the Libraries' collections through accurate inventory control, labeling of materials, and preservation of collections for present and future generations;*
- *Cooperating with other cataloging institutions to enrich shared databases;*
- *Maintaining in-depth knowledge of the principles of bibliographic description and access, and of national and international standards and their local applications, in order to serve the user community in problem-solving and advisory capacities;*
- *Creating a challenging, rewarding and positive work environment to attract a diverse, high-quality work force;*
- *Fully utilizing the rich and diverse contributions, skills, and abilities of staff by providing and supporting opportunities for personal and professional growth and accomplishments;*
- *Enhancing the work environment by fostering leadership, teamwork, empowerment, open communication, respect, trust, and fairness to all employees, and by maintaining a flexible attitude in expecting and accepting changing rules, technologies, and work assignments;*
- *Committing to Continuous Quality Improvement*

This mission statement would be considered too long by many TQM specialists; according to the literature a mission statement should be concise and focus on the essential purpose of an organization. In addition to the brief opening statement, however, many staff believed it was important to provide more specific statements regarding the department's core functions. In providing this additional guidance, it was recognized that the department balanced a diverse variety of essential functions. For example, it was noted that the vital, mutually reinforcing relationship between the libraries responsibilities to both the University Libraries' and the national (and, increasingly, international) cataloging community needed to be made explicit in the mission statement. It was thus felt that the relationship between national and university responsibilities also needed to be made clear.

The vision statement, promulgated at around the same time as the mission statement, complemented the latter and was conceived as a listing of primary qualities, or values, that informed the work of the department:

Cataloging Department Vision Statement

The Cataloging Department is considered by its customers to be:

- *Quality and Customer Driven*
- *Dynamic*
- *Effective*
- *Flexible*
- *Responsive*
- *Cooperative*
- *Providing Essential Services*

The Cataloging Department is considered to be the premier department in which to work.

Both the vision and mission statements have been reviewed in the following years, and while minor changes have been proposed, they have not been substantial enough for the department to embark on a formal revision of the statements.

Reorganization of Cataloging into Teams

It was clear from the start that the unwieldy division between the Bibliographic Processing and Original Cataloging Sections would be addressed as part of the CQI process. This division was unpopular among staff, and increasingly voices were heard that advocated a shift in favor of the format-based resource workgroups. Formal reorganization began in 1994 with the departure of the Head of Cataloging and the naming of three senior staff as cataloging coordinators, who together became known as the Cataloging Management Team. Another event that helped to set the stage for a sweeping reorganization was the purchase of individual computers and workstations for all cataloging staff. Thus ended the decade-long, tightly scheduled sharing of terminals, working in three staggered shifts, and the rigidity imposed by working under such conditions (the influence of technology in the CQI process will be discussed in a separate section below).

By 1994 two CQI teams in the Cataloging Department, the Pre-Order Search Team and the Label Requests Team had completed their work and their recommendations were implemented. The teams also shared their findings at the university-wide CQI Expo, an idea-sharing and networking fair that takes place annually at Penn State. The two teams represented the first organized attempt to work through process improvement using formal CQI methods. With the experience gained the concepts and practices of CQI were then practiced informally in additional process improvement groups within technical services, and to a smaller extent in the rest of the library system. Building on this experience, a number of groups in the division began following the steps used in the processes outlined by the first two teams. Acquisitions, in particular, vigorously pursued the process improvement course and quickly became the first library unit to formally reorganize into self-directed work teams.[9]

To coordinate the process of reorganization in the Cataloging Department, and to get it going on a larger scale, the Associate Dean for Information Access Services worked closely with the Cataloging Management Team, which was composed of the two librarian section heads (eventually reduced to one librarian) and a senior paraprofessional coordinator. All staff in the department were asked to study the issues of reorganization and to come up with an organizational proposal that would identify areas for process improvement, address workflows, increase production, reduce hand-offs and introduce self-management. This was a difficult time for staff because they were expected, for the first time, to accept self-sustaining responsibility for their organization and the roles they would assume in it. The Associate Dean made it clear from the start that success or failure lay entirely in the hands of all staff working together. Faculty librarians, who up to that time had been supervising higher-level cataloging staff and who represented authority figures in the department, were relieved of their supervisory responsibilities and were explicitly asked to step back from their positions of authority. The Dean of the University Libraries announced that cataloging faculty would relinquish their supervisory roles vis à vis the staff, and instead there would be a growing emphasis on their roles as 'resource persons,' in research, and in outreach within the library, the university community and the profession. The general departmental emphasis on decision-making thus shifted from individuals to groups who would collectively make decisions. It became apparent that moving from a diverse group of individuals to a team, and in making decisions through consensus, was going to be a learning process, and not something achieved over a short period of time. Indeed, consensus-building became one of the most important tools in the transformation of the department.

For the next year, the discussions surrounding reorganization continued without a clear consensus and without acceptable results. In retrospect, the primary reason for this was the leadership void left by the sudden flattening of the organizational hierarchy. While the department as a whole was still developing a modus operandi for team-based collaboration, a frustrating interim period ensued. A key lesson learned from this concerns the critical role that enlightened leadership continues to play throughout the CQI process, but particularly during the initial phases of an organization's transformation. The more leadership understands the process of transformation following the management principles embodied in CQI, the greater the chances of success. Leadership, in playing a stabilizing role during a period of major transition, must be present to assist in guiding the process through its various stages, and to insure that forward momentum is maintained. At the same time, leadership must be willing to accept the radical changes that will occur in an organization's authority structure, which for many can be difficult. In Penn State's case, the departure of the head of the Cataloging Department during the first phases of the process left a void that was difficult to fill during the time that the reorganization process had already begun. In effect, the newly appointed Cataloging Management Team was compelled to develop its function and role at a time when the department organization itself was undergoing radical change.

Nonetheless, the conditions under which change would occur–the 'environmental factors' in the language of TQM–continued to affect the composition and activity of the department. Several cataloging positions, including both faculty and staff, became vacant and were not filled in order to satisfy the Libraries' 10% operational budget reduction previously mandated by the University. The 1995 Cataloging Department budget meeting with the Dean of the Libraries focused on the continued perceived high cost of cataloging operations.[10] About the same time, in order to provide the department with attainable goals during the reorganization process, the Associate Dean for Information Access Services challenged the Cataloging Department to reduce referrals by 15%, increase cataloging by 15%, and to reduce all backlogs of uncataloged and minimally cataloged monographs and rare books. Interestingly, rather than create tension the department, as one would perhaps expect, these production goals provided tangible guidance and a timeline for progressing with the reorganization. For the most part, staff were eager to address productivity issues and to be additionally trained to complete the cataloging process, eliminating many referrals. This process of expanding cataloging competencies of qualified and experienced staff became a key strategic tool for the department for the next five years. Hence, the frustration on the part of staff surrounding what for them appeared as rather vague discussion on process improvement through reorganization dissipated noticeably once actual production goals were set by administration.

By summer 1995, the new organizational structure emerged. Working with the eleven original advisory workgroups, five core workgroups based on cataloging formats or type of material were established–the Maps Team, Monographs Team, Music/AV Team, Rare Materials Team, and Serials Team. Staff members themselves selected which group they wished to belong to, with some intervention from the Cataloging Management Team to assure that workload needs were adequately met. While initially the idea of having individual staff be members of multiple groups seemed desirable, and several at first did work in more than one group, in time it became apparent that this proved too unwieldy and difficult to sustain in practice. Gradually all but one staff member chose to devote their efforts to one team. The Physical Processing staff became the Catmarking Team and bindery operations moved to another unit. Without their supervisory responsibilities, the faculty librarians also associated themselves with a specific team based on their own specializations and experience. Though they were not expected to take on formal leadership responsibilities, the role of the faculty catalogers for each of the five cataloging teams, in addition to ongoing cataloging responsibilities, was defined as a "knowledge resource person." The latter referred to someone who would provide expertise in following and interpreting rules and procedures, as well as the person who would keep the team apprised of national developments. The three former supervisors also joined teams according to their format skills and preferences. The teams themselves decided, and were strongly encouraged by the Associate Dean for Information Access Services, to work toward becoming self-directed teams, functioning with a rotating team leader position rather than with permanent leaders. They finalized memberships, defined their own responsibilities, set goals, and established a meeting structure. To be formally accepted as viable organizational units, each team developed a five-month plan, emphasizing both production and self-management goals. The plan, as well as the goals, were then submitted to the Cataloging Management Team, who would work with them in finalizing a plan that would be submitted to library administration. The Cataloging Management Team itself took on a coordinating role in the department's activities.

The department-wide reorganization discussions were completed in about one year. During this challenging and at times difficult process, the entire department had an opportunity to experience first hand the principles of CQI–giving up former roles and embracing new ones; listening to and accepting the opinions of colleagues, regardless of rank and position; taking risks in trying new ways of working and instituting new processes; working together as a team; learning to work towards consensus in decision-making; accepting responsibility, individually and as a team; and accepting the concept of empowerment in making decisions. For many staff this signified a radical departure from the daily work routine they were accustomed to in previous years; this required significant adjustment for everyone. Not only was progress and development expected of the department as a whole, but each staff member individually needed to grow and develop personal skills in adapting to the changed circumstances. Both the university and library administrations were strongly supportive of the effort, and a large variety of workshops, training programs, and seminars were offered on an ongoing basis to assist individual staff in their own progress and development. In the end, a true indication of the Cataloging Department's success in reorganizing into teams is that no one individual, or even group of individuals, stand out as having 'led' the process. It truly reflected a group effort, with everyone learning that each staff member plays an important role in the ongoing success of the department.

The Transformative Power of Technology

The early 90s was a crucial period for computing technology. By this time American industry had spent billions of dollars in developing its corporate and manufacturing infrastructure using computers, and more and more critical voices could be heard, loudly claiming that little could be shown for this expense.[11] But slowly, progressively, personal computers were becoming more powerful, and software development was leading to applications more capable of truly rationalizing work processes across a broader spectrum of business and industrial fields. The question that had come to the fore in business theory was, could one now equate the *transformation in* technology with a *transformative power of* technology? It had become apparent by this time that the potential for this transformative power could not be tapped unless management and personnel structures were correspondingly adapted to make use of technology. This meant that new forms of organization were necessary that could respond quickly to the opportunities being made available by technology. Existing organizations were too static, and rigid workflows prevented them from introducing and making use of the transformative power of the computing and telecommunications technologies becoming available.

The above situation certainly applied to library technical services, and administration at Penn State was aware that changing the organizational culture following CQI principles and introducing new computer technology worked hand-in-hand. As such it was necessary to coordinate the two realms to realize the desired improvement of library services. In the winter of 1993-1994 library administration astutely resolved to allocate the library's first Intel 80486-class computers to the Cataloging Department, a unit that could make strategic use of these computers in improving productivity.[12] Eleven IBM Value-Point computers, each configured with 8 MB of RAM, a 200 MB hard disk, and 15-inch SVGA color monitors, were distributed among the cataloging staff who could most make use of the new computing technology in their daily work. A cataloging librarian with substantial computing experience was charged with coordinating the introduction and strategic use of the computers, and a plan for their implementation was quickly devised. A software suite was developed for each of the Windows 3.1 workstations, including office productivity software such as Microsoft Word, Excel, and Access, as well as an Internet client package composed of a telnet client (WinQVT/Net), an email client (Eudora), a graphic Web browser (Mosaic), and Gopher. Library administration had already expressed its commitment to provide each technical services staff member over the course of the next two years with a personal workstation, and so it was expected that this first phase of their introduction would be used to gain experience with managing their use as new machines were added to the department. At the same time, Cataloging Department management could work toward a reorganization that was structured around each staff member having a personal computer. The existing DOS-based computers remained in the department until a more powerful Windows machine had replaced them, or until they were no longer needed.

Though the specifications of these workstations may sound quaint by today's standards, the shift from a command-line oriented DOS working environment to the brightly colored graphics-based Windows operating system elicited a radical change in the way staff worked with computers. Along with the introduction of the ValuePoints the library's computing support office had recently installed the latest version of Novell for Windows networking software. The graphics-based representation of a computer, its functions, and its relationship to other computers on a network, made it much easier for staff to learn and orient themselves to the computer working environment. Whereas only a minority of staff had learned the non-intuitive commands for making use of the earlier DOS-based LAN, now the iconographical orientation to the network made it a much simpler process to use its power in sharing files and in developing a virtual organization of the department's documentation via the LAN. Though only in a limited way at first, staff could now begin thinking in terms of 'multi-tasking' one's work, and in carrying out a number of operations simultaneously. That multiple activities, represented as Windows applications on one's virtual 'desktop,' could be open and present to the cataloger at the same time, meant that data *between* applications could be readily shared via the copy and paste functionality available in Windows. When considered in the context of hundreds of such operations being made by staff on a daily basis, this ready means of sharing and moving data between applications had an immediate and profound impact on the time saved in carrying out these operations (not to mention the improvement in quality in avoiding rekeying data).

Indeed, it didn't take long for cataloging management to recognize that primitive computing technology played an important role in how the department was organized up to that time. Only a small minority of staff had their own PCs at their desks (predominantly the professional staff and the supervisors), and most staff had organized their workday around the schedule for the computer 'pods,' large communal circular desks with 4-6 workstations at each pod. The computers located at these pods possessed specific 'hard-wired' functions, such as those used for the OCLC or RLIN terminals. As at countless other libraries, these PCs were shared by staff, who each had an allotted period of time during the day to complete their work at the terminals. Thus, because of limited resources staff throughout the department had to organize their work around scheduling time for the computers.

With personal workstations at their desks staff could now use their Internet clients–in this case the telnet software–for using services like OCLC and RLIN at their discretion. At first interaction with the utilities was limited to searching with the generic telnet software, but shortly after the introduction of personal computers for individual staff both OCLC and RLIN introduced their own proprietary clients (Passport for Windows and RLIN for Windows, respectively), which allowed staff to carry out a much larger range of activities in the utilities. Responding to a growing number of libaries shifting to such individual workstations, the utilities gradually added new software functionality to their Windows-based applications, such as being able to readily import and export records locally. For a while insufficient computing power continued to be an issue. While the first delivery of ValuePoint computers could operate adequately as windowing workstations, it was with the second large delivery which included Pentium-class computers with 16 MB of working memory that a comfortable hardware platform had been reached. This was particularly an issue with the Library of Congress's Cataloger's Desktop software, where the 8 MB 486-class computers were barely sufficient for running the Folio software that formed the basis for the Cataloger's Desktop, as well as the other productivity applications necessary for cataloging.

The move to personal computers for all staff also led to a rapid growth and reliance on electronic communications and documentation in carrying out one's assignment in the library. At around the same time that the ValuePoint computers were installed in the Cataloging Department the graphic-based Web browsers Cello and Mosaic (soon afterwards Netscape) were becoming increasingly popular in libraries. Though the Web still possessed limited content (Gopher was much more prevalent in libraries at the time), Mosaic was installed as part of the initial suite of Internet applications on the departmental PCs. The advantages, as well as the ease of use, quickly led computer-proficient staff to propose that the Web be used as a platform for organizing and maintaining departmental documentation. In the summer of 1995 two working groups were formed, the Online Documentation Taskforce was created in June 1995, and the World Wide Web Homepage Working Group was called into being soon afterwards, in August of that year. The purpose of these two groups was in part to critically assess the use of printed documentation in the department, to recommend measures to rationalize the creation and use of documentation, and to study the feasibility of moving the department toward 'paperless cataloging.' It was estimated that well over 30,000 printouts were being generated monthly to control the flow of inventory through the department. Under the new conditions, and as the department underwent reorganization, a significant percentage of these printouts were deemed unnecessary, and other functions previously satisfied by the printouts were shifted to the online environment. Over the course of several months it was thus possible to reduce the printouts created to a fraction of the former amount.[13]

Earlier in the year Penn State had been selected as a beta site for testing the Library of Congress's Cataloger's Desktop, an important new product that brought together most of LC's documentation in online form as a Windows-based application. The two working groups–the Online Documentation Taskforce and the Web Homepage Ad hoc Working Group–coordinated their activities, and they pursued the goal of moving as much documentation as possible to the Web environment. Though the same software used for the Cataloger's Desktop, Folio VIEWS, was evaluated for its promise in managing local documentation, technical limitations of the software eventually prevented the department from moving to VIEWS for its own documentation. Though considered a problem at first, having some documentation on the Web, some on the network in various formats (Word, Excel, etc.), and the LC documentation in VIEWS format, staff quickly adjusted to using various online means of accessing needed documentation (the 8 MB of memory proved limiting, but adequate, for having multiple applications open, and the introduction of Pentium-class computers with 16 MB of memory soon relegated hardware issues to minimal significance).[14] At the same time, the Web homepage group quickly learned that the Web could be used to create a virtual, or metaphorical, representation of the department, and documentation, utilities, and other resources were organized by teams. Indeed, this led to the group recommending that each team should be responsible for its own part of the departmental Website, where meeting minutes, procedures, announcements, online reference tools, and other documentation would be maintained and kept current. In learning of the Web's ability to act as a graphical metaphor for a department's organization and services, the homepage working group proposed that the departmental Website could become an effective tool for outreach, that is, it could be utilized for communicating with its internal and external customers. For example, forms, procedures, and descriptions of services which were formerly maintained in paper form could now be transferred to the Web. This made these materials not only more accessible to the department's many customer groups, it was now possible to update these materials with the click of a button. Recognizing this potential, the department requested a document imaging scanner in 1994 to facilitate the digitization of its documentation to the online environment. The problem, which was a significant drain on departmental resources, of constantly printing updated documentation and forms was now minimized to a non-issue after the relatively brief transition to online documentation.

The commitment that every staff member would have a personal computer also led to email becoming a more integrated and essential means of communicating among staff. Rather than using the cumbersome and limited mainframe mail system for managing email, with Eudora for Windows it was possible to store and archive messages locally in folders on one's hard disk. Organizing meetings, distributing drafts of minutes, coordinating one's work with others, all of these group activities were made much easier and at the same time less intrusive on one's work and time. These personal resource materials, as well as personal email, could be intuitively organized into graphic-based folders, where they could be readily brought up and referred to when needed. This made it possible, for example, for the department to stop printing meeting minutes, and instead to distribute them electronically via email to staff (minutes were also posted to the department's Website).

The 'personalization' of departmental computing played a central role in facilitating the reorganization based on CQI principles. In freeing the department from the constraints of having staff share computers, it was now possible to truly think in terms of teams based on a variety of workflow-related characteristics: by subject of the material cataloged, format, physical characteristics, and so on. It represented a key factor in allowing the department to breakdown the unwieldy former organization based on the broad (and, in the end, rather vague) tasks of 'copy' and 'original' cataloging. Within the team framework, professional and non-professional staff could work closely together based on levels of experience and expertise. In addition, the move to online documentation was feasible only because management could make strategic use of the personal computers being allocated to every staff member. With their own computers, staff could now organize their own work lives, in terms of documentation, communication, and applications, in a personalized way that was impossible under the old organization. Rather than having to constantly refer to paper-based documentation on shelves elsewhere in the department, it was increasingly possible to have needed documentation readily accessible as part of the Windows desktop environment on one's computer. In effect, the use of networked personal computers that could multi-task made it possible to create a dynamic, interconnected virtual space in which staff could interact and carry out one's work. This interconnected space is both *personal*, as embodied in a staff member's PC, and *departmental*, as represented by the LAN. While this digital representation of the department remains present to staff in 'real time,' ready to be used when needed, the shift is to a deliberately more personal type of computing, in which each staff member can configure and manage his or her work as they wish. This personalization of computing was a prime reason why the shift to teams was possible.

OUTCOMES OF THE CATALOGING DEPARTMENT'S TRANSFORMATION THROUGH TQM/CQI, TEAMS AND TECHNOLOGY

Flattening of the Organization and Reducing Staffing

Prior to the beginning of reorganization in 1994 there were 45.5 FTEs (35 staff and 10.5 faculty FTEs) in Cataloging. By 1997 the number of positions in the department stabilized at 36 FTEs (28 staff, 8 faculty FTE). The Cataloging Department was leaner by 9 FTEs compared to 1994.[15] The department went from five levels of hierarchy to two levels: the Cataloging Management Team (consisting of two coordinators) and the teams. Staff generally accepted the new arrangement with little difficulty, though there was some turnover of staff and faculty positions, most notably with the faculty positions. Librarians speculated why there was a relatively high-turnover of faculty positions. With hindsight the best explanation is probably found in the increased emphasis on research and publishing, and in removing formal management responsibility from their assignments. Without a formal administrative means of maintaining status and recognition in the department, faculty librarians needed to sustain their position more through individual achievement, which included valued experience useful to the department, and through research and development of new services or technologies. This did not represent a radical departure from library culture at Penn State, since the university has a well-known and strong tradition of supporting the tenure-track faculty model for academic librarianship. The shift to a research focus also complemented the growing need for qualified staff to develop and introduce innovative ways of organizing, accessing, and otherwise bringing library resources under effective bibliographic control.

By reducing the departmental staffing and flattening the hierarchy from five to two levels, the Cataloging Department achieved several objectives. First, the department was able to support the University Libraries in achieving a number of budgetary goals, including the 10% budget reduction mandated by the University. An additional outcome was improved service–a flattened hierarchy permitted staff to respond much more quickly to customer needs. The empowerment of staff, i.e., the moving of operational decision-making to those closest to the work performed, resulted in improved processes, higher productivity and stronger identification of individual staff members with their work. Two of the reduced cataloging positions were used to fund the PromptCat service and other outsourcing initiatives, which helped to deliver some categories of materials to users with a much improved speed. Finally, many opportunities were created for staff to develop skills that the hierarchical organization did not provide.

Improving Quality of Service by Increasing Production

Even with a staff reduction of 9 FTEs, the Cataloging Department was able to significantly increase productivity levels. The production gains allowed the department to establish new priorities in terms of backlogs or uncataloged collections that for years had been waiting for action. Since 1995, over 17,000 titles from the rare books backlog (in addition to incoming materials) and nearly 4,000 incompletely cataloged monographs of various less-common languages and unusual types of material, which had accumulated over the years, now received full cataloging. Over 10,000 uncataloged Education Library materials (Penn State possesses a large textbook collection) were given online access. The cataloging of maps intensified and the uncataloged music and AV collections also received long-overdue attention. Statistics show an increase in demand and a growing user interest in these collections when online access was provided. In addition, currently acquired materials in all formats continued to receive full cataloging in a timely manner, in fact, the department was able to show a steady improvement in turn-around time. Besides reorganization into teams and application of CQI principles, other factors also contributed to these productions gains, such as optimizing the use of technology in the cataloging process and with judicious outsourcing.

With a quantitative increase in productivity one must always ask about the consequences regarding quality in other areas—will, for example, quality in terms of record accuracy and subject access suffer when the actual numbers of materials processed rise? This was an important issue that staff recognized needed addressing, and it was an issue that was discussed at several meetings. With CQI statistics represent a primary means of assessing quality improvement. In terms of numbers of items cataloged there was little doubt that the Cataloging Department could register marked gains in productivity. Also, the simple fact that large bodies of material previously uncataloged were now being cataloged was a clear indication that service in particular areas was being significantly improved. Each team developed a Web-based matrix that listed ongoing projects of the team, in addition to prioritizing them, and they used this matrix to systematically work through their cataloging projects. At the same time, however, the most significant indicator of improvement–a statistical comparison demonstrating improved record quality in terms of accuracy and better access–could not be produced. Just as problematic was the inability for the teams to implement structural safeguards to insure quality control, much like how the TQM-driven corporations in the manufacturing industry had been employing to insure quality levels in production. Certainly a system of quality assurance in the creation of cataloging records could have been devised in the department, but the fact that such a system was not instituted is in large part a reflection of the values and priorities that came from library administration, which in challenging the department to increase productivity by 15% did not mention quality assurance at all. It should be noted, however, that this problem is a general one in librarianship today; since patrons typically do not recognize poor records when searching a database, and in most cases do not know when lack of success in searching is a product of poor quality in a library catalog, quality assurance has a low priority with a large number of library administrations across the country.

While little could be shown in terms of statistical comparisons, however, the department could point to a number of factors that facilitated an ongoing commitment to record quality. Most of these factors revolved around the nature of self-directed teams. Working more closely and collaboratively, team members have greater opportunities to support and monitor one another's work. The faculty catalogers, for example, instituted a regular review of one another's cataloging, which included looking at a random selection of five to ten cataloged items per cataloger, and a group discussion of the issues raised in each of the materials evaluated. In addition, team members were strongly encouraged to consult with one another regarding unfamiliar materials or cataloging issues. Training and review of new and junior staff was carefully coordinated to insure that the necessary skills were learned before a staff member assumed new responsibilities. Key to the success of such a supportive environment is to cultivate an open, non-threatening culture of mutual support. Staff should not feel threatened by going to colleagues when uncertain of particular cataloging issues or rules. As a rule, most staff have developed a general attitude of it not being possible to ask too many questions, and this has gone far in assuring that a general level of quality is being maintained in the department's operations. This climate, and the general attitude of mutual trust that results, is of course possible because of the relatively stable and long-term nature of the Cataloging Department's staffing. With many years of experience working with MARC formats and AACR2 it has been a relatively easy process to promote staff through additional in-house training.

Becoming a Customer-Driven Organization

A strong focus on customers is one of the primary tenets of TQM/ CQI. As a behind-the-scenes operation with little direct contact with 'external' customers (students, faculty and other library users), the Cataloging Department relies primarily on public service faculty and staff (the internal customers) as interpreters of the library users' needs. Thus, being responsive and working closely with the public service areas is of singular importance for the department. Because cataloging teams were given responsibility to work directly with their constituents in public services (a number of cataloging staff also work a couple of hours a week at a public service desk), most teams have developed very close relationships with those whom they serve. Instead of remaining behind the scenes and only cataloging materials as they arrived, the cataloging teams are pro-active in finding what needs to be cataloged in the format for which they are responsible. Emphasis has been on finding ways to address backlogs while still keeping short turn-arounds for incoming materials. The teams communicate directly with their public service 'customers' regarding what work needs to be done, how workflows can be streamlined, and which steps eliminated. By working closely with their internal customers, cataloging teams have developed a strong sense of quality of service defined by user expectations for timeliness of access, as well as through a need for flexibility and continuous improvement of services as needs change. To underscore this shift in the department's focus, several years ago the Cataloging Department changed its name to Cataloging Services.

Changing Expectations and Expanding Competencies of Staff

In the earlier sections, mention was made of the necessity for staff to continuously learn new skills relating to TQM/CQI concepts and to the application of new technologies to cataloging. The reorganization of the department into self-directed teams responsible for distinct cataloging workflows based on formats also engendered new expectations, as well as creating new opportunities, for staff. Because the cataloging teams function without a supervisor or a permanent team leader, the individual team members have assumed responsibility and accountability for monitoring their own time, managing their own workloads, and, ultimately, adhering to standards of cataloging. The team members are also expected to assume responsibility for their own self-development, as well as for keeping informed about and participating in changes relating to local policies and procedures. Shared responsibility for the team's decisions and activities means that everyone on a team needs to develop leadership and facilitation skills. Team members are also responsible for developing personally to function well in a participatory and collaborative environment.

The team members as a group assumed the responsibility for management and administrative activities previously handled by supervisors and section heads. These responsibilities include: achieving cataloging goals, analyzing and improving processes, implementing and assessing process improvement, maintaining quality control, monitoring and adjusting workflows, managing shifting priorities, planning and monitoring projects, and communicating with customers. In addition, the team members participate in interviewing and hiring new staff, in training activities, and in writing documentation for cataloging processes. Team members also take part in the management of the team activities, as well as in serving as team administrators (or 'team leader') on a rotating basis. This responsibility includes coordinating communication among the team members, preparing and distributing weekly agendas, chairing team meetings, documenting team discussions and decisions, and acting as a team spokesperson. The team members also serve as representatives to various groups inside and outside of Cataloging Services. Faced with these new responsibilities, some team members embraced them and quickly excelled, others have had a more difficult time adjusting to these expectations.

In practicing CQI techniques such as strongly focusing on reducing hand-offs and improving quality of service, it naturally must also provide opportunities for staff to expand their cataloging competencies. To be able to complete as much work on a title as possible (a kind of 'whole book' cataloging, at least in spirit), staff members have been given additional cataloging training in a variety of areas. In order to provide adequate support for timeliness of original cataloging of current materials and for getting backlogs of complex materials cataloged, several experienced non-professional staff were trained in original cataloging and subject analysis. These staff members had demonstrated analytical and language skills, and they possessed the requisite college-level education in appropriate subject areas. Over a period of three years, eight paraprofessional staff members were trained to perform original cataloging of monographs, rare materials, maps, music and serials. In addition to assuring that incoming materials needing original cataloging receive timely attention, this support for original cataloging has made it possible to effectively handle backlogs, thus continuing to make inroads with the still sizable uncataloged collections.

Changing Roles and Expectation of Faculty Catalogers

As noted, the reorganization into teams and the strategy of training experienced staff in original cataloging resulted in major changes in the role of faculty catalogers, who traditionally have been responsible for supervising paraprofessionals and for all original cataloging. By giving up their hands-on, day-to day supervisory responsibilities, and instead to serve solely as resource persons for the teams and as mentors for staff in developing their cataloging skills, the faculty catalogers could direct their energies to other endeavors. Under the new circumstances their role was to continue performing complex original cataloging as well as to introduce to the department new national developments, such as those occurring in the cataloging and management of electronic resources. They were also expected to expand their roles as librarians within the library by taking on additional activities like collection development responsibilities, mentoring of new librarians seeking tenure, increasing their presence on campus by participating in inter-disciplinary programs in their fields, and in directing their energies toward professional development and contributions at the national and internationals levels.

PROBLEMS AND DIFFICULTIES ASSOCIATED
WITH GOING TO TEAMS

Challenges Confronting Staff in Adapting to the New Environment

With teams came the issue of 'retooling' staff into roles they were not always willing–and many unprepared–to accept at first. Closely allied with this challenge involved motivating staff to develop the skills needed to succeed in the new culture of empowerment. Some staff welcomed the opportunity to learn and develop new skills, as well as to participate in decision-making activities. Others preferred not to and continued to focus most of their attention on the type of cataloging they performed before the reorganization. Those that did not readily embrace the expanded duties as team members resented what they considered an unfair intrusion on their day-to-day cataloging work. Regardless of the level of commitment to the teams, each person had to be willing to assume a leadership role. For many, this was the first time in their careers that such activities were expected of them. Addressing personnel issues related to different levels of willingness to fully participate in team activities proved an important part of the transition to the new working environment.

Training and Continuous Organizational Commitment to CQI and Teams

It is generally acknowledged by writers on TQM/CQI and team-based organizations that the number one ingredient for success is a strong, continuing commitment to continuous quality principles at all levels of the organization, and particularly at the highest levels. The hierarchical nature of many institutions, with decision-making powers concentrated at the top levels, is not easily replaced with a collaborative team-based organization.[16] The shift from entrenched hierarchies to a team-based organization requires sweeping change with many aspects of an organization, including accountability, reporting structures, communication, and expected conduct. Extensive training in the fundamental concepts and methodologies is thus needed for staff at all levels. Attaining commitment to teams on the part of each individual is of utmost importance. This is often overlooked when the emphasis is on quickly getting results. The ensuing resentment often leads to resistance to change, and hence not all the benefits of a team-based culture can be realized. Everyone involved, regardless of rank and grade-level, must be expected to learn significantly different work styles and to commit to a participatory work place.

Inadequate investment in training of the proper fundamentals for the team environment was one of the problems of the reorganization process at Penn State. While the reorganization of the Acquisitions Department took place a year earlier, when a healthy training budget was present, the funding dried-up by the time the Cataloging Department embarked on formal reorganization. Though staff was in need of full immersion in team management techniques, limited funding made it difficult for the department to make use of formal training programs and seminars.[17] Indeed, another problem was that a small minority of staff was resistant to the very notion of training as a means for developing skills (these tended to be the same individuals who were averse to attending meetings or working in groups at all). To be effective, training must come at the right time and must be recognized as relevant to those being trained. With hindsight it is always easier to identify when the appropriate training was timely and necessary. The situation was aggravated by the existence of a broad range of experience and skills represented by the staff. As a result of early training failures, a number of staff developed a healthy skepticism to the usefulness of training sessions. Because of either inadequate funds for team training, or because there simply did not exist appropriate types of training tailored to a library environment, the department was constrained to use the University Human Resources ready-made training sessions for teams, and these forms of training were not always appropriate for the existing circumstances. Even the day-long sessions with outside consultants did not always succeed, mostly because the consultant came in with a canned team-building program, rather than attempting to tailor the training to the department's specific situation. Again, with hindsight, a common thread to the less successful training sessions was the inability of the trainer to adequately characterize the purpose, need, and utility of a given training session. The successful training programs were those that were well prepared, and were focused on specific issues confronting single teams. Also, those conducted over a longer period of time (often continuing over several weeks or even months) tended to be more successful.

Teams versus Hierarchy

Another factor complicating the success of the team environment within technical services at Penn State was the fact that only half the library reorganized into teams. The Associate Dean for Information Access Services was a strong advocate of CQI and team-based organization. Thus technical services departments reorganized into teams while public service areas decided, paradoxically, that CQI was not appropriate for pubic service departments (there is much irony in this, of course, since the primary purpose of CQI is to improve customer service). There were some cross-sectional process improvement teams established in public services to address specific problems, and some work groups referred to themselves as teams, but the organizational structure for that part of the library remained a strict hierarchy. This half-team and half-hierarchical environment was not an ideal situation in regard to the library as a whole. The staff and faculty in other areas of the library were not familiar with team practices and originally mistrusted, or were somewhat hostile, to the team culture. The attitudes exhibited did not make the switch from hierarchy to teams easier in technical services. Technical service teams were perceived as spending too much time in meetings rather than in production-oriented activities. Even when obvious gains in cataloging production were taking place, some staff in the public service areas continued to be uncomfortable with the team structure, and they frequently preferred to think that these gains "just happened" and were not a direct result of the team environment.

On the other hand, public service areas that worked closely with the cataloging teams, such as the Rare Books Room and the Maps Room, became strong allies and supporters of the cataloging teams. These public service units experienced first hand the high level of commitment of the teams to its cataloging goals and saw their backlogs literally disappear. The changes in communication patterns in the team environment in technical services also generated some mistrust and confusion in other areas of the library. While one half of the library continued to communicate issues and problems only through supervisors and librarians, in the other half of the library the new style of open communication within and outside the teams was being established. When staff from technical services began using the new CQI-related vocabulary, other staff tended to react negatively, often considering it jingoistic or faddish. This split culture made achieving the full benefit of teams in technical services more difficult.

Pay Equity

The team environment created a need to address possible position upgrades associated with increased duties of staff in teams. With the roles and responsibilities of so many staff changing dramatically, a plan was devised to gradually review job descriptions for staff in technical services. Because this turned out to be a lengthy process, some departments completed the job reviews and had some of their positions upgraded within a reasonable time after going to teams, while teams in other departments had to wait. As the lengthy process of reviewing positions in teams continued, it became apparent that responsibilities of all staff in the library, not just those associated with the teams, had changed due to the advances in technology and the increased demands on keeping up with these new developments. Thus another plan was devised to review every position within the library every five years on a rotating basis. While the overall plan seemed reasonable, keeping the process on track was much more complex. Positions that had changed substantially were prioritized as the first to be reviewed. Funding was budgeted for the review process and had to be increased to meet the review goal. Only those positions identified as high priority were actually reviewed. Other positions that had also changed demonstratively were put on a hold to be budgeted each year. This plan caused further equity issues and some discontent among the staff in teams that have had to wait for their position reviews much longer than their co-workers. The library administration, however, remains committed to continue working on and budgeting for position reviews and upgrades over the coming years.

Performance Appraisal

Recognizing and rewarding team as well as individual performance in team-based organizations is an issue that does not lend itself to an easy solution. For a variety of reasons, some team members contribute to the team goals more than others. Furthermore, some individuals have a very strong need to be singled out as outstanding performers, while others are happy with the satisfaction they derive from the team accomplishment and recognition. The difficulty in recognizing individual performance has been noted as one of the shortcomings of the team approach.[18] The issues of team versus individual performance appraisal have been particularly thorny at Penn State, since performance appraisals serve as a means of recognizing staff and faculty for outstanding achievements. The performance appraisal is graded and this grade determines the merit raise that will be given. In a team-based environment the assessment of both the team and the individual performance appraisals do not easily translate into a number. Achieving a balance between rewarding the team and individual performance in a formal evaluation process has been a challenge, and will certainly continue to require attention over the coming years.

KEEPING THE TEAM CULTURE ALIVE AND WELL

An issue of enormous relevance for team-based operations is keeping the commitment to the team culture alive. Often new staff come into the team environment with vague or erroneous notions about what it means to work collaboratively in a team. They need to be trained in appropriate behaviors, communication styles, problem-solving, facilitation techniques, self- and team-management, and in handling conflicts. Basic skills in interviewing, hiring, performance assessment and evaluation, which formerly resided with the supervisor's position, also need to be acquired. Team management skills need to be continually developed and cultivated. Participating in some level of group training needs to be continued to reinforce and improve group dynamics. It should not be assumed that these skills will be developed and maintained without some level of organized training. In this regard the Penn State Human Resource and Development Center has offered invaluable support through training, consultation and facilitation for individuals working in teams. Having professional support to keep the culture healthy is a key asset for a team-based organization. It is advisable that a training package for new members of teams is developed and offered periodically so that new staff develop and maintain the necessary commitment to team goals and responsibilities.

Personnel changes in higher administration can also lead to diminished organizational support for the team environment. Administrators who come from traditional hierarchical organizations are often not even familiar with, let alone committed to, CQI and team organization concepts. They tend to be uncomfortable with the level of empower-ment and decision-making that staff in the more advanced teams are capable of performing. They are more comfortable with the traditional accountability patterns and hierarchical decision-making, and they are likely to question the functionality of teams. They may not understand the commitment and ownership staff have to the workplace when responsibility for work processes rest at that level. Mature teams dem-onstrate a work ethic previously seen only at higher supervisory and administrative levels. New administrators need to be educated about teams successes and accomplishments and informed about the benefit to the organization as a whole. These issues are of course not unique to library technical services, and here libraries can learn a good deal by making active use of the strategies and techniques employed in private industry.

CONCLUSION

Penn State's Cataloging Services in 1999 is a vastly different place than the Cataloging Department was in 1994, before the process of transformation began with the implementation of TQM/CQI prin-ciples, reorganization into self-directed work-teams, and the applica-tion of the latest computing technologies. While the changes discussed in this article are too numerous to summarize succinctly, there can be no doubt that, as difficult as some of these changes were, enormous benefits have resulted from them. The cataloging staff and faculty benefited, the University Libraries as a whole benefited, and most importantly, the users of the Libraries resources–Penn State students, faculty and staff–have benefited as well. The fundamental shifts in methods of working, in personal acceptance of self-directed responsi-bility, and in accepting change as a normal part of one's work will continue to bear fruit in the future as we face new challenges.

NOTES

1. Several good books and articles have appeared reviewing the literature on TQM in libraries. For an introductory overview of TQM applications in a library set-ting see: "Quality Improvement in Libraries: Total Quality Management and Related Approaches," by Joanne H. Boelke. *Advances in Librarianship*, vol. 19, 1995.

Another useful monograph which provides a general context for libraries is: *Total Quality Management in Academic Libraries: Initial Implementation Efforts: Proceedings from the 1st International Conference on TQM and Academic Libraries, April 20-22, 1994*, editors Laura Rounds, Michael Matthews (Washington, D.C.: Office of Management Services, Association of Research Libraries, 1995). Also, Rosanna O'Neil's *Total Quality Management in Libraries: A Sourcebook* (Englewood: Libraries Unlimited, 1994) provides a now somewhat dated, but still useful bibliography on the topic. Also useful is the collection edited by Susan Jurow and Susan B. Barnard entitled: *Integrating Total Quality Management in a Library Setting* (New York: The Haworth Press, Inc. 1993). A more recently published article on TQM in cataloging is by Zahiruddin Khurshid, "The Application of TQM in Cataloguing," *Library Management*, vol. 18, nr. 6, 1997: p. 274-279.

2. Dorothy Gregor and Carol Mandel, "Cataloging Must Change!" *Library Journal*, April 1, 1991.

3. A more trenchant article on the need for change in cataloging was written by Ellen J. Waite a few years later. Also appearing in Library Journal (November 1, 1995), it was entitled "Reinvent Catalogers," and was conceived as a response to Michael Gorman's Library Journal article "The Corruption of Cataloging" (September 15, 1995). Indicative of the level of interest arising from the topic, this was a Library Journal cover story that engendered much discussion afterwards.

4. In his book *The Trouble with Computers: Usefulness, Usability, and Productivity* (Cambridge, MA.: MIT Press, 1995), Thomas K. Landauer delivers a still useful critique of the high overhead, and unfulfilled promises, of computing in the 1980s. Unfortunately for the longevity of his research, his work was carried out just as the World Wide Web was developing momentum. Though as an historical analysis his book still has much value, the validity of many of his more critical, general claims regarding the utility of computing was swept away in the latter part of the 90s.

5. Both of the 'gurus,' and acknowledged founders, of Total Quality Management, Joseph Juran and W. Edwards Deming, have been repeatedly quoted as estimating that 80-90% of the problems dealing with quality and productivity can be traced to management, and not to workers. Bill Creech's *The Five Pillars of TQM: How to Make Total Quality Management Work for You* (New York: Truman Talley/ Dutton, 1994) also focuses on the shortcomings of management in identifying quality and productivity problems in organizations. This book is also an excellent introduction to TQM.

6. See Landauer for a more detailed characterization of this phenomena for computing in general. See also Janet McCue and Roger Brisson, "Technical Services Workstations in a Library Environment," *Encyclopedia of Microcomputers*, vol. 18, (New York, Marcel Dekker, 1996) for a description of how personal computing can be strategically integrated into library technical services.

7. Donald Riggs was an early advocate of employing TQM in library administration. See his "Strategic Quality Management in Libraries," *Advances in Librarianship*, vol. 16 (New York: Academic Press, 1992).

8. Irene Owens, "The Impact of Change from Hierarchy to Teams in Two Academic Libraries: Intended Results versus Actual Results Using Total Quality Management," *College & Research Libraries*, November 1999, p. 573.

9. Nancy Stanley and Lynne Branche-Brown, "Reorganizing Acquisitions at the Pennsylvania State University Libraries: From Work Units to Teams," *Library Acquisitions: Practice and Theory*, 19, 1995: no. 4, pp. 412-425.

10. As an aside, it is interesting–and revealing–to note that in giving a total dollar amount for technical services expenditures by the library for the previous year, the Dean wished to emphasize the overly high cost of technical services. The large number of technical services staff attending the meeting, however, interpreted the amount quoted to indicate how inexpensive technical services operations were in relation to the value provided by the library!

11. See Landauer's book for an incisive critique of computing up to the mid-1990s.

12. Mark Stover. Leading The Wired Organization: The Information Professional's Guide To Managing Technological Change. New York: Neal-Schuman, 1999. For a more specific overview of the strategic advantages in the change to Windowing workstations, see Brisson, Roger, "The Cataloger's Workstation and the Continuing Transformation of Cataloging, Part 1" *Cataloging & Classification Quarterly, vol. 20*, nr. 1. 1995, and "The Cataloger's Workstation and the Continuing Transformation of Cataloging, Part 2" *Cataloging & Classification Quarterly, vol. 20*, nr. 2 1995.

13. Roger Brisson, Online Documentation in Library Technical Services, *Technical Services Quarterly, vol. 16*, nr. 3, 1999.

14. Ibid., p. 14.

15. Staff responsible for bindery activities is not included in the 1994 figures; in 1997 they were part of a different unit.

16. Owens, Irene, The Impact of Change from Hierarchy to Teams, p. 579.

17. It should be noted here that the Cataloging Department did continue to have a budget for training, but in general formal training programs, in particular from those companies with national reputations, are very expensive investments.

18. Owens, p. 580.

Flexibility in the Management of Cataloging

Claire-Lise Bénaud
Elizabeth N. Steinhagen
Sharon A. Moynahan

SUMMARY. Cataloging managers at the University of New Mexico General Library, feeling under pressure from colleagues and administrators to become more efficient, have introduced a flexible management style in the traditional Catalog Department. Instead of pushing staff to work harder and faster, they developed a point system, or quota, for staff catalogers. This allowed them to implement flextime and other liberal options, such as working at home, or in other campus libraries. Expectations of quality and quantity of production have been clarified, and staff morale, generally, has improved, as people feel they have more control over their work. Although still cataloging in the traditional mode, managers feel that improved flexibility will allow them to become more proactive and tackle anticipated changes in a positive manner. *[Article copies available for a fee from The Haworth Document Delivery Service: 1-800-342-9678. E-mail address: <getinfo@haworthpressinc.com> Website: <http://www.HaworthPress.com>]*

KEYWORDS. Flexible management, cataloging, quotas, flextime

Claire-Lise Bénaud, MLS, is Head, Catalog Department and Elizabeth N. Steinhagen, MA, MLS, is Head, Ibero-American Cataloging Section at the University of New Mexico General Library. Sharon A. Moynahan, MSLS, MALAS, is a special projects cataloger most recently assigned to the Clark Field Archive at the University of New Mexico.

[Haworth co-indexing entry note]: "Flexibility in the Management of Cataloging." Bénaud, Claire-Lise, Elizabeth N. Steinhagen, and Sharon A. Moynahan. Co-published simultaneously in *Cataloging & Classification Quarterly* (The Haworth Information Press, an imprint of The Haworth Press, Inc.) Vol. 30, No. 2/3, 2000, pp. 281-298; and: *Managing Cataloging and the Organization of Information: Philosophies, Practices and Challenges at the Onset of the 21st Century* (ed: Ruth C. Carter) The Haworth Information Press, an imprint of The Haworth Press, Inc., 2000, pp. 281-298. Single or multiple copies of this article are available for a fee from The Haworth Document Delivery Service [1-800-342-9678, 9:00 a.m. - 5:00 p.m. (EST). E-mail address: getinfo@haworthpressinc.com].

On the threshold of the 21st-century, the cataloging community feels under attack. This crisis was brought on, in part, by a new technology which affects both the format in which information is produced and the way in which libraries organize, store, and deliver information. The latter has also raised users' expectations for instant identification and access to resources. In this environment, cataloging departments, which still need to support the old paradigm, deliver products whose complexity seems excessive to administrators and which, never-the-less, do not fully provide the level of access needed by users. Even though these greater forces are at work, catalogers cannot neglect print-based materials; they need to find a way to effectively maintain the traditional products that have always been associated with libraries.

Even though dealing with electronic resources is exerting increasing pressures, the cataloging managers at the University of New Mexico General Library (UNMGL) decided to address the proper functioning of the traditional MARC environment. Circumstantial evidence suggests that cataloging departments are being downsized. At UNMGL, this translated into not filling vacant positions, while at the same time diverting funds to the growing areas of systems, education services, and library development. Staff attrition in cataloging over the last decade and the desire to change the environment provided the impetus for innovation. Concerned about being marginalized, cataloging managers decided to become more proactive. Rather than rehashing old models, the Department gradually struck out in new directions on several fronts. It focused on delivering the products needed by public service in a more efficient and timely manner. This was achieved by reevaluating the "old way" of doing things, which perpetuated workflows and routines that were no longer relevant. Flexibility became paramount. The steps taken covered a wide spectrum of options, including flexible scheduling and work locations, quotas supported by a point system, redefined expectations, entrepreneurship, and a variety of staffing options. Instead of working faster and harder to meet administrative and budgetary demands, it made sense to work more creatively. This article describes the changes implemented by UNMGL to support the traditional functions of the Catalog Department. What follows developed in response to local circumstances.

BREAKING OLD RULES AND TRADITIONS

Background

The Catalog Department at the General Library consists of four sections each managed by a section head: General Cataloging which is responsible for English and foreign language monographs other than Spanish and Portuguese; Ibero-American Cataloging; Serials Cataloging; and, Bibliographic Control, responsible for database maintenance and authority control. UNMGL also belongs to a New Mexico online catalog consortium, LIBROS, consisting of mainly academic and special libraries.

Both staff and faculty perform copy and original cataloging, ranging from Library of Congress to original records. Staff in cataloging sections are primarily exempt from the Fair Labor Standards Act while staff in the database maintenance section are generally in the non-exempt category. Faculty catalogers are governed by the university's faculty handbook, and their performance evaluation takes into account research and service in addition to librarianship. These differences in status affect the way the Department manages catalogers. The four section heads assist the department head in management through the Catalog Management Group (CMG) which looks at all policy, technical, and personnel issues affecting the Department. In response to the multiple, and seemingly unrelated, internal and external pressures–to become more productive, to become more accountable, to offer staff more control over their own worktime, to modify cataloging workflows, and to utilize staff expertise differently–CMG investigated a number of new ideas, such as outsourcing, staffing reassignments, and addressed such long-standing unresolved issues as flexible scheduling and cataloging quotas.

Flextime

Until recently, the Department followed University guidelines which stipulated that staff members had to work their hours Monday-Friday between 7:00 am and 6:00 p.m. Staff members also had the option of working a 4-day week. Faculty catalogers always had more leeway than staff but usually followed similar workday patterns. Past attempts to accommodate individual needs, such as personal biorhythms, a second job, child- or elder-care, or the desire to work the same hours as a spouse had produced problems for the cataloging managers. Varying arrival times, messages for absent staff and make-up time surrounding these variant schedules had created red tape. Further complicating matters, section heads applied the policies differently. There was also concern for security when staff worked at odd hours. Supervision was difficult, and it became evident that the Department was not able to support flexibility under these rigid rules. These attempts at accommodation were subsequently abandoned but the idea of having more flexible work hours remained.

Finally, in the fall of 1997, CMG decided, with the approval of the Associate Dean, to introduce a new flexible scheduling option. Determined to start afresh and not to get bogged down with past problems, or anticipate new obstacles, the group accepted the fact that some problems, such as petty theft, could not be resolved. After discussing various possibilities, including a set of core hours when everybody had to be at work, the group decided to eliminate virtually all scheduling restrictions and to interfere only in the event of serious safety or security problems. Staff could work whenever they wanted, including nights and weekends, as long as they attended section and department meetings. Exempt staff, on a monthly schedule, could take full advantage of this new system while non-exempt staff still had to work no more than 40 hours each week. Within these restrictions, however, they could choose when to work. In order to facilitate face-to-face communication, participants were asked to post a schedule indicating when they would most likely be at work.

Once the decision had been reached to allow for maximum scheduling flexibility, another method for accountability, other than hours at work, had to be devised. CMG worked long and hard to come up with a point system which took into account all duties required of staff catalogers–the system was not applied to faculty–which would measure production, complexity of cataloging and support activities in a fair manner.

The Point System

Traditionally, there were no hard and fast rules governing cataloger productivity. Based on the Department's history, managers knew who was a slow cataloger, a good cataloger, or a fast cataloger. Lore rather than data was the measurement tool. Catalogers were compared with each other in ambiguous ways, but the "winners" were the ones with the highest monthly statistics. Issues such as language of the catalog record, non-Roman script, or format were taken into account inconsistently and impressions were often tempered by personality or style. Production figures were kept but size of the backlog played a big role in UNMGL's perception of its Catalog Department. The more compelling issues of the times, such as migrating to a new online catalog, data load problems, conversion of records, new policies and procedures required by the OPAC occupied everyone's attention. Catalogers' productivity, while never truly overlooked, was on the back burner.

A gradual change took place. First, in the early 1990s, individual statistics became public information and were recorded in monthly reports. Later, catalogers were asked what their expectations were of themselves. Production numbers varied widely and "wildly" among catalogers. Department members knew that the quality of copy, the language, the often erratic speed of OCLC's dedicated lines, and peripheral activities interfered with productivity. Early discussions helped clarify who was responsible for what type of cataloging and what constituted an acceptable record. The quest for perfect records in LIBROS had to be balanced against time constraints. The decision was made to accept more of the records found in OCLC, based on their improved quality. National and consortial cataloging standards were determined in advance and were not negotiable.

Devising a simple and fair system representing all duties and activities performed by staff catalogers was daunting. Cataloging per-se, support duties, and general office activities had to be taken into account. Because staff catalog a wide variety of materials, different point values were assigned depending on the complexity of the cataloging required. Monographic cataloging was divided into four categories: original, OCLC member copy, pre-AACR2 DLC copy, and full AACR2 DLC copy. Serials cataloging and maintenance were given a single, comprehensive point value, while monographic cataloging was further broken down to include authority work, database maintenance, and the like. Cooperative work such as upgrading and enhancing records, contribution to NACO and BIBCO were also assigned point values. Non-book and non-roman script titles were given additional points.

Staff meetings, workshops, training, selection and supervision, were documented in units of time as translated into points.[1] General duties such as e-mail, writing reports, consulting with co-workers, perusing cataloging tools, dealing with computer problems, learning to use new network applications, and other incidentals were assigned a flat rate per day. Cataloging points and units of time, as translated into points, were calculated and a minimum average of 240 points per month was established.

The proposal was then presented to Department catalogers. After lengthy discussions, some of the point values were revised and the system was put in place for a trial period in the spring of 1998. Since it was quite controversial, the point system was optional at first but in fact most catalogers chose to participate. Participants, who contracted for a 240 point monthly minimum, found the goal attainable and enjoyed being able to leave when their work was done. Flextime was an instant success. Some tinkering and revisions over the next year fine-tuned the system and since then, all staff catalogers are expected to earn the minimum points.

FLEXIBLE LOCATIONS: ADJUSTING CATALOGING TO THE NEEDS OF COLLECTIONS AND CATALOGERS

Flextime and quotas, combined with quality standards, whether imposed by national agreement or local decisions, essentially removes the need to closely monitor catalogers' activity. The flexible scheduling option of letting employees set their own schedules led easily to the next step of letting catalogers work at remote locations. This could mean working at a remote library site on or off campus. "Today we construct and maintain workgroups ourselves, and not all members are in a contiguous environment. Organizations . . . that encourage remote work styles need to devote resources to building a fully functioning communication infrastructure to foster all employees' effective use of that infrastructure."[2] The point system, the requirement of attending sectional and departmental meetings, and clear standards for record quality allowed this additional flexibility. The Catalog Department went a step further and also experimented with telecommuting on a small scale.

Cataloging at Remote Sites on Campus or in Other Libraries

At one time all cataloging work was done at a central cataloging department. It was usually believed that the best cataloging, closely monitored, came from these cataloging operations, and that any work from outside contributors, even the branch libraries, was of lesser quality. Although this attitude still lingers in some quarters, pragmatism and consortial mentality make it impractical. When materials were moved around among branch libraries on campus, these usually had to go through the Catalog Department for processing. Hiring additional staff to catalog these collections was usually not an option.

Improved telecommunications, online tools such as LC's *Catalogers' Desktop* and *Passport for Windows,* Internet and dial-up access to OCLC and other databases now allow catalogers to work remotely, as well as in a central facility. For instance, the National Library of Medicine determined that it was the final product that counted and whether the work was completed by in-house employees at the central site or elsewhere by independent contractors made little difference.[3]

UNMGL has used three approaches for collections at sites that are not administrative branches of the Library. In one instance, a department cataloger, paid by the Library, cataloged the collection of the Clark Field Archive and Library. This collection, owned by a museum association and operated by the UNM's Department of Anthropology, is extensive, and the backlog and retrospective conversion of the shelflist was a multi-year project. Work was done primarily at the site, with the museum association providing the hardware, and UNMGL providing the software and the cataloger. Another arrangement, for the Native American Studies Department, used grant monies to hire several UNMGL catalogers to moonlight. Work was done in the Catalog Department using library equipment and the participants were paid additional wages by Native American Studies. A third approach involved the UNM Alliance for Transportation Research Institute Library, which has paid UNMGL for the services of one of its regular cataloging staff. This cataloger moved to the Institute and works regular but flexible hours. The Institute supplies the hardware and the Library contributes the software and the expertise. These various arrangements reflect a more business-like attitude, since the Catalog Department is no longer able to subsidize cataloging at affiliated consortial libraries.

Such arrangements provide several tangible advantages. Materials do not need to be carried to the central Catalog Department for cataloging. There is no need for direct supervision of the employee, although some adjustments may have to be made for differing conditions. The materials continue to be available to users at the remote sites, and departmental routines are not disrupted. The cataloger works in the same environment as the end-users and is in a position to see how materials are being accessed, and can act as a resource person for those needing a wider range of information. This experience can make cataloging decisions more appropriate and user friendly. There are also some trade-offs. These include slower communications lines, less than optimum working conditions, lack of adequate work-space, noise form users at the remote site, and the fact that some tools and resources are available only in the Catalog Department.

Telecommuting

Cataloging standards, quotas, and expectations that evaluate cataloging done at remote sites, also serve as guides for catalogers who telecommute from home. The needs and desires to telecommute extend far beyond the early stereotypes of being able to spend the workday in a bathrobe.[4] Women are more likely to seek telecommuting options–family considerations are most often cited, and women still appear to have the most responsibilities in this area–and libraries are staffed mainly by women.[5] Disabled staff, or those for whom a long commute is stressful, also seek this option. Yet the option to telecommute has been slow to arrive in libraries. A poll conducted by *Library Personnel News* noted that of 60 libraries polled, only 12 allowed it, with academic libraries more likely to support it than public libraries.[6]

Several circumstances led to telecommuting at UNMGL. One faculty cataloger's child care considerations prompted her to request part-time telecommuting. A months-long renovation project was going to put additional burdens on the Department. It was suggested that all her responsibilities be handled from the remote departmental library, whose collection she was cataloging, or from her home. Having worked at home during a previous, non-cataloging assignment, required hardware and software were in place and work routines established. Past experience with telecommuting had and solved the typical problems of distractions and household interruptions. Since jobs with quantifiable standards that do not require public interface or direct supervision are most easily adapted to telecommuting, working at home posed no disruption to Departmental routines.[7] Having clear objectives and goals was essential. In fact, quotas, while not applied to faculty catalogers, helped alleviate two of the typical disadvantages vex telecommuters. First, since cataloging has a never-ending backlog, the quotas indicate not only when to keep going but also when to stop. Secondly, the fact that family considerations prompted the request to telecommute, it did not turn out to be detrimental to career advancement considerations since goals were met.[8] Statistics and standards speak for themselves, thus the isolation inherent in telecommuting impacts catalogers less than those in other fields.[9]

The second instance of telecommuting was the result of a disability. Telecommuting allows the employee to "adjust time to coincide with optimum effectiveness."[10] This is especially true of employees coping with illness or injury. In this instance, the Library contributed the hardware, the software, and a faster communications link. The employee works at home full time, coming in for meetings and to pick up and drop off work. While her primary job is authority and quality control, additional assignments have included cataloging. The work gets done, and expertise and experience have been retained by both the employee and the Department. However, working off site did mean that the disabled employee could not perform supervisory duties, and this resulted in a lower job classification.

Since these two instances of telecommuting have caused minimal disruptions, and since telecommuting has been used in other departments at UNMGL, future requests might be considered. However, barring a disability, the Library cannot afford to contribute the hardware and faster telecommunications links to all. Thus, this option will only be available to those who can afford it.

FLEXIBILITY IN CATALOGING SERVICES: BUYING AND SELLING CATALOGING

Traditionally, catalog departments have outsourced selectively, e.g., federal documents, special formats, or retrospective conversion. Over the years UNMGL has outsourced the conversion of sections of its shelflist to OCLC, its name and subject authority control, and the cataloging of government documents. However, it has been taken for granted that "regular" purchased and gift materials should be cataloged in-house. Until the early 1990s, vacant cataloging positions were re-advertised and filled almost automatically and the Library typically had a large backlog of uncataloged materials. From the mid-1990s on, several hiring freezes were put in place and the Catalog Department lost nearly a fourth of its positions.

Administrative pressure started to mount to outsource some cataloging. Cataloging is often a good target for outsourcing because, unlike other departments, it is production-oriented. It is easy to quantify output and to specify the number of records that can be purchased. While libraries can buy cataloging records from various vendors, increasingly, they can purchase a full package of products from a single vendor including the book, the matching records (bibliographic, authority, and/or item), as well as physical processing.

Following these traditional patterns, the Department thus decided to outsource what it estimated could be done more cheaply by a vendor, i.e, cataloging 270 Sanskrit monographs. Lack of language expertise made the job expensive to do in-house. Ironically, at the time of the proposal, there were no extra funds to pay for the outsourcing of this collection so the Department had to backtrack and selectively catalog them in-house. Interest in outsourcing is rising again, this time, for approval plans and firm orders, the high-volume and less expensive titles. However, it is not clear where the funding for outsourcing will be found.

More recently, the Department found itself in the reverse situation, that is, selling cataloging to a consortium library. In the past, smaller consortium libraries had contracted with individual catalogers, but in 1998 the UNM Alliance for Transportation Research Institute library signed a formal year-long contract with the Department for the cataloging of its collection. The Department "lost" a staff member for a year but the funds received were used for much needed office furniture and equipment. This move was rather controversial, especially in times of general belt-tightening but at the end of the project, the cataloger will return to a regular assignment. Other consortium libraries are also interested in similar arrangements and discussions are underway.

FLEXIBILITY IN THE ORGANIZATION OF PERSONNEL AND INFORMATION

In the early 1980s, some predicted that "today's professional work may migrate to the level of library specialists, technicians or others," to achieve enhanced workflow and productivity.[11] Throughout the 1990s, the library literature focused on the expanded job responsibilities of paraprofessional catalogers, while noting that the roles of librarian catalogers shifted to management, supervision, training and systems duties. Mary M. Rider writes that "Changes in cataloging practices and philosophies, new technologies and vendor services, and enhanced efficiency and productivity" have allowed us to become more effective as catalogers by organizing personnel, information and materials in new ways.[12]

Staffing Re/Assignments

At UNMGL, responsibilities were reassigned to different levels of staff and students, in and outside of the Catalog Department, depending on the complexity of cataloging needed. Historically, paraprofessionals at UNMGL have edited OCLC member records for the local system, have input full level original records, and have created authority headings. These staff also cataloged DLC copy, using virtually the same procedures as with other non-DLC member copy. Yet studies that have looked at the quality of copy catalog records have found them good enough to be accepted without revision.[13] During the re-evaluation process, CMG decided to draw the line between complex and simple cataloging, and assigned "vanilla" DLC copy to lower level staff in the Bibliographic Control Section. Additionally, some staff in the Acquisitions/Serials Department volunteered to assist with this level of cataloging.

The Ibero-American Cataloging Section, on the other hand, decided to utilize the language expertise of graduate students from the University's strong programs in Spanish and Portuguese language and culture. There is ample evidence in the literature that the use of student assistants in academic libraries is a well-established and essential practice. In fact, a whole issue of *Journal of Library Administration* is devoted to the theme of "Libraries and Student Assistants: Critical Links."[14] For the most part, though, the articles discuss the students' roles in public service departments such as circulation, periodicals, stack maintenance, or reference departments. To judge by the current literature, no in-depth studies have examined the use of students in copy cataloging.

Over the years, Ibero-American Cataloging had employed a number of student assistants for the more routine tasks of sorting, counting and shelving new titles, of keeping statistics, searching for authorities, and verifying literature call numbers. Copy cataloging, which usually requires years of training and on-the-job experience, had been considered too specialized an activity. However, the language expertise needed to correct typos and other inaccuracies made it practical to consider the knowledge of either or both languages to be more important than cataloging experience. These students now catalog all DLC copy. This practice has been in place for over three years and it has been successful. The Section has been able to reduce its backlog of over 10,000 titles to under 2,000. The fundamental drawback of employing students in cataloging is their rapid turnover as they graduate, a factor that some authors have called "variability."[15] This indeed proved to be a problem in the Ibero-American Cataloging Section and the continuous training and revision have taxed the Section's resources.

Defining Standards and Expectations

In conjunction with the point system, cataloging managers developed several documents to help catalogers decide how much or how little to edit member copy. Catalogers were given lists of MARC fields to check against local and national authority files. Standards for cataloging DLC AACR2, pre-AACR2, and non-DLC copy clearly indicated which fixed and variable fields to edit. Depending on the type of copy found, authority work is either done pre- or post-cataloging. On the other hand, original catalogers are expected to create "perfect" records since UNMGL is a BIBCO participant.

One of the first changes in departmental workflow was the implementation of post-cataloging authority control for copy cataloging. Daily exceptions lists generated from the OPAC report new and/or erroneous headings. Topical subject headings, and single surname authors listed are searched and conflicts resolved by maintenance staff. A sampling indicated that these two categories seldom present significant problems and that handling them post-cataloging eliminated considerable searching. Compound and corporate names and series are still searched and resolved at the point of cataloging. Managers are presently discussing the pros and cons of expanding post-cataloging authority work to all headings

Despite this streamlining, managers have encouraged staff to participate in national cooperative efforts. As a major research library, UNMGL has an obligation to contribute quality cataloging at the national level. However, while the Department participates in NACO and BIBCO, not all catalogers are obligated to contribute. It is left to the individual's judgement to make the additional effort required for compliance with national cooperative programs. As both output and national level contributions generate points, both choices are re-warded.

Other efficiencies were introduced by creating collection level records and by changing analysis practice. Pamphlets, related minor titles bound together, and ephemera often had been fully cataloged; cataloging culture focused on the individual piece rather than on the big picture. Such materials at UNMGL are now being examined carefully and decisions have been made to catalog many as collections. Similarly, virtually every title in a series used to be analyzed. However, with the loss of positions over the years, this practice was also put under the microscope. While the Department will usually follow LC's analysis practice, managers are reexamining local decisions and many titles are being recataloged as serials.

The adoption of the core record generated discussions between technical and public service librarians. Ironically, the same public services librarians who found full cataloging unnecessarily complex and time-consuming worried about the loss of access points, notes, and subject headings and did not support the adoption of the core record at the local level. After the Library of Congress announced that its default would be to catalog at the core level, some collection development librarians at UNM recommended that DLC records be upgraded from core to full. However, since DLC copy is now handled by lower level staff and students, cataloging managers decided that those records had to be accepted.

OUTCOMES OF FLEXIBLE MANAGEMENT

No matter how thorough the planning for such complex processes, some results can be unexpected. While it is possible to plan for and predict changes in workflows and in processes, it is the human element that produces the most surprises.

Intended Outcomes

The introduction of flextime gave catalogers almost full control over their schedules, which may be the greatest single benefit to staff. The benefits to the Department were equally important: increased efficiency, realistic production expectations, and improved ability to predict staffing needs.

Under the point system, the most efficient catalogers became even more efficient. They fully embraced the point system and were able to radically reduce their work hours. For a few, it made little difference. Most catalogers fell somewhere in the middle range and benefitted from the flexibility of choosing their own pace. Catalogers have become more efficient in the way they catalog and production levels are no longer an issue. Time gained from reassigning cataloging tasks, from rearranging workflows, and from using the latest technologies was diverted to increased production and new ventures. These included processing uncataloged backlogs and providing access to such diverse materials as electronic resources and pamphlet collections.

Since the automatic filling of vacant positions no longer occurs, cataloging managers can respond to requests for work on projects such as retrospective conversion, or special collections cataloging, with accurate data in terms of personnel needs, time requirements, and productivity. Managers have a better sense of how much cataloging the Department can deliver. In addition, inquiries from anywhere in the library system regarding outsourcing options can also be answered much more accurately. Comparing costs for in-house vs. offsite cataloging and processing has become less of a guessing game.

Perhaps the most difficult aspect of this new approach was to give up the old ideal of fully cataloging every work in the collection. Does every piece or byte the library owns–or can provide access to–need the painstaking, detailed cataloging work that we have traditionally lavished on them?

Unintended Outcomes

Unintended outcomes were both positive and negative. On the positive side, catalogers' work practices, scheduling, and the use of sick leave turned out even better than expected. Some faculty catalogers have also changed their attitudes as a result of this change in culture.

Since catalogers were allowed to take control of their time on the job, and some discovered that by using shortcuts and macros extensively, they could work more efficiently. They could achieve their cataloging production and earn the required points with less time in the Library. Catalogers showed great creativity in this area. Also, a few good production days meant time off for outside interests. Concurrently, catalogers' tolerance for aging hardware, disk crashing, or slow response time has been reduced considerably.

Odd schedules did not prove to be a problem. Moreover, eliminating the red tape involved in tracking attendance proved a huge blessing to supervisors. Phone messages, made-up time, doctors' appointments, and other scheduling arrangement were eliminated. Supervisors did not realize how long it took to monitor schedules and welcomed the chance to let go of this aspect of management. However, a year into the program, a restriction was imposed. The Library administration felt the need to restrict night-time work–even though no catalogers wanted to work only at night.

Although faculty catalogers had not been bound by standard schedules, most had kept regular office times, generally between 8:00 and 5:00. However, after the flexible scheduling and point system was introduced for staff, some faculty also started keeping more variable hours and started to look at their output in terms of the expectations applied to staff catalogers.

The use of sick leave was cut by half. When people feel tired or have an off-day, they can go home and then choose to work when rested or recovered. Staff no longer use sick leave for doctors' appointments for themselves and their families.

There was also a down side. The division of cataloging among different levels of staff eliminated all the easy copy cataloging for higher level staff, with everything remaining requiring either more complex editing or original cataloging. Much of the complex copy requires some research and the creation of authority headings, which adds to the time it takes to complete the cataloging process, adding interest but also stress to the job. The opportunity to learn from easy DLC copy–and even to kick back–is no longer available.

Since some of the DLC copy cataloging is done outside the Catalog Department, training and supervision are more difficult to accomplish and politically delicate to handle. It is difficult to direct and evaluate staff that one does not supervise. Training and re-training staff who do not catalog full-time takes more time, and enforcing quality control requires considerable diplomatic skills.

By far, the most surprising outcome was a striking change in socialization. When flextime and the point system were first introduced, there was some sense of isolation among staff, with a silence that could be deafening. Where there once had been camaraderie and conversations–too much at times–catalogers preferred to go home after they had earned enough points. The same was true for library-wide or campus-wide events, such as "Diversity Day," for example, which staff became less likely to attend. However, as they got used to the system and learned how to monitor progress towards their monthly goal, catalogers' social interaction is slowly returning to normal.

CONCLUSIONS

Most changes introduced in the Catalog Department have come about pragmatically, in response to local conditions and personalities. There was no grand scheme, no mission statement, no goals and objectives, other than getting more work done with less pain. No time was spent in building a theoretical framework, because cataloging production had to continue; glitches were solved in real time. Even though changes were achieved in a piece-meal manner, the Department kept its focus at all times.

Bringing flexibility to one area made it easier to be flexible in others. Many options are now available: catalogers work when they are most productive, they work in different locations, and they work at home. This approach allows performance evaluations to be based on a neutral point system rather than by comparing catalogers to one another. Catalogers go to work with a different attitude, morale is generally higher and fritter time, which does not generate points, has moved offsite. Greater flexibility also helped the Department comply with ADA with minimum disruption. The Department took a fresh look at its processes and at how catalog records are used and made changes in several areas. Defining standards and expectations for local and national cataloging, using technology more effectively, allowing staff outside cataloging sections and students to participate in copy cataloging, helped the Department redefine itself.

Supplying cataloging to campus libraries was an eye-opener. The managers, in true cataloger tradition, had assumed that these libraries wanted what catalogers knew how to do best, i.e., full MARC cataloging. The cost associated with this level of cataloging astounded one campus library and perhaps it should have forewarned the Department as well. In view of this reaction, the Department will be looking at other, cheaper options in the future, such as minimal level records linked to digitized text, or even non-MARC based access.

Even though the Department has made drastic changes, it can only go so far given current cataloging rules and technology. Although much has been achieved already, we are still in a period of transition and it is discouraging to realize that we have only scratched the surface. Processes and perspectives change, but catalogers must seriously consider what it is that we do, rather than how we do it. That will be the hard part, because it will entail breaking with principles and traditions that are embedded in our culture. So far, the cataloging community has been tweaking the formats and the rules–i.e., minimum level cataloging, core and/or collection level cataloging, including tables of contents–but needs to define alternatives. While technology has so far allowed us to duplicate the catalog in a new medium, the OPAC is still unable to adequately provide what users are really after, content rather than a bibliographic citation. The OPAC has been relegated to second place while web-based resources provide the user with instant content. Cataloging rules, designed for a more linear and static environment, cannot adequately be applied to the dynamic hyperlinked Web environment. True flexibility in cataloging will remain limited until–and if–current formats and rules adapt to an Internet model. UNMGL's exercise in flexible management has allowed us to look at this future in a positive light.

NOTES

1. Claire-Lise Bénaud, Sever Bordeianu, and Mary Ellen Hanson, "The Quantification of Cataloging: Documenting Productivity in a Flexible Scheduling Environment," to be published in *Technical Services Quarterly*.

2. Susanne Bjorner, "Changing Places: Building New Workplace Infrastructures," *Online* 21 (November/December, 1997): 10.

3. Fred Hamilton, "Rethinking the Workforce and Workplace: Alternative Ways of Getting the Job Done," *The Serials Librarian* 25, no. 3-4 (1995): 256.

4. Joshua Cohen, "Home Work: the New Job World,"*Library Journal* 122 (May 1, 1997): 51.

5. Jeanette Woodward, "Commuting from Electronic Cottage to Virtual Library," *Library Administration & Management* 10, no. 4 (Fall, 1996): 226.

6. "At-home Work Uncommon in Libraries," *Library Personnel News* 4, no. 1 (Winter 1990): 2.

7. Hamilton, "Rethinking the Workforce," 257.

8. Patricia Mokhtarian and Carol Mandel, "The Impact of Gender, Occupation, and Presence of Children on Telecommuting Motivations and Constraints," *Journal of the American Society for Information Science* 49, no. 12 (October, 1998): 1126–1127.

9. "Eight Keys to Managing Telecommuters," *Library Personnel News* 10, no. 5 (September–October, 1996): 5.

10. Hamilton, "Rethinking the Workforce," 257, and Judy L. Johnson, "Flexible Staffing Through Use of Telecommuting: A Report of the ALCTS Creative Ideas in Technical Services Discussion Group Meeting, American Library Association Midwinter Meeting, Washington, D.C. February, 1997," *Technical Services Quarterly* 15, no. 3 (1998): 83.

11. Mary M. Rider, "Developing New Roles for Paraprofessionals in Cataloging," *Journal of Academic Librarianship* 22, no. 1 (Jan. 1996): 26.

12. Rider, "Developing New Roles," 26.

13. Rider, "Developing New Roles," 28.

14. "Libraries and Student Assistants: Critical Links," William K. Black, guest editor, *Journal of Library Administration* 21, no. 3/4 (1995).

15. Donald G. Frank, "Management of Student Assistants in a Public Services Setting of an Academic Library," *RQ* no. 1 (fall 1984): 52.

Management by Action:
How We're Embracing
New Cataloging Work at Tufts

Lyn Condron

SUMMARY. Preparing for new cataloging such as metadata beyond MARC and thesauri beyond LCSH, is an exciting and daunting challenge for university libraries. Advancing technologies, as well as a growing demand for quality information with rapid access is fueling the need for technical services departments to restructure their work to accommodate the evolving world of information management. Catalogers who have been following the same procedures and practices for many years may find this change particularly difficult. Team leaders are often faced with breaking through skepticism and resistance to this new work in order to enable necessary progress. We found that discussions and gradual introduction of new directions is important to acceptance by team members. However, just as important is the implementation of an action plan to ensure that progress is ongoing. Reengineering Acquisitions and Cataloging into Current Processes and Information Management Initiatives, along with forming several focus groups to investigate and evaluate cataloging work, is proving successful for embracing

Lyn Condron, is Head of Cataloging/Web Manager, Tufts University Tisch Library, Professors Row, Medford, MA 02155 (E-mail: lyn.condron@tufts.edu). She holds an MLS from the University of North Texas.

My thanks to two Tisch Library team members for participation and assistance in preparing the reengineered model for Technical Services: Paul J. Stanton, Director of Administration for Information Technology and Libraries in the School of Arts & Sciences, and Anthony Kodzis, Head of Acquisitions, Tisch Library.

[Haworth co-indexing entry note]: "Management by Action: How We're Embracing New Cataloging Work at Tufts." Condron, Lyn. Co-published simultaneously in *Cataloging & Classification Quarterly* (The Haworth Information Press, an imprint of The Haworth Press, Inc.) Vol. 30, No. 2/3, 2000, pp. 299-313; and: *Managing Cataloging and the Organization of Information: Philosophies, Practices and Challenges at the Onset of the 21st Century* (ed: Ruth C. Carter) The Haworth Information Press, an imprint of The Haworth Press, Inc., 2000, pp. 299-313. Single or multiple copies of this article are available for a fee from The Haworth Document Delivery Service [1-800-342-9678, 9:00 a.m. - 5:00 p.m. (EST). E-mail address: getinfo@haworthpressinc.com].

299

new cataloging at Tufts University. *[Article copies available for a fee from The Haworth Document Delivery Service: 1-800-342-9678. E-mail address: <getinfo@haworthpressinc.com> Website: <http://www.HaworthPress.com>]*

KEYWORDS. Management, supervising, catalogers, professionals, teams, restructuring, reengineering, technical services, cataloging, acquisitions

In November 1998, I began a new position as Head of Cataloging/ Web Manager at Tisch Library, Tufts University. Tisch is the library for the School of Arts, Sciences, and Engineering, in a private Massachusetts university with approximately 6000 students enrolled in the School. I was excited about the new challenges facing me, and was anxious to learn how this department worked. Though this was my first position as a department head and I knew I would be learning on the job, I was confident that my years of experience managing in other capacities, coupled with my training in this area, would serve me well in this new endeavor. Simultaneously, major changes were also occurring in the library world, and I was eager to explore and implement these with the staff. Soon I began to realize, though, that initial openness to a new team leader was deteriorating into skepticism about my ideas, particularly as they related to these emerging technologies. Continuing to overcome this resistance to change is proving to be a critical and often difficult portion of this journey. My first year in this position has been one of many challenges and sometimes discouragement, but on the whole, one of growth and team success. Progressive technologies, policies, and procedures are beginning to reshape both the actual work results, as well as learning opportunities for the staff.

BACKGROUND

Upon my arrival, the Tisch Cataloging Department was comprised of four professionals, two library assistants at level III (Tisch's highest), four at level II, and the department head. Longevity ranged from six months to over four decades, with all four professionals having been in their current positions for more than a decade. These ten positions had been standard for several years, and were necessary for the workflows that were currently in place. In acquainting myself with the policies and procedures of the department it soon became apparent that local cataloging practices had not been adequately evaluated in many years. Since Tufts has had only one automated library system (acquired in the mid 1980s), the natural tendency to stay with procedures designed in conjunction with this radical change was deeply embedded. Workflow and procedural evaluations take lower priority when things appear to be working well. Additionally, emerging technologies, along with the increasing demand for more rapid access to information was making Tisch, along with all libraries, reevaluate virtually all aspects of our work.

Initial discussions with the department staff revealed that most felt the procedures were as streamlined and efficient as possible, given the need to maintain the level of quality to which Tisch was committed. This belief was particularly strong in team members with the greatest longevity. The department had been without a head for nearly two years, and the environment was more one of individual contributors with separately designed objectives rather than of a team with cohesive goals. One of my first priorities was to bring leadership back to the department and to guide members toward a more unified structure.

As a step toward achieving this, I began deliberately and consistently to alter some language. History has shown that while seemingly subtle differences exist in many of our language's apparent synonyms, updating terms is often a catalyst toward achieving shifts in individual and group thinking. The past quarter century particularly is replete with examples–"worker's comp" to replace "workman's comp" being only one of a myriad. I quickly began using the term "team" instead of "department."[1]

I also embarked on the somewhat controversial practice of referring to "customers" instead of "patrons." While I do understand the objections to this term in the library field, it is becoming ever more apparent that libraries, particularly in universities, are in an increasingly competitive environment. Technology, especially the web, has made it possible for potential students (customers) to evaluate educational institutions more rapidly and thoroughly. Universities' libraries have always been and continue to be a vital part of this evaluation process. Additionally, libraries at the turn of the twenty-first century are competing with the likes of Amazon.com, where the relatively small monetary price is often seen as a viable option for students needing information quickly. Other competitors we've not faced before are also to be found via the web–the volume of information available with a few mouse clicks is astounding. Librarians must take a more assertive role in educating our customers that we are able to help them locate *quality* information amidst this sea of "stuff." Increasingly, entrepreneurs are finding that libraries' past and current customers are willing to expend funds to insure rapid access to quality information–traditionally a major challenge for many libraries. The fact of the matter is, if we don't provide our customers with the services they want, they *will* go elsewhere. Ultimately, without shifts in our thinking and practices, we librarians could be forced into new careers. Practicing true *customer* service instead of the standard patron service is vital for every member of any library's staff in the twenty-first century.

Persisting with these language changes proved to be one of the smallest challenges; guiding a team to reevaluate policies and procedures in which they were deeply invested was and remains one of the biggest. Additionally, emerging cataloging technologies and practices were not yet seen by many team members to have much value. There was no real collective reason for progress because, in fact, Tisch's cataloging practices were working. And if it ain't broke. . . . "Not broken" and "working well," however, are far from synonymous. While Tisch Cataloging had always performed well qualitatively, our workflows inadvertently insured a longer than necessary turnaround time of materials cataloged, as well as more staff than were needed. We were cataloging for catalogers instead of for customers: recataloging acceptable copy, oververifying, and investing too much time on non-access points. To be sure, our practices mirrored those of many other excellent libraries, and were formulated during a card catalog environment and before the majority of Library of Congress and member copy available in OCLC was of an acceptable quality. I, too, had been reared in this school of cataloging and had begun my career based on the realities of the time. But realities change, and certainly ours in libraries have changed drastically in the past several years. Tisch Cataloging had not successfully kept current with the progress in the field. No doubt, a major cause for our static environment rather than a dynamic one was our only having had one local system. This in and of itself, of course, is not necessarily a detriment. But while libraries are always informed of changes and upgrades to their local systems, only major ones generally become absorbed into the workflow. Without a deliberate reevaluation of customer needs, policies, workflow, *and* an examination of the new technology available in the local system, it is highly unlikely that any technical services team could hope to attain peak performance.

Couldn't all the team members see this as clearly as I did? Shouldn't my proselytizing about the wonders of cataloging for customers instead of catalogers be enough to persuade any potential holdouts? Needless to say, my analyses and solutions were generally not met with enthusiasm. And really, why should they be? Things *were* working given the environment that most of the team members had been in for many years. Obviously, many felt, the new department head was the big bad wolf sent here to blow the house down, a house that had been standing for a long time. "Yes, but the house was made of straw" was hardly an acceptable evaluation on my part. I was branded a change agent; brought in to make change to the status quo. Change just for change's sake is not necessarily a good thing. However, progress is. "Progress professional" is beginning to replace the popular "change professional" of the past few years, particularly in the business literature. Perhaps in this new century we will see librarians' (virtual) business cards proudly displaying this title!

Part of this resistance was due to the American working environment at the time that many staff members had joined Tisch. Management theories, like many others, are cyclical, and philosophy in the 1970s and early 1980s focused more on what made the employee feel good than on performance results. The 1990s has seen a turn toward more personal responsibility and accountability. It was no wonder that this change in direction was an uncomfortable one for many staff.

Despite resistance, the department head's responsibilities still included streamlining our procedures. Spurring this necessity was the loss within two months of three staff members due to resignation, retirement, and illness. Three more team members left within a few more months. Certainly each individual had specific personal reasons for leaving, but there is little doubt that the new environment and direction we were moving toward played a role in some of the decisions to resign. Change–even good change–as we're told repeatedly, is seldom easy.

Action Phase I

Much of my management training and experience seemed to be failing me. Additionally, while I could locate information and assistance on change resistance, I was having less success finding information in the literature on managing professionals–quickly becoming my downfall. Time and again, the only viable option was to move forward, even if only in a test environment, over the objections of many team members, particularly the professionals. The culmination of the resistance came in June of 1999, when we moved forward with testing student assistants performing DLC (Library of Congress) cataloging. This one task seemed to represent the core of much of the trepidation: "If students are able to do our work, we won't have jobs." True and not true. Advances in practices and technology have made DLC cataloging so much more routine than it was even a few years ago that libraries are now able to take advantage of the opportunity of having students perform this task. I attempted to assuage fears by discussing the more complex work that we were currently faced with–and could not handle because our time was invested in routine cataloging. And what about this exciting new field in cataloging spawned by the emergence of the web? Catalogers, I joyously reiterated, are in the best positions to transition our MARC (MAchine Readable Cataloging) skills into other metadata, and our knowledge and experience with LCSH (Library of Congress Subject Headings) into other thesauri. We would not be losing our jobs; we would be gaining opportunities to enhance them. Again, though, it is unrealistic for a team leader to expect staff who have been working well in the same way for several years to accept changes easily.

Besides the fear of loss of status, a real concern was that quality would be compromised. This is an especially difficult issue for catalogers; after all, not so long ago we had had full control over virtually every aspect of the catalog–those beautiful cards! Gradually, most team members are accepting that neither Tisch, nor any library, will have a perfect database; that while we definitely should do what is necessary to maintain authority control and accurate access points, the time spent oververifying and overediting work results in little added value for the customers.

Empowering team members to design and implement the pilot project of students performing DLC cataloging was a key factor in gaining acceptance, however reluctant, to conduct this test. Contacting other libraries who had implemented similar plans provided some much needed input from a source other than "the new department head." In addition, we had conducted some informal interviews with other catalogers to gain insight into their workflows and procedures.

With the onset of Tufts' new fiscal year on July 1, 1999, it was time for each team member to set individual goals. Coincidentally, my first experience in goal-setting with this team was simultaneous with the implementation of a completely revamped performance evaluation process at Tufts. The new @WORK Program outlined specific steps in setting SMART goals (specific, measurable, attainable, relevant, and time-bound) for all Tufts employees. This program also includes five competencies: expertise, interaction with others, continuous improvement/customer focus, resourcefulness and results, and leadership.[2] While all Tisch staff had set annual goals for many years, most Cataloging Team members, particularly the professionals, had not previously set measurable (quantitative) goals. Though it was clear that this change in the goal-setting process was university-wide, there was much resistance to the concept of professionals being held accountable for measurable goals. Cataloging, particularly, is a much easier task to quantify than many others in the library field. Just as libraries know frequently to the dollar how much of the budget is allocated annually to new materials, they must also be able to gauge with a fair amount of accuracy how many titles will be cataloged within a year. While all who perform original cataloging understand that some titles are more complex than others (and therefore require a larger investment of time), cataloging teams can and should be responsible for advising administrators on expectations of work to be completed. This cannot be accomplished successfully unless individual team members are accountable for measurable goals.

Action Phase II

The dawn of Fiscal Year 2000 also provided us an opportunity to outline an action plan. The Director of Administration for Information Technology and Libraries in the School of Arts & Sciences and I realized it was time to present the team with a visual explanation of the direction we were taking. I prepared and presented a number of slides (Figure A) as a blueprint, with most of the details deliberately omitted. These were yet to be specified, and an introduction of our direction was plenty of new information for team members to digest at one time. Major themes of this presentation included team work, increased personal responsibility and accountability, cataloging for customers, and

Figure A (7/12/99 Presentation)

Slide 2: Emphasizing the importance that organizational objectives are the driving force behind the development of individual goals was a reversal in practice for many team members.

Slides 3-4: Understanding we serve internal customers, including peer team members, as well as external customers, is a vital shift in thinking.

Slide 5: It was critical to reinforce that these changes were not unique to Tisch, nor were they being derived by the team leader or administration.

Slide 7: Automatable titles: Those easily performed by paraprofessional staff, student assistants, or receiving shelf-ready titles. Much of our record editing had resulted in cataloging for catalogers; i.e., no true value added for customers.

Slide 10: We had been investing much valuable time performing tasks that at best, would potentially serve a small portion of the Tufts community.

Slide 11: Training, initial and ongoing, is paramount to the success of any team.

Slide 14: One team member felt offended at the car mechanic example in this slide. Others, though, felt this to be a good analogy.

Slides 14-16: Clearly outlining expected qualities of team members was an important step in delineating expectations to which we had previously merely alluded.

Slides 17-21: These were perhaps the most important slides in the presentation. Individuals and groups need incentives to change.

Slide 18: I deliberately used the phrase "career security" instead of "job security."

Slide 19: Many catalogers have often felt that we were the stepchildren of the library. It is up to us as catalogers to change that perception by increasing the value of our work.

Slides 22-24: "Metadata"–Perhaps the most negatively-charged concept in the cataloging world since removing those oak cabinets with the precious little drawers threatened to ruin our lives! This visual explanation helped alleviate some fears about our upcoming new work.

Slides 25-35: A few more details are presented here, including a framework for a timeline. However, the nuts and bolts of the new work are purposely omitted.

Slide 33: This definition showed perhaps the most important aspect of the team work. Focus groups (see presentation of 9/16/99) derived in part from this concept.

having routine work performed by lower-level staff and student assistants. Though I had been hired with the title of Head of Cataloging and Web Manager, there was no real home for the web work. Various staff members and student assistants had handled the maintenance at various times, but we had realized that adding new web sites was a responsibility that generally did not lend itself well to student assistants, as more continuity was required than could be maintained with students who frequently worked for only one semester. It had never been the intention that I would perform the technical work, but clearly it was important for us to ensure the validity of this work by putting responsibility for it on the same team as the Web Manager.

A major purpose of the July presentation was for me to visually reinforce ideas I had espoused since my arrival; i.e., that catalogers must learn new skills to empower us to catalog in the new millennium. Names of teams and positions were presented as suggestions only, to be determined by the team. A deliberate attempt was made to include areas which would directly address questions which all team members were most surely pondering: what's in it for us.

We had an immediate discussion after the presentation, and scheduled another one for a week later. Feedback from those sessions revealed a deeper resistance than I had assessed–based in large part on skepticism about a "digital library" ever coming to fruition. Indeed, Tufts, like many universities, had just begun the process of discussing our digital library a few months prior to the July presentation. Understandably, it's difficult to see how individual daily work will change when the concept itself is still in its abstract form. Team members also wanted more details.

We agreed to a follow-up session in September. In the meantime, I asked all team members for ongoing feedback on the direction we were heading, our team goals, and concerns or suggestions about how individuals fit into this new plan.

Action Phase III

Over the next two months, the Director of Administration, the Head of Acquisitions, and I developed an action plan to implement the goals outlined in the July presentation. While we would not be actually merging Acquisitions and Cataloging into one team, we knew that there were many areas of redundancy, as well as tasks being handled by inappropriate levels of staff, (e.g., professional catalogers performing routine, non-complex cataloging). By shifting some responsibilities and focusing on Current Processes (CP) and Information Management Initiatives (IMI) instead of Acquisitions and Cataloging, we were able to streamline work and eliminate many redundancies, ensure appropriate levels of work, reduce total staff, and build in time for new work (specifically that having to do with digital libraries and reviewing workflows). CP would be performing all DLC and other routine cataloging; IMI would be performing complex cataloging, as well as focusing on new work.

In September of 1999, I presented the team with a new visual outline–this time in much more detail. The Head of Acquisitions presented it to his team as well, and we each had individual and group discussions. The slides for this presentation (Figure B) have been altered only in the omission of staff names and issues local to Tufts/Tisch. The position titles of "Prof" and "Parap" are in order of appearance in the presentation, not in ranking or seniority order.

This restructuring of teams' and individuals' responsibilities was a radical change from our previous paradigm. Moving the routine work, including DLC cataloging and physical processing of materials, over to Current Processes left obvious gaps in work for those in Information Management Initiatives. Tisch, like most libraries, is acquiring more and more electronic resources. Additionally, while we do not yet know exactly when and how, there is no doubt that we will be working soon on digital library processes. It is critical that libraries not repeat the mistake with digital libraries that most inadvertently made in not preparing quickly enough for the emergence of the web and its impact on our work. Catalogers need to begin educating ourselves on other metadata, thesauri, and technical aspects with which we will soon be working.

Perhaps the most important function emerging from the plan presented in September was the formation of several focus groups. Those performing the daily work (i.e., team members) should be the same ones responsible for investigating, evaluating, and recommending new workflows. Time must be allowed for this. Just as importantly, staff must understand that this work is considered a high priority and that performance evaluations will be reflective of individuals' participation. We deliberately used the term "facilitator" for these focus groups, and structured them so that the "expert" in the field would not be in the capacity of facilitator for that group in order to help break

Figure B (9/6/99 Presentation)

Slide 4: We had altered the name of this team slightly from Information Management Services to Information Management Initiatives. While we had solicited suggestions for alternative names, none had emerged.

Slide 5: Further emphasis that goals must be developed in conjunction with the University's mission first, then Tisch Library's.

Slide 6: Workshops range from in-house expertise and Tufts' Human Resources staff to those available through the Boston Library Consortium, etc.

Slide 9: We will be reviewing individual and team goals quarterly (partially as required by Tufts' @WORK Program).

Slide 11: We have since lost our intern and made the decision to shift this work to paraprofessionals.

Slide 19: Ongoing training is now written into these paraprofessionals' job descriptions.

Slide 20: This slide outlines the core of responsibilities for focus groups.

Slides 21-24: The position underlined is the facilitator for that focus group. Soliciting input from those outside Technical Services is a vital factor to the success of these investigations.

Slide 22: The facilitator for Focus Group 6 is the exception to our model of not having the "expert" facilitate the pertinent group; other metadata is so new to all the staff that we felt it important to have a facilitator who had begun some training in this area.

Slide 23: Focus Group 7 (web) was the only one that had previously been in place.

Slide 24: The two professionals in IMI are each facilitators of three focus groups, and participate on an additional one. The only paraprofessional who had not been hired during this quarter was given responsibility for facilitating one focus group and participating in three others.

resistance to change in well established procedures. For example the cataloger mainly responsible for authority control is a member of the focus group on authority control, but is not the facilitator.

The outline in September was presented as a working plan, with only the first two quarters (beginning in October) having specific tasks. Much of the work is ongoing, particularly actual cataloging. The focus groups are anticipated to have short lives, from a few months to a year, depending on the needs and results of the investigations within the groups. However, we will be adjusting or adding focus groups as needed.

Some changes having much impact in this new model involved responsibilities of two professionals. One, a part-time cataloger, was moved to the CP Team.[3] The major reason for this shift was that we needed a strong cataloging expert on the CP Team to act as a bridge between the "non-catalogers" in CP, and the trained catalogers in IMI. Additionally, since focus group meetings and assignments would require a large time commitment from members, it was decided to only have full-time staff working on these groups. This CP cataloger was assigned to one focus group.

The other professional with the most dynamic change was the music cataloger. For many years, Tisch had devoted a full twenty percent of the cataloging staff exclusively to the cataloging of music materials, though music comprises a relatively small percentage of our total collection.

While music cataloging is generally more complex and therefore requires a higher level of skill as well as time, this was one area where an examination of the actual procedures revealed many redundant and unnecessary steps. We had streamlined much of this work in the past several months, but we felt it was important to have a focus group including input from the music librarian.

In order to make room for the new work, particularly metadata, we had to take a close look at our current needs. The music cataloger was given the additional responsibility of metadata, initially in a learning mode. Tisch administration had targeted funds specifically for training IMI staff in new work; workshops and other training forums on metadata have proven invaluable since IMI's inauguration in October 1999.

To truly show our commitment to the new work, team leaders and Tisch administration had to find a way to build time into current team members' job descriptions for responsibility and accountability for performing new work. Priorities were closely examined. Preliminary streamlining of procedures had already released some time previously spent performing the same amount of work. Additionally, we ceased or tabled some projects that were not as critical to our work,–i.e., not as critical for the customers–to enable the necessary time for the new work. This commitment to the new work was explicit in slide 25, where we clearly showed that we were building time for a full fifty percent dedication to new work into job descriptions. While this may seem radical, it is important to keep in mind that all library positions already include varying amounts of time spent in meetings, etc. So in real time, we were allowing for approximately an additional twenty-five percent of time for each IMI team member to spend participating in focus groups and assignments resulting from them, university-wide digital library meetings, etc. It was expected that fifty percent of each team member's time would be spent in actual cataloging.

The September presentation was much more detailed than the July one. However, we iterated that it was a working plan and that many specific assignments would be discussed with team members. This was particularly true for paraprofessionals I, J, and K. We were recruiting for these three positions at the time of the September presentation. Since members of the IMI Team would be performing the more complex work, established and new, we hired all three open paraprofessional positions at the level III rank. We had an excellent opportunity to match tasks with skills in hiring these three team members at the same time; after initial training, we reassigned specific areas of responsibilities as best fit the needs of the team and the individuals. A level II paraprofessional position was added to the CP Team to handle some of the ordering and receiving work previously performed by paraprofessionals who would now be adding DLC and other routine cataloging to their responsibilities.

Reaction was mixed, but generally the new model was not well received by staff in Cataloging. Follow-up group and individual meetings uncovered even further resistance by some team members. However, a turning point was in our actually putting into action the concepts we had been discussing over the past year. Trepidation was definitely still rampant, but in the short time since the emergence of Current Processes and Information Management Initiatives, there has been clear progress–not just in the work itself, but in a sense of openness to new ideas.

Action Phase IV: Progress to Date

Major highlights of the past three months include hiring and training three new IMI team members, as well as participation in Tufts and external workshops on change management, team building, and specific cataloging functions such as authority work, digital libraries, and metadata.

CP team members were generally enthusiastic about cataloging, as my training with them continues to reveal. Several of the focus groups have begun, with guidance from team building workshops and literature assisting us in this new endeavor. We knew actual production would decrease in this first quarter: existing team members had to go through major adjustments, and new team members were in training. A senior paraprofessional has discovered an enjoyment and strong capability in training that she had not previously realized. One professional has embraced the new metadata, now leading others in learning this new field. Visions, and subsequent practices, are beginning to broaden into focusing on customer service rather than "cataloging by the book" (*AACR2*, of course!).

I have learned much in my first year as Head of Cataloging/Web Manager at Tisch, and certainly have much more to learn. Learning and implementing emerging cataloging technologies and practices alone would be enough to keep any cataloging team busy with new work. Add to this the appointment of a new department head who has ideas for progress in areas of well-established work. One overriding theme of this year has been that while team leaders and administrators must introduce new directions to those most affected gradually, allowing for feedback and input at every step, it is equally important at some point to put a plan into action so that these changes can begin to occur–whether acceptance is yet high or not. New processes can and mostly should be begun in a test environment, with continual reassessment along the way. Team members in all capacities are generally interested in learning new work, if given appropriate leadership to help them achieve those goals. While it is understandable that staff who have been performing the same tasks in basically the same way for a number of years would be resistant to change, it is critical for leaders not to be discouraged to the point of preventing us from forging ahead with action plans. Progress can and will begin to be evident in the teams' performance results, and most importantly, in the quality of customer service we catalogers provide for this new era of information gatherers.

NOTES

1. While I prefer the title "Team Leader," I remain "Department Head" to maintain consistency with other peer team leaders at Tisch.

2. Tufts University, *@WORK Guidebook for Performance Development and Compensation Programs*. 1998, p. 17.

3. This professional was offered the option of continuing to report to the Head of Cataloging. She chose to report instead to the Head of Acquisitions, as was suggested in the new model.

AUTHOR NOTE

Due to a publishing error, this article was sent to press without copies of the slides included. Figure A (page 306) and Figure B (page 309) refer to these slides. The full article with the slides included is available in *Cataloging & Classification Quarterly*, volume 32, issue 2, 2001.

Cataloging in Three Academic Libraries:
Operations, Trends, and Perspectives

Kuang-Hwei (Janet) Lee-Smeltzer

SUMMARY. This article describes the cataloging operations and management in three medium-sized academic libraries–Oregon State University, University of Houston, and Colorado State University. It provides an overview of the staffing and organizational structure of the cataloging department in each library. Faced with similar challenges from constantly changing environments brought about by technology and institutional pressure to achieve more with less, library technical services in these three libraries, cataloging in particular, are developing some common strategies for coping. These trends include: (1) changing the roles and responsibilities of both professional and support staff, (2) designing workflow around library systems and limited personnel resources, (3) mainstreaming government documents cataloging and processing into technical services, (4) using technology to increase cataloging efficiency, and (5) dealing with bibliographic control of current electronic resources and moving into digitization and metadata arenas. *[Article copies available for a fee from The Haworth Document Delivery Service: 1-800-342-9678. E-mail address: <getinfo@haworthpressinc.com> Website: <http://www.HaworthPress.com>]*

Kuang-Hwei (Janet) Lee-Smeltzer, MSLIS, is Coordinator for Bibliographic Control and Electronic Resources Services, Colorado State University Libraries, 210A Morgan Library, Fort Collins, CO 80523-1019.

The author would like to acknowledge Debbie Hackleman, Head of Cataloging Department at Oregon State University Libraries; Patricia Smith, Coordinator for Acquisitions Services at Colorado State University Libraries; and Tom Wilson, Head of Systems Department at University of Houston Libraries for their help in the revision of this article.

[Haworth co-indexing entry note]: "Cataloging in Three Academic Libraries: Operations, Trends, and Perspectives." Lee-Smeltzer, Kuang-Hwei (Janet). Co-published simultaneously in *Cataloging & Classification Quarterly* (The Haworth Information Press, an imprint of The Haworth Press, Inc.) Vol. 30, No. 2/3, 2000, pp. 315-330; and: *Managing Cataloging and the Organization of Information: Philosophies, Practices and Challenges at the Onset of the 21st Century* (ed: Ruth C. Carter) The Haworth Information Press, an imprint of The Haworth Press, Inc., 2000, pp. 315-330. Single or multiple copies of this article are available for a fee from The Haworth Document Delivery Service [1-800-342-9678, 9:00 a.m. - 5:00 p.m. (EST). E-mail address: getinfo@haworthpressinc.com].

KEYWORDS. Cataloging management, cataloging operations, cataloging trends, academic libraries

INTRODUCTION

With the introduction of MARC (MAchine-Readable Cataloging), bibliographic utilities and shared cataloging, and integrated library computer systems, we have seen a fundamental change in cataloging operations and management. The development of the Internet and the World Wide Web presents new challenges for the world of cataloging and organization of information. These factors have caused some common themes to emerge in the three libraries at which I have worked–Oregon State University, University of Houston, and Colorado State University.[1] All three institutions are medium-sized academic libraries.

Located in Corvallis, Oregon, Oregon State University (OSU) is a land-grant, sea-grant, and space-grant institution. It is a Carnegie 1 Research University with an enrollment of about 16,000 (fall 1999), a $370 million budget (FY 97/98), and 2,728 FTE faculty and staff. The university libraries include the main library on campus (the Valley Library) and the Hatfield Marine Center Guin Library in Newport, Oregon. The Libraries hold 1.5 million volumes and employ 71 FTE staff (32 Faculty and 39 classified staff). The library budget is $7 million (FY98/99).

The University of Houston (UH) is the doctoral granting and largest campus in the University of Houston System. Located in Houston, Texas, UH has an enrollment of 32,296 (fall 1998), a $482.9 million budget (FY2000), and 4,022 FTE faculty and staff. The University of Houston Libraries, a member of the Association of Research Libraries (ARL), include the main library (M.D. Anderson) and four branches–Architecture/Art, Music, Optometry, and Pharmacy. In November 1998, UH Libraries celebrated the 2 million-volume milestone in collection size. The current budget is $10.9 million with 122 FTE staff (47 librarians and 75 support staff).

Colorado State University (CSU) in Fort Collins, Colorado, is a land-grant, space-grant, and Carnegie 1 Research university with 22,782 students, 5,200 faculty and staff, and a $465.5 million budget (FY99). Colorado State University Libraries include the main library (Morgan), the Engineering branch (closed in December 1999), the

Atmospheric Sciences branch, and the Veterinary Medicine branch. A member of ARL, the Libraries currently hold 2 million volumes and employ 128 FTE staff (41 librarians and 87 support staff). The total expenditure for FY 98/99 as reported to ARL was $10.5 million. On July 28, 1997, as a renovation and addition to Morgan Library was nearing completion, a devastating flood filled the lower level of the building damaging more than 462,000 volumes. Acquisitions, Cataloging, Database Maintenance, and Preservation in Technical Services are still heavily involved in the flood recovery.

STAFFING AND ORGANIZATIONAL STRUCTURE

The cataloging operation fits within technical services in all three libraries although the organizational structure varies. Currently, technical services at OSU Valley Library include the Cataloging and Acquisitions departments.[2] Prior to 1995, the Automation Department and the Materials Preparation Unit were also under technical services. The mending and binding operations in Materials Preparation were later integrated into Acquisitions, while the physical processing of materials became part of Cataloging. In 1995, the Oregon State University Libraries, Computing Services, Telecommunications, and the Communication Media Center merged and formed Information Services (IS). IS was then reorganized into teams. Staff in the Automation Department were reorganized into various teams under IS except for those who were responsible for maintaining Oasis–the Libraries' online catalog. They remained part of the Libraries Technical Services.

At the time of writing the UH Libraries' technical services, as part of the Bibliographic and Access Services division, is composed of the Acquisitions Department (for monographs), the Serials Department (for serials acquisition), Cataloging Services, and the Database Maintenance Unit. Cataloging Services and Database Maintenance are separate and independent units. The head of each unit reports directly to the Assistant Dean of Bibliographic and Access Services.[3]

At CSU, cataloging (formally Bibliographic Control and Electronic Resources Services since 1996), Acquisitions Services (for monographs and serials), and Preservation Services form the Technical Services Division. Cataloging departments in both OSU and CSU libraries include original cataloging, copy cataloging, and database maintenance. In contrast, copy cataloging is a unit in Acquisitions at the UH Libraries.

The cataloging operation is centralized in all three libraries, (i.e., OSU, UH, and CSU). However they fall administratively, catalog librarians and copy catalogers in the main library are responsible for the cataloging of monographs, serials, and non-print formats, including electronic resources, as well as materials for branch libraries.

At Colorado State University, Bibliographic Control and Electronic Resources Services is composed of four faculty, including the coordinator of the services, eleven state classified staff, and several student assistants. Each of the three cataloging faculty has a specialization in monographs, serials, and database maintenance. The eleven classified staff include four copy catalogers, one retrospective conversion specialist, and six (including one half-time) database maintenance staff. Both copy cataloging and database maintenance units are headed by classified staff.

Cataloging Services at University of Houston Libraries consists of three catalog librarians, including the manager of the services. This unit is responsible for original cataloging, cataloging of non-print formats, and other complex copy cataloging referred from the copy catalogers. The copy cataloging unit (Bibliographic Edit) in monographic acquisitions composed of seven classified staff and two to three student assistants is managed by a librarian. Although at one time the copy cataloging unit was under the cataloging department, the current structure has not changed for at least ten years. Placing copy cataloging in acquisitions is one approach in designing organizational structure and workflow around the integrated library system in which one bibliographic record is used for verification at the pre-order stage ordering, receiving, cataloging, and OPAC for circulation.

From 1993 to 1995, the Cataloging Department at OSU consisted of the head of the department, the assistant head, two catalog librarians, and eight and a half classified staff who were primarily responsible for copy cataloging. Two of the classified staff also had database maintenance duties. An additional catalog librarian was hired in 1996. During the merger and reorganization, the Cataloging Department formed three teams: Monographs, Serials, and Oasis Database Maintenance. The staffing and organizational structure have changed again since 1996. The assistant head position was eliminated and the cataloger in that position became a personnel manager for IS. Most of the team-based structure in technical services has been dissolved although the team concept of soliciting staff input for work-related issues is still in practice. A serials cataloger position was reinstated in 1998 bringing the number of professionals back up to five.[4]

COMMON TRENDS IN CATALOGING

Despite the differences in organizational structure and staff levels, all three libraries share similar challenges from new technologies and demands to become more efficient. Common responses to these challenges can be observed as cataloging operations within these institutions adapt to meet new demands. Using technology in cataloging operations and designing workflow around the functionality of the integrated system is one common strategy for efficiency and has major impacts on the roles of professional and support staff. Mainstreaming cataloging and processing of federal government documents into technical services has become another strategy for more effective use of limited human resources and providing enhanced access to these materials. All three libraries are faced with the challenges of providing organization of and access to electronic resources and moving into the arenas of digitization and metadata albeit each library is at a different stage.

Changing Roles of Professional and Classified Staff

MARC, cooperative cataloging, bibliographic utilities, and library automation are among the major forces contributing to the changing roles and responsibilities of professional and classified staff.

Being able to exchange bibliographic data through MARC records fostered cooperation in cataloging and the establishment of international bibliographic utilities such as OCLC. A title needs to be originally cataloged only once, the record can then be shared and used by many other libraries. The result is a dramatic increase in copy cataloging and decrease in original cataloging. The average amount of original cataloging in academic libraries is very low, mostly for local, special, esoteric materials, and theses and dissertations from the university. While librarians are still responsible for original cataloging and some complex copy cataloging, the majority of the copy cataloging has been shifted to the support staff–copy catalogers.

Although cataloging on copy in general is not as formidable as original cataloging, it does require a considerable level of knowledge and expertise in MARC encoding and cataloging rules and practices. Since none of these three libraries is big enough to have separate units or staff specializing in subjects, formats, or languages, copy catalogers are usually required to catalog materials on all subject areas, in most print and non-print formats, and in foreign languages. They are taking on more complex work and making certain judgements and decisions that previously were made by professional librarians.

Professional catalogers in these three libraries, in addition to performing original cataloging and complex copy cataloging, are often involved in developing and formulating local cataloging policy and procedures. They resolve cataloging related problems. Because of their knowledge and expertise, some are also involved in training. At UH Libraries, catalog librarians have regular hours on the reference desk as well as collection development responsibilities. One also helps out in the Interlibrary Loan Department.

Catalog librarians are also involved in issues and decisions related to the library online system such as implementing new system functions and making collaborative decisions with the public services librarians on how MARC fields are indexed and displayed in the OPAC. For example, the catalog librarian at CSU who specializes in database maintenance is also a member of two library-wide groups dealing with the Libraries' online system (Innopac): the WebPAC Group and the Sage Group. Sage is the name given to the local system. The Sage Group is composed of representatives for different functions of the Innopac system such as acquisitions, circulation, cataloging, and OPAC.

Professional development is another important part of catalog librarians' work life in these three libraries. Librarians at both OSU and CSU libraries have tenure-track faculty appointments which means devoting a substantial amount of time to research and publication. This is especially true for junior faculty. Service in professional organizations, the university, and the community is also an integral part of the job description. Librarians at UH Libraries are "library faculty" and must go through promotion. Although the promotion process is not as strenuous as tenure-track, a considerable amount of time and effort on professional development activities is still expected.

Designing Workflow Around Library Systems and Limited Personnel Resources

Cataloging workflow design has become increasingly important as libraries look for ways to improve efficiency and minimize the cost. Changes in priorities and workflow can be a constant for coping with the increased workload with no addition in positions. Often the workflow is designed around the functionality and capabilities of the library's integrated system. Libraries are taking advantage of some systems' capability of downloading records from a bibliographic utility or vendor for ordering, receiving, and cataloging. The goal is to utilize the integrated system, such as Innopac, to achieve a seamless approach to ordering, receiving, and cataloging, thereby making the whole process more efficient. This approach also reduces the cost for searching and cataloging and offers the possibility of creating a cross-functional workforce and making receiving and cataloging a one-step process. The advantages go beyond purely operational. Once the record is downloaded to the local system, the bibliographic information and status of the title are instantly accessible to the library users.

Both UH and CSU are Innopac libraries and are making full use of this functionality although the workflow and the division of labor are quite different. At UH Libraries, pre-order searching for firm-ordered materials in the local Innopac system is done by the ordering staff, but the pre-order searching in OCLC and exporting records to Innopac are done by the copy catalogers. Ordering staff then attach orders and receive on the same bibliographic record. The record in Innopac is also used for cataloging unless a discrepancy is found between the item received and the record downloaded in which case OCLC is searched again. Searching and copy cataloging for the case above and for other categories of materials such as approval orders, gifts, etc., are done in OCLC by copy catalogers. For approval titles, brief records supplied by the approval vendor with orders already attached are loaded into the local database upon the receipt of the approval shipments. These brief records are overlaid with full OCLC MARC records when copy cataloging on OCLC is completed and records are exported in the Bibliographic Edit Unit. All titles needing original cataloging are referred to the catalog librarians. As of January 2000, the workflow remains the same.[5] Under this model, the copy cataloging unit works closely with the ordering and receiving units in the

Acquisitions Department, Cataloging Services, and Database Maintenance Unit.

In contrast to UH, at CSU, the Acquisitions Monographs Section is responsible for most of the searching in both the local Innopac database–Sage and OCLC. For firm orders the Monographs staff perform pre-order searching in Sage and OCLC including exporting records to Sage. They also search in OCLC for cataloging copy for approval books, gifts, etc., after they are received and before moving them to copy cataloging. CSU also loads brief vendor records for approval titles. The vendor records are overlaid once cataloging is done on OCLC and records exported to Sage in the Copy Cataloging Unit.

The current workflow at OSU has similarities in different areas with both UH and CSU.[6] OSU has recently migrated from Geac-ADVANCE to Innopac. Similar to CSU, the Acquisitions staff do the pre-order searching for firm orders in both the local system and OCLC including exporting bibliographic records. The Acquisitions staff also performed pre-order searching and exporting for approval orders until recently. The current cataloging workflow for approval titles is similar to that at the UH Libraries. A work group consisting of Cataloging and Acquisitions staff is being formed to further define the process in the Innopac system.[7]

Even when copy cataloging is under the cataloging department, the unit has a close working relationship with the staff in the acquisitions department. At CSU, a search/fast cataloging workflow was implemented a few years ago to expedite the searching and cataloging process of newly-received approval books with straightforward Library of Congress copy. This process involved Acquisitions Monographs staff in doing some copy cataloging. During 1998, the Acquisitions and Cataloging departments at CSU experimented with another combined workflow–Cataloging at Receiving (CAR). CAR was an attempt to test the feasibility of a more streamlined workflow by making receiving, invoicing, and cataloging a one-step process for firm order books. CAR was not fully implemented because of a problem with Innopac's invoicing system. A new approach of creating a more flexible joint copy cataloging unit consisting of higher level classified staff from both departments for searching and cataloging is currently being investigated. Changes in workflow and job reassignment for classified staff often bring up personnel issues that need to be addressed such as training and reevaluating job classifications.

Mainstreaming Federal Government Documents Processing and Cataloging

The option of buying depository item cataloging records for post-1976 federal government publications from a vendor, such as MARCIVE, and loading them into the local online database resulted in some libraries mainstreaming into technical services the cataloging and processing of these materials, work was previously done manually in the documents department. All three institutions described here are depository libraries for federal government publications. Both University of Houston Libraries and Colorado State University Libraries dissolved their government documents departments and mainstreamed document processing and cataloging into the regular technical services workflow. OSU is at the beginning of this mainstreaming process.

UH Libraries started loading MARCIVE GPO records in 1995. It was not until the fall of 1998, however, that the integration of processing and cataloging of federal documents into technical services was fully implemented. Monographic acquisitions started receiving and checking in (on the shipping list) government documents. Physical processing is done by student assistants in the Bibliographic Edit Unit. MARCIVE records are tape-loaded into the Innopac database monthly. Prior to 1999, all the MARCIVE records were suppressed from public view in the catalog upon loading until they were "cataloged." The copy catalogers performed copy cataloging of all the monographs that had MARCIVE records in the database, unsuppressed these records and completed the item records. They also sorted out serials and forwarded them to appropriate staff in the Serials Department, Database Maintenance Unit, or Cataloging Services for further handling depending on if the serial title needed a check-in card, if the item was an added volume to an existing record, if there were cataloging related problems requiring decisions from the cataloger, etc. During the summer of 1999, it was decided that all MARCIVE records should be unsuppressed. The decision was based on two reasons: better patron access and integrating Clear Lake campus (another campus in the UH system) library's records into the same database. The Documents Department was officially dissolved when the document specialist position from the department was transferred to the Database Maintenance Unit toward the end of 1997. The mainstreaming and initial workflow design involved coordination from the Acquisitions Department, the

Serials Department, and Database Maintenance Unit, as well as the government documents coordinator who is still responsible for the collection development aspects of the government documents.

A similar reorganization occurred at Colorado State University. CSU started loading MARCIVE records in 1989. As with the case at UH, not much was done with these records. Government Documents Department processed all the documents and maintained a manual shelflist. The situation changed when the activities of the department were divided into public services and technical services. The reorganization was implemented in phases. A position from Government Documents was transferred to Database Maintenance Unit in Cataloging in 1995 when maintenance and quality control of MARCIVE records were integrated into Database Maintenance.[8] While there is no longer a government documents department, the Government Documents Specialist remains responsible for collection development of the federal documents. In order to provide users with immediate access to newly received titles, CSU started subscribing to the MARCIVE Shipping List Services (SLS) for monographic titles in 1997 and loading these short records into the local online database weekly. The mainstreaming process was completed when the receiving and check-in became part of Acquisitions Services in October 1997.[9]

Currently, two and a half FTEs in Database Maintenance are responsible for government documents. The titles received are checked against SLS records for the accuracy of bibliographic and location information. The SLS records are then overlaid automatically in Sage when the MARCIVE full bibliographic records are loaded. Manual review by staff is required only when problems occur. The workflow is still being refined and yet to be finalized.

OSU started loading MARCIVE weekly and monthly records into the online system (Geac-ADVANCE) in 1995. After a lengthy MARCIVE profiling this practice continues in the Innopac system. OSU's situation was complicated by their earlier practice of classifying many government documents in Library of Congress (LC) rather than SuDocs classification system. As part of the profile MARCIVE is flipping the SuDoc stem to a LC call number in many cases. They are currently in the process of integrating the cataloging and processing of government documents into the Acquisitions and Cataloging departments. Selection will continue to be done by the documents librarian. One classified staff member and some student hours have been transferred to Acquisitions Serials and another position is under review to determine how many hours will be transferred to technical services.[10]

Government documents present many challenges in physical processing, cataloging, and maintenance. The increased number of documents available through the Web adds the validation of URLs (Uniform Resource Locators) to the already labor-intensive maintenance. MARCIVE records come from GPO cataloging. GPO cataloging is often inconsistent in quality and practice. Quality control and database cleaning after MARCIVE loads are tremendous, not to mention the inventory and retrospective conversion of the prc-1976 titles. There are some definite advantages in mainstreaming the processing and cataloging of government documents into technical services such as the consistency in cataloging quality, more effective use of staff, and better access for users to these materials. It is, however, evident in both UH and CSU libraries that staff are overwhelmed and stretched thin with the additional workload associated with government documents without an adequate increase in staffing.

Using Technology for Increased Efficiency in Cataloging Operation

Technology not only influences the organizational structure and the design of cataloging process and workflow, it also forces a very different layout of the physical working environment. OCLC dumb terminals chained in clusters are replaced by a new generation of Technical Services Workstations. These multitasking workstations are loaded with a combination of cataloging tools available electronically, graphical cataloging interfaces, windowing environments, and customized programs and macros. The three libraries discussed here provide high-end workstations and support for their staff. In this new cataloging environment, appropriate hardware, software, and support are absolutely essential.

Technology also has an effect on the make-up of the workforce. Computer skills and the ability to handle a variety of tasks using different software and application programs are essential. Staff also need the ability to perform work with a higher level of complexity since the clerical work such as typing cataloging worksheets and filing have mostly disappeared with the implementation of library computer systems. Both professional and support staff in all three libraries perform various searching and editing functions in OCLC and local library systems with different sets of commands. It is not uncommon for staff to compile statistics and write procedures and manuals using software such as spreadsheets and word processors. In addition, communicating through email, surfing on the Internet for work-related resources, and consulting cataloging tools such as Library of Congress Cataloger's Desktop and Classification Plus have all become part of the daily work routine.

In addition to a higher level of computer skills, because the integrated library system tends to connect different technical services functions and activities, the staff also need to have broad-based knowledge about the whole of technical services functions. For example, the cataloging staff need to be familiar with the acquisitions processes and should know how to read order records.

Facing the Challenges of Electronic Resources and Moving into Digitization and Metadata Creation

The advancement of information technology and the phenomenal growth of electronic resources have increased accessibility of information. On the other hand, these forces have also created new challenges and issues for libraries in the areas of collection development and bibliographic control, particularly in determining how best to present resources in an organized and understandable fashion to the users.

Electronic resources come in different forms: CD-ROM databases, Web-based databases, subscription-based electronic journals, valuable Web sites that are free, etc. As more electronic database producers are moving from CD-ROMs to Web access through the Internet, libraries face new issues in cataloging, database maintenance, workflow, personnel, and systems because of the dynamic nature of Web-based resources. Cataloging Internet resources using the current cataloging rules and MARC formats is problematic. Electronic resources can be monographic or serial. Cataloging them requires expertise in both areas as well as knowledge of the unique qualities of electronic resources that are fundamentally different from those in the print format. Maintenance of the URL for each electronic resource is labor-intensive and may involve staff from other units and departments of the library. For aggregated databases keeping up with constant adding and deleting of individual titles by the vendors presents another challenge.

Unlike print and other physical formats, Internet resources do not come in tangible physical pieces for moving through the process. The workflow has to be designed to insure that when an electronic title is added to the library collection, there is a mechanism for notifying appropriate staff in technical services for providing cataloging and user access to the resource. If the library's policy is to catalog electronic resources and include them in the local catalog, how these records are displayed in the catalog; whether to create check-in, summary holdings, and item records; and how to facilitate the link to the resource itself through the catalog are among the most important issues to consider. Developing policy and procedures for dealing with electronic resources is the critical first step and should involve staff from both public and technical services.

The Assistant Department Head at Oregon State University Libraries had developed a written selection policy. The policy was reviewed and accepted by the Collection Services Team. She participated in the OCLC Intercat project and cataloged a few titles. OSU Libraries, however, had yet to integrate the cataloging of electronic resources into the routine workflow when I left in 1996. All three libraries have now made considerable efforts to catalog electronic journals which are acquired through purchased subscription and to include them in the local catalog. All three libraries also provide access to long lists of other electronic resources which are not "cataloged" through their home pages. Although the discussion on issues concerning access to electronic resources at UH Libraries involved reference librarians as well as the catalogers, CSU formed a formal committee of public and technical services librarians that produced a written document recommending the policy for provision of access to electronic resources. Acquisitions and catalog librarians followed up with another document detailing the cataloging policy and procedures for access to electronic resources in different categories. At OSU, a group was formed recently to develop policy and procedures for acquiring and cataloging electronic resources.[11]

Related to electronic information dissemination and access, libraries find themselves moving into the areas of digitization and metadata creation. The Special Collections Department at OSU Libraries has begun digitizing the collection of Linus Pauling papers, one of the most important scientific archives of this century. Listing of individual items in the collection is accessible through a finding aid on the OSU Special Collections Web page. The full text and image of each item, however, can not be viewed due to unresolved copyright issues. Other digitization projects are in the preliminary planning stages at OSU.[12] UH Libraries started digitizing a historical Houston postcard collection in Special Collections and Archives recently. Methods for access are to be determined.[13]

As mentioned before, the uniqueness of electronic resources and amount of information on the Internet make the traditional cataloging practices less than ideal. Although considerable efforts have been made in revising the current cataloging rules and MARC formats, other metadata approaches for organizing and providing access to these resources, such as the Dublin Core (DC) initiative from OCLC, have generated much discussion and interest in the field. As a member of the Colorado State consortia, Alliance, CSU Libraries is a participant in the OCLC CORC (Cooperative Online Resource Catalog) project. CORC explores the feasibility of having different record structures, such as MARC and DC, in the same database.

CSU Libraries also participates in a state-wide digitization effort–the Colorado Digitization Project (CDP). Technical Services staff have been taking the lead in the Libraries' involvement in the project. CSU Libraries is represented by a cataloging faculty member on the CDP Metadata Working Group that develops and shapes the metadata standards for CDP. The Libraries is one of the designated regional scanning centers for CDP and will advise other project participants on digitization and the creation and use of metadata. Faculty and staff in Technical Services are expected to have some involvement. Two experimental digitization projects are also being planned and developed in-house to gain experience in implementing a digitization project including creating Dublin Core records through CORC.

CONCLUSION

Donald Riggs stated "change is occurring faster today than ever before in the history of academic libraries."[14] Technology has caused this constant change in libraries and has influenced all aspects of cataloging operations and management. It will continue to be the driving force of change for libraries and for shaping the organizational structure and management of cataloging in the future.

This article attempts to document some common themes in cataloging in three medium-sized academic libraries resulting from the dwindling resources and the constantly changing technological environment. The issues and trends highlighted in this paper, however, do not describe all the changes and challenges faced by cataloging departments in academic libraries today.

Resources for cataloging will stay lean for academic libraries. There will be more reliance on outsourcing of certain cataloging functions for cost-effectiveness. Managing digital information will remain one of the biggest challenges for library technical services and cataloging. The need for designing more streamlined and cost-effective cataloging operations by using technology, creating flexible organizational structures, and employing and developing a staff with skills and capability for performing more complex work will continue to be critical in cataloging management in academic libraries. Providing value-added access to information in all formats focused on user-centered services will be the only guarantee for the survival of technical services and cataloging.

Organizational Paradigm Shifts from NACUBO (National Association of College and University Business Offices) suggests that:

> The organization of the future will be characterized by much less rigid distinction between units . . . organizational principles need to shift toward processes being performed and the customers being served . . . The greatest challenges lie not in determining the boxes on a table of organization, but in sustaining the vision and commitment required to realize the benefits of these changes.[15]

Cataloging operations and management will continue to evolve and may indeed look very different in the future. The mission and core functions of cataloging which are identifying, describing, organizing, and providing access to information in all formats will remain the same and become even more critical in the 21st century.

NOTES

1. The author was a Catalog Librarian at Oregon State University Libraries, 1993-1996, and the Copy Cataloging Manager at University of Houston Libraries, 1996-1999.

2. Communication with Debbie Hackleman, Head of Cataloging Dept., Oregon State University Libraries, in December 1999.

3. Communication with Mary Beth Thomson, Head of Acquisitions Dept., University of Houston Libraries, in January 2000. `

4. Communication with Debbie Hackleman, Head of Cataloging Dept., Oregon State University Libraries, in December 1999.

5. Communication with Mary Beth Thomson, Head of Acquisitions Dept., University of Houston Libraries, in January 2000.

6. Communication with Debbie Hackleman, Head of Cataloging Dept., Oregon State University Libraries, in December 1999.

7. Communication with Debbie Hackleman, Head of Cataloging Dept., Oregon State University Libraries, in December 1999.

8. Fred C. Schmidt and Nora S. Copeland. "Mainstreaming Government Documents Technical Processing: the Colorado State Experience." *Colorado Libraries* 24, no. 1 (Spring 1998): 7.

9. Ibid.

10. Communication with Debbie Hackleman, Head of Cataloging Dept., Oregon State University Libraries, in December 1999.

11. Communication with Debbie Hackleman, Head of Cataloging Dept., Oregon State University Libraries, in December 1999.

12. Communication with Debbie Hackleman, Head of Cataloging Dept., Oregon State University Libraries, in December 1999.

13. Communication with Tom Wilson, Head of Systems Dept., University of Houston Libraries, on December 23, 1999.

14. Donald E. Riggs. "Creating and Managing Change: Some Controversy, Some Level-Headedness." *College and Research Libraries* 57, no. 5 (Sept. 1996): 402.

15. "Change As a Constant." Excerpts from *Organizational Paradigm Shifts* (Washington D.C.: National Association of College and University Business Offices, 1996).

Cataloging Plus: Philosophy and Practice at a Small College Library

Y. Mei Mah

SUMMARY. Many small college libraries place tremendous importance on personal service to end users. The staff at small college libraries usually perform a wider variety of tasks than their counterparts in larger libraries, who tend to be more specialized. Catalogers at small college libraries often perform functions normally associated with public services; they must be librarians first and catalogers in addition. Through their work with end users, they may develop appreciation for users' difficulties with the catalog. Web technology can be a boon to catalogers who wish to develop user-oriented tools to complement the catalog. *[Article copies available for a fee from The Haworth Document Delivery Service: 1-800-342-9678. E-mail address: <getinfo@haworthpressinc.com> Website: <http://www.HaworthPress.com>]*

KEYWORDS. Small college libraries, philosophy of cataloging, management of cataloging, cataloging, Warren Wilson College

INTRODUCTION

The threshold of the new millennium seems to find libraries under unprecedented pressures from within and without. In the literature and

Y. Mei Mah, MA, MS, is Catalog Librarian at the Pew Learning Center and Ellison Library, Warren Wilson College, P. O. Box 9000, Asheville, NC 28815-9000 (E-mail: mmah@warren-wilson.edu).

[Haworth co-indexing entry note]: "Cataloging Plus: Philosophy and Practice at a Small College Library." Mah, Y. Mei. Co-published simultaneously in *Cataloging & Classification Quarterly* (The Haworth Information Press, an imprint of The Haworth Press, Inc.) Vol. 30, No. 2/3, 2000, pp. 331-342; and: *Managing Cataloging and the Organization of Information: Philosophies, Practices and Challenges at the Onset of the 21st Century* (ed: Ruth C. Carter) The Haworth Information Press, an imprint of The Haworth Press, Inc., 2000, pp. 331-342. Single or multiple copies of this article are available for a fee from The Haworth Document Delivery Service [1-800-342-9678, 9:00 a.m. - 5:00 p.m. (EST). E-mail address: getinfo@haworth pressinc.com].

in professional discussions, we encounter what seems to be a litany of difficulties. Our anxieties run the gamut. We lament the myriad problems which seem to beset us–inadequate resources, burgeoning workloads, runaway developments in technology, various foolish boors who would destroy us–and wonder what our future might be. Some of us have even suggested that libraries and librarians as we know them will cease to exist. Granted, our problems are many, real, and persistent. Granted, also, there are no easy or swift remedies, perhaps no remedies at all. Although these are times of trouble and change, the landscape of our profession is not dominated by the Slough of Despond. Surely, problems are not alien to us. Gorman observes that there seems never to have been a time when libraries were not under one gun or another.[1] Libraries and librarianship have survived and thrived for millennia because librarians have responded to the challenges of their times with commitment, talent, imagination, and intelligence. These time tested qualities will continue to serve us well in the future.

Ours is an exciting time. Even as we paddle to keep our heads above water, good news is around us. Developments in technology have opened the way for us to provide services impossible just a few years ago. New tools are available to help us work more efficiently. Alongside the range of anxieties is ample evidence of librarians thriving in shifting sands and facing uncertainties with dedication, creativity, and wisdom. At such a troubled time, the most effective strategy for ensuring a future may be to keep our eyes on the central truth of our profession: libraries exist to serve users. For most of us, it is truly that simple. But there ends the simplicity. Where we stumble is over how we define the future and how we achieve it.

No library should take its future for granted; and one way a library can enhance its chances for achieving its desired future is for its stakeholders to identify and agree on that future.[2] Each library has to find its own way, struggle with its own afflictions, develop its own strengths, and deploy its own strategies. Even within a single library, each of its various functions repeats this paradigm, as does each librarian. Although we can learn from one another and benefit from the experiences of others, there are no sure-fire formulae. Mindful that library environments are diverse and that my general observations will necessarily contain many exceptions, I nevertheless offer some thoughts from the perspective of a catalog librarian in a small, private, liberal arts college.

THE CONTEXT

Warren Wilson College has an enrollment of approximately 750 undergraduate and 80 graduate students. Located on the outskirts of Asheville, North Carolina, the college grants BA and BS degrees, as well as a Master of Fine Arts degree. The educational program consists of a combination of liberal arts academic study, required community service, and participation in a campus-wide work program. Since the founding of the college in 1894, students have been its work force. During each academic term, all resident undergraduate students are required to work fifteen hours each week on 111 crews which essentially operate the college. The use of student labor is a major component of the educational mission of the college. Student workers at Warren Wilson receive grades for their work performance similar to their grades for courses and can be placed on probation or suspended from the college for poor work performance.

Over 90 percent of the undergraduates live on campus, as do about half of the full-time faculty and staff. Because students, faculty, and staff live, work, study, and serve together, a strong sense of membership infuses the campus community. All members of the community participate in the governance of the college and have a voice in most policy-making decisions.

The size and nature of the campus community profoundly affects the environment of the library. The cultural emphasis on service and community is reflected in the values and attitudes of the library, which supports a curriculum including a low-residency graduate program in creative writing and fifteen undergraduate majors.

STAFFING THE LIBRARY

The library staff at Warren Wilson College consists of five professional librarians, two paraprofessionals, and a student crew of about twenty. The library staff organization at Warren Wilson College is relatively flat, with few layers of hierarchy. The whole staff, professional and paraprofessional, reports directly to the Library Director, who reports to the Dean of the College. Members of the staff enjoy considerable autonomy in planning and executing their work.

While the library's collection is modest, one of its chief strengths is the staff's commitment to service. The small number of staff members and their active involvement in community and curriculum issues and other aspects of campus life make them and their work very visible to library users. In a campus culture which encourages community participation, they receive formal and informal feedback on their performance and try to be accountable to users and responsive to their needs.

Every staff member performs a wide variety of tasks and works directly with end users, whether his or her primary responsibility be in technical or public services. The professional librarians have faculty status and carry the responsibilities incumbent upon it. All the professional librarians, regardless of their official job titles or areas of primary responsibility, share reference duties and provide bibliographic instruction. All staff and students, regardless of their specific departmental assignments, serve circulation functions and must have sufficient familiarity with library equipment such as photocopiers, microform machines, computers, and printers to provide basic servicing of these machines as necessary.

Our service ethic essentially requires all staff to assist library users with a wide range of needs. Professional assistance is available virtually all hours that the library is open, including weekends and nights. Although some functions, such as cataloging, are performed only by professional librarians, few distinctions are made between professional and paraprofessional work. Thus, a professional librarian may find herself answering a reference question one minute, clearing a paper jam from a photocopier the next, and helping a user check his email after that.

Because there is considerable overlap in responsibilities, communication is critical. Anyone on the staff can have input in any decision, as most decisions are made at staff meetings attended by the entire staff, professional and paraprofessional. It is normal for technical services staff to participate actively in discussions and decisions on matters normally considered the purview of public services. Much of the work in the library is achieved through collaboration. Position descriptions tend to be fluid, as every member of the staff must be willing to do whatever needs to be done, even work which does not fall within his or her position description.

While team work and trust are important in any library, they are vital in an environment of fluid job descriptions and communal decision making. In addition to maintaining reasonable currency in their areas of primary responsibility, staff members must keep informed of changes in several areas. On the local level, they need to keep current with trends and changes in the academic programs and the curriculum.

The staff must be nimble: ability to learn quickly, openness to try new ideas, and willingness to perform a variety of tasks are valued highly, as is a cooperative attitude toward colleagues and library users. Personal qualities are crucial, perhaps more than specific expertise. In times of change, libraries need staff who can evolve as the needs of the organization change.[3]

THE CATALOGING DEPARTMENT

The Warren Wilson College library is a member of OCLC and of the Mountain College Library Network (MCLN), a consortium of fourteen libraries in the region. The members of MCLN work cooperatively but autonomously. Seven of the members are private liberal arts colleges, six are community colleges, and one a health science library.

Six of the liberal arts colleges that participate in MCLN share an integrated online DRA catalog, with each library responsible for cataloging its own materials and maintaining its records in the catalog according to its policies and practices. Two of the six, including Warren Wilson College, use LCMARC as their primary source for bibliographic records and OCLC as an additional source; the other four use OCLC exclusively. Due in part to this considerable diversity, communication is important to balance the need for consistency with the need to respect the autonomy of each member, and so the cataloging staff of member libraries discuss policies and processes, share ideas and information, and assist one another in various ways through periodic meetings, by phone, and by e-mail.

At Warren Wilson College, the primary cataloging staff consists of a librarian who also provides some reference service and bibliographic instruction. She is responsible for copy and original cataloging of a range of materials for the library, including monographs, serials, audio-visual materials, software, and selected items for the college archives. Another librarian, whose primary responsibilities are inter-library loan and reference, is responsible for cataloging items for the reference collection and selected gift books. Two student assistants provide cataloging support.

Serial subscriptions are cataloged, regardless of format. In addition, the library has access to over 4,000 full text titles available online through a statewide licensing program called North Carolina Libraries for Virtual Education (NC LIVE). These titles are not cataloged but are listed and accessed through links from the library's home page.

Like many libraries, Warren Wilson College no longer maintains a standing shelf list. As appropriate and feasible, the Catalog Librarian generates customized reports by extracting fields from the bibliographic and holdings databases for inventory, collection development, and other purposes.

THE REMOTE CATALOGER

As creators and maintainers of a product (the catalog), the purpose of which is to make it possible for the consumers (library users) to find materials, catalogers should train our focus on the habits and needs of these consumers. But in a profession dedicated to serving people, catalogers are perhaps the furthest removed from the end users of our product. Other library staff, even technical services staff such as collection development librarians, work more closely with users.

Many possible reasons account for the gulf between catalogers and library users. A major one is inherent in the nature of our work. Catalogers claim, with much truth, that cataloging is an art and a science. So is engineering. For cataloging work in an age of networking and resource sharing must include a preponderance of data and detail, accordance and accuracy, standards and systems. Like engineers who build roads which enable travelers to reach their destinations, we build and maintain infrastructures which enable the users of a library to find its materials. Like engineering, our work requires using complex tools and rules to create the contents and to build the structures of the catalog. Indeed, catalogers more resemble engineers than customer service representatives.

Of course, catalogers are not oblivious to the importance of the catalog to library users. We are concerned with the quality of our product, and virtually all of us would agree that its *raison d'être* is to enable users to find library materials. To paraphrase Ranganathan's first law, library catalogs, like the books they represent, are for users. Most catalogers recognize the importance of assisting users yet do not consider this activity a component of cataloging functions. Many of us view our cataloging responsibilities as defined by our duty to produce and maintain a good catalog. By that we usually mean a catalog the records of which meet standards, accurately describe the holdings of the library, contain the requisite and desirable access points, and provide information on the locations of items. To assist users, we use devices such as controlled vocabulary and authorized headings and provide tools such as cross references and uniform headings. Advances in library technology, such as keyword searching and web technology, have provided additional tools for catalog users.

Still, catalogers generally consider reference service, user education, and bibliographic instruction duties which fall outside the bailiwick of cataloging. This separation, however, is largely a matter of administrative convenience in small college libraries where responsibilities overlap freely. Catalogers in these environments often wear a human face and traffic directly with library users.

OUTREACH FROM THE BACK ROOM

Referring to the frames librarians build, Charles Martell suggests that some of our frames are paradigms such as that of ownership and access.[4] Traditional librarianship has also constructed frames around technical and public services, between cataloging and reference. But the relationship between cataloging and reference has been a theme in librarianship since the early 1900s.[5] Recent publications include considerable discussion on the roles of and relationships between technical and public services.[6] Professional organizations, too, are paying attention to the fading of distinctions between technical and public services.[7] Predicting that library service of the future will not divide neatly into bibliographic vs. advisory or research services, Intner believes that technical services staff will need reference skills, reference staff will need in-depth bibliographic skills, and good professionals will use an integrated set of skills to meet user needs.[8]

To many small libraries which provide a variety of services with a small staff, indistinct separation between cataloging and reference has long been customary. The two are but the obverse and reverse of a coin: one creates a product, the other facilitates its use, a reality which is readily apparent to catalogers who provide reference service. Also readily apparent is the difficulty many users have with the catalog.

For catalogers, serving at the reference desk can be eye-opening.[9] Catalogers worship standards and consistencies, yet our users perceive our product to be the work of arbitrary and capricious minds. Our principles are unassailable, yet they appear arcane. We believe that our product works most of the time as we intend; but to our users, they are intrusive infrastructures which always seem to go wrong.[10] The catalog we labor to create is a good product, yet it often fails its users. The reality, as many in our profession have observed, is that many undergraduates have little understanding of the catalog and its uses.

What, then, can catalogers do about this problem? One justifiable response is to do nothing. After all, our catalog meets the industry standard and is constructed based on sound principles; it is the users who are deficient in library skills. Decrying that the mind-set of the 1933 Chicago World's Fair ("Science finds, industry applies, man conforms") still dominates our world today, Norman notes that the design of technology requires people to behave in machine-centered ways, ways for which people are not well suited. And when errors occur, we tend to blame the person.[11]

At Warren Wilson College, where user assistance is a function of cataloging operations, we try to meet users on their terms. The Catalog Librarian is scheduled at the reference desk for an average of eleven hours a week and also provides bibliographic instruction to some classes. In addition, the cataloging department provides value-added services as extensions of our cataloging operations. We are suited to provide these services, accustomed as we are to managing databases and to manipulating records and fields.

One of these services is a classified list of our video holdings, which is updated monthly and available through the library's home page. Although searching the library's online catalog for videos is a simple procedure, users often have difficulty isolating these records. And so the list was created in response to user requests. The printed list of video holdings was generated several years ago as a text file containing only call numbers and titles extracted from holding and bibliographic records in the catalog. After the library developed its web site, the file was converted to HTML and published on it. Recently, responding to faculty suggestions, we began including descriptions and running times as we added new titles.

Another value-added service we provide is a monthly list of new titles cataloged for the collection. For decades, the classified list has been distributed to the heads of academic departments and any faculty or staff member who requests to be on the mailing list. In the early days, the list was typed on a typewriter. Later, it was manually keyed into a wordprocessor. Still later, as the technology became available, the list was generated by extracting certain fields from the bibliographic and holdings records and writing this information into a file. Student assistants reformat and edit the file as necessary. Although a printed list is still distributed to some faculty and staff, our mailing list is becoming curtailed as the list of new titles is now posted on the library home page and widely available.

Publishing on the web allows us to update our lists more frequently than would be the case for print. It reduces our printing costs, extends our reach, and enables users to take advantage of web technology for searching and browsing.

MANAGING CATALOGING FUNCTIONS

Cataloging at small college libraries often differs from other organizations in several respects. Cataloging functions are frequently defined broadly and seen in the context of library operations as a whole. The small size of the libraries and consequent visibility of its staff and work can prevent their cataloging departments from becoming insular.

Where the catalogers are concerned primarily, but not solely, with cataloging operations, they must be librarians first and catalogers in addition. The variety in the duties of such catalogers can offer valuable perspectives into the life of the library and help them to appreciate the interdependence of various functions. These catalogers must be able to see beyond the immediate concerns of cataloging and be sensitive to the perspectives of other departments of the library. They must be good planners but also able to respond quickly to changing conditions and needs.

Cataloging operations in small college libraries usually handle a variety of materials and formats in a variety of subject areas. Their catalogers tend to be generalists rather than specialists and are expected to be jacks-of-all-trades who can work with the range of materials which make up the collection of an undergraduate library. While there are clear advantages to being jacks-of-all-trades, there are obvious drawbacks as well.

It is difficult to develop and maintain expertise and specializations, particularly in an environment of rapid change. A major challenge in the varied work environment for catalogers in small college libraries involves managing competing demands. Planning, ever a major part of professional responsibility, is especially important to catalogers who must meet this challenge and set priorities to ensure that cataloging operations receive warranted attention. Continuing education, networking, and professional development are crucial to catalogers in small colleges because they often have few in-house colleagues with whom to discuss the fine points of cataloging.

At Warren Wilson College, cataloging support is provided by student assistants; there is no paraprofessional cataloging staff. Each of the two student assistants works in the cataloging department for 6-9 hours a week. Our dependence on student labor poses special challenges and has obvious implications for management. Cataloging support is parttime and largely inexperienced. Turnover is high as students leave for various reasons. Unlike paraprofessional staff in a more conventional setting, our student assistants are not selected by the library staff.

The Catalog Librarian must commit considerable resources to training, motivating, supervising, and evaluating student assistants. For before any task can be transferred, the skill requisite for performing the task must be transferred.[12] Although recent professional literature and discussion seems to show support staff assuming responsibility for increasingly complex tasks, such delegation is generally limited in our situation.

Quality control, a major issue in any cataloging operation, is even more important in our situation where student assistants constitute the support staff. The Catalog Librarian is responsible for supervising the student assistants in her department and delivering prompt feedback to reinforce good work performance and to correct deficiencies. At the end of each semester, she provides a formal evaluation of each student assistant's work performance and assigns a work grade for that semester. She discusses the evaluation and grade with the student assistant before submitting it to the Work Program Office. In return, her student assistants complete and submit to the Work Program Office a formal evaluation of her performance as a teacher and supervisor.

Although, like many small college libraries, Warren Wilson does not have production quotas and does not require submission of formal plans, the Catalog Librarian benefits from developing plans which include taking stock of achievements, analyzing needs, setting priorities, and developing strategies for meeting goals. As a member of the faculty, she is required to submit to the Dean of the College an annual report and self evaluation which addresses her performance in several areas. Preparing this report offers opportunity for reflection, assessment, and planning.

CONCLUSION

In 1883, R. R. Bowker wrote in *Library Journal* that librarians "classify and catalog the records of ascertained knowledge, the literature of the whole past, and so bring the books to readers and the readers to books. He is the merchant, the middle man, of thought." [13] Bowker's insights, articulated in an environment quite different from ours, remain as fitting today as when they were expressed. It is still the work of catalogers to connect the users of a library with its holdings, regardless of the format of its catalog. Willard Mishoff said in 1932 that the issue is whether or not the catalog "is to continue to be a product of the catalogers, by the catalogers, and for the catalogers, in which case it may deserve to perish from the earth." [14]

For undergraduates, library catalogs often fall short of their intended efficacy. And so the cataloging department at Warren Wilson College tries to provide tools and services to complement the standard catalog. Human service to human beings and communities is the prime reason for a library to exist. [15] Even for catalog librarians, traditionally sequestered from public services and preoccupied with the particulars of bibliographic management, opportunities exist for reaching and assisting library users. And in the long run, it is our users who will sustain and nourish us and ensure us a prosperous future.

NOTES

1. Michael Gorman, preface to *Future Libraries: Dreams, Madness, & Reality*, by Walt Crawford and Michael Gorman (Chicago, IL.: American Library Association, 1995).

2. Richard M. Dougherty, "Getting a Grip on Change," *American Libraries* 28, no. 7 (1997): 41-42.

3. Roy Tennant, "The Most Important Management Decision: Hiring Staff for the New Millennium," *Library Journal* 123, no. 3 (1998): 102. Suggesting that it may be more productive to choose staff based on their personality traits than on their specific skills, he lists and describes several qualities which will help build a library for the new millennium: The capacity to learn constantly and quickly, flexibility, an innate skepticism, a propensity to take risks, an abiding public service perspective, an appreciation of what others bring to the effort and an ability to work with them effectively, skill at enabling and fostering change, and the capacity and desire to work independently.

4. His "A Fold in Time," *College & Research Libraries* 60, no. 3 (1999): 108-109, calls for librarians to pay attention to the content and context of information. "Let us move beyond digital libraries to build whole earth libraries."

5. Ruby E. Miller and Barbara J. Ford, "A Relationship Between Cataloging and Reference," *Texas Library Journal* 66 (summer 1990): 48-49.

6. Mary F. Salony, "A Selected Bibliography of Recent Publications on the Relationship Between Public Services and Technical Services," *The Southeastern Librarian* 40, no. 4 (1998): 30-33.

7. Marilyn Myers, "Blurring the Lines: Mingling Technical and Public Service Responsibilities; Report of the ALCTS Role of the Professional in American Technical Services Discussion Group Meeting," *Technical Services Quarterly* 15, no. 4 (1998): 67-70.

8. Sheila S. Intner, "The Good Professional: A New Vision," *American Libraries* 29, no. 3 (1998): 48-50.

9. See, for example, Loanne Snavely and Katie Clark, "What Users Really Think: How They See and Find Serials in the Arts and Sciences, *Library Resources and Technical Services* 40, no. 1 (1995): 49.

10. For a discussion of the role of infrastructure and the need for human-centerd product development, see Donald A. Norman, *The Invisible Computer: Why Good Products Can Fail, the Personal Computer is So Complex, and Information Appliances Are the Solution* (Cambridge, MA: MIT Press, 1998).

11. Norman, Donald A., *Things That Make Us Smart: Defending Human Attributes in the Age of the Machine* (Reading, MA: Perseus Books, 1993), 9-11.

12. Jennifer A. Younger, "Support Staff and Librarians in Cataloging," *Cataloging & Classification Quarterly* 23, no. 1 (1996): 42.

13. Quoted in Crawford and Gorman, *Future Libraries*, 3-4.

14. Quoted in Miller and Ford, "A Relationship Between Cataloging and Reference," 48.

15. Crawford and Gorman, *Future Libraries*, 182.

Staff Assignments and Workflow Distribution at the End of the 20th Century: Where We Were, Where We Are, and What We'll Need to Be

Jane Padham Ouderkirk

SUMMARY. Innovative procedures and new cataloging tasks have resulted in modified workflow distribution and evolving work assignments. In addition to the functional skill set required within each job level, specific behaviors and personality traits are necessary for success in meeting the demands of multiple priorities and activities. *[Article copies available for a fee from The Haworth Document Delivery Service: 1-800-342-9678. E-mail address: <getinfo@haworthpressinc.com> Website: <http://www.HaworthPress.com>]*

KEYWORDS. Job descriptions, skill sets, personality traits, history, roles

WHERE WE WERE–
A BRIEF HISTORY OF 20TH CENTURY BIBLIOGRAPHIC RECORD PRODUCTION

The Artisan Era

Those who began their careers in aged library systems when card catalogs were the access tool of choice may have run across elegant

---

Jane Padham Ouderkirk, MLS, MS is Head of the Cataloging Services Department, Widener Library 88, Harvard University, Cambridge, MA 02138 (E-mail: ouderkir@fas.harvard.edu).

[Haworth co-indexing entry note]: "Staff Assignments and Workflow Distribution at the End of the 20th Century: Where We Were, Where We Are, and What We'll Need to Be." Ouderkirk, Jane Padham. Co-published simultaneously in *Cataloging & Classification Quarterly* (The Haworth Information Press, an imprint of The Haworth Press, Inc.) Vol. 30, No. 2/3, 2000, pp. 343-355; and: *Managing Cataloging and the Organization of Information: Philosophies, Practices and Challenges at the Onset of the 21st Century* (ed: Ruth C. Carter) The Haworth Information Press, an imprint of The Haworth Press, Inc., 2000, pp. 343-355. Single or multiple copies of this article are available for a fee from The Haworth Document Delivery Service [1-800-342-9678, 9:00 a.m. - 5:00 p.m. (EST). E-mail address: getinfo@haworthpress inc.com].

antique cards, penned in library script, nestled among the mass-produced cards of later decades. Objects of beauty that provided searching enhancements far beyond those of the book catalog, handwritten cards were the epitome of labor-intensive catalog production methods.

The Industrial Era

The industrial revolution in cataloging was in full gear at mid-century. Mechanical support and assembly line practices lead to divisions of labor between catalogers and clerks and in larger institutions between clerks as well. There were clerk-typists who produced cards and file clerks who filed them in the catalog–usually "above the rod" until a cataloger could verify that they were filed correctly. At some institutions, catalogers filled out (usually handwritten) 3 × 5 slips of paper called p-slips (p for preliminary cataloging) or flimsies (referring to the weight of the paper in comparison to card stock) and forwarded them to clerks who typed the card sets. The advent of the IBM Selectric™ self-correcting typewriter with a card holding platen brought joy to many a cataloging department of the '70s. Acquisitions staff were using multi-part order forms the early versions of which had carbon paper between each layer. The advent of the carbon-less multi-part order form was considered a minor miracle that made acquisitions work much less messy. In their simplest form the order forms which were also in 3 × 5 format had 3 parts, 2 flimsy layers and one heavier paper. One copy was sent to the book jobber, one was filed in the on-order file, and the sturdiest copy was filed under main entry in the card catalog as a temporary record. A variety of outsourcing vendor services for catalog card production were offered by agencies outside the library. In addition to the Library of Congress, several library companies provided card sets for purchase by libraries. Local editing was done directly on the cards using razor blades, electric erasers, or buff tinted WhiteOut™ to remove information so that corrected data could be added. Some libraries used cameras attached to frames that fit over the pages of the *National Union Catalog* to photograph entries. The film was sent to vendors who returned card sets ready for added entries to be typed. Production of card sets for original cataloging was similarly convoluted. Some libraries produced a single main entry card for each new title and sent it to a specialty company that would reproduce the number of cards needed for a set. When the set was returned to the library, clerks would add the headings.

The Electronic Era.

At the beginning of the electronic era, few of us imagined how quickly the rate of change would accelerate. When the bibliographic utilities first emerged, they provided a way for us to use the cataloging work of others by buying copies of their cards, and we had the ability to do our original cataloging online with full card sets appearing in the mail within days. Any necessary editing was usually done on the card sets because they were considered the end product of the process. The result of our short-sightedness and unwillingness to pay for revised card sets meant that an institution's holdings in the utility's database could be so variant from the card catalog that even libraries with MARC records for substantial proportions of their collections still found it necessary to incorporate database maintenance activities as a considerable component of retrospective conversion projects and on-line catalog implementation.

Bibliographic input and searching were initially considered professional level tasks. As card catalogs were closed and replaced with online databases of library holdings, the electronic version of clerical tasks became paraprofessional or library assistant (LA) work. Catalogers filled in worksheets instead of writing out p-slips and handed them on to support staff for input instead of typing. Eventually copy cataloging became a support staff activity. As increasing numbers of libraries began to add their holdings to the utility databases, there were irrational predictions about the demise of cataloging as a professional activity because "there would be copy" for everything. Copy is available only after someone performs the original work and contributes it to the database–it does not spontaneously generate itself, as some in our profession seemed to imply. Forecasts of the demise of cataloging were wrong. Only the tiniest libraries can find copy for all the titles they own or access. Large research libraries that pride themselves on unique collections cannot be expected to find copy for titles that are not owned by others. Although today's catalogers have spent either all or most of their careers in the electronic era, we are still in the dawn of development of electronic publication and electronic catalog management tools.

WHERE WE ARE

Cataloging tasks have traditionally moved along a continuum. In the innovation phase, new processing techniques are usually pegged at professional level. When those techniques have become routine and the next innovation has appeared, the same procedures become paraprofessional tasks. Now however, there are tasks that can be assigned to electronic support systems. Copy cataloging has moved the length of that continuum. First assigned to professional staff, searching for copy became the core job for cataloging support staff, but the most basic level of searching is now performed automatically by specialized applications programs. The process of original cataloging has also been moving piecemeal down the same continuum. Most large research libraries assign some portions of original cataloging to paraprofessional staff. Some have access to cataloging software which captures available information and fills in the blanks on templates for bibliographic and authority records thereby automating a basic portion of original cataloging by eliminating the need to key in the same data repeatedly.

Tiered Work Flow Distribution at Widener Library

The Harry Elkins Widener Memorial Library is Harvard University's social sciences and humanities research library. The following descriptions of staff assignment and workflow distribution refer to the practices and methods of monographs cataloging in Widener Library. We regularly investigate improved methods of automated copy cataloging and have achieved major gains in productivity using the methods developed so far. As much as possible, we exhaust all methods of automated copy cataloging before performing book-in-hand searching on the utilities as the last step before original cataloging. At the time of order, our local catalog (HOLLIS) is checked for order duplication, for a matching record in the Library of Congress Books File, or for a match produced by another of our libraries. The latest four years of the Library of Congress Books File (LCBF) is also available in HOLLIS.

1. If no match is located in HOLLIS, a technical services client macro saves the contents of the search and checks OCLC for copy. If copy is found, the record is downloaded for use as an order record. If no copy is available, a provisional record is created using the data originally entered for the search.

2. Provisional records are machine matched against HOLLIS and the LCBF on a regular cycle and are overwritten with full copy if found.

3. If only provisional order record remains in HOLLIS at the time of receipt, a macro searches OCLC again to find copy that may have appeared between the time of order and receipt. If no copy is located and the title is not designated a priority for original cataloging, the title is shelved in the cataloging backlog, equal in volume to the number of titles cataloged in a year.

4. Searches for copy in HOLLIS and the LCBF continue to cycle until the title is cataloged. Additional copy is harvested by downloading ISBNs from the "older" provisional records to a file that is loaded into OCLC's Microenhancer software and searched against OCLC.

5. Records for those titles that remain no-hits are processed through RLG's Marcadia Service to locate any additional copy.

6. Titles whose records have been processed through each tier of the automated search routines are sorted for original cataloging either by library staff or by OCLC's TechPro service. Before original cataloging is initiated, titles are searched in HOLLIS and on the utilities with book-in-hand by staff to locate any copy that automated searching operations may have missed as a result of inconsistencies or insufficient information in the provisional order record. Original cataloging workflow is divided into two streams. Titles judged to be "of relatively less scholarly interest" to the researchers of today are sent to OCLC for TechPro cataloging. Included in this category are ephemeral materials and "gray" literature acquired to support the research of future social historians. Our cataloging staff completes the work on the remaining titles.

We have six levels of staff assigned to monographs cataloging–three paraprofessional and three professional categories.

The core work of ***Library Assistants IV (LA IV)*** is copy cataloging. Staff at this grade:

- work with existing bibliographic data, matching the appropriate record to the individual title. Bibliographic data may be found in our local system files, in remote vendor files, or on major bibliographic utilities.

- create provisional cataloging records using information culled from the title in hand and may create name authority records.
- are able to identify inaccuracies and inconsistencies requiring correction or referral to other staff for resolution.
- create the piece specific information for the item record.
- may also assist in training and assigning work to other support staff and casual assistants.

Processing added volumes, works-in-parts and creating original series authority records for unnumbered series are examples of tasks performed by LA IVs working with English materials, but rarely by those working in other languages where the complexity of the language structure and/or publication patterns adds another degree of difficulty. A college degree and previous library experience are preferred when hiring LA IVs. Reading knowledge of a foreign language and/or knowledge of a particular subject matter and basic knowledge and experience using personal computers are also required.

The core work of the **Library Assistants V *(LA V)*** is assistance with cataloging of materials within established guidelines and the resolution of problems resulting from incorrect, incomplete, or conflicting bibliographic data. Staff in this group:

- perform moderately complex copy cataloging such as editing variant bibliographic records.
- are expected to have comprehensive knowledge and experience in LA IV tasks and are able to recognize, resolve, or refer copy cataloging problems referred by other staff.
- are assigned responsibility for original descriptive cataloging of straightforward works and for supervised subject analysis and classification of materials within designated types, such as local histories or works of literature, within defined projects and within specific formats.
- create name authority records and series records for numbered series.
- are expected to have strong analytical skills, a knowledge of the culture of the country whose works are being cataloged, and sufficient language expertise to accurately identify the subject(s) covered in the assigned works.
- are able to recognize whether the form of a heading is correct and whether the description of content is accurate.

- may be assigned to catalog material, which would normally be performed by higher-grade staff in order to learn new skills and to exhibit potential for future promotion. In such cases all work is closely supervised and revised.
- serve as a source of information on established policies and procedures and may oversee day-to-day processing functions and maintain related records and statistics.
- may hire, train, and supervise student and casual staff and may assist in training and directing the work of support staff.

A college degree is preferred and previous library or related work experience is required. Language facility, subject or technical competence and/or supervisory ability may be required. Basic knowledge and experience using microcomputers is required.

The core work of *Library Assistants VI (LA VI)* is a combination of original cataloging and classification for materials designated as appropriate to skill and language ability and copy cataloging of the most complex nature. The highest grade paraprofessionals, they:

- are expected to have achieved a comprehensive level of knowledge and experience in LA IV and V tasks and are able to instruct and supervise others in the performance of those tasks.
- are required to have extensive knowledge of specific subject areas and of the culture of the country whose works are being cataloged as well as comprehensive reading ability in the language(s) assigned.
- are fully aware of the systems and policies, which support workflow and participate in the development of those systems and policies, and serve as recognized sources of information on the rationale as well as the content of cataloging policies and procedures.
- are expected to have advanced skills with multiple software programs used to perform cataloging and to manage cataloging data and its quantification and analysis.
- may hire, train, and direct the work of student and casual staff.
- may also train and direct the work of other support staff and participate in performance evaluations.

The LA VI is also expected to contribute to the job beyond performance of the core work by participating on College and University committees and task groups. A college degree is preferred and substantial library or related work experience is required. Language ability, subject or technical competence, and/or supervisory ability are required as is extensive knowledge and experience in the use of cataloging applications on microcomputers.

Catalogers perform: Original cataloging of works in several languages and formats; are trained in local practices of subject analysis and classification; take part in continuing training in more complex aspects of the job; remain current in review of rule changes, new cataloging software applications, technology changes; contribute to local cataloging policy; work within the context of a team; by attending local and system-wide meetings; and training or supervision of support staff and student copy cataloging. Attendance at regional and national conferences is valued and is expected of those staff seeking promotion to the next level. Requirements at time of hire include two years relevant experience, an MLS or equivalent work experience, standard cataloging skills and solid working knowledge of one or more foreign languages and of cataloging rules and tools.

Senior Catalogers perform: Original cataloging and authority work in one or more foreign languages in all bibliographic formats; work independently without review; serve as resources for difficult cataloging questions and problems; develop and recommend local policies and procedures as well as review and comment on national draft policies and proposals; review and revise work of other original catalogers and library assistants. They are also expected to participate in local, regional, and national technical services committees and working groups and may conduct job-related research and publish the results. They may be responsible for supervision of other staff. An MLS or equivalent degree is required and a second specialized advanced degree may be preferred. Two to four years experience, advanced knowledge of one or more foreign languages and/or a subject specialty, advanced knowledge of cataloging standards and practices, and demonstrated familiarity of emerging publishing and cataloging technologies are additional requirements for Senior Catalogers.

Cataloging Team Leaders are expected to carry the duties of Senior Catalogers and to: Manage a team of professional and support staff; hire, train, evaluate, recommend promotions and terminations; develop and implement, prioritize, and reorganize workflow to accommodate changing needs; recommend cataloging procedures, software adaptation and database selection for catalog management; collaborate and negotiate with colleagues at Harvard and other institutions. Team Leaders are expected to demonstrate a detailed understanding of theoretical and technological changes in the profession, predicting and advocating for change through teaching, publishing, and service on planning committees. Additional responsibilities include: monitoring expenditures; regular participation on technical services committees; conducting job-related research or engaging in other professional development activities particularly those which enhance the prestige and importance of the library profession; and preparing manuals, directories and reports. Requirements include those listed under Senior Cataloger plus advanced communications skills, supervisory experience, and a solid working knowledge of acquisitions, collection development and cataloging management. Team Leaders are Senior Catalogers with management and administrative responsibilities.

The once distinct lines between paraprofessional and professional cataloging responsibilities have become relics of the past. "While at one time there may have been general agreement that librarians performed the intellectual work of cataloging and paraprofessionals the routine tasks, it is no longer clear that this is where the distinction between 'professional' and 'paraprofessional' work lies."[1] Many routine tasks are now automated. If non-MLS staff are able to attain the skills necessary to create consistently satisfactory bibliographic records, then the requirement for an MLS for all catalogers is an artificial barrier to productivity. Although there are often claims that allowing paraprofessionals to do "our work" downgrades the profession, I believe that holds true only if we fail to provide appropriate compensation for the intellectual effort required to do the work.

There is little turnover among library assistants in comparison with previous decades. Although there was always a contingent of long-term staff committed to support level work as an occupation, they were a minority until about ten years ago. We used to have staff who stayed for two or three years while they or their spouse completed graduate work. Now most library assistants are committed to library careers. In order for us to take advantage of individual skills and the training and experience that the library has provided, it is in our best interest to design paraprofessional career paths and to make known our expectations and staff requirements to be promoted to higher level positions.

There is a degree of crossover in the responsibilities of the highest-level library assistants and the first level professional position where skills and salaries are comparable. It is possible in Widener Library for a library assistant to be promoted to a professional cataloger position. We differentiate between professional catalogers and professional librarians. "Because it is a graduate degree, requiring an ALA-accredited master's degree does not guarantee that applicants will have any specific practical skills needed by the employer."[2] Cataloging requires on the job training for both professional and paraprofessional staff. All staff at the senior cataloger and higher levels are required to have an MLS and are expected to maintain their knowledge of issues effecting areas of the profession within and beyond technical services. There is also a difference in expectation of professional development activity. All staff are encouraged to attend local meetings, workshops, and seminars related to their work. Professional development activity is a requirement of higher level positions and is a component of the annual performance review process.

WHAT WE'LL NEED TO BE

Expectations have changed for both new staff and long term staff. Our jobs change even if we haven't changed jobs. It will be increasingly important to enhance our skills so that we remain competitive in tomorrow's job market. There are few jobs left for the "lone cataloger" of the past and those jobs that do remain will be in outsourcing agencies. Long term career planning means monitoring new postings for jobs similar to yours, especially those within your organization to check your own skill set against new requirements.

Hiring managers must emphasize the need for a balance of skill sets within their work units. Often staff who are most innovative become bored with implementation and evaluation while less creative staff may excel in those areas. You'll need to rely on both types to maintain management viability. The workplace also needs early adapters who can "sell" innovative methods through their ability to frame new concepts within the context of the individuals responsible for implementation. Even the best ideas will meet with initial resistance from some quarters.

"MLS catalogers should do more than just catalog faster than others and they should be able to do that as well. They'll also need to be creative and visionary, taking a more active role in managing their own and the library's affairs, with an eye to doing more than defending the status quo."[3] "Catalogers must start being better managers of time and resources."[4] Sheila Intner's "new kind of Good Professional" makes the best use of the library's resources, meets deadlines, acts objectively, shoulders responsibility, is open-minded and seeks to learn from others, reads widely, wants to experiment, empowers staff and inspires trust. "The Good Professional of the future won't feel obligated to maintain the status quo or to value the past over planning the future. He or she will not fail to understand the lessons of the past while considering tomorrow.[5]

In their examination of the evolving and expanding roles of catalogers in academic libraries, Lois Buttlar and Rajindar Garcha conclude that "professional catalogers no longer are defined merely on the basis of performing their traditional roles of original cataloging, authority work, and assigning call numbers and subjects" and that "perhaps the term professional cataloger will have to be replaced by another term or title that would cover a variety of position responsibilities carried on by the cataloger of the future."[6] Instead of renaming ourselves, perhaps we can redefine the term, "cataloger," so that the full scope and range of activities for which we are responsible is more broadly understood.

Because our job content changes so frequently, and because task assignments are redistributed among levels of staff over time, it may be more important to hire staff with specific characteristics that will support their ability to change in response to organization need over time. Adaptability and flexibility are essential traits for staff at all levels within the library. According to Roy Tennant, the personality traits of the staff you hire are at least as important as the skills they bring to the job because; "it may be more productive to choose staff who can evolve as the needs of the organization change." The traits that Tennant recommends for digital librarians are also important qualities in cataloging staff candidates:

- Ability to learn continually and quickly
- Flexibility
- Willingness to take risks and skill at enabling and fostering change

- Collegiality and team player skills balanced with the ability and desire to work independently. [7]

Joan Giesecke and Beth McNeil have identified twelve core competencies–"the skills, technical knowledge, and personal attributes"[8] which apply to all library staff with some variation within categories depending upon the specific position:

- Analytical Skills/Problem Solving/ Decision Making
- Communication Skills
- Creativity/Innovation
- Expertise and Technical Knowledge
- Flexibility/Adaptability
- Interpersonal/Group Skills
- Leadership
- Organizational Understanding and Global Thinking
- Ownership/Accountability/Dependability
- Planning and Organizational Skills
- Resource Management
- Service Attitude/User Satisfaction

Our continued success will be dependent on our capacity to manage multiple programs, projects and priorities. It is important not only to acquire cataloging skills, but also to develop the ability to recognize trends and opportunities for better resource management and to proactively enhance the skills that will be necessary when the next innovation develops and our work assignments move down the continuum of change.

NOTES

1. Mohr, Deborah A. and Anita Schuneman. "Changing roles: Original cataloging by paraprofessionals in ARL libraries." *Library Resources & Technical Services*, v. 41, no. 3 (July, 1997), p. 205.

2. Fallis, Don and Martin Fricke. "Not by library school alone." *Library Journal*, v.124, no. 17 (October 15, 1999), p. 44-45.

3. Steinhagen, Elizabeth N. and Sharon A. Moynahan. "Catalogers must change! Surviving between the rock and the hard Place." *Cataloging & Classification Quarterly*, v.26, no.3 (1998), p. 3-20.

4. Ibid.

5. Intner, Sheila. "The good professional: A new vision. " *American Libraries*, v.29, no. 3 (March 1998), p. 48-50.

6. Buttlar, Lois and Rajinder Garcha. "Catalogers in academic libraries: Their evolving and expanding roles." *College & Research Libraries*, v. 59, no. 4 (July 1998), p. 311-321.

7. Tennant, Roy. "The most important management decision: Hiring staff for the new millenium." *Library Journal*, v. 123, no. 3 (February 15, 1998), p. 102.

8. Giesecke, Joan and Beth McNeil. "Core competencies and the learning organization." *Library Administration & Management*, v. 13, no. 3 (Summer 1999), p. 158-166.

The End of an Era Builds New Team Spirit: Team Playing at Its Best

Andrea L. Stamm

SUMMARY. Northwestern University Library has recently migrated from its locally-developed mainframe NOTIS online catalog to Endeavor's Voyager. A history of the migration is discussed and includes choosing a new integrated library system, planning for the new ILS, workflow analysis, impact on staff, and the resulting reorganization in technical services. Particular attention is paid to the management of monographic cataloging, but acquisitions is also discussed. *[Article copies available for a fee from The Haworth Document Delivery Service: 1-800-342-9678. E-mail address: <getinfo@haworthpressinc.com> Website: <http://www.HaworthPress.com>]*

KEYWORDS. NOTIS, Voyager, migration, cataloging, acquisitions, reorganization

INTRODUCTION

One of the major trends in libraries at the onset of the new millennium approaches is the migration from one online catalog to another. This article will discuss and analyze Northwestern University Library's migration from NOTIS to Endeavor's Voyager. It will pay

Andrea L. Stamm, MLS, MA, is Head of the Catalog Department, Northwestern University Library, Evanston, IL 60208-2300 (E-mail: astamm@nwu.edu).

[Haworth co-indexing entry note]: "The End of an Era Builds New Team Spirit: Team Playing at Its Best." Stamm, Andrea L. Co-published simultaneously in *Cataloging & Classification Quarterly* (The Haworth Information Press, an imprint of The Haworth Press, Inc.) Vol. 30, No. 2/3, 2000, pp. 357-372; and: *Managing Cataloging and the Organization of Information: Philosophies, Practices and Challenges at the Onset of the 21st Century* (ed: Ruth C. Carter) The Haworth Information Press, an imprint of The Haworth Press, Inc., 2000, pp. 357-372. Single or multiple copies of this article are available for a fee from The Haworth Document Delivery Service [1-800-342-9678, 9:00 a.m. - 5:00 p.m. (EST). E-mail address: getinfo@haworthpressinc.com].

particular attention to planning, workflow analysis, and impact on staff, especially monographic cataloging staff of the Catalog Department. The factors affecting the management of a large cataloging unit will also be considered in the second part of the article.

BACKGROUND:
NOTIS ROOTS

In an era when library processing was still very much manually performed, and libraries still relied on the Library of Congress and the National Union Catalog as their primary source of cataloging copy, Northwestern University Library (NUL) was already thinking into the future when it pioneered the development of its own mainframe-based integrated library system (ILS), NOTIS. Since the late 1960s, the Library was fortunate to count amongst its ranks a dedicated team of computing staff to first create and then refine NOTIS for its local needs. The circulation module was implemented in 1970, and all technical services operations, including cataloging, acquisitions and serials control, began in 1971. Improvements continued, even as the University marketed NOTIS to other libraries, eventually spinning it off as NOTIS Systems, Inc. in 1987. Local enhancements to NOTIS continued, especially in cataloging and OPAC functionalities. In 1994, the Library's authorities librarian and programmer, Gary Strawn, developed a revolutionary workstation level product which he called CLAR, or the Cataloger's Toolkit.[1] In its local version, 54 buttons provided us with the ability to perform many activities with greater speed and accuracy. Examples of Toolkit functionalities included bibliographic and authority record verification and validation, automated creation of authority records, and the automatic assignment of a call number, to name just a few. It should come as no surprise that our catalogers were enthralled with the Toolkit and the cataloging efficiencies it afforded us.

CHOOSING A NEW ILS:
PLANTING THE SEED OF GOOD TEAMWORK

In the spring of 1996, University administration informed the Library that we would need to move NOTIS off the University's mainframe computer and adopt a new ILS that used client-server architecture. The library then formed a task force, the NOTIS Replacement Task Force (NRTF), to recommend a new ILS. Representatives included stake holders from the main library at the department head level as well as representatives from the Law and Health Sciences libraries (in Chicago), and from the United Library of Garrett and Seabury Seminaries (which shares our online catalog but is not affiliated with Northwestern University). The NRTF was given an unorthodox charge from our main library University Librarian: do not follow the customary pattern of asking for a Request for a Proposal. He wisely explained, and we readily agreed, that this process often entices vendors to promise something that they may or may not be able to deliver. His counsel was that we should ask vendors what they have now and show us how it works in some detail. After the NRTF drew up lists of essential and desirable features and functionalities for each ILS module, we then were ready to contact vendors. At the 1996 American Library Association annual conference, NRTF members attended six specially arranged vendor demos. There we made two important discoveries: first, not all of the vendors offered true client-server systems; second, some of them had little to demonstrate to us other than explain how their client-server system might work once they put more development efforts into it.

By October 1996, the NRTF arranged for four vendors to come to NUL for in-depth three-day demos. Each demo would consist of half-day sessions for cataloging, serials and acquisitions, circulation, OPAC; a technical session with our systems and programming people; and a meeting with the NRTF. One vendor withdrew from the selection process when they realized that they could not give us the demo on their client-server system. The NRTF now had to choose from among the three remaining vendors. What a delightful surprise occurred when the task force, after consulting with all interested staff who with considerable spirit had grilled the vendors during the demos, unanimously recommended the migration to Endeavor's Voyager, to be implemented no earlier than the summer of 1998.

PLANNING FOR THE MIGRATION

Planning for the migration began in earnest in the spring of 1997, after the letter of intent was signed and while contract negotiations were still ongoing. In April, selected members of the NRFT visited both the University of Rochester and Syracuse University to observe how Voyager was currently running at larger academic libraries. From this visit, we gained useful insights which helped us understand current features and desirable enhancements. Contract negotiations with Endeavor continued through the spring and into August when the contract was finally signed. The contract also contained a long appendix which included specific desired functionalities and concerns from each of the four modules represented in Voyager, along with the promise by Endeavor representatives of when each item would be addressed. Each item on the list was discussed with Endeavor senior staff and Library representatives. Of all of the modules, it was agreed that the cataloging module needed the most attention. We specified in our contract that cataloging representatives would meet with Endeavor staff to explain our view of issues related to the cataloging module. This meeting occurred in the fall of 1997 but did not yield as much as we hoped. At this time, we knew pretty well what we could expect from Voyager by the time we migrated the following summer.

In August 1997, a new task force, the Voyager Implementation Committee (VIC) was formed with an eye to representing all of the key players in our shared online catalog. The 11 representatives included a coordinator for each Voyager module (cataloging, acquisitions, circulation and the OPAC) as well as the head of the Library Management System Department. Representatives from beyond the main library included two people from the University Computing Center, representatives from the University's separate Law and Health Sciences libraries, and a representative from the seminaries of the United Library. The main library's head of technical services chaired the VIC.

Each of the four VIC module chairs also formed a sub-group to assist in planning and decision-making. In the case of cataloging, an already existing group, the Cataloging Policy Committee (CPC) became the module implementation team. CPC members represented each cataloging unit within our online catalog. This included considerable overlap between the VIC and the CPC since it also included the same representatives from Law, Health Sciences and United. The end result was fuller cataloging representation on the broader committee, VIC.

The CPC performed a major role in planning for the migration. It was obvious that the CPC would be most knowledgeable about cataloging functionalities and possible future enhancements and it would produce the list that was eventually forwarded to the NRTF. It was not nearly as obvious that the CPC should mastermind data migration. Who else is so intimately connected with the mysteries of the MARC record? Who else would understand data mapping from system to system? Who else would be blamed if we did not get it right? For these reasons, we spent much time working out the most minute details of data migration. The CPC was also asked to oversee the mapping of several system-wide features, such as location codes and owning libraries which would be used at the time of migration when we performed our time-consuming and complicated system configuration.

In preparation for the migration, the CPC developed a testing plan for cataloging. This included the approach to setting up the test database, the delineation of responsibilities for testers, the method of detecting and logging errors, as well as deliverables including dozens of test cases and test scripts, and the creation of a problem/error report form. The CPC also created numerous templates to be used in the creation of bibliographic, holdings, and authority records.

Selected technical staff received the first official training from Endeavor early in 1998. Module chairs received our first Voyager training in the spring of 1998. This consisted of "functional training," a four day overview of all the modules. For this particular training, Endeavor required that the same chosen people attend all sessions so that they receive a complete system overview and understand the implications of a decision in one module on another module. Cataloging and OPAC each took a half-day, while acquisitions and circulation each took a day and a half. Later on in the spring, selected NU people received "train the trainer" instruction at Endeavor's headquarters.

At this point, we were ready to sink our teeth into formulating a training and documentation program tailored to our own local needs. Each module team was responsible for determining the level of training for all staff in that module. For the cataloging module in the main library, this translated into hands-on training for catalogers and acquisitions staff as well as a cataloging overview for public service and collection management staff. We also thought that cataloging staff would understand the new ILS better if they received training in the acquisitions and OPAC modules. Little did we realize how essential this additional training would turn out to be for the catalogers. All of the Voyager training was given in the final weeks before migration.

Key in our minds at this time was the belief that as successful as any of our training might be, working in Voyager could only be successful if we also tailored our cataloging documentation to the Northwestern environment. Thus the trainers willingly agreed to write NUL-specific cataloging documentation.

One of the key challenges for the trainers and documentation writers involved the unfortunate timing of Voyager releases. Although we had received training and had practiced on a separate training database using Release 97.1, we were, in fact, going live on Release 97.2 which was loaded only days before our migration. We knew in advance that the biggest changes between the two releases would affect the cataloging module. This situation caused considerable angst because the cataloging trainers had to scramble around at the last minute to make sure that their training scripts and their documentation would give accurate information for the current release. The end result was easy-to-follow, accurate, and up-to-date documentation filled with numerous prints of all of the important Voyager screens: bibliographic, holdings, item, and authority records. We now realize that the next time we undergo another migration, we should attempt to time it so that we avoid migrating so soon after receiving a new release.

With only a few months remaining before our much-anticipated migration, some staff felt that they were not informed about how the migration was progressing. Towards the end of June, our VIC public relations representative therefore arranged for a staff introduction to Voyager. Speakers included each of the module chairs who gave brief presentations about how Voyager differs from NOTIS in each module, problems encountered in the migration process, and accomplishments of each team.

Administrative support for the migration was clearly articulated when the University Library Director informed staff that the Library's primary goal for the summer and fall of 1998 was to prepare for the migration to Voyager. These were clearly extraordinary times. All "but the most necessary activities" were suspended during this period.[2] For the first time in NUL's history, committee and task force meetings were severely limited unless they related to the migration.

Negotiating the exact migration date was more problematic than might be otherwise expected because of the two different fiscal years and three academic calendars of classes used by the various libraries represented in the VIC. Migrating in the middle of a quarter would have been intolerable because of the possible disruption to our users. Fund accounting would have been very difficult if we switched vendors in the middle of a fiscal year. Migration was arranged to begin on June 30, 1998 and take approximately one month.

GAP PERIOD

Endeavor staff warned us that we would need several weeks to configure the Voyager system once we received Release 97.2. They suggested that during this time, after we froze updates to NOTIS and before we completed the migration, we might want to stop cataloging. As an alternative, we could continue cataloging single volume monographs that were not represented in NOTIS. Endeavor would load these bibliographic and holdings records and create item records at the last minute, just before Day 1. This period came to be called the "gap." Cataloging managers were somewhat torn about making this decision to continue cataloging the materials that fell into the guidelines just mentioned. We had to exclude much of our normal cataloging activity from the gap period because Endeavor could not handle updates to existing records, be they bibliographic, holdings, authority, or order records. This meant that even our cataloging backlog was out of bounds for the gap period. We did manage to catalog during the gap, although there were some data migration problems that only came to our attention after migration. If we had to do it all over again tomorrow, we would probably choose to stop cataloging during the gap period.

REACHING DAY 1

We were well prepared for the migration when it was completed in early August 1998, in time for the beginning of the new school year and a new fiscal year for the University. Instead of phasing in, module by module, as some sites do, we implemented all four modules simultaneously on Day 1. That was a wise decision for us, since we all wanted to be able to begin work on the new system as soon as possible. We experienced no ill effects from that decision.

Cataloging managers in all three departments of the main library were delighted that staff was easily able to perform cataloging functions within the first couple of days after migration. Our considerable efforts in planning, as well as our provision of tailored training and documentation, were much of the reason for the smooth transition.

COPING WITH CATALOGING STAFF MORALE

None of this could have been smoothly accomplished if we ignored the issue of morale. From the cataloging perspective, we had just migrated from a library system which was tailored to our every need. If a cataloger had an idea to improve cataloging workflow in NOTIS, it was often, sometimes within minutes, possible to ask our resident magician, Gary Strawn, to implement the idea.

All of this changed with the adoption of a new "out of the box" online system. Northwestern was now just another customer. We could request enhancements, but there was no guarantee that Endeavor would favor our ideas over their own or over those of other customers. Those of us in management positions took on new leadership roles. It was more important than ever to motivate staff and build a team spirit. We needed to help the staff develop new skills needed in Voyager. We were not afraid to counsel staff, to let them know that if we did not know the answer immediately, we would find it for them. We kept in constant touch with our staffs, taking action where needed, and following up periodically with the less vocal cataloging staff. We were leading by example, working in the cataloging module so we would be prepared to answer any and all questions.

We also had high hopes that at least some of the NOTIS Toolkit functionalities would eventually reappear in Voyager. Because Endeavor staff has assured us that we will be able to write local programs (such as the Toolkit) that will interface with Voyager, we have been able to maintain staff morale.

FACTORS AFFECTING THE MANAGEMENT OF CATALOGING

An Embarrassment of Riches

Who could have predicted that our migration would coincide with one other important factor beyond our control in Technical Services?

For years, despite annual budget requests, the Library's collections budget had been gradually eroded by the rising costs of serials and inflation. Not until University President Henry Bienen launched his "Highest Order of Excellence" Program and billion dollar capital campaign was the Library blessed with a major influx of funds. By some strange quirk of fate, by the time the Library migrated to Voyager in August 1998, we suddenly were faced with an embarrassment of riches. The income from a new $10 million Library endowment combined with budget increases for inflation and collections budget left over from the previous fiscal year meant that at the beginning of the fiscal year, we had over $1 million dollars more in the collections budget than the previous fiscal year! The Library administration decided not to make any permanent changes in staffing until we could examine workflows and assess the true impact of the Voyager migration.

Taking on New Responsibilities

Before describing how Technical Services began to cope with this situation, it might be useful to first describe the functions performed in each of the three departments. The Serials and Acquisitions Department (SAS) was composed of serials acquisitions, serials cataloging and monographic acquisitions. In the Bibliographic Records Services (BRS) Department, monographic books were searched and copy cataloged. Some "special purchases" not acquired via firm order or approval were received and searched and all were cataloged if copy was available. The Catalog Department was composed of original monographic catalogers, catalog management staff, the authorities librarian, the backlog manager, and physical processing staff. Thus cataloging activities were occurring in all three departments.

In a matter of weeks after the migration, it became clear that there were problems in the acquisitions end of Technical Services. In the Serials and Acquisitions Department, serials staff had two new major tasks ahead of them. First, since our open orders did not migrate to Voyager (for migrations after ours, Endeavor has been able to migrate open orders), SAS staff had to create manually a new purchase order for each of our approximately 15,000 active serial titles. They also wanted to take advantage of Voyager's predictive check-in feature which utilizes serial subscription and prediction patterns for each serial title checked in. In October, several monographic original catalogers began to assist SAS by spending an hour a day checking in current periodicals. A few also received training in the creation of serial patterns and serial purchase orders. Serial cataloging was reduced to an absolute minimum so that catalogers could spend their time on the more urgently needed tasks mentioned above. Acquisitions staff could not keep up with the orders to be placed on behalf of the many selectors with their increased budgets.

In the Bibliographic Records Services Department, prior to the migration to Voyager, there were regular ebbs and flows of work between SAS and BRS. There was, at times, not enough work to keep the acquisitions staff busy while at other times they were swamped. Technical Services managers realized that it was now time to examine workflow and consider reorganizing to take advantage of the possibilities of the new ILS. The heads of Technical Services, SAS and BRS spent considerable effort analyzing current staffing functionalities and needs. They decided to experiment with cross training in BRS and the monographic side of acquisitions. Some copy catalogers would learn to order or receive and pay for monographic books. Some monographic acquisitions staff would eventually learn to perform copy cataloging. This experiment began in the fall of 1998, just after migration.

Since the cutoff date to place monographic orders for the 1997/98 fiscal year had been moved up because of the migration, when selectors were again allowed to submit new orders in September 1998, orders flooded into BRS. As a temporary measure, BRS stopped copy cataloging because it was deemed more essential to acquire the books in a timely fashion. Copy cataloging could wait until the flow of orders abated. Monographic orders were becoming logjammed. Acquisitions staff was also slow to unpack the books received and create an invoice primarily because of the increased time it takes to create an invoice in Voyager.

What was happening in the third area of Technical Services, the Catalog Department? We could have continued to "do our own thing" since we were able to perform all of our functions in Voyager and we were, by and large, not directly impacted by the migration. However, Catalog Department staff was more than willing to assist the other technical services units if that was what was the best for the Library. As already mentioned, our first new duties involved assisting with serials work. Then to assist BRS, the original catalogers were asked to spend several hours a day performing copy cataloging. These new responsibilities continued for about six months. Books began to overflow our existing shelving units. New space had to be found to accommodate the recently acquired uncataloged materials. Gradually books were beginning to accumulate all around Technical Services and additional shelving had to be constructed in the cataloging backlog area.

By 1999, other more drastic measures had to be taken. The attempts by copy catalogers to alleviate the monographic order situation were not nearly enough. It was clear that the Library would not come close to spending the annual collections budget by the end of the fiscal year. It was clear that in addition to the copy catalogers, original catalogers needed to pitch in and create monographic orders. In February original catalogers began to place orders on a half-time basis, temporarily halting their copy cataloging assignments. Finally, after several months of this order creation, we could see light at the end of the tunnel. With due diligence, we would come close to spending the entire collections budget.

Organizational Changes Finalized

The cross-training experiment at the front end of Technical Services was working well and was accomplishing several important goals. One does wonder how much the increased budget impacted on this new lack of peaks and valleys of work. SAS and BRS staff were kept busy at all times, so we were now making better use of our existing staff. From a managerial perspective, cross training also builds more flexibility into staff positions. From a staff point of view, it has the added benefit of giving the staff more variety in their assignments so they feel that their work is more interesting and less routine. We have also now eliminated some of the excessive handling of books. We have currently eased the bottleneck of orders at the point of acquisitions, but we also wonder what will happen midway through the current fiscal year if more drastic organizational changes are not made.

In January 1999, BRS and SAS reorganized, changing both their structures and names. Some staff from SAS joined BRS to form the Monographic Acquisitions and Rapid Cataloging (MARC) Department, responsible for ordering, receiving, invoicing, and copy cataloging of monographic titles. The remaining staff in SAS formed a new Serials Department, responsible for serials acquisitions and serials cataloging. The Catalog Department remained unchanged. As before the reorganization, cataloging operations are still taking place in all three Technical Services departments.

Making the Best Use of Catalog Department Staff

Some pre-migration background might be useful in order to understand how well the Catalog Department is currently functioning. For the past several years, the University Librarian had been (through attrition) moving staff out of Technical Services and into Public Services. In the months immediately before migration, the Catalog Department lost two of its eight original catalogers. In the fall of 1998, we were permitted to refill one of the two positions and were fortunate to rehire an experienced former member of our own Department. It was recently agreed that his cataloging time would be further cut back as he assumed some of the selection responsibilities for a retiring bibliographer. Despite these cutbacks, we are able to maintain a core of original catalogers, each with his or her own knowledge of foreign languages and subject disciplines.

Since 1995, NUL has also been a contributor to the Program of Cooperative Cataloging's (PCC) bibliographic record component, BIBCO. The editing of records (bibliographic and authority) in NOTIS was easier than in OCLC itself, so we cataloged the BIBCO item locally in NOTIS and exported it to OCLC. This saved the cataloger time and performed some additional validation of data while it was being uploaded and also at OCLC's end. Since our migration to Voyager, we have continued to catalog BIBCO candidates locally and export them to OCLC. For NUL, a Dewey library, all BIBCO records must have a complete Dewey call number. In fact, this one BIBCO requirement is particularly vexing to our catalogers who only classify to the fifth digit beyond the decimal point and, when appropriate, classify an item according to a special scheme for Africana materials. The cataloger therefore must often classify a single book two times, once for our local needs, and once according to national BIBCO guidelines.

In the fall of 1996, when the PCC core standard was nationally approved, NUL began to contribute PCC core records. Cataloging managers had hoped that the adoption of the core standard as our "default" level of cataloging would mean that we would be able to catalog that many more items. In spite of efforts to promote core level cataloging with catalogers, selectors and reference librarians, core level cataloging has had little impact at NUL. Most original catalogers, despite repeated urgings, would rather perform full level cataloging or a locally developed minimal level cataloging. Several of them are subject to "core creep," i.e., adding one more note or field to make the record comply with the full level PCC cataloging standard. In the three years since we instituted core level cataloging, we have received only one complaint that can be traced to a core level record. Public services staff appears to have taken seriously the instructions to suggest to users the occasional need for keyword searching. Our BIBCO contributions, both full and core level, have gradually decreased over the past three years. This is due, in large part, to the push to catalog as many items as possible before migration, and the assistance the original catalogers have provided to the other two departments since migration.

In the Catalog Management Section of the Catalog Department, a variety of tasks are performed. The primary Catalog Management project for the past two years was the completion of retrospective conversion (recon) of one of our collections of distinction, the Transportation Library, which had not taken part in the earlier retrospective conversion project for the main library. Due to the tedious nature of recon, two experienced support staff members requested that they be given release time from that project in order to perform copy cataloging. Since we obviously could use the copy cataloging help, and we knew that morale could only be improved by this move, we readily agreed to their proposal. They have served us well in this capacity. Now that the recon project has been completed, most Catalog Management staff will permanently continue to perform some much needed copy cataloging.

NUL had a long and rich history of database maintenance in NOTIS. Most of the database maintenance routines and programs enjoyed by other NOTIS customers were originated at NUL by Gary Strawn and others. Once we migrated to Voyager, all of this changed. We no longer have an acceptable batch correction capability. Precious little database maintenance is now performed except on an "as encountered" basis by individual copy and original catalogers. We expect this situation to change in the year 2000 since we have a base upon which to build new database management tools, staff eager to do the work, and a promise from Endeavor that they will provide us with the ability to write local programs that will interface with Voyager from release to release.

Regardless of which of the three Technical Services departments a cataloger works in, the original or copy cataloger performs authority record creation at the time of cataloging. In 1977, the Catalog Department, as part of an NEH and Carnegie Corporation grant called the Northwestern Africana Project, began an experiment with the Library of Congress in the decentralized creation of authority records.[3] Northwestern's original catalogers continued to create new Africa-related national-level name authority records on behalf of the Library of Congress until the creation of the Name Authority Cooperative Project (NACO) which we joined in 1980. For a number of years, we sent in hand-typed workforms to the Library of Congress. By the 1990s, with our Toolkit, we could make use of machine capabilities to create the complete authority record, including all appropriate fixed and variable fields as well as suggested cross-references. We were also easily able to export the records to OCLC, so that our NACO contributions were easier to create, more accurate, and resulted in increased NACO contributions. When we migrated to Voyager, we hoped to keep many of these functionalities. In fact, with the help of Gary Strawn, Voyager does create authority records automatically.[4] We can export or import authority records (and bibliographic records, of course), so our NACO contributions are currently only limited by our ability to find appropriate NACO candidates and the time constraints, such as committee work and other assignments, of each original cataloger.

Where Do We Stand One Year After Migration?

Because of the migration, it was assumed that cataloging production during the first year after migration would be down in all three Technical Services departments. Interestingly enough, in the Catalog Department, the total number of items cataloged remained constant between fiscal years 1997/98 and 1998/99.[5] The type of cataloging is what differed. Our original cataloging decreased while our copy cataloging increased since we were regularly performing a considerable amount of copy cataloging for the MARC Department. Understandably, cataloging production of the MARC Department declined significantly since they were overwhelmed with acquisitions work (ordering and receiving) which was deemed to have a higher priority than copy cataloging.

In spite of the best efforts of the two monographic cataloging departments, MARC and Catalog, a "frontlog" of uncataloged books developed. Because most of these materials have some sort of cataloging copy, they were not integrated into our cataloging backlog. We can already see the pendulum swinging back and forth as the frontlog swells and diminishes according to other influences such as the submission of orders by the selectors. Copy cataloging takes a back seat to acquisitions when orders pile up during peak times of the fiscal year. Original cataloging time is reduced by the need to catalog the growing number of books with copy. Growth of the frontlog has become a major concern because there is little remaining free shelf space to house these current materials.

We are just beginning to understand the impact in Technical Services of our migration. It is now clear that we must make some changes in workflow and consider additional organizational changes. While Technical Services is now more of a group effort with common goals and a better understanding of the whole technical services process, there is no "magic pill" to improve productivity. In our quest for better service, we have just begun to experiment with two new services: OCLC's Prompt-Cat and EDI (Electronic Data Interchange). With PromptCat, we expect to receive timely monographic cataloging copy from our primary domestic vendor, Yankee Book Peddler. We have also just successfully loaded our first electronic invoices for serials from one vendor and hope to have similar results with four more before the year 2000. It is hoped that these two experiments will free up much needed staff time to perform other critical tasks in technical services but it is too soon to tell.

Future Directions?

In the next two to three years, we expect to see new efficiencies in future releases of the Voyager cataloging client, particularly as Endeavor works towards tearing down the wall between the cataloging and acquisitions modules. While we wait for those improvements, we continue to examine workflows and aim towards improving processing efficiencies. Towards that end, we are exploring workflow changes with the Collection Management Division to make the acquisitions process and Voyager fund structure more efficient. Work also continues in recasting for Voyager as many of the NOTIS Toolkit functionalities as we can.

CONCLUSION

As the 21st century approaches, the need for cataloging is still very much in evidence at research libraries such as Northwestern. We still need to maintain a solid core of original catalogers with varying language and subject expertise. In our case, cooperation amongst the three Technical Services departments was an essential component of a successful migration. Workflow analysis has played and continues to play an important part in our daily life. In fact, the key to the management of a successful cataloging operation today consists of three important factors: flexibility, the willingness to take risks and try new things, and the acceptance of the inevitability of change.

NOTES

1. Gary L. Strawn, *User's Guide to Accompany CLARR, the Cataloger's Toolkit.* Evanston, IL: Northwestern University, 1995. Also available: *<http://www.library.nwu.edu/clarr/home.html>*, 14 Dec. 1999.

2. Letter of David F. Bishop, University Librarian, Northwestern University, to Library staff dated 3 June, 1998.

3. Janet Swan Hill, "The Northwestern Africana Project: An Experiment in Decentralized Bibliographic and Authority Control," *College & Research Libraries* 42 (July 1981): 327.

4. Cindy Miller, Voyager Users Group Meeting, 1999, Rosemont, IL., 22 April, 1999.

5. Andrea Stamm, *Catalog Department Annual Report, Fiscal Year 1998/99.* Also available: *<http://www.library.nwu.edu/catalog>*, 14 Dec. 1999.

Cataloging at Yale University in 2000: Challenges and Strategies

Joan Swanekamp

SUMMARY. There are significant challenges in managing a large and distributed cataloging operation as the one at Yale University. This paper describes the current environment and trends, and goes on to outline the challenges facing the Catalog Department and possible strategies for addressing them. Technology plays heavily in improving processes and developing the most effective workflows. The biggest challenge is original cataloging capacity and how to increase it. *[Article copies available for a fee from The Haworth Document Delivery Service: 1-800-342-9678. E-mail address: <getinfo@haworthpressinc.com> Website: <http://www.HaworthPress.com>]*

KEYWORDS: Cataloging, workflows, process improvement, original cataloging, Yale University

INTRODUCTION

The pace of change in libraries during the last twenty-five years has been dramatic, and the world of cataloging has been no exception. Today, cataloging as a profession bares little resemblance to the field I entered in 1975. In 1975 I would have been unable to predict even a

Joan Swanekamp, MLS, MM, is Chief Catalog Librarian and Head of the Catalog Department, Yale University, 111 Memorial Library, P. O. Box 208240, New Haven, CT 06520.

[Haworth co-indexing entry note]: "Cataloging at Yale University in 2000: Challenges and Strategies." Swanekamp, Joan. Co-published simultaneously in *Cataloging & Classification Quarterly* (The Haworth Information Press, an imprint of The Haworth Press, Inc.) Vol. 30, No. 2/3, 2000, pp. 373-385; and: *Managing Cataloging and the Organization of Information: Philosophies, Practices and Challenges at the Onset of the 21st Century* (ed: Ruth C. Carter) The Haworth Information Press, an imprint of The Haworth Press, Inc., 2000, pp. 373-385. Single or multiple copies of this article are available for a fee from The Haworth Document Delivery Service [1-800-342-9678, 9:00 a.m. - 5:00 p.m. (EST). E-mail address: getinfo@haworthpressinc.com].

small percentage of the developments that have occurred, and I can only begin to imagine the library of 2025. I can however, comment on current trends at Yale and in the environment, outline the challenges as I see them, and chart out a plan for the bibliographic control of resources for the next few years.

ENVIRONMENT

Yale University will celebrate its Tercentennial Anniversary in 2001, and as might be expected in an institution of this age, the Library is one of great richness and depth. The Library also comes with a wide range of complexities and traditions, and often finds itself torn between viewing itself as one library or a federation of libraries. Cataloging at Yale is no different. The vast majority of cataloging occurs in the central Catalog Department in Sterling Memorial Library, but our technical services environment is a distributed one with assorted acquisitions, cataloging and binding functions occurring in many of the school and department libraries, and in some of the special collections. Several of the school and departmental libraries have completely independent technical service units and manage all of their cataloging. The Divinity Library, the Music Library, and the Medical Library follow this model. The Law School supports its own Library and Catalog and its operation is completely independent from the rest of the Library. A number of the school and departmental libraries do some, but not all of their cataloging–the science libraries and the Social Science Library are examples of this model. In addition to the cataloging performed in the Catalog Department, new titles with matching Library of Congress copy are cataloged on receipt in the Acquisitions Department. Several of the Library's area curatorial collections also manage their cataloging operations. Included in this category are the Near East Collection, the East Asian Collection and the Southeast Asian Collection.

The Catalog Department is organized into cataloging teams with subject or language as the organizing feature. The teams include Arts and Science, History and Social Science, Rare Books, Latin American, Slavic, Hebraica, and Networked Resources. The Catalog Management Team has general oversight for retrospective conversion activities, automated authority control and catalog maintenance. The Catalog Department consists of 55 staff, about equally divided between professional catalog librarians and supporting cataloging assistants. The cataloging team administrative structure was put in place more than ten years ago and continues to serve the Library well. Each Team has a combination of professional, support and student staff. Each team manages its own workflow and backlog, though the Library recently created a non-public Frontlog that combines the backlogs of the Arts and Science and History and Social Science Teams. Each Team Leader has liaison responsibilities with the selector(s) or curator for the materials that the Team catalogs, and most of the catalog librarians also have specific cataloging assignments and work closely with the appropriate selector or public service librarians in their area. The teams handle materials in all physical formats, and each team has someone responsible for serials cataloging. This organization has proved to be the most efficient structure for the management of a large department. The Catalog Department catalogs approximately 90,000 titles annually. The Library receives approximately 150,000 volumes annually.

The Chief Catalog Librarian is the Head of the Catalog Department with responsibility for the general oversight and management of the Catalog Department, and also system-wide leadership for cataloging policy. Those responsibilities extend to insuring the ongoing quality of the Library catalog.

TRENDS

A review of recent budgets, annual statistics and staffing patterns would predict, at least for the next few years, a stable budget and staff size, with an increased level of productivity. The total number of staff has remained stable for the last 4-5 years, though a number of retirements, at all levels, loom on the horizon. The Library's Collections budget continues to be healthy and the number of volumes received actually seems to have risen slightly in the last few years. We are however finding it increasing difficult to fund new innovations and hope to generate the necessary funds through process improvements and reallocation.

The Catalog Department has and will continue to devote energies to making improvements in workflows and processes, and to seek automated solutions whenever possible. During the last two years the total number of titles cataloged increased despite a number of lengthy staff vacancies. With some workflow improvements and the added opportunity to research some of our backlog through automated processes, the Library has come closer to realizing the optimal cataloging efficiency for materials with cataloging copy.

The trend that is perhaps most bothersome, is the lack of the capacity to keep up with original cataloging. This is a trend we share with some of our large peer institutions. It could be that Yale is acquiring more truly unique materials or, the limited number of libraries purchasing these materials all have the same capacity problem, and the same book is sitting in all of our backlogs. Most likely the latter is the case. Most of the titles in the Arts and Science and History and Social Science Team backlogs requiring original cataloging and 3-8 years old, are in English and western European languages, published by recognized publishers, and distributed through our standard vendors. It is unlikely that Yale has the only copy.

Yale set a goal some years ago to provide full cataloging of materials within 18-24 months after receipt. Backlogging titles without copy and re-searching them in RLIN and OCLC still results in a significant number of titles requiring original cataloging after 24 months. The total titles without copy is well beyond the number of titles that the department can accommodate. The Catalog Department staff perform original cataloging on receipt for priority titles: serials, multi-volume sets, reserves, requests and materials designated as probable high use. We also do not backlog computer files and other non-print materials (excepting microforms). Pressure continues to find ways to reduce the growth of the backlog and expedite the cataloging of materials from it.

Recent evaluation of workflows in the Arts and Science and History and Social Science Teams has led us to convert two vacant support staff positions to 1.5 professional positions with an eye toward increasing our original cataloging capacity. This shift will not eliminate the problem, but should help it. Future improvements in cataloging with copy may also lead us to re-examine positions as they are vacated.

CHALLENGES AND POSSIBLE SOLUTIONS

The Yale University Library, like most libraries, will face a whole range of challenges in the years to come. They will include human resources issues as recruitment of new catalog librarians and qualified support staff, and staff training and development. We will continue to strive to increase our cataloging production, rationalize workflows, and better manage our backlogs. Issues of catalog management will include retrospective conversion 'clean-up' projects to insure the accuracy of our online holdings, and a mandate to insure the ongoing quality of the Catalog. External forces will include opportunities for new services from vendors, and the challenge of making cost-effective use of our shared bibliographic utilities that are changing in nature. A new Library Management System will offer new opportunities to evaluate our practices and provide solutions to old problems. Digital resources will force us to question our standard definitions of a library collection and its catalog. Incorporating methods for providing access to and control of electronic resources will most likely need to occur within current budget guidelines. The changing nature of library service will, without doubt, have an impact on cataloging and how cataloging staff members respond to their role as internal service providers. The management and leadership challenges will be many. We will find ourselves juggling many new priorities; actively recruiting from a smaller pool of new catalog librarians; providing training and staff development opportunities for staff who must be constantly adapting to new technologies and changes in the workplace; partnering with peer institutions and vendors; and finally, we must continue to market the value of cataloging.

Recruiting, Training and Staff Development

The challenge of recruiting new catalog librarians is one of the biggest challenges that libraries will face. With fewer library schools and even fewer courses in bibliographic control, classification and subject analysis, there are fewer potential catalog librarians making their way to the job market. Twenty-three years ago the Dean of a well-respected Library School remarked that cataloging was a dead profession–the machine would do it all. Unfortunately, a number of library school administrators continue to hold this view, and fail to direct students to cataloging as a rich and rewarding, and very viable profession.

After recruitment, staff training and development will require continued attention. Staff must adapt to new and changing technologies both in the materials that they catalog, and the tools that assist them in performing their work. Staff development and training for cataloging support staff will help prepare them to function at the highest levels in our changing environment.

An important goal will be to assist staff in finding the right balance between attention to detail and appreciation for the larger picture. We need to help them place a value on their time and use it wisely, recognizing the cases where it is appropriate to go the extra mile, and knowing when to move on.

Colleges and Universities are centers for learning and so is the Catalog Department. But, it is not always easy to create a learning environment, and helping staff perform to their fullest in a learning organization is an incremental process. It requires new training methods and techniques, and creating an atmosphere where learning is nurtured and rewarded.

Increased Cataloging Productivity and Effectiveness

Every library will strive to increase cataloging productivity and Yale is no exception. We will continue to increase our use of technology to do our work more efficiently and effectively. The continued employment of automated re-searching techniques as those supplied by OCLC and RLIN will reduce our recycling costs. We hope to expand our efforts to include the development of a local program to automate the re-searching of our locally mounted Library of Congress resource file.

We will seek to make improvements through revised processes and the rationalization of many of our exceptional workflows that were designed long ago. Most of these special processes and workflows are expensive, no longer serve a purpose, and prone to error. Over the years, each school and department library set different requirements for the cataloging and processing of their materials, and each specialized process had an important function or served a special purpose. But for many years now, we have had shared a catalog and its associated bibliographic records, and most of these exceptional processes no longer serve a critical purpose. The creation of a standard set of processes for materials flowing from the school and departmental libraries would serve many purposes. It would first make for more efficient processing and cataloging and reduce professional staff intervention. Staff would be required to follow one set of procedures rather than many, making staffing more flexible, and training easier. If cataloging assistants were required to apply fewer exceptional procedures, it is also likely that they would make fewer errors and the overall quality of cataloging would be improved. This will all be complicated by a system that has historically placed a high value on customized processes.

Cataloging with copy will be more effective as support staff receive additional training to enable them to better analyze complex copy, and deal with a broader range of copy cataloging situations. In response to changes in the publishing practices, staff will also need training to understand how these changes effect the materials that they handle. We will need to expand our variant edition and Cataloging-in-Publication completion cataloging procedures to accommodate changes in the publishing world. As more English language materials are cataloged on receipt in the Acquisitions Department, we should look to fill vacated support staff positions with new staff with good foreign language and computer skills. Most of our higher-level support staff perform original cataloging of belles-lettres materials since subject analysis is not usually required. Continuing to build on this practice will ease the burden on the professional staff.

The challenge of increasing our capacity to provide original cataloging is complex. Some might argue that the only way to achieve results is to throw more money at it, i.e., hire more catalogers. Most of us do not have this luxury and instead will need to be more creative in our approach. We recently made a decision to convert two support staff positions to 1.5 professional cataloger positions and are in the process of filling the new positions. That alone will not solve the problem. We will need to insure that the professional staff members are engaged in the truly professional work, i.e., original cataloging, the knotty copy cataloging problems, and classification and subject analysis. We need to expand our portfolio of accepted cataloging records to include a range of standards for different categories of materials, and especially to gain general acceptance for the core record standard.

Active participation in national cooperative cataloging activities by as many libraries as possible, will surely add to the pool of high quality cataloging records that can be used by most libraries with little or no modification or postponement. The Program for Cooperative Cataloging has taken the lead in this area, and through BIBCO and CONSER has demonstrated that cooperative cataloging according to an accepted standard can work. Under the auspices of the Program, the *Core Record Standard* was developed as a means to insuring a base standard that libraries could accept for copy and commit to create. An added advantage to using PCC BIBCO records is that all the headings are represented in the National Authority File, and the headings for those titles will be claimed automatically through our authority control service. Yale, already an active NACO contributor and a contributor to BIBCO on a limited basis, will expand its BIBCO contributions early in 2000. The future success of the PCC programs will only be insured if large numbers of libraries agree to participate, not just as users of the records, but also as contributors. Yale will continue to be a strong supporter of the Program for Cooperative Cataloging, but it will also encourage its peers to participate in an effort to insure the continued success of the Program.

Backlog/Frontlog Control

Backlog management is a fact of life in most libraries, as they cannot catalog all new titles on receipt. And so, we are all faced with the problems of backlogs with minimal access, and the public relations problems they cause. Some libraries have found at least a partial answer in publicly accessible frontlogs, and while we have considered the possibility, it is unlikely that there will be stack space available for at least two years. In the meantime, faced with space considerations in our own closed backlog, we must look for ways to limit backlog growth and insure the timely recycling of materials.

We can make some reductions in the number of titles going to the backlog by expanding our use of OCLC to some additional categories of materials that will most likely be represented there, rather than in RLIN. In some cases, searching both databases will be more cost efficient than searching one and backlogging the title. Processing titles for the backlog, shelving them and then re-searching them is not without costs. We would also see some improvement if we trained staff to do a more thorough examination and evaluation of records from the utilities. The increasing presence of tape loaded records from vendors and national libraries, and the wider array of codes to identify these records, has only added to staff confusion. In some cases, titles with acceptable, but not easily identifiable cataloging copy are routinely being forwarded to the backlog.

OCLC and RLIN both offer services to re-search titles and supply libraries with the corresponding MARC records. We have just recently begun to make use of OCLC's service and we are still experimenting with workflows and processes. Based on successes at peer institutions, we expect to see improvements in our ability to handle the recycling of backlog titles in a more expeditious fashion. We have also made a concerted effort to improve the quality of our backlog records, thereby assuring better quality access, and increasing the accuracy of the matching records. In the near future we also hope to develop a local program that our Systems Office can run at regular intervals, matching our backlog against our copy of the Library of Congress resource file. We expect this would yield an additional 25-35% of the titles with copy at no additional cost for the records. Our goal continues to be to reduce the time a title is in a backlog to 18-24 months.

Changing Nature of Our Bibliographic Utilities

Our national bibliographic utilities, OCLC and RLIN, are critical to our ability to catalog effectively. But, in recent years they have taken on an international flavor and the bibliographic records represented in them range from fully cataloged records with English language AACR2 cataloging to vendor records in a variety of languages. They are now repositories for records created according to a whole range of standards, and they also include large numbers of records for digital resources created according to evolving, and often confusing standards.

Support staff in particular, will need to become better versed in bibliographic record evaluation. Bibliographic descriptive work for digital resources will become more routine and regularly assigned to support staff. However, since our rules for the cataloging of these materials are still under development, staff will need a firm grounding in basic concepts for the cataloging of these materials, and an awareness of how their properties affect the description and identification.

Another change to be noted in our major bibliographic utilities is that while they include more types of records, they often include the holdings of fewer libraries, or lack the timely inclusion of holdings. When libraries cataloged directly in OCLC or RLIN, catalogers could depend on finding copy for a specific title immediately after it was cataloged. As libraries moved their cataloging operations to their local systems, the lag time between record creation and its appearance in a bibliographic utility increased. The installation of new library management systems has only increased this problem. Libraries have unintentionally returned to the time when we all cataloged the same book over and over. The solution here, and one which requires the highest level of commitment from all libraries and the utilities, is the more timely export of records back to the utilities. In the meantime, we will need to make adjustments to our recycling schedules to accommodate the delayed records.

Retrospective Conversion and Authority Control

The completion of the Yale retrospective conversion project is projected for early 2002. With the completion of the planning and development of specifications, our minds turn toward clean up, including conversion of the non-JACKPHY vernacular titles and cryptic cards from another era. Volume holdings will also need to be verified and recorded for the titles in the school and departmental libraries. Quality assurance is high on our priority list. Bibliographic and holdings accuracy is critical to the success of our off-campus Library Shelving Facility, and must be insured for campus-wide acceptance of an integrated online catalog. We have viewed authority control to be an integral part of retrospective conversion, and have implemented a project that has every converted record passing through the OCLC Authority Control Service. Critical to success, is our ability to manage the retrospective conversion and authority control clean up in tandem. This will require us to develop new efficiencies and automated procedures.

New Library Management System

A new library management system is planned for late 2002 or early 2003. The next few years will involve evaluating, contracting, planning and implementing. With a new system will come the opportunity to re-evaluate processes and practices and to make improvements. We see it as offering an opportunity to increase our use of technology to do our work more efficiently and effectively. The challenge for the Library will be to maintain daily operations while actively engaged in the planning and implementation process.

Digital Resources

The advent of electronic resources representing a number of classes of materials (print text, image, numeric) has presented catalog departments with a unique set of challenges. The question has not just been how to catalog or provide bibliographic access, but what to catalog, at what level, who decides, and how to find the right balance. The options are numerous, each with it's own benefits and drawbacks:

- full OPAC access
- minimal OPAC access
- web page
- database
- AACR2 MARC, Dublin Core, or other metadata standard

Our general approach has been to catalog titles in our collection or those we license, in our NOTIS online public access catalog. We have used web pages as pointers to titles that we do not consider part of our collection, though some of our cataloged titles also appear on web pages.

The introduction of digital resources requires us to think differently about staff cataloging assignments, and specifically about our support staff positions and the management of less complex digital cataloging. Our professional staff includes an Electronic Resources Catalog Librarian position. The position has responsibility for developing digital cataloging strategies, and documenting decisions and practices. The actual cataloging of digital resources is a responsibility shared by a number of catalog librarians. In the next year, we will need to do a closer examination of the expanding digital workload with an eye toward assessing our support staff needs in this area. With the assistance of our Library Systems Office staff, we have developed a program to check for broken URL's and it has been a great help in insuring the integrity of the links in the catalog. In the coming years we will need to build on these early efforts to develop a full maintenance program for records of digital objects. I see no easy answers to the questions of selection for cataloging or access, and I expect that we will continue to wrestle with how to provide a trigger or routing for a title in need of cataloging.

The Library currently supports separate databases for image materials, some digital texts and special collections finding aids, each supporting different metadata standards. A Metadata Task Force has offered a possible solution for linking these rich and diverse collections and hopefully that plan can be brought to fruition in the near future.

A new art image cataloging position was recently created, and while the cataloging work will be done in the art image database using the VRA core standard, we have agreed that the new Librarian and the Catalog Department staff would all benefit from closer ties. We have agreed to house the new position in the Catalog Department rather than the Art Library.

Service Issues

One of the most important questions facing us is how to define our collection and our catalog. With it we must redefine the relationship of the Catalog to the Library, to the University, to our peer institutions and to the world. If we think narrowly we could define the catalog very much as we did the card catalog. But most of us see many new opportunities. The Catalog can link to a wide range of reference sources, full texts, images, numeric data, reserve collections, unpublished works, and university resources. From the catalog we can invoke programs to assist us in performing text and numeric analysis, and link to other Library's catalogs. With so many options, it is inherent upon catalogers to help shape and articulate this new definition of the Catalog for our user community.

It will be an added challenge for all of us to understand how our communities use the Catalog and respond to their needs. In most large institutions we will depend on our public service colleagues to keep us apprised of reader comments, but it is also important for us to seek out the answers, to understand problems, and to develop creative and responsive solutions. We must insure that cataloging staff members view themselves as a service provider and respond appropriately.

Management and Leadership

The management of the Catalog Department and library-wide cataloging operations will require a program of continual review of processes and costs, with an eye to improving processes and continuing to become more effective. It is most likely that the Library will continue to fund new initiatives from its own budget, and it will be necessary to reallocate resources without reducing any services.

Training and staff development opportunities will be critical to insuring a well-trained and responsive workforce at a time of sweeping change. As we find ourselves in a tight labor market, recruiting for all levels will be a challenge. Successful recruiting will require us to offer competitive compensation and benefits for the best-qualified candidates, and an inviting, stimulating, and nurturing work environment.

We will find ourselves increasingly reliant on vendors for a wide range of services. Good management skills will assist us in managing contracts and licenses. We will also benefit from an ability to partner with peer institutions to develop innovative programs and influence vendors and other service providers. The cultivation of consortial arrangements will assist in our ability to influence costs and services.

Finally, we will need to continue to market the value of cataloging, both in support of traditional bibliographic control needs, but also as an approach to organizing and controlling our increasing complex collections of digital resources. As the nature of our Collection and Services change, it will still be the Catalog that will define the Library.

Index

Numbers followed by an "f" indicate figures.